FLY NAVY

ALSO BY ALVIN TOWNLEY

Legacy of Honor
Spirit of Adventure

FLY NAVY

Discovering the Extraordinary People and Enduring Spirit of Naval Aviation

ALVIN TOWNLEY

THOMAS DUNNE BOOKS

St. Martin's Press

New York

THOMAS DUNNE BOOKS.
An imprint of St. Martin's Press.

www.thomasdunnebooks.com
www.stmartins.com

Library of Congress Cataloging-in-Publication Data

Townley, Alvin.
    Fly Navy : discovering the extraordinary people and enduring spirit of naval aviation /
Alvin Townley. — 1st ed.
        p. cm.
    Includes bibliographical references.
    ISBN 978-0-312-65084-1
    1. United States. Navy—Aviation—History.   2. Air pilots, Military—United
States—History.   3. Air pilots, Military—Training of—United States.   4. Aircraft
carriers—United States   5. United States. Navy—Sea life.   I. Title.
    VG93.T68 2011
    359.9'40973—dc22

                                                                        2010054435

Book design by Phil Mazzone

First Edition: May 2011

10 9 8 7 6 5 4 3 2 1

To those who have served America so honorably during the first one hundred years of naval aviation, and to those who will carry this legacy into its second century

CONTENTS

FLY NAVY

INTRODUCTION

I STILL REMEMBER FIRST WATCHING the phantom figures of crewmen moving through the ghostly steam of an aircraft carrier's catapult, and
seeing the silhouettes of F-14 Tomcats taxiing slowly across the windswept
deck of the USS *Enterprise*. The image of wings unfolding, crewmen lock-
ing aircraft into position, and jets straining against blast deflectors will
never leave me. I'll always remember that sense of anticipation, and I'll never
forget the raw thrill that shot through me when I first saw those big fighters
thunder into a dawn sky.

Like many people, my introduction to naval aviation came with that opening scene of *Top Gun*. When those Tomcats leapt off the deck, they left an
entire nation enchanted by the individuals, aircraft, and ships that comprise
the high-stakes world of naval aviation. The power of jet engines and the
sheer excitement of flight operations captivated us. Millions of Americans
have now seen the film; we love its characters and know the lines by heart. Its
heroes—Maverick, Goose, Viper, Iceman—have come to represent the camaraderie, adventure, and greatness for which we all hunger. We think that the
people on carrier flight decks just might be privy to a secret that the rest of us
were never told, and in truth, some part of us longs to join their fraternity, be
part of that great undertaking, and perhaps strap into a cockpit ourselves.

Naval aviation has fascinated me since the first time I watched the film years ago, but I am not *of* naval aviation. I've never worn an aviator's wings of gold. I've never raced across a flight deck to ready a jet for launch, nor have I endured a long deployment that carried me oceans away from home. My place lies with other civilians, forever observers to one of the world's greatest pageants.

Before watching *Top Gun*, I had little personal knowledge of carrier aviation. Mine was not a military family. I didn't know the nineteen-year-olds who worked the flight decks, the veteran leaders who trained the crews, or the aviators who flew the missions. Consequently, I never understood the real people who comprised the extraordinary team that sends aircraft screaming off a flight deck. But even *Top Gun* didn't reveal the entire story.

I will always appreciate the 1986 blockbuster for being what it is—a great and inspiring film. Over time, however, I've come to recognize what it is not. The film had left me with the impression that naval aviators were polished demigods who won glory for themselves. I assumed that deck crews had insignificant roles, and I viewed aviation as a one-on-one sport, with the fictitious Top Gun trophy as its prize. That woefully inaccurate perception remained unchanged for many years, but then I finally stood on a carrier's flight deck and saw for myself what transpired on its four acres. In those unforgettable minutes, my view of naval aviation changed forever.

Three F/A-18E Super Hornets flew through a clear Pacific sky just off the Hawaiian Islands, toward the homeward-bound aircraft carrier USS *Nimitz*. As they roared overhead, just off the carrier's starboard (right) side, my friend Lee Amerine's jet gracefully peeled away from the formation and crossed over the unplowed sea before the ship's bow. He flew Aircraft 212 down the length of the flight deck, one mile off the port side. Nearly parallel with the deck's end, the twenty-eight-year-old lieutenant banked into another 180 degree turn that placed him squarely behind the carrier, three hundred and fifty feet above her churning wake. He continued his bank until he lined up with the landing strip that ran right to left at a slight angle across the ship's deck.

From Lee's viewpoint, the carrier seemed like an impossibly small stripe of gray in an endless sea of blue. He would have to land his Rhino (as Super Hornets are also known) on this short, narrow, gently pitching runway. He had to set his tailhook onto a 150-foot-long by ten-foot-wide portion of that runway so it could catch one of the four arresting cables that would bring him to a halt. Really, he was expected to catch the optimal number three wire. That gave him a precise fifty-foot by ten-foot slice of deck to target with his steel tailhook, which hung from the jet's tail, fifty feet behind the cockpit. Aircraft and hook were moving at more than 140 miles per hour, and Lee had to lay them into that tiny groove.

Even after landing on the *Nimitz* almost daily for six straight months during his deployment to the Arabian Sea, Lee's muscles still tensed as he settled his plane onto the glide slope; the rapidly approaching deck before him consumed his entire focus. Many flight deck veterans call carrier landings "controlled crashes" for a reason, and almost nothing presents a greater challenge to a pilot. Naval aviators don't gently settle their planes onto the landing strip after a long straight approach; they are only lined up with the centerline behind the boat for fifteen seconds. They effectively slam their planes onto a small, crowded deck, mere feet from the crew and parked aircraft, hoping to catch the wire. At least Lee was making this landing on a calm, sunny day. The dark of night or heaving decks that can rise and fall more than twenty feet will drive aviators' pulse rates even higher.

I was Lee's guest for the weekend and from my vantage point near the rear of the flight deck, I watched a green light flash on the Landing Signal Officer's platform indicating that the deck was clear for landing. From that crowded platform on the carrier's aft corner, a team of pilots responsible for safely landing aircraft watched the Super Hornet approach, ready to help if needed. Lee continued descending toward the deck, using the jet's expansive flaps and stabilators to supply lift as he maintained 140 miles per hour—a relatively slow airspeed that would still carry him over the deck so fast that ship, deck markings, aircraft, and crew would all pass by in a blur. Landing gear down and trailing two curling brown plumes of exhaust, Lee rapidly closed the remaining distance to the ship.

The engines of Aircraft 212 roared over the stern and Lee's wheels squeaked onto the steel deck. His wingtips cleared the line of planes and crew next to me by ten feet; he had no margin for error. In a movement too quick for me to see, the tailhook caught its target: the third of four arresting wires. The thick steel cable began spooling out behind the thundering plane. Lee had pushed his throttle forward in case his hook missed the wire and he had to get his forty-four-thousand-pound jet airborne before he shot over the end of the angled flight deck, which he reached in just two seconds. His afterburners flared and his two turbofan engines blasted the deck with heat, noise, and the unmistakable perfume of jet exhaust.

His hook held its grip and the black line of arresting cable pulled taught, slowing the charging jet. Beneath the deck, a powerful hydraulic system unleashed a deafening hiss as it used oil fluid pressure and a series of levers to exert just the right amount of tension on the wire—enough to stop the Super Hornet within three hundred feet, but not enough to rip the tailhook away from its body. Less than three seconds after his hook caught the wire, Lee's jet came to a halt just yards shy of the deck's end. With his engines whining at idle, he raised his hook and let out a long sigh of relief: safe recovery, successful trap. The cable retreated to its original position to receive the next jet, and a yellow-shirted plane director caught Lee's attention and motioned him forward and out of the way.

By the time I arrived planeside, Lee had opened his canopy and stepped onto the wing. A small crowd of crew members had gathered to meet him. He shook their hands and thanked each of them when he reached the deck. They seemed like teammates after Lee had scored a game-winning shot— and in this moment, I began to understand something new about the true character of naval aviation. The men and women in the cockpit did not own the show. They played but one part on a carrier's inspired team of 5,000 warriors who work together so that 120 aviators and aircrew can go off the deck in planes and helicopters to execute their missions. Every time Lee returned to the carrier, the mechanics and technicians in the squadron knew they had done their job. They had spent long hours checking the jet's vital electronics, fine-tuning its weapon systems, and meticulously repairing and testing its complex engines. Their preparation had carried Lee safely home. I realized that the men and women occupying aircraft cockpits were but the very tip of a long spear made up of a proud line of dedicated individuals.

Lee made his way to me and noted my surprise. He explained, "Everyone in Strike Fighter Squadron Fourteen [VFA-14]—the Tophatters—is part of this. Mine isn't the only name on the jet."

He pointed to the landing gear door, which proudly bore the name and hometown of the jet's plane captain—the young enlisted airman in charge of the aircraft. "Fourteen is a team. *Nimitz* is a team. Everyone on this ship supports us in flying our missions. From the galley to the radar to the crew chiefs, everyone here supports us in getting off this deck.

"In our squadron, we have two hundred twenty-somethings and a great group of chief petty officers who are dedicated to keeping twelve F/A-18E Super Hornets fighting-ready. And there's a cadre of fourteen pilots who go out and fight. Those two hundred young men and women bust their tails, work day in and day out, heaving thousand-pound bombs up onto our wings so that they get everything on this jet perfect. There's no way I could pre-flight this whole jet.

"I know that nineteen-year-old kid," he said, pointing at the plane captain who was busy making sure 212 was secured to the deck. "I've seen him progress from being in training to a full plane captain. I trust him. I know what he did. When the plane captain or chief petty officer in charge says their jet is safe for flight, I have complete confidence up and down the chain that this jet is ready to go flying.

"And the thing is," Lee continued, speaking loud enough for me to hear over the ubiquitous engine noise, "the parents of the guys who work pumping the fuel into these jets are just as proud as my parents. Everybody is proud to be out here and doing this. So it's very, very, very humbling. I get touched so many times when I'm on the flight deck and I look around and there are a hundred people dodging jet exhaust and propellers just to get me off the deck. And it doesn't matter if we're in the Persian Gulf where it's a hundred and twenty degrees on the flight deck or if we're off Korea and it's close to twenty degrees and snowing. Rainstorm? Doesn't faze 'em. They work twelve-hour days and live in 170-man berthing. To have that kind of dedication is just awe-inspiring. It keeps me going and it's unbelievable, it truly is. When I get out of the aircraft I try to shake as many hands as I can. To me, it's a real honor that I'll remember forever, these young men and women running around busting their tails so I can go fly. That's teamwork. That's how we fly in the Navy."

Several days later, *Nimitz* neared her home port of San Diego, California. Spirits were high as the five thousand men and women of the ship's air wing and crew neared the end of a six-month deployment. They had packed their belongings into boxes, bags, and crates, many of which would soon be stacked high in the hangar bay. The Tophatters' briefing center and home base aboard the ship—their ready room—now held its fair share of boxes and its walls were almost bare. The atmosphere reminded me of the last day of school, and the two hundred men and women of Lee's squadron were graduating.

Late that evening, Lee and I were the only two souls in the ready room, the other pilots either having a late-night meal or already asleep in preparation for an early briefing before *Nimitz* returned her entire complement of fifty-five planes and seven helicopters to their respective bases on land. We talked about my week as his guest aboard ship and about his long deployment. Then I asked about why—really, *why*—he had chosen naval aviation; he had no navy or aviation tradition in his family and grew up nowhere near the ocean. Further, it was a choice that entailed significant personal sacrifices, the foremost being months away from home.

"Most of us were raised a certain way," Lee said. "Growing up, we learned that we're part of something bigger than ourselves. We wanted to be extra-ordinary. Out here, we're all part of this team that shares a mission important to our country and to our families back home."

Lee explained that his fellow aviators and everyone on board joined the navy with different motivations. Some are deeply patriotic, earnestly aspiring to serve the United States. Others simply feel a responsibility to provide for their families. Some seek excitement and the company of professionals who excel at their jobs. Many seek discipline, a steady job, or an opportunity to be part of something truly significant. Regardless, these men and women volunteer to spend long months at sea, protecting those at home. In the process, they become part of the small, proud, and exceptionally skilled group of Americans who make naval aviation possible.

Young people over the past hundred years have sensed the adventure and opportunity offered by aviation at sea, and they've become part of this special family. These individuals—peacetime volunteers and wartime draftees alike—have come from every background imaginable. Some were born to privilege, others were born to poverty. Some joined and became officers after graduating from college Naval Reserve Officers Training Corps (NROTC) programs or the U.S. Naval Academy. Others completed Officer Candidate School and thus became part of the officer corps. As officers, they would progress from ensign to lieutenant (junior grade), to lieutenant, to lieutenant commander, to commander, and perhaps to captain. A small group remains in the navy and attains the stars that accompany the prestigious ranks of rear admiral, vice admiral, and admiral.

A majority of the navy's men and women enlist fresh from high school, hoping for excitement, discipline, or income. Some join as recent immigrants, aspiring to serve their new country. Regardless of their background, they become apprentices or airmen then progress through the ranks of third-, second-, and first-class petty officer before earning the revered title of *chief* petty officer. Perhaps they might eventually become senior or master chief petty officers. Others become technical experts and earn the blue marked bars of a chief warrant officer. Rich or poor, officer or enlisted, these men and women all come together in their squadrons and aboard their ships to work together, united in that great undertaking of getting aircraft off the deck.

In executing their missions, they may find themselves in cockpits of F/A-18 Super Hornets, repairing the twin turboprops aboard early warning E-2C Hawkeyes, hauling chains across a sweltering flight deck, leaping out of SH-60 Seahawk helicopters to rescue those in trouble, monitoring air traffic from the bridge of a carrier, or performing any of an almost endless list of functions all critical to the mission of the United States Navy.

Whatever their reason for first stepping aboard a ship or aircraft, and whatever their role, the people of naval aviation have crafted a lasting legacy, defined by a unique set of characteristics that recur across generations. Experiences in the skies and on long deployments have shaped explorers like Alan Shepard, the first American in space, and Neil Armstrong, the first man on the Moon. They also inspired leaders like Medal of Honor recipients Jim Stockdale, Thomas Hudner, and David McCampbell. And carrier flight decks have helped launch the careers of innovators like Jack Taylor, the founder of Enterprise Rent-A-Car—which he named for his World War II aircraft carrier—and Leroy Grumman, whose namesake company has produced some of history's greatest aircraft along with the newest *Nimitz*-class aircraft carriers. Today, naval aviation continues to hone our rising generation of leaders, using its time-proven and combat-tried system to instill those rare yet vital qualities of devotion, honor, and citizenship. During the one hundred years since we first began landing aircraft aboard ships, thousands of unsung men and women have proudly sailed the world's oceans aboard America's carriers and found themselves changed forever.

During the same century, the navy's aircraft have served our country proudly and effectively in countless theaters and oceans the world over. Aviators and crew have selflessly fought for America, their families, and their fellow servicemen and women. They've taken the good fight to the skies above the vast Pacific, the U-boat–patrolled waters of the stormy North Atlantic, the icy peaks of Korea, the jungles of Vietnam, the deserts of Kuwait, the mountains of Afghanistan, and lands across the globe where freedom was threatened or the helpless were in need. Their actions in those skies have saved countless lives, won America's battles, and inspired their fellow countrymen.

As they served America in these far-flung places, the hard and dangerous work, important missions, and shipboard fellowship began to shape ordinary men and women into something extraordinary. They inspired one another to perform at higher and higher levels. They became warriors and trusted teammates. The capable individuals who joined the navy and deployed with carriers and squadrons would return to port as a team marked by greatness.

I began to wonder about that process, those values, and how they marked the individuals who have joined this century-long drama. The actors have certainly changed since naval aviation's birth in 1911, as have the machines and missions. Yet, this ever-changing cast has answered the same alluring summons of sea and sky. They have heeded the call to challenge themselves, inspire others, and serve their country. And as they served, they became something truly special.

The people of naval aviation share a unique but undefined spirit that has transcended ranks, roles, eras, and oceans. They offer a rich story much deeper than what *Top Gun* or any single film could ever capture. Nor could any single book effectively convey the uniquely different cultures of Marine Corps and Coast Guard squadrons, which are also part of naval aviation; I quickly learned they have their own special roles and proud heritage. Yet I knew that even by exploring just the navy's squadrons and ships, I still could never hear all the stories that came from thousands of deployments and countless sorties. So I decided to explore this one-hundred-year heritage through some of those who have walked across flight decks during those past decades—and who have truly helped define naval aviation. With that aspiration, I set out across the country and around the world to uncover one of America's most inspiring legacies and noble callings.

PART ONE

HOME PORT

1

A JOURNEY BEGINS

SOME TIME AFTER MY VOYAGE on the *Nimitz*, I found myself looking across the waters where naval aviation's century-old tradition began. Nothing about this particular place resembled the warm, sun-washed cruise across a smooth Eastern Pacific Ocean that I had experienced with the VFA-14 Tophatters (their VFA designation stands for fixed-wing [V] Fighter Attack [FA]). The Pacific of my transit was a summer lake compared to the wintry Chesapeake Bay that I found off the shore of Hampton Roads, Virginia. Whitecaps danced on the churning gray water and ominous clouds above made the water grayer still. A biting wind howled across the channel and cut straight through my jacket.

One hundred years ago, on a similarly inhospitable November day, a ship very unlike the *Nimitz* carried a plane very unlike an F/A-18 out into this very channel. The lone aviator aboard the USS *Birmingham* couldn't swim, didn't like the water, and was known to get seasick. Instead of a polished, carbon fiber helmet with an electronic display like the one worn by Lee Amerine, Eugene Ely wore a leather football helmet along with shoulder pads, and looked more like a turn-of-the-century linebacker than the world's first maritime aviator. His training, attire, and aircraft differed from what I encountered in the men and women aboard the *Nimitz* in almost every conceivable way—but Ely had exactly the same spirit.

Wilbur and Orville Wright also shared that spirit, and on windy Atlantic dunes near Kitty Hawk, North Carolina, they had performed the first great feat in modern aviation history—simply getting airborne. Thus, in 1903, the Wright brothers had opened an entirely new and unconquered realm to pioneers and daredevils alike. In the air, records waited to be broken; new dares awaited the brave. There were plenty of takers, and Eugene Ely would become one of the most famous.

Eugene was eighteen when the Wright brothers flew, and he had already become fascinated by the internal combustion engine and the speed, danger, and freedom it could offer. In the late 1800s, when automobiles were quite rare in Eugene's rural corner of Iowa, he began driving and maintaining cars for a local Catholic priest who rightly saw cars as the future of transportation. Eugene became a crack mechanic and standout driver in the process, expert at repairing cars and pressing their limits. From his first minute behind a steering wheel, he loved speed, and Father Smyth only encouraged him. The pair ruffled feathers throughout the community as they flew over the local roads, the accelerator pressed to the floorboard.

"Ely got a little too smart for the old priest," remembered Iowa minister Louis Rohret, who knew Ely as a boy. "[He] used to take the priest's car away with the intent of making some difficult repairs to it. Instead, Ely would run races at the country fairs. The fact that Ely was running in these races finally got back to Father Smyth and he fired him."[1]

Chastened but not in the least discouraged, Eugene struck out for the West to make his mark. He arrived in San Francisco in 1904 where he used his knowledge of engines to become a respected mechanic. His entrepreneurial spirit soon led him to start a car rental company, forerunning naval aviator Jack Taylor's Enterprise Rent-A-Car by half a century. Ely operated the business out of San Francisco and remained by the Bay long enough to marry the petite and attractive Mabel Hall. Then the couple left for Oregon where Eugene indulged his growing interest in aviation—which proved well-matched for his adventurous nature and relish for risk.

In early 1910, Ely flew his first aircraft—a Curtiss biplane—and promptly crashed it. Completely unbowed, he bought the plane from its owner, repaired it, and taught himself to fly. He was simultaneously an airplane mechanic, engineer, and pilot. All the skills that aviation would require, he possessed;

he played the roles of the modern navy's enlisted ranks and officers alike. All the men and women involved in flying and maintaining navy aircraft can trace their roots to this young man from Iowa.

Eugene was a pioneer, expert, and daredevil who rapidly built a reputation as a skilled pilot and expert maintainer. But by late 1910, he had yet to distinguish himself from the other young bucks of aviation who were aiming for distance and altitude records. He began working with entrepreneurial aircraft designer Glenn Curtiss, who had designed the first plane Ely crashed. Curtiss was an exceptionally creative inventor who had designed and raced motorcycles before he began building aircraft. Together, he and Ely devised a plan that could transform aviation.

The two men had met in Winnipeg, Canada, during a demonstration show. Ely's keen interest in the mechanics and theories of flight caught the attention of Mr. Curtiss, who was regarded as the day's leading aviator and plane manufacturer. Curtiss recognized talent and immediately hired Ely as an exhibition pilot.

Curtiss well understood the possibilities of aviation; he also had interest in profiting from it. With a mutually beneficial contract in mind, he began to approach the U.S. Navy, which had been resisting overtures to develop a real aviation program. To encourage their consideration, he spoke out publically, saying, "The battles of the future will be fought in the air. The aeroplane will decide the destiny of nations. . . . [America's battleships] cannot launch air fighters, and without these to defend them, they would be blown apart in case of war."[2]

He emphasized his point by using aircraft to successfully bomb ship-shaped targets off the coast of New York. That needled the well-established ranks of battleship admirals and also caught the attention of Captain Washington Chambers, the man responsible for exploring aviation's potential for the navy.

The three men—Curtiss, Chambers, and Ely—met at a New York air show late in 1910 and discussed launching and landing an airplane aboard a navy vessel. Chambers knew that a German company had plans to do the same, and the three felt a mutual sense of urgency—they wanted themselves, along with their country, to be first. The truth was, however that, like Wilbur Wright, Glenn Curtiss thought flying off a ship might be too dangerous for a pilot to attempt. But Eugene Ely had lost neither his confidence nor his desire to put himself in the record books. Ely and Curtiss proposed staging the flight free of charge and Chambers agreed to build a runway aboard a ship. So it came that seven years after the Wright brothers' landmark flight on North Carolina's Outer Banks, twenty-four-year-old Eugene Ely would earn his place among aviation's pioneers by flying a plane off a ship.

At its base in Norfolk, Virginia, the U.S. Navy had constructed an eighty-three-foot-long wooden platform on the bow of the cruiser USS *Birmingham*. From his plane's position at the platform's end, Ely would have fifty-seven feet for takeoff. The navy had craned aboard the *Hudson Flyer*, a Glenn Curtiss–designed biplane already famous for a record-setting flight, and on a blustery November morning, the world's first aircraft-carrying vessel sailed into the Elizabeth River. Crowds had gathered in boats and along the Hampton Roads shoreline to see if Curtiss and his pilot could pull off their feat, which many observers considered more stunt than military experiment. Time would prove them quite wrong.

Several storms rolled across the Chesapeake early that afternoon and the *Birmingham* dropped anchor to await better conditions—a decision that agitated Ely considerably. The aviator had spent months preparing for this moment and now felt much like a focused, well-prepared runner who arrives at the starting line only to have officials delay his race. He wasn't the only one frustrated by the inaction. Captain Chambers had risked his reputation on this venture and he feared that if Ely couldn't launch, the observers from Washington would leave scoffing at his idea.

A window in the weather finally appeared and the aviator pressed the opportunity. The ship's captain complied and issued the order to begin raising the anchor. Ely's momentary relief evaporated when he discovered the agonizingly slow pace with which the ship reeled in foot after heavy foot of anchor chain. His impatience and frustration returned. Over the next half hour, he fidgeted, paced, and fumed; he checked and rechecked his plane. He was ready, his engine was ready, his plane was ready, and the weather— for the moment—was also ready. So what if the ship's anchor wasn't? He decided to launch.

At 3:16 P.M. on November 14, 1910, Ely gave his idling engine a final rev. Just like modern aviators before a launch, he flexed his rudder and elevators. He signaled a crewman to release the fasteners holding the plane. The crewman hesitated, knowing the captain had not issued an official launch order. Ely repeated the command more emphatically and the crewman complied. The biplane's fifty-horsepower motor pushed it down the slightly inclined deck toward the cold, gray river and a good deal of uncertainty. The primary question in Ely's mind as he rattled forward was whether the little biplane would have enough speed and power to clear the water. Since the ship wasn't under way and thus wasn't generating any wind, Ely prayed his wings would have enough lift to get airborne. He'd find the answer at the deck's end.

The plane's wheels cleared the deck. Instead of rising, however, the biplane began dropping quickly toward the river. The possible and quite unwelcome answer to Ely's question flashed into his mind, but he wasn't giving up. He pulled hard on the controls, using every bit of his skill to avoid a crash—which he did, barely. The wheels dipped into the water and the furiously spinning propeller scraped the waves, slightly damaging the blades. Cold water sprayed over Ely, but he continued urging the plane upward, and thankfully, the determined little biplane slowly began rising away from the water. Ely worried about the effects of his brush with the water and heard the engine begin to vibrate disturbingly. Being a nonswimmer, he had no interest in remaining over the bay any longer than necessary and he scratched his original plan to land at the Norfolk Navy Yard. Instead, he landed on a nearby beach five minutes later, having opened a new era of sea power.

Ely and Curtiss set themselves to accomplishing the other half of their plan. They realized that simply flying a plane from a ship would not truly open the sea to aviation—they needed to make a successful shipboard landing as well. Two months later, the twosome traveled to San Francisco to make history once again.

January 18, 1911, dawned overcast and chilly but at 11 A.M., the weather lifted and Ely took off from Selfridge Field, just south of the city. He winged his canvas, wood, and wire biplane toward San Francisco's crowded waterfront where the cruiser USS *Pennsylvania* waited offshore with a 127-foot by 32-foot wooden landing platform on its stern.

Before he embarked on this day's mission, Ely's primary challenge had been to determine how to stop his plane on the short platform before he crashed into the ship's superstructure—the decks that rise above the ship's hull. A similarly short landing had never been accomplished, so he had no existing model to guide him. Interestingly, or perhaps amazingly, he devised a system that has fundamentally remained unchanged for one hundred years.

Ely had lined up a series of sandbags along each side of the landing platform. Between each pair of bags stretched a length of rope. A pair of rails ran parallel along the length of the platform, raising the perpendicular ropes so special hooks on Ely's landing gear would catch them. As the landing gear snagged more bags, the increasing drag would slow and stop the plane—in theory. If not, a barricade waited at the platform's end. Today's system of hydraulic arresting cables and a tailhook, while more advanced, stems from Ely's initial ingenuity.

Eugene was at once a thrill-seeker and an astute risk manager. He outfitted his plane with pontoons to prevent it from sinking into the bay should it crash. He used a set of bicycle inner tubes as a life preserver. He also saw that a canvas net girded the landing platform in case the plane veered overboard.

That morning, Ely's biplane approached the waiting ship, circled over the choppy water, and then began its final approach, coming in at approximately thirty-five miles per hour. A sudden updraft lifted the plane above Ely's desired glide slope at the last moment, and he had to recover quickly. He skillfully put the plane back on slope and set his wheels down near the middle of the landing strip. The plane snared half of the deck's sandbags, and Ely stopped short of the barricade, having made history's first arrested landing.

Captain C. F. Pond, the *Pennsylvania*'s commanding officer, called Ely's feat "the most important landing since the dove came back to the Ark."[3]

The young pilot landed a celebrity, and Captain Pond hosted a lunch for the attending dignitaries before Ely returned to his plane, started its engine, and rolled forward toward his second shipboard takeoff. On this occasion, he easily cleared the water below and rose into the sky above San Francisco Bay.

Upon landing amidst a throng of cheering soldiers at Selfridge Field, Eugene said, "It was easy enough. I think the trick could be successfully turned nine times out of ten." Then the soldiers carried off the young civilian aviator in triumph. The next day, the *San Francisco Examiner* proclaimed, EUGENE ELY REVISES WORLD'S NAVAL TACTICS.

Naval aviation's journey had begun.

Looking over San Francisco Bay a century later from the deck of the retired aircraft carrier USS *Hornet*, I contemplated how far naval aviation had progressed. I stood on a flight deck nearly eight hundred feet longer than the temporary wooden structure that had received Ely. *Hornet*'s deck had launched thousands of bomb-laden planes on missions against Japan in the Pacific. It had felt the heat of supersonic jets leaving for missions over Vietnam, and it had welcomed home Neil Armstrong and his crew after mankind's triumphant first steps on the Moon. In all, the carrier had launched more than 115,000 missions during her 30-year career.

Yet today, even the imposing forty-thousand-ton *Hornet* seems small compared to a modern goliath like the *Nimitz*, with her twin nuclear reactors, ninety-seven-thousand-ton displacement, and air wing comprised of state-of-the-art aircraft. Having walked the decks of both ships, I realized how far innovation and spirit like Eugene Ely's have brought naval aviation.

No guides or rulebooks existed for the pioneers who sought to link aviation with sea power. Theirs was an entirely new discipline, with no forerunners to lead the way. Consequently, many men gave their lives trying to push the limits of flight. Less than one year after making history on San Francisco Bay, Eugene Ely died when his plane crashed during a demonstration flight in Macon, Georgia. Today, aviation still claims lives; it will forever exist as a discipline on the cutting edge of capability, technology, and safety. As one modern instructor reminded a group of aspiring aviators, "Every time you strap that aircraft onto your back, it's trying to kill you." For reasons both complex and naturally simple, the tantalizing opportunity to master that wild beast has attracted the best and most daring of every generation.

After his plane's success on the *Birmingham* and *Pennsylvania*, Glenn Curtiss established a flying school on North Island in San Diego, California. Lieutenant Theodore "Spuds" Ellyson volunteered to leave the submarine service and report to Curtiss's school and soon thereafter, he captured a *New York Times* headline when he became the first naval officer to fly, on January 29, 1911. He was designated Naval Aviator Number One in April. In May, Curtiss finally received his sought-after contract, which was for two A-1 Triad seaplanes. Their purchase marks the true birth of U.S. naval aviation.

During 1911, the navy began sending Curtiss its first aspiring aviators, who were a unique and slightly renegade group of young officers with a taste for adventure and the nontraditional. They bucked the established surface warfare path, giving up their posts on prestigious battleships and cruisers. They consequently suffered the condescension of many peers and most commanders, but they didn't care. They wanted to fly.

By 1914, these early pioneers had earned the reluctant respect of Navy leadership, although they had to struggle mightily to attain it. Stubborn battleship admirals still stinging from Glenn Curtiss's humbling aerial bombing demonstration against surface ships would admit little strategic use for airplanes in the navy; and any strategic use they could foresee would only threaten their established order. On another front, some politicians and army leaders advocated for a single United States air force that would combine the navy's aviation assets with those of the U.S. Army Air Service. They argued, quite well but ultimately without success, that the navy did not need a separate aviation program.

Even though most of the navy's leadership still refused to view naval aviation as of central importance, they certainly didn't want the army to own aviation entirely. They agreed to provide their air force with a home. For its location, they chose the old navy yard at Pensacola, Florida. For its leader, they called upon Naval Aviator Number Three, John H. Towers.

Jack Towers was Eugene Ely with a uniform. The two young aviators shared the same adventurous spirit and zest for risk. The native of Rome, Georgia, graduated from the U.S. Naval Academy in 1906 and jettisoned a promising battleship career as soon as he heard about the navy's new aviation program. He did so despite stringent protests from his senior officers, who wanted the talented young officer to remain with them. On June 26, 1911, he left his shipmates to join Spuds Ellyson and Glenn Curtiss in a still-dangerous and unproven endeavor that was claiming lives of many aspiring pilots—aviation.

"I am sure many of my shipmates thought it *was* really and finally Farewell and that a small allowance should be put aside for later flowers," Jack remembered of his departure. His family in Rome thought "he had prepared to commit suicide."[4] He was risking his life as well as his career.

Jack learned to fly under the instruction of Spuds Ellyson near Glenn Curtiss's Hammondsport, New York, home. In 1912, he reported to North Island off San Diego and became an instructor. It was there that some of his students established one of naval aviation's great traditions: brown shoes, which have since distinguished flyers from their black-shoed surface warfare counterparts. Everyone found that North Island's dusty environs made it impossible to keep their standard-issue black shoes well-shined, and a group of students began wearing brown shoes instead; the brown tended to hide the dirt. From that point on, naval aviators have been called "brownshoes."

Jack proved exceptionally adept at teaching and flying. Soon, he began pursuing altitude, flight time, and distance records that impressed the navy brass. They began developing a begrudging respect for aviation and for the navy's emerging "senior aviator." Then Jack almost died.

Lieutenant Towers and his copilot, Ensign William Devotie Billingsley, were flying a Wright Brothers B-2 hydroaeroplane over a stormy Chesapeake Bay when an unexpected gust suddenly pushed the plane into a sixtydegree dive. The movement threw Billingsley from his seat and he crashed into the flight controls. Planes had neither seat belts nor parachutes at the time. The plane dove and accelerated toward the bay. Billingsley was knocked out of the plane and plummeted 1,500 feet to his death, becoming the navy's first aviation fatality.

The initial gust also knocked Jack from his seat, but he managed to grab a support strut on the wing. He tried to kick the steering controls to stop the plane's dive, but to no avail. Fortunately, updrafts slowed its descent and Jack held on tightly as he rode the B-2 down. The crash knocked him unconscious and injured one of his arms. When he came to, he lashed his good arm to the plane's pontoon so he'd stay afloat should he pass out. The stormy waves hid him from the crash boat on its first pass, but Jack's dog, which had accompanied the rescuers, began barking furiously at the scent of its owner. The boat circled back and fished the badly wounded aviator from the water. After Billingsley's death, Towers helped make sure all navy planes had seat belts.

That was 1913. The next year saw him arrive in Pensacola as executive officer of the navy's new Gulf Coast airbase. There, he developed the first formal training syllabus for navy pilots and set about getting the base in order so it could begin producing the aviators he envisioned the navy would soon need. He was distracted from his duties when, in April, he led a contingent of aircraft into combat over Veracruz during the Mexican Revolution. In an important first, naval aviators scouted hostile positions for navy and marine forces during America's occupation of the port city. During this time, he became friends with Lt. Commander William Moffett, who, as a rear admiral, would team up with Jack to lead naval aviation during the 1920s.

In the years before and during World War I, Jack served as the de facto leader of the young aviation department. Then in 1919, Towers embarked on a great adventure he'd been plotting for years. He led a contingent of three Navy-Curtiss (NC) flying boats on the world's first transatlantic flight. The big 20,000-pound biplanes each had four powerful engines, a five-man crew housed in the forty-five-foot center hull, and a pair of 126-foot fabric-covered wings. They were forerunners to the widely famous and slightly smaller PBY Catalina seaplanes used so extensively in World War II. While made for flight, they were designed to land and take off from large bodies of water. Ten "Nancies" were built, four of which were designated to fly the Atlantic—NC-1 through NC-4. NC-2 was used for spare parts, and NCs 1, 3, and 4 set out from Rockaway Beach, New York, on the afternoon of May 16, 1919, aiming to cover 4,106 nautical miles before arriving in Plymouth, England. Since transoceanic airplane navigation did not exist, the threesome followed signals set by a long line of destroyers spread out along the flight path, which included several refueling stops.

Jack Towers commanded the mission from his flagship NC-3, and held his three planes together until Newfoundland. On the longest hop—Newfoundland to the Azores on May 17—the planes encountered rough weather that cut visibility to one hundred yards. They became separated and NC-1 landed on the North Atlantic to verify its position. Jack Towers and NC-3 did the same. Neither plane realized that ten- to twelve-foot swells crisscrossed the surface. NC-1 succumbed to the waves soon after landing; its five-man crew was rescued by a passing Greek merchantman. The heavy seas damaged NC-3 too badly to fly again, but the machine remained afloat, albeit two hundred miles southwest of the Azores. The plane's radio transmitter had failed several hours before—unbeknownst to the crew—and nobody knew where NC-3 was on the vast, stormy Atlantic. Even when searches began, nobody looked so far to the southwest.

Jack had one option: sail NC-3 to the Azores. They had no communication and their scant supplies wouldn't last more than a day or two. Their only drinkable water was radiator water, which pooled in the bilge, tainted with oil and rust. Waves and heavy rain battered the craft, which was made for travels in the air, not on the open sea. With no other options, they began to sail the stricken seaplane toward the Azores. The large hull, canvas wings, and struts caught the stiff wind and carried the flying boat over the seas with surprising speed. They also made intermittent use of the engines and propellers.

The crew used two buckets as sea anchors to stabilize their ungainly ship as it plowed through the storm and ten-foot seas at thirteen knots—about fifteen miles per hour. Jack expertly kept them on course by making sextant sightings on the sun and stars. They took care to move northeast while also keeping their bow to the waves, which would swamp them if taken sideways. The storm increased its temper overnight, and swells grew upward of twenty-five feet. The rain and waves began to batter the intrepid plane to pieces. The sea ripped off the pontoon on the port (left) wing and the men began taking turns sitting on the end of the starboard wing to ensure the opposite wingtip—no longer supported by a float—stayed clear of the water. Should the greedy waves catch the wingtip, they would pull it under and swamp the entire plane along with its crew. The men also punched holes in the fabric wings to keep water from collecting and dragging them down. At the same time, their hands were growing swollen from pumping water from the hull, which had sprung several leaks.

The waves subsided on May 18—their second day afloat—which allowed the pilots to motor their craft toward the island of San Miguel in the Azores. Jack continued taking bearings to ensure they were on course. Should they miss the island, they wouldn't make landfall until they reached Europe, 760 miles to the east. Each crew member knew they'd never survive that scenario. They had to rely on their battered boat and Jack's skill as a navigator and leader.

The storm resumed and continued dismembering the ship during their second night afloat. It sent the men scurrying about the wings tightening bolts and lines that the jarring waves had loosened. The pumping continued, draining energy they could replenish with neither food nor rest. Their provisions quickly ran low and the constant bucking and cold spray conspired to keep the men awake around the clock.

Towers estimated they were nearing San Miguel on the morning of May 19. Another storm pushed them temporarily off course, but they recovered and soon sighted the peaks of an island. His sighting put them forty-four miles distant.

"The effect on all hands was astonishing," Towers recalled. "After two days without seeing any sight of a vessel and expecting to go down any moment, to have land in sight! It was still rough, and we didn't know if the old wreck would hold together long enough to make shore. But there was hope, spelt with a great big H."[5]

The commander hoisted their American flag and mission pennant. He would sail a beaten and battered ship—a flying boat with shredded wings, really—into the harbor, but he would do it proudly. At 4:12 P.M. they were seven miles off the harbor entrance and were finally spotted.

"We crabbed in under the eastern end of the breakwater, and into the harbor," Towers said. "That place was perfect bedlam. Whistles were blowing, flags flying everywhere, and boats chasing about like mad." Everyone thought they'd surely met their end at sea.

Several days later, NC-4, the only plane in Towers's command that was still serviceable, would leave to complete the crossing—although for curious reasons, the Secretary of the Navy (against protests from Assistant Secretary Franklin Roosevelt) ordered that Towers not pilot the flight himself. Jack dutifully swallowed that bitter pill and offered his encouragement as Albert C. "Putty" Read and his crew took off on May 25 in NC-4, bound for Portugal. Two days later, they arrived in Lisbon, becoming the first men to cross the Atlantic by air. The Secretary of the Navy later apologized to Towers for his mistake.

All the NC aviators became celebrities and were feted in Europe and America alike. The transatlantic feat earned mission commander Towers and naval aviation itself new respect, and Towers continued his rise as one of the young discipline's greatest protectors, advocates, and strategists.

He progressed through the ranks quickly, reaching captain in 1930, and commanding the carriers *Langley* and *Saratoga* during the next decade. Many peers called him the Prince of Naval Aviation.

In 1932, Jack sailed to Hawaii in command of a navy task force assigned to simulate an attack on Oahu in a joint exercise with the army. He sailed the carriers *Lexington* and *Saratoga* into position one hundred miles north of the island and launched his first wave of planes against Pearl Harbor before dawn on Sunday morning, February 7, 1932. That was the navy's first night-time launch.

The navy aircraft caught the rival Army Air Corps and all of Pearl Harbor entirely unaware. The army managed to launch one wave of planes, but they couldn't catch the navy attackers. The army pilots returned to their base at Pearl Harbor. Towers had predicted exactly that, and a second wave of navy planes descended upon the army base just as its last plane returned. The army howled that a Sunday morning attack was most unfair, but the navy's victory was complete. Unfortunately, by Sunday, December 7, 1941, everyone except the Japanese had forgotten Towers's lesson.

As a brown-shoe aviator in a black-shoe-run navy, Jack Towers waged a continual campaign to enhance the role of aviation within the fleet. Many friends encouraged him to leave aviation if he valued his career; he didn't even consider it. The established order of battleship admirals developed a strong distaste for Towers, but as his tactics helped lead naval aviation (and the entire Pacific Fleet) through World War II, he finally won their respect. But before the war, their hostility to him was such that the promotion board—comprised of unfavorable surface admirals—pointedly denied him the rank of admiral. President Franklin D. Roosevelt had seen the results of Towers's work, however, and he personally intervened, naming him Chief of the Bureau of Aeronautics, which automatically elevated him to the flag rank of admiral, meaning a starred flag would fly from the mast of any ship on which he sailed. By the end of his career, he would earn four stars and serve as Commander-in-Chief, Pacific Fleet. From 1911 until his retirement in 1947, he remained naval aviation's greatest advocate and its true champion.

Tactically, Jack Towers's lifelong tenacity and unflinching vision helped prepare naval aviation for its pivotal role in World War II and beyond. On a more personal level, he set an example of daring, innovation, and leadership that generations of naval aviators would follow. Today, his spirit still guides the aviators and airmen who arrive each year at the base he helped found—Naval Air Station (NAS) Pensacola—to receive their introduction to this special fraternity.

2

THE CRADLE OF NAVAL AVIATION

As NAVAL AVIATION MATURED OVER the decades, so did Pensacola. When aviators first arrived at the converted navy yard along the Gulf of Mexico, they launched and landed on the waters of Pensacola Bay in biplanes rigged with pontoons. Airmen routinely carried the first aviators to their planes so their boots wouldn't get soaked in the surf. Seaplane ramps began lining the waterfront and planes were stored under canvas tents. After 1915, expansive hangars for the navy's blimps and airplanes sprang up around the base. Then the concrete seaplane ramps began to see less use and the blimp hangars stood empty as the navy's focus shifted to carrier operations. Runways soon covered Pensacola's sand dunes and scrubs while new brick buildings replaced the base's early makeshift facilities. When the jet age arrived in the 1950s, the shorter airstrips disappeared, replaced by Forest Sherman Field. The airfield, named to honor the former Chief of Naval Operations who helped orchestrate America's World War II victory in the Pacific, now operates props and jets year-round on its three runways, which each stretch well over seven thousand feet.

Pensacola was indeed one of naval aviation's starting points and the base has been called the "cradle of naval aviation" for decades. But in addition to nurturing the fledgling discipline of naval aviation itself, Pensacola has also forged generation after generation of aspiring pilots, aircrew, and others who play a role in naval flight operations. The base trains almost every type of sailor or aviator needed to run a carrier air wing: ordnancemen, rescue swimmers, mechanics, aircrew, and pilots for jets, prop planes, and helicopters. From that storied base flows the continually replenished stream of highly trained men and women who *are* naval aviation.

With its moss-draped live oaks, green lawns, and two golf courses, however, NAS Pensacola can seem more a university campus or resort than a military installation. The heart of the base sits along the brilliantly white sands of crystal-clear Pensacola Bay, and classic brick buildings with crisp white trim make the base one of the country's most beautiful. Not everyone appreciates the serenity and beauty of the grounds, however. Aesthetics were the last thing on the mind of eight students who'd assembled before 7:30 A.M. for a notoriously strenuous morning workout at the Search and Rescue (SAR) Swimmer schoolhouse.

This particular day began with one of those springtime Florida mornings that heralded the coming of a hot and humid summer. Bright sunshine coated the grassy drill field in front of the SAR building and pool, where enlisted sailors prepare for jobs as aircrew aboard the navy's helicopters. Eight current students had reported early for their daily physical training session, and exercises had scarcely begun when sweat started pouring from Jace Piper's shaved head. The sweat soon began to seep through the nineteen-year-old's stark white T-shirt, which was stenciled front and back with PIPER. Drill instructors circled him like sharks and their shouts broke the morning quiet. All this transpired under a serene blue sky, to which Jace paid no attention. He was looking straight at the ground.

Airman Apprentice Piper held his back ramrod straight and veins lined the two tanned and muscled arms that strained to keep him off the ground. He had already pounded out sixty push-ups, but the instructors wanted more. Piper had quickly become a favorite among the cadre of instructors at the SAR schoolhouse; he would tackle every task and give it everything he could. Nobody worked harder during PT.

"Sixty-one," his partner called out as Piper rose from the grass again and locked his shaking arms. He mechanically lowered and raised himself again. "Sixty-two."

Piper paused, winced, and took two deep breaths.

"You are *not* tired," boomed an instructor several inches from Piper's sweat-beaded head. "You are *not* tired!"

"Let's go, keep going," yelled another instructor who stood on Piper's other side.

Piper pounded out sixty-three.

He went down for sixty-four, then began to struggle.

"Do not lay on that deck, Piper! Get up!"

He slowly rose and locked his arms again. Sixty-five. His partner—a classmate—joined the instructors in asking for one more push-up. Piper complied, then it was over.

"This is my workhorse," said Petty Officer First Class Jake Brandon proudly, pointing at the exhausted rescue swimmer candidate. "He's a machine."

Judging by his appearance, so was Petty Officer Brandon, a SAR instructor and my escort that morning. Jake stood five feet, nine inches tall and his body had the solidity of a brick. He wore a pair of sunglasses that made him look anything but friendly. That, of course, was the impression he hoped to give his students.

"You don't like any of your instructors when you go through here," the SAR veteran told me later. "And if you do, there's a problem because we're not providing the intensity that's supposed to be there. We're simulating the real intensity that'd be out there on a real rescue."

Together, we watched Piper and seven fellow sailors stand up together and face their lead instructor. He led them through a series of stretches to reset their burning arms and help prevent any injuries as the PT session continued. Impressively, the instructors did many of the drills alongside the students. Even though they were many years removed from their own basic training, they still kept in top shape—the kind necessary to leap from a helicopter, swim through rough seas, and rescue a downed pilot or crew member. Navy helicopters conduct almost two hundred rescues each year, and many of those require a swimmer to jump or lower from a helicopter and plow through heavy seas to save people in distress. In the SAR schoolhouse, instructors prepare future swimmers mentally and physically so they'll never hesitate and always bring the victim home safely.

The stretching ended and the instructor announced the next cycle, or evolution as they called it: sit-ups. Four white shirts put their backs on the grass and crossed their arms over their chests. Four others grasped their feet and pressed down.

"Go," said the instructor, looking at his stopwatch. The yelling commenced again—coming mostly from the instructors who walked among the students like teachers proctoring a high school exam—except that they were sweating and yelling. Cries of encouragement from the other students to their partners joined those of the instructors.

"The yelling is motivation to get their intensity up," Petty Officer Brandon explained, in between his own yells of encouragement. "And it's not just us yelling; they're yelling for each other. Sometimes the students aren't loud enough so we let them know they need to yell louder. Motivation is key here at the schoolhouse; it'll help you get through a lot of evolutions."

The instructor called time on the first group, all of whom immediately collapsed onto their backs, closing their eyes in exhaustion and wincing with each breath they sucked in. Their stomach muscles burned.

The respite, of course, did not last long and the instructors quite pointedly motivated them to their feet. The other four students then lay on the ground for their turn. Their still-huffing partners knelt to grab their feet. The lead instructor looked at his watch and called, "Go!"

Rescue swimmer candidate Airman Apprentice Fales grabbed Piper's feet and Piper began his sit-ups: up and down, up and down with astounding speed, pace, and precision. He was every bit the machine Petty Officer Brandon had described. His legs remained stock-still, his back almost rigid. Up and down, up and down under the eyes of two instructors who lorded over him, casting shadows across his face as his head bobbed. Piper's face showed no emotion.

He cruised past thirty and forty. The yelling grew more intense. Fifty. Sixty. He began to wince and slow his pace. Sixty-five.

"Get up, Piper, these are easy," one instructor yelled. "Are you going to let Fales beat you? Come on—pull up! Pull up! Get up, Piper!"

"Get up, get up, get up," another laid into him. "Come on, Piper, you're like an obese old lady trying to do a sit-up!" The lead instructor mercifully called time. Piper collapsed onto his back. His chest heaved. His eyes closed tightly against the bright sun.

Petty Officer Brandon stood expressionless, his arms crossed, and took in the scene. As the students recovered, he turned to me and said, "When they class up that first week, we let them know this isn't a five-week tour; this is a lifestyle change. You have to like PT; you have to like pushing your body beyond its limits. If you don't, this program isn't for you."

Brandon clearly relished his job of instructing new students *and* being paid to keep himself in top shape. He did admit that staying in shape seemed harder after he recently turned thirty. Regardless, he continued to show up for PT at 7:30 every morning, staying in every bit as good condition as his much-younger students. His commitment to the SAR mission had never wavered.

"We try to instill in them a program," he said, "a workout routine they can continue to use throughout the remainder of their career, be it four years or twenty. One of the biggest things we preach to them is that you've got to stay in shape for the remainder of your training so when you get to a squadron, you're ready to go jump out of an aircraft and save someone's life."

That was why Jace Piper was on that field. That's why he had accepted the challenge. That's why he was pounding out push-ups every morning. When I met him the preceding day, he had confided that he wanted to make a difference in someone's life. He viewed becoming a rescue swimmer as his calling.

"I want to be that hope that saves them when they're out in the ocean, thinking they might die," he said. "I want to be the guy who makes a difference.

"The navy search and rescue swimmers' motto here is 'So others may live.' Everybody is a really giving person and cares about everyone else. We know that we'll all do whatever we have to do to make sure you come home alive. Even if it's giving our own life, you're coming home."

A bugle call broke the morning stillness and rang out across the base: *Morning Colors.* Its staccato notes marked the official beginning of the day— a day that had started an hour earlier for these students and instructors who stopped in their tracks and turned toward the distant flagpole at the base headquarters. They stood at attention as the notes of the national anthem played and the flag rapidly climbed to its perch. Finally, the last note sounded and echoed across the dewy fields.

"Team, fall in," cried Piper, breaking the momentary trance that had settled over the group. He raised his hand and his six classmates fell in behind him and Airman Apprentice Fales, whose name led to all the creative taunts you might imagine.

Together, Piper and Fales bellowed, "D team, running formation, get there!"

As one, the entire team responded, "D team, huh!"

Together, Piper and Fales shouted, "D team, forward march!"

As one, the entire team responded, "And step!"

"Forward at a double time," the leaders shouted, and the team let out a collective "Hoo-yah!"

"March," ordered Piper and Fales, and the team hustled to the pull-up bars on the shaded west side of the schoolhouse.

Piper and Fales sang out, "D team, pull-up bars, get there!"

As one, the team responded, "D team, huh!"

Two students leaped up, grabbed two opposing bars, and began the repetitions. The six other airmen yelled encouragement. The four circling instructors added their voices to the chorus.

After each class member had seemingly left everything on the pull-up bar, the group re-formed and jogged to the paved trail that ran along Pensacola Bay. They had exhausted their arms, abs, and backs. Now the instructors would work their legs.

On the way to the shoreline, I jogged with Jace.

"I can't believe someone doesn't quit every day," I said.

He replied, "It's a lot harder to quit when people are yelling at you, sir."

I laughed—somehow he had energy enough to let a smile spread across his sweat-streaked face. "I just remember as long as I keep breathing, I'll be fine," he said. "As long as I'm breathing, I'm alive and it can't be that bad. But just breathing and being loud isn't enough. You're not going to graduate this school by yourself. You've got to become a team and you've got to work as a team, help each other along."

During their five weeks in the SAR schoolhouse, students commit to their mission and the lifestyle it demands. Those who aren't committed won't last; roughly 35 percent wash out before they graduate from the SAR program. And not only do these young men and women commit to the navy and the SAR program, they learn to commit to one another.

Several minutes later, Airman Apprentice Piper and his classmates were hustling down the shoreline on a timed run. Even at this early hour, the sun was baking NAS Pensacola and drawing prodigious amounts of sweat from students and instructors alike. As their forms grew smaller in the distance, Petty Officer Brandon drifted over to me, his arms still crossed and his dark glasses still on. With the students gone, his face wore an easy grin. He remembered being in Piper's shoes.

Unlike Piper's hometown of Monrovia, Indiana (population 628), Petty Officer Brandon hailed from Southern California. He graduated from high school and began playing baseball for a junior college. "But apparently you have to go to class to be on the baseball team," he said, and his grin became significantly more pronounced. With his grades in the proverbial tank, he left school and tried construction. It wasn't for him and so he tried his parents' career path: the U.S. Navy. His recruiter asked if he liked to swim.

"Of course," he'd replied.

"How about in the ocean," came the next question.

Even better. He was, after all, from Southern California.

The recruiter put him in the rescue swimmer program, explaining it was like being a lifeguard on a boat—plus some other stuff.

"I signed up and had no clue what it really involved until I got down here and started figuring out what this schoolhouse is all about," he confessed, laughing at his twenty-one-year-old self.

"I started figuring out that this is going to be some tough training! But as it turns out, I'm really fortunate to have been placed in this position. They get you in shape and if you stick with us long enough, you'll be in the best physical shape of your life.

"You get a few freaks of nature who'll do twenty-four pull-ups, which is a lot, but overall I'd say ninety-nine percent of the time we're a lot more physically fit than the students, even though we're older. We still have to maintain. Like you saw back there, we do PT with them every time they're doing it."

Physical fitness serves as the base requirement to enter the SAR program. In the fleet, Petty Officer Brandon explained, following directions and paying attention to details are the difference between accomplished missions and failed missions. And like every other instructor at Pensacola, the SAR instructors train their sailors to succeed in the fleet.

"One more thing," he said. "Most instructors here have it in their mind that they're not going to let anything beat them. You don't want to lose and that's the mentality you have to have: 'Nothing here can break me. I'm not going to die. I can beat this school hands down.'

"Of course it's a lot of work along the way, but you have to have that 'I'm not gonna quit' attitude and that's what we expect in the fleet. You're going to be tasked, probably in the middle of the night, with having to go pull eight guys out of the water. We want somebody who jumps out of that helicopter and says, 'I've got all eight of these guys. They're all getting back home safely.' That's what we want: a no-quit attitude. If you even *think* you can't do it, you've already defeated yourself."

As I would observe in many others, Jake Brandon seemed supremely happy in his job. He'd found an adventure with a purpose and appreciated every second.

The SAR swimmer program graduates anywhere from three to twenty students per class, sending them into a fleet where they are needed aboard almost every helicopter the navy flies. And today, the navy has almost as many helicopters as fixed-wing aircraft. Its thirty-eight fleet helicopter squadrons execute underwater mine countermeasure missions, transport supplies, hunt submarines, provide combat air support, and perform search and rescue. Forty-five percent of naval aviators currently go through helicopter training. By 2013, more than 50 percent of naval aviators will fly rotary-wing aircraft. The SAR schoolhouse will have to keep up with the increased demand for aircrew.

The swimmers stand out as members of their helo crew and as members of the ship's company for several reasons, but one in particular. I remember trotting along the flight deck of the USS *Dwight D. Eisenhower* toward the spinning SH-60F Seahawk that waited to carry me over the Indian Ocean. When I saw the helo, I immediately noticed a pair of bare legs hanging out the door. Everyone on the flight deck wears long pants. Except the SAR swimmers. They take immeasurable pride in wearing canvas khaki shorts that most people generally agree are terribly out of date and much too short. But they wear these outfits to show their commitment to readiness and service.

"The shorts—UDTs, we call them—are a source of pride," Petty Officer Brandon tried to explain.

But, he admitted, the rough shorts haven't changed much since the navy's Underwater Demolition Teams (hence UDTs) began wearing them during World War II. Now, SEALs, SEAL instructors, rescue swimmers, and SAR instructors wear them regularly. Wearing UDTs has become a tradition, but not a particularly functional one.

"You have to earn your UDTs," Brandon said, "and that means making it through rescue swimmer school. On their last run before they graduate, students get to wear their UDTs for the first time. We instructors know the shorts will start rubbing and we've built up a tolerance. Students get a huge rash on the inside of their legs—that canvas chafes and rubs them raw and they're dying at the end of the run! That's earning their UDTs. That's pride."

After they graduate basic training at Naval Station Great Lakes in Illinois, almost every enlisted sailor or marine pursuing an aviation career path comes to the Navy's Aviation School—A-School for short—at the Naval Aviation Technical Training Center (NATTC), which sits on the eastern side of the base. Each arrives in Pensacola as an airman, airman apprentice, or airman recruit—depending on their experiences prior to enlisting. Generally, everyone just calls them airmen or maintainers. Their classes at NATTC teach them specialized skills which they'll later hone in squadrons. Some will learn how to fix jet engines, some will specialize in electronics and radars, others will study survival equipment, and yet others will learn to maintain an aircraft body. Their instructors ensure they learn completely and quickly. Before Jace Piper or Jake Brandon set foot in the rescue swimmer schoolhouse, they had to complete their coursework at A-School.

The navy spends numerous hours maintaining aircraft for every hour of actual flying time. Their thousands of working parts require constant attention. Sometimes, mechanics and technicians will work extra-long hours, fixing an issue or "gripe" and returning the aircraft to flight status. Without proper—and frequent—maintenance, these complex machines don't leave a carrier deck and missions don't get accomplished. Without the same maintenance attention, the carriers can't sail at all. The navy's engineers, repair technicians, and mechanics form a large and absolutely critical piece of the naval aviation team. The navy's enlisted aircraft maintainers fight their war with tools instead of rifles, but their contributions are as valuable as those made by soldiers on the ground or pilots in the air.

When these aspiring airmen arrive at NATTC, they find a new campus that looks like a modern branch of a large university. The buildings have brick facades and metal roofing, and they surround a horseshoe-shaped quad that bakes cars and airmen alike in the summer heat. Chevalier Hall, also called the Mega Building, dominates the campus and holds much of the classroom space. The palm trees outside give the buildings and barracks a decidedly unmilitary atmosphere. That resort-like atmosphere stops at the doors.

Inside a Chevalier Hall classroom, I found nineteen newly arrived students, seated quietly in their blue and gray camouflage uniforms awaiting a visit from their Leading Chief Petty Officer. Soon, Chief David San Angelo swept into the room, striding up the aisle toward the front.

"Good morning, shipmates," he said as he carried his solid six-foot-two frame up the aisle.

"Good morning, Chief," the students boomed in response.

He reached the front of the classroom and turned to face the students—the most recent nineteen of the eleven thousand who come through the program annually. "Welcome to Pensacola," he began, in a matter-of-fact voice, marked with a slight Southern accent. Then he jumped straight into his message:

"This training will be unlike any other training you've ever received. Who did not graduate from high school?"

Two hands were raised.

"Who here has had some college?"

Several other hands went into the air.

"Okay, in high school and college, you have literature, math, and science for one or one and a half hours per day. In the navy, you train on one subject, eight hours a day, five days a week. That's forty hours of instruction per week—that's a lot of stuff being put into your heads. To get that much instruction in one subject in high school or college, you'd go to school for two months. We're going to pack it into five days."

He let that fact hang in the air.

"Some of you will be here for two, three, six months, and it'll get boring—guaranteed. What I need you to do is find *your* motivation. Find your motivation for learning. This is your job. This is what you get paid to do—to learn."

Eventually, they'd all have to find their own inner drive, but today, Chief San Angelo stood before them in his crisply pressed khaki uniform and delivered them an initial dose, in his own well-practiced style.

"You did *not* join the navy to push a broom on a deck that doesn't need to be swept for eight hours a day," he began. "You didn't join to wipe down a wall that doesn't need to be washed. This isn't barracks support duty. This is the real deal. You have to get the skills developed now to do your job in the fleet.

"Let me tell you right now, every single one of you will be an aircraft maintainer. You're going to be working on aircraft. It's not like being an auto mechanic. Auto mechanics work on cars and if they make a mistake, ninety-nine percent of the time the driver can pull that car over to the side of the road safely. In naval aviation, if you make a mistake, there'll be a malfunction in flight—and someone's gonna die. These aircraft are flying at five hundred or twelve hundred miles per hour. When there is a malfunction in flight, they can't correct it, they're moving too fast and they're too high. Those pilots depend on you to know your job. And the only way you get to know your job is by paying attention in here eight hours a day, five days a week, until we're done and you've learned this stuff. Their lives depend on you.

"I guarantee you, when you're working on that flight deck, a pilot will come up to you, look you dead in the eye and ask you, 'Did you fix this aircraft?'

"You're gonna look them dead in their eye and say, 'Sir, ma'am, this aircraft is good to go. From nose to tail, I fixed this aircraft. You can fly this aircraft to *Hell* and it will bring you back. I guarantee it.'

"Then they'll look in *your* eye and say, 'Aye, aye,' and get in that aircraft and take off. They're putting their lives in your hands.

"And it's not just them that are depending on you," the chief expounded. "Most of our pilots have spouses and children. Their children expect Mom and Dad to come home every single night or come home from every single deployment. They depend on you as well.

"Not only that, navy and marine corps aviation has a fifteen-minute response time. We have boots on the ground saying, 'I need air support; I need air support now.'

"If you don't have those airplanes fixed and ready to go, we cannot launch them from a flight deck to provide that support to our brothers and sisters in arms. It's on you. You've gotta pay attention now."

He looked around the classroom, making sure that he held everyone's attention. He saw nineteen pairs of eyes intently trained on him. He continued.

"The navy and Marine Corps are the most formidable force in the entire world," he explained with no small trace of pride. "Let me say that again. The navy and Marine Corps are the most formidable force in the entire world. The navy currently has eleven aircraft carriers and the navy and Marine Corps are the only two services in the world that operate on land, sea, and air. We are the only service in the world that can be almost anywhere in fifteen minutes. In fifteen minutes, we will receive one phone call, load a bird on a catapult, launch it off the end, fly a hundred miles, and drop an ungodly amount of ordnance on the enemy with more precision and accuracy than anybody else. That's what we can do in fifteen minutes—land, sea, and air.

"This country depends on your ability to maintain that force. You're going to be out there defending the liberties and freedoms of this great country and it all starts here and now by paying attention and learning what we teach you. I need you to pay attention. I need you to learn this material.

"Can ya'll do that for me?"

"Yes, Chief," the class boomed again.

"Hoo-yah?" he asked, using the familiar navy expression.

"Hoo-yah!" the class answered emphatically.

"Ooo-rah?" he asked the marines in the group.

"Ooo-rah!"

"It was a pleasure talking to y'all," he said, concluding the day's motivational session. Then his tone and still-youthful thirty-two-year-old countenance softened. Like he was confiding a great secret in the class before him, he said earnestly, "If you ever need to come talk to me for whatever reason, come see me. Personal, financial, school; I'm here to help you. My job is not to yell at young sailors and marines. That's not why I became a chief. My job is to help you give a hundred percent. You got personal issues or financial issues at home? Then you can't give me a hundred percent and I need a hundred percent and you'll need a hundred percent on the flight line. When you're standing on that flight line and you only have ninety-nine percent focus, you may cost somebody his life."

He looked across the nineteen faces one last time. Satisfied that he'd made an impression, he said, "Thanks, shipmates, y'all have a good afternoon," and walked down the aisle and into the hallway.

I left my seat on the back row and met him in the empty corridor. We walked toward his office, past door after door leading to classrooms like the one we just left. Chief San Angelo had visited almost every one to make sure the next generation of airmen has a real commitment to their jobs and the navy's mission.

"When I was in front of that class," he explained, "I was doing everything I could to motivate them. But while they're in school they're going to lose all that motivation. They'll get so bored with the curriculum and the same monotonous day. I was here in A-School for six months and it was like one long day. It was the same thing every day: wake up at five a.m., go to physical training, go to school, go to lunch, go to school, go to sleep. Six months, the same day, over and over again. After a while, you don't really understand why you're in or why you even *want* to be in the navy. But when you get to the fleet, it's entirely different—entirely different. In the fleet, people will come up with their own ideas of why they're here. They'll get a good deployment and feel they're serving their country; they'll be part of something with their best friends beside them. Or maybe it's just that guaranteed welfare check we get on the first and fifteenth of the month. That stability keeps a lot of people in, too. They're always able to provide for their family or themselves."

For Dave, family tradition had led him into the navy after high school, but he left not long after he enlisted. As he put it, "I was focused more on liberty time than work time. I was basically immature."

Leaving the navy at eighteen didn't help his maturity any and he grew increasingly unhappy with his life's direction. He needed discipline—not the harsh, knuckle-rapping variety but rather some structure, purpose, and direction. Chastened and seasoned by life outside school and the military, he returned at age twenty-one. Thankfully, he said, the navy took him back. He repaid them by becoming one of the younger chief petty officers in the fleet, making the rank in just nine years, not the more average thirteen.

"But when I came through at twenty-one years of age, I was still lacking a lot of responsibility," he said. "When I came back, the navy showed me how to be responsible, to take care of a job, and manage all that goes along with that. When you look at any sailor, you're looking at someone who'll be at work on time all the time. Accountability—that's something bred into us from Day One. Our sailors will be held accountable for their actions and the consequences will be dire—and it's not the consequences to *them* that will be dire. It's the consequences to *others*; consequences to the mission."

Dave's responsibility was training these young men and women for the fleet and preparing them to perform at the highest levels. He had to inspire them, make sure their instructors delivered lessons well, and see that the airmen learned their jobs. If he accomplished his goals, these women and men would help America's warplanes execute their missions successfully and safely. If Chief San Angelo failed in his job, there would be consequences. The motivational scenarios he laid out in the classroom applied to him as well. If he didn't do his job well, a soldier or sailor could lose his life; a young child could lose their father or mother.

Because the chief realized that, he did everything in his power to help his students succeed. When he invited them to bring their worries to him, he meant it. He can't let troubles distract them, so his door remains open.

"You wouldn't believe what comes through my door," he said. "For some students, I have to be a father figure. For others, I have to be a sounding board because they're frustrated. I have to lead some of them by the hand to get their life squared away. It's the *Jerry Springer Show* all the way to some of the most intricate investment questions you can imagine."

Recently, a twenty-three-year-old sailor had come to see him. She faced a mountain of debt that had started to accumulate when she was only fourteen years old. That's when her parents began putting utility bills in her name and not paying them.

She dropped out of high school at age seventeen to care for her younger siblings after her mother became a state prisoner. A tax preparer had badly mishandled her taxes and another relative wrongfully claimed her siblings as dependents, leading to trouble with the IRS. She joined the navy to escape her situation and find stability, security, and a purpose. When she enlisted, however, utility companies, debt collectors, and the IRS were still chasing her. She came to see the chief.

"She needs to get a security clearance and she can't get that with a whole lot of debt," Chief San Angelo explained. "I ended up taking her to the IRS—drove her myself—and sat down with her at the IRS to figure out what was going on. We brought her back here, filed rebuttals for her utility bills, and talked about some credit card debt she needs to take care of herself. She's accountable for that piece. Now we have a plan and in two weeks, she'll be in much better shape. She came into the office owing ten thousand dollars. Now she owes four hundred and fifty."

The same week, the chief chased down an estranged husband who wasn't paying his child support. His student, who was caring for a child while going through A-School, didn't have any contact information for her husband; all she knew was his army unit and that he had deployed to Kosovo.

"Do you know how hard it is to get the phone number for an army unit in Kosovo?" Chief San Angelo asked me with a grin. "It took me three-quarters of a day to get in touch with his camp. I talked with this deadbeat's first sergeant and my sailor and her child started getting their support.

"Those things are my job as chief here. She's worried about her child and she can't focus on her work here. I need them all to focus."

"Considering everything," he said, "this is the greatest job in the world and I wouldn't change it for anything. Those students will ask me, 'How much longer you got in, Chief?' I tell them forever. I'll retire one day—and then come in to work the next day! They'll have to kick me out."

That seemed to prove a common theme among the instructors at Pensacola.

Inside the hanger of Training Air Wing Six—one of the buildings that line the endless Forest Sherman airstrip—I met another instructor who shared the chief's sentiments about her current job. Flight navigation instructor Lieutenant Amber Dempsen trained Naval Flight Officers (NFOs), the skilled officers who serve alongside pilots as navigators, bombardiers, and weapons and electronics experts aboard an array of aircraft.

Students on two tracks pass through the Aviation Preflight Indoctrination (API) program: those who will become pilots and those who will become NFOs. In API, all students at Pensacola learn the basic fundamentals of flight, engines, systems operation, navigation, survival, and risk management. Their performance and aptitudes, along with the needs of the navy, help determine the paths they each will follow later. After completing six weeks of API, aspiring navy and marine aviators pursue either fixed-wing platforms or rotary-wing platforms—airplanes or helicopters. After they complete the next phase of flight training, pilots and NFOs receive assignments to begin learning their specialty. On the fixed-wing side, pilots primarily learn to fly jets (F/A-18 Hornets and Super Hornets, EA-18G Growlers, or EA-6B Prowlers) or turboprop-driven E-2C Hawkeyes, C-2 Greyhounds, C-130s, or P-3C Orions. Most rotary-wing pilots learn the SH-60/HH-60/MH-60 Seahawk platform, which fly without NFOs. Those individuals pursuing the navy's NFO path begin training for missions as navigators and weapons officers in the same airplanes with the exception of the single-seat Fleet F/A-18s.

"Before students arrive in our classroom, they haven't had any interaction with NFOs," Amber said, "so we bring them into the NFO community. They're still new to the navy, so we also train them to become good officers and help them learn to survive in aviation. And part of our particular role as NFO instructors is teaching our students to be a leader even though they're not the pilot. A pilot or an NFO can be the mission commander. And when I serve as mission commander, I'm responsible for anything on that plane. Just because you're not at the controls doesn't mean you're not commanding the mission."

When I met Lt. Dempsen, she was sitting across the table from a student who was just starting the long trek to become an NFO mission commander. The student was about to take his sixth training flight. Instructor and student squared off in a cramped conference room, with an aeronautical chart spread across the table and a whiteboard full of preflight information on the wall. The student—a twenty-three-year-old ensign who looked slightly too small for his olive flight suit—showed just a trace of nervousness as his instructor began the preflight brief. The preceding five flights and mountains of classroom work had given him a fair amount of confidence and he fielded question after question, providing the answers as rapidly as the questions came at him.

Amber spends much of her time preparing students for worst-case scenarios. On this day, she covered the three areas of aviation safety and operational risk management: Man, Mission, and Weather. Were the pilot and NFO trained, briefed, and ready? Did they know the routes, altitudes, and goals for the mission? What was the weather and how could it change? She made sure her student was prepared for anything, especially the worst. She also led him through a review of the seven skills that prevent mishaps: decision making, assertiveness, mission analysis, communication, leadership, adaptability, and situational awareness.

The two then walked through the entire flight, covering the possible emergencies that might arise on the ground, during takeoff, en route, over the target, on the return, and on final approach. How would he salvage the mission—and his life—should an emergency occur? What would he do if a fire broke out while taxiing? What if they lost an engine during the flight?

For all their bravado, pilots and NFOs are serious risk managers. Even the most boisterous among them get serious as they review contingencies that could mean life or death. They carefully assess the dangers of each flight and plan carefully to avoid them so they can safely return from the mission with the aircraft and their lives.

"You can't fly a mission blindly," Amber explained. "We go through what to expect, what to do in event of emergency. That's not just something we do in training; we'll also spend hours briefing in the fleet. We'll talk with intel officers and other crews that have flown the same mission—what are the threats, what should we do for given scenarios? Guys will be flying jets at five hundred knots; they can't think about what to do. You have to know already. Considering the mishaps we've had—and that we could have—I talk about one real mishap during each brief to reinforce why all these procedures are important. These procedures are written in blood."

That day, Amber and her student briefed for a low-level flight that would take them from Pensacola to the coast of Alabama, up toward the Georgia-Florida border, then back to Pensacola. They'd be flying a T-1 Jayhawk from NAS Pensacola over the Gulf of Mexico to a point just southwest of Mobile Bay. There, at the appointed time, they'd begin their run inland to the target. Amber reached over the chart and pointed to the start of the run.

"Okay," she said, "where are we here?"

The ensign replied with altitude, time, and a landmark.

"Right," his instructor confirmed. "Now walk me through what we'll be looking for going north. And tell me what can kill us—remember, we'll be flying low."

Her student traced the route, pointing out the landmarks—bridges, towers, river bends—that would indicate their position or that could pose a threat. She pointed out the power lines that he missed. Unshaken, he continued walking through the mission, noting his altitude and estimated airspeed for each point of the journey. He finally walked through the "course rules" approach and the final turns of the landing pattern at NAS Pensacola, or the "Pensacola break" as it's known to pilots. He was ready and Amber sent him to get his flight gear.

As we waited for him to return, Amber explained, "We always make them consider everything that can prevent us from completing the mission. If you don't talk about things that can go wrong, you won't be prepared, and something will go wrong every flight.

"Particularly in the air, I always try to let the student make the mistake and give him the opportunity to correct it before I jump in there. I always hated when an instructor would tell me what to do a second before I did it. I'm trying to train them how to be a mission commander, so I give them the reins and give them the opportunity to make mistakes so they can fix them."

The ensign emerged from his final preparations, carrying a clipboard and his helmet in a green bag. Together, we walked down the long corridor toward another briefing room where we met the civilian instructor who would serve as the pilot for the day's mission. The ensign would serve as navigator for their T-1 training jet. As a navigation student, the ensign would have a pilot, instructor, and a jet aircraft devoted entirely to his training. The navy dedicates prodigious resources to training its flyers, and the results show in their widely respected performance.

The day's pilot—a retired air force officer—led his navigator through yet another briefing and touched many of the points Amber had covered minutes before. The student gave his answers confidently and correctly. Satisfied his navigator knew his stuff, the pilot said, "Well, it's a perfect day to fly. Let's go."

Amber and I dropped behind the pilot and student on our way to the flight line where the T-1 awaited, fueled and ready. We walked through a pair of tinted glass doors and emerged into the bright sunlight that reflected off the concrete tarmac and the metal hangars. Our ear plugs helped drown out the jet noise that seemed ever-present in Pensacola. You become accustomed to the ubiquitous smell of jet exhaust.

"Our mission in the T-1 program—today and overall—is basically how to get on target on time with enough gas," she explained over the noise. Part of doing that entailed thoroughly preflighting the aircraft. Amber and her student walked around the jet, checking its surfaces, engines, and electrical connections for any trouble. Satisfied, they climbed inside where the student reviewed the dials, gauges, and displays he'd use on the upcoming flight. Shortly, they closed the hatch and taxied toward the runway.

Unfortunately, Amber had to give her student a failing mark on the flight when they returned later that afternoon. It was a graded mission and her student just didn't have everything together. He missed key landmarks and failed to identify several hazards during the flight. He also overlooked procedures that, while they didn't threaten the life of the plane's crew, could have jeopardized a combat mission.

"I spent a long time—a really long time—debriefing him," she told me later. "I could tell he had it in him, he just needed to prepare more. There is nothing more important than preparation, whether you're a student, an instructor, or out in the fleet.

"I helped him with how to study and how to chair-fly the mission. We went over our mission then chair-flew it again together—sitting in our chairs and doing the entire flight. I really wanted to help him succeed, so we spent a lot of time on it."

After his debrief, the ensign had five days to prepare for a flight with a senior instructor who would determine his future. When the flight came, Amber reported that he knocked it out of the park. "That's why we had such a long debrief—he just needed to spend more time on it and hopefully he learned that he'll always need to spend that much time preparing for a flight. It's a serious business."

But it's also fun, and Amber realizes her good fortune. Many aviators and NFOs earn their wings at Pensacola and immediately begin hoping to return as an instructor. Only a relative few have that opportunity.

In her last months of flight school, Amber selected the P-3C Orion program, which prepares aviators and NFOs to crew the navy's long-range patrol aircraft. After she earned her wings at Pensacola, she began training for the maritime missions of the big, four-engine Lockheed-made aircraft.

Since they were introduced to the fleet in 1962, the land-based Orions have patrolled high above the world's oceans gathering intelligence and, most often, searching for hostile submarines. The 135,000-pound planes played a critical role in monitoring the Soviet fleet during the Cold War, using countless sonobuoys and their ability to remain over targets for more than twelve hours to track the enemy.

A former tactical coordinator with Patrol Squadron Nine (VP-9), Jim Winchester recalled a typical Cold War mission, hunting for a new Soviet submarine dubbed the "Philippine Sea Phantom."

"Our admiral learned that the new *Charlie*-class was on patrol near the Mariana Trench," Jim recalled. "So we flew search patterns and dropped listening devices set for different levels, then we stayed on station for ten to twelve hours looking for it. We'd drop sonobuoy patterns, localize him, drop more, then localize. We finally found the Phil Sea Phantom. Then we followed it for twenty-four hours a day for an entire month—we never got a day off. That was the reward!"

Flying in Orions off Vietnam, Guam, and Alaska during the peak of the Cold War, Jim also learned skills that he'd use long after he left the navy. "The navy taught you to appreciate the value of the assets they're putting in your hands and that you had a responsibility," Jim said. "Then they held you accountable. They taught you that there are all types of people that'll work for you: educated but not motivated, uneducated and motivated, et cetera. They'll have different lifestyles and most aren't going to be like you. As a leader, you're expected to educate and motivate them all."

Jim, now president of Quikrete, reflected on one of naval aviation's unexpected gifts to its veterans and America in general. "I still use those skills every day," he said. "The navy taught us how to manage people and run organizations, and that had impact long after I left the service."

Amber Dempsen had learned the same lessons even as she flew in Orions during very different missions.

On her first fleet deployment, she and her eleven-person crew performed ISR—Intelligence, Surveillance, and Reconnaissance—in support of Operations Iraqi Freedom and Enduring Freedom in Afghanistan. From their post above the deserts, cities, and mountains, her Orion crew fed video and tactical information to soldiers and marines on the ground. In recent years, fewer Orions are performing the antisubmarine duties so vital in the Cold War, and instead spend more time patrolling conflict zones in the Middle

East, the pirate-infested waters off Somalia, and the drug routes off South and Central America.

Recently, other service branches have borrowed navy personnel to fill specific missions—particularly as operations in Afghanistan and Iraq have strained their resources. In Amber's case, the army had few people trained for electronic warfare and they began using crews from the navy's P-3C Orions. Thus, Amber began an Individual Augmentation tour where she helped the army install and use electronic devices on their vehicles in Iraq that effectively jam signals that can detonate remote-controlled roadside bombs. Working on the ground proved a very different experience and while she'll never know exactly how many detonation signals her devices foiled, she knows her work definitely saved lives.

"The navy teaches us to be flexible, and it was a great chance to use our skills to help soldiers on the ground in a different way and a particularly meaningful way," Amber reflected. "We were helping our guys survive on the streets. We helped shield them from IEDs so they could complete their missions safely and come back home. We worked with a team, which is something I'm used to doing being from the P-3 community. On our planes, we have a crew of eleven men and women—officers and enlisted. A really unique relationship develops between that team. Even though the P-3C is a good-sized aircraft, you're sharing it with those eleven other people during some long flights. You trust each other and work with each other in way that's pretty unique in the military. When you're flying with those guys for three years, you become a family."

When her tours with the fleet and army ended, she faced a slew of non-flying shore duty options. Fortunately, she wrangled one of the few available flying positions. As an instructor at Pensacola, she flies almost daily and understands that she may be training an ensign who might fly with her when she leads a squadron herself in the future, so she takes a vested interest in the success of her students.

"This is the greatest job in the world," she told me with noticeable relish. "I would not trade it for anything. You prepare these students for the fleet and to shape the future of our navy."

———

The classrooms, drill fields, pools, aircraft, and instructors of Pensacola—and other navy training installations around the country—equip the newest members of the naval aviation family with the concrete skills they need to perform their jobs safely. During their time along the Gulf coast, these young men and women also learn something deeper. Their leaders and instructors instill a set of values just as important as the procedures they study in their textbooks.

That of course happens by design. Jack Towers started the training process almost a century ago and generations of leaders have tailored and improved it to meet the demands of a changing navy and world. The Chief of Naval Air Training (CNATRA—pronounced *Sinatra*) oversees the navy's flight training programs and shoulders responsibility for making former civilians true parts of naval aviation.

As CNATRA, Rear Admiral Mark Guadagnini brought a loaded résumé to the flight training headquarters in Corpus Christi, Texas. The U.S. Naval Academy graduate had commanded Strike Fighter Squadron Fifteen (VFA-15) and Carrier Air Wing Seventeen (CVW-17), completed tours as a test pilot and instructor, served on flag (admiral) staffs in Washington and Pacific Fleet headquarters, and worked as a liaison between the Office of the Secretary of Defense and Congress. During his career, he'd flown missions from twelve aircraft carriers in every major operation since Desert Storm—and in the process inspired two of his sons to pursue his career path. He had an easy way about him that was somehow complemented by his nearly shaved head and the dark moustache that stretched to each corner of his mouth, curling every time he smiled.

His years in the fleet also taught him about the common characteristics that define the diverse people involved in launching aircraft off a flight deck. He discovered that the work of naval aviation doesn't just accomplish tactical missions. It also empowers its people with a powerful set of values. As one of Mark's fellow admirals described it, naval aviation creates the whole sailor.

Men don't have wings, so flying has always been a dangerous endeavor; being airborne is not a natural state for man. Add to that the challenge of launching aircraft from the crowded deck of a pitching carrier or escort ship. Then consider flying, landing, and maneuvering at night in bad weather. Combat adds yet another element of fear. Only courage enables men and women to overcome that fear and still accomplish their mission.

"To function as a human being, to function as a warrior and do those things that are required to be successful in combat takes courage," Mark said in his measured and resonant voice. "That's very different from being fearless. There's no place for fearlessness in naval aviation. We need courage."

Naval aviation also needs people who can get the job done, no matter if enemy bullets are flying, temperatures rise above 100 degrees, or flight decks are caked with ice and snow. Having what the admiral called a mission-accomplishment mind-set takes knowing exactly what the mission requires and knowing what both your team and your opponent are capable of doing. Then you must have the dedication to see your job through to the end, no matter what. If you don't do it, who will?

"I call the third trait 'disciplined aggression,'" he said. "If you're going to win a fight, you've got to take that fight *to* somebody. Be aggressive. You can't sit back and be passive. If you do it in a reckless way, however, you lose teammates, you lose equipment. If you do it in an undisciplined fashion and you don't pay attention to the rules of engagement or the recognized rules of warfare, you end up doing more damage to our country than good."

He moved to another point: adaptability. The navy's training programs teach students proper procedures and planning, but instructors know that a plan rarely survives in a heated engagement. The weather may change, a piece of equipment can malfunction, or a flight deck crew might need to launch a backup jet. Once arriving on-scene, a pilot might discover an entirely different situation than was forecasted. To succeed in combat, the navy's people must be able to adapt quickly and smartly.

"Over all of this," the admiral said, "is integrity. Integrity is what we need to deal with each other and be able to communicate in a timely and necessary fashion when you're in a combat situation. You have to know that the person you're talking to is trustworthy and honest; that the information you're getting from them is accurate so you can act on it and get your job done.

"Without that basic integrity, we fall down. I've been in for thirty-four years and I don't stay in because of the flying. I stay because of the people—people whose word I can take to the bank. I know if they say they'll get this job done, they'll get it done or die trying. I like dealing with people like that, people who are problem solvers. They're excited, they're patriotic. Those are the types of people in our navy."

Despite completing the finely honed training regimens at Pensacola and other bases, however, most new airmen and aviators don't arrive at their fleet assignments possessing all of the qualities Rear Admiral Guadagnini described. Courage, discipline, adaptability, and integrity take root with experience. That experience comes during years of training, or more appropriately, apprenticeship. Once they graduate from the classrooms of Pensacola, their real training begins as a succession of mentors brings them into their assigned community and helps them along their personal journey.

"All of naval aviation is really a grand apprenticeship," Mark told me. "The only way you can really learn this discipline is by getting taught by someone else in an apprentice fashion. So it's passed down from generation to generation . . . Not only those skills required to survive in the air and to succeed in combat, but also those values."

Pensacola has always called itself the cradle of naval aviation because it incubated the nascent navy flight program during the early twentieth century. Today, it deserves the title for another reason. In the nearly one hundred years since naval aviators began training along the Gulf coast, thousands of patient instructors have brought hundreds of thousands of young men and women into their special fraternity. They have endowed them with purpose, given them discipline, sharpened their sense of duty, and built bonds between them. In Pensacola's classrooms and airspace, these teachers have prepared and equipped their students to begin a life of service to the fleet and to others. The skills, values, and unique spirit of naval aviation have thus been handed down through generations, each inspiring the next to reach new levels of excellence. For its men and women, naval aviation becomes a journey of self-improvement that can last five years, ten years, or a lifetime. And for nearly a century, almost every one of those journeys has started here.

3

HIGH TRUST

Blue angels number five and Six roared overhead, wing-to-wing. Their twin General Electric engines startled the crowd and laid down four streaks of exhaust over NAS Pensacola's Sherman Field and the small stands filled with family and friends.

"Oh no, this is the one maneuver I can never watch," Bethany Weisser said to me, turning her face away from the sky and her husband's Number Five jet. "Frank terrifies me every time he does it."

The pilots in the two radiant blue and yellow F/A-18 Hornets were executing one of their perennially favorite tricks: the tuck-away cross.

The crowd had recovered from the initial surprise of Five and Six flying over them, and now followed the jets as they streaked straight away across the runway. Suddenly, the planes rolled in opposite directions then continued their roll back toward each other, looking as though they might crash. The crowd cringed. Then the jets suddenly crossed paths at an impossibly close distance. The crowd gasped collectively; it looked as if they would collide. Trick completed, the two blue jets streaked away and disappeared into the sky.

"That's one of my favorite maneuvers," Blue Angel Number Five, Lieutenant Commander Frank Weisser, would tell me afterward, in amusing contrast to his wife's sentiments.

Blue Angels Five and Six, the "solo team," demonstrate the astounding aerial capabilities of the F/A-18 and the precision flying that it allows. Their maneuvers are not as simple as they may seem from the grandstands. For the tuck-away cross, the two jets roar over the crowd with their wingtips three to five feet apart. As the pair hustles away from the crowd, Frank maintains his precise position by looking ninety degrees to his left and from his vantage point, keeps his partner's wingtip aligned with the middle of the "U" in the "U.S. Navy" emblazoned on his partner's fuselage. Frank doesn't look forward; it's his partner's job to fly the right course, altitude, and airspeed. Then like a magician performing a sleight of hand, Frank slowly slides back so that the crowd won't realize that the two planes are now uneven. Then he calls out a cadence to Number Six and on his command, the two jets roll away from each other; neither pilot can see his partner. They roll upside down and begin to right themselves, looking like they'll actually roll into one another in the process. That draws the first gasp from the audience. Then the two pilots pull hard on their sticks and the jets suddenly cross paths, one passing just feet behind the other. Inevitably, the crowd gasps again, thinking the two planes will finally collide.

"We're about five or ten feet away from each other if we do it correctly," Frank explained, not mentioning that the planes are flying just two hundred feet above the runway at speeds over 400 miles per hour. "It's my job to ensure I'm not going to hit Number Six; it's his job to fly the right profile." He laughed. "Really, he trusts me not to hit him. He *has* to trust me. He doesn't have time to worry about me. He has to roll the right number of degrees, set his wings, add power, and pull at the exact same time so our circles are the same size.

"We have even closer wingtip separation before I slide aft. But the closer you are, the more you minimize the variables. I have more specific reference points the closer I am. The farther away you get, you have less fidelity in your checkpoints."

That's why during some maneuvers, the jets are only eighteen inches apart. If the pilot in the low slot of their four-man Diamond formation had no canopy, he could do a pull-up using the wingtips of the two jets above him.

I'd learned that for different maneuvers, the Blue Angels sight off particular parts of one another's jets. For example, flying one formation correctly means that from Frank's vantage point in the cockpit, the tip of his wing covers the "-rnet" in the yellow letters spelling "F/A-18 Hornet" on his wingman's fuselage. As pilots, they're that precise.

As showmen, they love entertaining the crowd and making the masses think—for just a second—that the planes might crash. That precision and showmanship combine to make the U. S. Navy's Flight Demonstration Squadron—the Blue Angels—world famous and truly legendary. An elite group of maintainers and crew keep seven F/A-18 Hornets and one big C-130 Hercules transport perfectly tuned and spotlessly clean. An equally elite group of six jet pilots, clad in distinctively blue flight suits, electrifies crowds across the country and around the world as they represent the very spirit of the United States Navy.

As volunteers left the military in droves after the Second World War ended, the navy struggled to maintain its air forces. Chief of Naval Operations Admiral Chester Nimitz and Secretary of the Navy James Forrestal ordered the creation of a new aerobatic team to help promote the navy to the postwar public. They selected Pacific ace Roy "Butch" Voris to lead the new team, which they slipped into the navy training command's purview, thus establishing the team's home at NAS Pensacola. Butch was a strapping, well-liked aviator who had earned the name "Old Yellow Hat" in a fleet squadron because his head proved too large for the standard helmets and he modified a football helmet for the job and painted it yellow. His size and superb conditioning helped him wear the mantle of leadership easily and he quickly built a crack team of aerobatic pilots that would arguably become the world's most renowned squadron. During the ensuing decades, the team saw action over Korea while they were deployed aboard the USS *Princeton* as Fighter Squadron 191 (VF-191)—Satan's Kittens. Afterward, they resumed their air show performances and continued building a sterling reputation for teamwork and excellence.

Upon seeing the team perform three months after its inception in April 1946, future admiral Jimmy Thach—the renowned World War II aviator who developed the highly successful "Thach Weave" combat tactic for fighters— became one of the first to realize that the team demonstrated much more than an airplane's capabilities. He told the press, "I don't think you realize what was demonstrated here this morning. It was teamwork."[1]

The exacting precision their brand of teamwork demands binds the members of the Blue Angels squadron together like few others and kindles a level of trust rare in any organization.

"I've heard it called 'high trust,'" said Blue Angel Number Five Frank Weisser after his morning flight. "It's an exceptional amount of trust that I hadn't seen before I came here.

"For us, there are a lot of points throughout the show where Number Six is trusting that when we come in for our opposing crosses, I'm going to be on the right line, at the exact right altitude. He's not looking at the ground; he's only looking at me. And I'm trusting that he'll maneuver his aircraft with the exact same pull and roll rate, and then set his wings at the same place on the horizon every time. I know he's going to get as close as he can without hitting me."

When the Blues fly in formation, they base their movements off the leader—one plane always leads and the others will always follow. The lead plane must maintain course and speed and also keep the route safe for the others. The pilots following him have one basic job: not to check their instruments or horizon and trust the lead pilot.

"When you're as low and as close as we are together," Frank explained, "if you look away even for a quarter of a second to check your speed or altitude you're already out of position and maybe dangerously so. You don't even have to move your head. Sometimes my head is looking one place and I just move my eyes—that'll be too much time because when you're flying that close, you can't bring your eyes inside to check anything."

During maneuvers, a Blue Angel pilot must maintain such absolute focus that he can't look away from his wingman even for a split second. The Blue Angels equate some of their formation maneuvers to driving at night, at eighty miles per hour, in pouring rain. Now imagine doing it in heavy traffic at 400 or 500 miles per hour. Then imagine cars streaking along mere feet above and below you.

"When we solo guys—that's Five and Six—join up with the Diamond [the other four Blue Angels who fly the Diamond formation together], we're third man out and we're flying in an echelon. I'm flying off of someone who's flying off someone else. Any mistake made by Number One is magnified by Number Two or Three, and is then doubly magnified in us. Our focus has to be even higher because we have to watch someone who's watching someone else.

"In those formations, you feel yourself getting lower and lower to the ground and the trees go ripping by or the water goes ripping by and you're on the inside of a turn and you're descending and you're speeding up and when you're at two hundred or three hundred feet, you feel like you're skimming the water, trees, or ground. And if you were to look away to make sure you're not going to hit something, you might hit the other airplane in that split second because they're turning into you. There's a lot of trust to place in whoever's leading."

Imagine six planes all eighteen inches from one another. Imagine them turning together at more than 300 or 400 miles per hour, then descending toward the ground. Only the lead pilot watches the ground to maintain the safety and heading of the formation. The other five pilots watch only their reference points on the aircraft next to them. They feel the entire group plummeting toward the ground at increasing speeds; they know the runways, trees, and lakes below are growing ever closer, ever closer. But they can't look. They have to focus on their wingman. They have to trust Number One.

"You can *never* look at the ground," Frank stressed, "but your periphery sees it. Your periphery can be your nemesis. All of us who have a desire to continue living have this survival instinct. You want to look, but you know through experience that you just can't."

To make this all the more difficult, when they're up there, they fly ahead of the jet—their term for thinking ahead. They go methodically from one maneuver to the next, but when they're flying a machine that moves with such speed, they can't fly it in its current position. They're flying a mile or two miles ahead of their airplane.

"We put the plane where we want it to be," Frank said simply enough. And they trust their wingmen will be there to meet them.

When the final six-plane delta formation flew over the crowd that had gathered for that particular day's practice session, the Blue Angels peeled into the carrier break landing pattern and touched down one after another, exactly fifteen seconds apart—much closer than the typical sixty-second intervals aboard carriers. The aerial show had ended, but the ground show resumed as the six jets taxied almost nose-to-tail back to the original flight line where their crew chiefs waited in formation.

The six crew chiefs wore fitted dark blue uniforms with U.S. NAVY BLUE ANGELS embroidered on the back. They had matching yellow headphones and dark sunglasses. They were arranged as they had been at the beginning of the show, in a perfect line, precisely spaced. The crew chiefs stood rigidly with hands clasped behind their backs. The first mechanics—first mechs— knelt on one knee, between their respective crew chiefs and jets. One knee touched the ground, their heads bowed down, and their palms rested on the concrete.

The crew chiefs raised their hands in unison, signaling the pilots to turn toward their final position. In unison, the blue jets pivoted, stopping where the first mechs knelt. Each crew placed chocks around their plane's front wheel, and then prepared to receive the pilot.

Six canopies opened simultaneously and the pilots removed their polished yellow helmets with mirrored visors. A predetermined number of seconds later, six crew chiefs walked smartly to their respective plane's port wing and lowered the pilot's ladder. Then they marched to the nose of the plane and stood firm, together with their first mech, while their pilots descended their ladders. Soon their pilot met them at the nose and shook their hands, congratulating his team on another successful mission.

The three people who were Blue Angel Number Five stood together at parade rest, until the announcer called Frank Weisser's name and he began walking toward the stands, joining with other pilots along the way. They walked in lockstep with one another—an unbroken line of bright blue flight suits and khaki garrison hats—until they reached the end of the row and began laughing and shaking hands. At last, they could relax.

After the show, I walked down the line of sparkling royal blue planes, to Number Five. There, I found the crew chief, Petty Officer Alicia Raper, dutifully checking to see if the most recent flight had caused any damage to her airplane.

"Most of us crew chiefs refer to the jets as *our* aircraft," she said as she took off her protective headphones, which slipped easily over her light brown hair, tightly drawn into a bun. "We own it for twenty-three hours a day and they get to fly it for an hour!"

She laughed. "The pilots are trusting us that they have a great aircraft, a safe aircraft, to go flying in. And we're trusting them to come back with that plane and not break it!"

Alicia had been trusting Frank—Mr. Weisser or Lieutenant Commander Weisser as she alternately called him—with her airplane for two years, or seasons as they call them in the Blue Angels. As crew chief, she serves as the lead maintainer for the aircraft and shoulders responsibility for its every nut, bolt, and circuit. The hours of inspections and repairs she vigilantly oversees ensure Frank can bring Number Five home safely on every flight.

Both Frank and Alicia came to the team at the same time and began working together in their second year. She became his crew chief on Number Six, the "opposing" solo jet. Then she followed him to Number Five, the "lead" solo jet, for the current season. The two had developed a real trust in each other. And not only does Alicia trust Frank with her airplane, she trusts him with her life: he'd taken her for a ride in the two-seater Number Seven plane at the Blue Angels' winter camp in El Centro, California.

"I was a little nervous," she said of the flight, "but that was about my own well-being, not the pilot. I didn't want to pass out!"

Blue Angel pilots deal with g-forces every day; their passengers will never be as comfortable as they. When planes suddenly scream upward or pull into tight turns, gravitational forces (thus the term "G") press—or crush—pilots and passengers into their seats. During maneuvers, their bodies can double, triple, and quadruple in weight. Sometimes, they can scarcely lift their arms and legs. The powerful forces also drive blood away from the brain and toward the legs; an unprepared passenger can black out. Most fleet aviators are required to wear g-suits, which apply pressure to their legs and abdomen to keep blood in their upper body during high-G maneuvers. Instead of g-suits, Blue Angels must rely solely on practice and strength to maintain control and consciousness. For all pilots, but especially the Blue Angels, performance flying requires hard training and exceptional conditioning.

Before he took Alicia up in Number Seven, Frank shared some hints to help her cope with the pressures. She laughed as she recalled Frank putting her through the ringer.

"Mr. Weisser is pulling these maneuvers and I'm sitting in the backseat going, 'Hmmmeerrrrr . . .' You grunt to keep from passing out. You're also flexing all your leg muscles and ab muscles to keep the blood in your head. I'm doing everything I can to not pass out—making those noises—and he's just carrying on plain as day!"

She laughed again. "He's been my pilot for two years now. I couldn't imagine working with anyone else, and there's nobody else I'd rather fly with."

Growing up in Cherokee, Iowa, Alicia knew little about the navy, but felt a call to be a part of something greater than herself. Seven years ago, she enlisted, finished A-School down the street from where we stood, and thereafter arrived in Whidbey Island, Washington, to begin training as an Aviation Ordnanceman. During her tour there, she visited Seattle and by chance, saw the Blue Angels perform over Lake Washington. She returned to her base and immediately began the application process. Not long after, she received orders to Pensacola.

"It's an amazing duty and a chance to do something different," she said. "Not only do you have the honor of representing every sailor and marine, you also have the honor of being stateside and showing the U.S. what its navy and Marine Corps are doing overseas.

"And when you work in places like this—or any aviation command—each and every person is contributing to get those flights in the air. You're just one person on a big team. Everybody's gotta do their part so it all goes smoothly."

As a Blue Angel alpha crew chief, Alicia bears responsibility for jet Number Five and for training her "bravo" crew chief, who learns to mirror her so either of them can serve as chief for a given mission. Frank should only notice one difference: his alpha has long hair and his bravo doesn't.

Most important, Alicia oversees every bit of maintenance done to Number Five. On a good day, she'll spend five hours working on the jet—replacing shorted wiring, fixing a weak landing strut, installing a new fuel pump, or dismantling part of an engine for a safety check. Other times, her team will work throughout the night to fix a problem so the jet can fly in the next day's show.

"The Blue Angels fly the oldest F/A-18s in the fleet," she said, "so there are always issues. They come to us after they've done so many carrier hours that, by navy regulations, they can't land on a carrier anymore. They've gone to a land base and then they finally come to us."

When the jets arrive at the Blue Angels hangar, they receive the distinctive blue and yellow paint scheme and an assortment of modifications that allow them to fly at the true limits of their capabilities. The maintenance team fits each new jet with an inverted fuel tank so they can fly equally well upside down or right side up. They also place a spring on the control stick that exerts forty pounds of pressure, so pilots can make the most minute of corrections to their jet's control surfaces—the stabilators, rudders, and ailerons that affect airflow and thus alter the plane's position in the sky. Those precise adjustments allow the Blue Angels to maneuver in such close formation.

Once the jets are fitted with those modifications, the day-to-day process of maintenance begins and continues for the life of the jet. Alicia and her fellow crew chiefs receive their engine turn qualification, memorize emergency procedures, and learn every system on the plane. In her case, it was quite a learning curve for an ordanceman who had formerly focused on armaments and weapons systems. Other crew chiefs arrive—handpicked—at the squadron with equally varied backgrounds, but they're soon experts on every hinge and switch on the Hornet. They know how to test it, break it, and fix it again.

"I've learned the whole jet—end to end—and turn the engine up before the pilot flies," Alicia explained. "I basically try to break it so when Mr. Weisser takes it up he doesn't have any problems.

"And we do that daily. Every day. For us, it's a challenge. Switching up your routine, the way you walk around the jet, makes sure your eyes stay sharp."

In addition to ensuring the jet maintains a perfect state of readiness, they work tirelessly on their flight line routine. As I'd just seen, the crew chiefs' movements on the ground are as precise as the pilots' movements aloft, and they critique each other often. By the time they're on the flight line performing, they mostly rely on muscle memory.

"We're all perfectionists!" Alicia said. "We want each show to be the best show possible. Here, attention to detail is so important. You notice things that you might not otherwise catch and that's the most important thing when you're looking over a jet before you send it flying."

Frank trusts his crew chief with more than just jet maintenance. Alicia performs the final check of the entire airplane, including examining a dizzying number of dials and setting an equal number of switches inside the cockpit. In typical squadrons, pilots perform a lengthy preflight inspection of their aircraft before they fly a mission. They walk slowly around the plane, checking the control surfaces, the fuel state, the weapons, and the landing gear. They carefully double-check the switches and settings in the cockpit before they power up. Blue Angel pilots can't do that. They have an air show to put on and crowds to entertain. Nobody wants to watch pilots spend fifteen minutes preflighting a jet before the show, so the crew chiefs do the final checks.

"They're excellent at it, by the way," Frank said. "When we climb up there, the crew chief helps us strap in, and then we shake their hand and they say, 'Jet's ready, sir. Have a safe flight.' You have to absolutely trust this person that they've checked everything."

Particularly since the pilots fly upside down at 500 miles per hour while putting several Gs worth of stress on their aging aircraft, everything has to be functioning just right.

Both Frank and Alicia do all of this for the crowd. The crew chiefs share their pilots' desire to please the tens or hundreds of thousands who gather for each major show. Every year, millions of men, women, and children spend their Saturday or Sunday watching the Blues perform.

Shaking her head with mild disbelief at the life she created for herself, she added, "I have the coolest job in the world. You see the general public's reaction to the flights; you see the little kids' interest in naval aviation. They're filled with questions; they're so curious about it. And all the communities we've been to are so supportive. We spend much of our careers deployed overseas and it's nice to travel in the States and see how much people appreciate the military. People constantly come up to members of the team at shows and thank us for our service. It definitely hits you in the heart.

"It's a great honor, too," she added. "You know, the navy's core values are honor, courage, and commitment. And we definitely represent all of them. It's an honor for every person on this team to go to the Midwest where they don't really know the navy—you may be the only time they've ever seen the navy. Then you have to have the courage to be a model sailor, a model citizen. Especially being here, people are going to judge the entire navy based on us. We want to be the best role models we can be. And for us, we're committed to our country and committed to showing people in the U.S. what guys in the real fight overseas are doing."

The other critical part of Blue Angel Number Five, Frank Weisser, felt exactly the same.

"We're a recruiting arm of the navy and our goal is to motivate and inspire," Frank said. "And we do it by putting on a show where kids look up and say, 'That looks amazing. How can I have that in my life? I want to have that precision, I want that professionalism, I want that excitement, I want that adventure. I want that in my life; how do I do that?'

"I knew that was part of the Blue Angels, but what I *didn't* understand until I arrived was how badly you want to represent the men and women who can't be here. All of our friends right now are overseas flying off carriers, at night, in bad weather, over hostile territory. People are shooting at you; they're certainly not clapping for you and you're certainly not flying over sunny Pensacola or Key West. We get out of our airplanes and people are clapping for us and want to talk with us, and we want those crowds to know that our brothers and sisters in arms are doing the same things but off of a boat, at night, in combat. There's a desire to do right by them because they can't be here to tell the story themselves."

After the Blue Angels had entertained the crowd with the day's practice flight, Frank and the team sequestered themselves in the one particularly unique room in their otherwise ordinary squadron hangar: the Blue Angels' briefing room. The team spent nearly three hours watching slow-motion video of their morning practice on the room's flat-screen monitor. They sat in comfortably padded chairs, embroidered with their plane numbers, and squared off around a long wooden conference table. Polished wood, glossy photographs, and shelves for trophies and trinkets covered much of the wall space.

Foremost among the awards stands a wooden pedestal supporting a silver cup topped with a silver airplane. The plaque affixed to the vase proclaims: SOUTHEASTERN AIR SHOW AND EXPOSITION; JACKSONVILLE, FLA; JUNE 15, 1946; U.S. NAVY EXHIBITION TEAM. At the bottom: AWARDED FOR THE FINEST EXHI-BITION OF PRECISION FLYING. It was the Blue Angels' first trophy.

The evening after their 1946 win, Butch Voris's fledgling three-man team began the Blues' tradition of thorough debriefings, which serve to build the high trust that leads to their peerless teamwork. The current Blue Angels have not strayed from that original practice, although today's debriefs are slightly more regimented than the 1946 discussion that transpired over a meal at Giupponi's Spaghetti House in Jacksonville. At the beginning of every debrief, each Blue Angel lists his mistakes, most of which the public audience can't even perceive. The team discusses the errors and learns what they can from each. By the time they dissect and analyze the entire flight, they are often exhausted and sometimes irritated, but they never let it show.

"You can't have too many big personalities in a small room like this," Frank said when we sat down at the long table after the day's debrief had ended. "Everyone has to be able to work with other folks and take criticism and give criticism—and those are equally challenging skills. It's hard enough to take responsibility for your own mistakes, much less to have someone else tell you that you're making mistakes and take it on board and do better next time rather than being hurt or offended by it. It's an equally challenging skill to look another professional in the eye and tell them that they screwed something up and they need to fix it. But that's what we do in naval aviation. It's too dangerous of a business not to improve every day."

The Blue Angels have, without question, one of the best and most respected assignments in naval aviation. They are chosen for their character as well as their skill in a cockpit. However, they admit they don't appreciate the job as much as they should. Because they are such a driven group of perfectionists, they constantly push themselves to improve—every day, every flight. In their business, coasting or losing the edge can lead to disaster. Nineteen of their predecessors have died in crashes.

Each of the 270 pilots who have flown as a Blue Angel since twenty-seven-year-old Butch Voris led the very first team in 1946 has felt that desire to continually improve. Generations of aerobatic perfectionists have created a world-renowned reputation for excellence that has not only endured, but has grown. The teams have honed their skills in F6F Hellcats, F8F Bearcats, F9F Panthers (their first jets) and Cougars, F11F Tigers, F-4 Phantom IIs, A-4 Skyhawk IIs, and their current plane, the F/A-18 Hornet. During their nearly sixty years of service, they have performed for more than 400 million people worldwide.

Shortly after I visited the Blues, a panel of former commanding officers met with the current Blue Angels team and chose Commander Dave "Mongo" Koss as the forty-third trustee of that impressive legacy. I had first encountered the good-natured, six-foot-four pilot aboard the USS *Nimitz* where he'd served as executive officer and later skipper of VFA-14, the Tophatters. When we met in Hawaii, he thought he was near his profession's peak—he would soon command a carrier-based Super Hornet strike fighter squadron and he flew missions almost daily. But he had dreamed of flying with the Blues ever since his father, an A-7 Corsair pilot in Vietnam, began taking him to air shows as a boy. Even so, he never truly thought he might fly Blue Angel Number One—a role considered by many as the top flying post in naval aviation.

Once he'd received the honor, his thoughts quickly turned to the challenges he faced. First, he had to lead the team, but had never flown such precise aerobatics. He would spend the coming January and February training in the squadron's winter home at Naval Air Facility (NAF) El Centro, California. For two months, he would fly six days a week, three missions each day, and work harder than anyone so he could be ready to lead the squadron in his first season. Dave would fly the Number One plane as he led the Diamond formation in harrowing dives toward the ground, pulling up with just several hundred feet to spare. Every other Blue Angel pilot would be flying off him, trusting his every move.

As the new skipper, he also felt the weight of sixty-five years of history. "The Blue Angels are a national treasure," he said. "Through the years we've had different officers, different crew chiefs, different planes, but that level of excellence has been maintained. And it's been maintained because each generation constantly strives to get better—and that's on my shoulders now. That's what the Blues are about—that's what naval aviation is about. We're always pushing ourselves so we can represent the navy and its people, and ultimately, encourage others to join us and be part of this great mission, this team of exceptional people—and I'm not just talking about the Blue Angels. I'm talking about all of naval aviation."

4

SHARPENING THE SWORD

LEE AMERINE WAS FIVE YEARS old when *Top Gun* hit theaters. Of course, there wasn't a theater anywhere near the Amerine home, which sits outside Paris, Arkansas (population 3,700). Nor was there an ocean within five hundred miles. But as soon as he saw the film, Lee—like thousands of other American boys—decided on his life's course: he wanted to fly jets for the navy.

And like any older brother, he pulled along his younger siblings. Growing up, Lee, Travis, and Denver called themselves Maverick, Goose, and Iceman. As their mother Carol drove the boys down the winding roads outside Paris, she had to endure constant sounds of jet engines and sharp commands to "break right" or "break left!"

"For the three aspiring aviators in the backseat, the curves of that windy road were high-G turns requiring the max performance of our make-believe aircraft and the maximum power of our make-believe throttles," Travis remembered. "As for the calls of 'Fox one' or 'Fox two' that Mom heard on those routine car trips, those were my brothers and me shooting down every unsuspecting vehicle that met our criteria for hostiles: driving the other direction."

The allure never wore off. "From those car trips to local air shows, our dream to fly only grew stronger," he said.

The brothers all bunked together in one room of their two-bedroom house on Mt. Magazine until they each left Arkansas to pursue their shared dream at the U.S. Naval Academy, which Lee entered in 1999. Travis followed in 2001 and Denver walked onto the Yard in Annapolis in 2003. By 2005, Travis was serving as brigade commander, the highest-ranking midshipman at the Naval Academy. All three brothers excelled there and in flight training, which earned each of them a seat in the cockpit of a navy jet. Lee and Travis flew the F/A-18E Super Hornet and Denver was about to qualify in the navy's newest jet, the EA-18G Growler, a Super Hornet modified with electronic attack capabilities that detect, jam, and destroy enemy communications, radar, and guided missiles.

The Amerine brothers came from neither a military family nor a wealthy one—but certainly a patriotic one. Carol and Perry Amerine taught their boys to respect their country and support each other. In that small house and in the woods outside, they developed an exceptionally tight bond that has only grown stronger as Lee, Travis, and Denver all became naval aviators. They know every facet of each other's personality. Around the Amerine brothers, the ribbing often gets merciless but always ends in laughter. Even with the two years of age that separated each, they did everything together as they grew up, including Scouting. All the brothers earned the high rank of Eagle Scout. From Scouting, the military was an easy jump.

"Like Scouting, your background doesn't matter in the military," Lee said. "With a good set of morals and drive, you can do anything. It's a merit-based society. You live by a code and take care of others around you. When a pair of single-seat Hornet guys are flying, you've got to watch each other's back in a fight. The most important man should be the one next to you."

In naval aviation, the three Amerines found a place where they could excel on a level field, on the basis of merit alone. They found a way of life that embodied the values they'd learned under their parents' roof. And they sensed the raw excitement offered by a flight deck.

"The initial attraction is going Mach Two with your hair on fire," Lee Amerine joked, referencing the famous comment *Top Gun*'s love interest Charlie (played by Kelly McGillis) made to Maverick. "But then you realize the military is about serving others. *Top Gun* got us going, but this sense of duty and purpose made us stay."

I had first met Lee at NAS Meridian, Mississippi, while he was training in T-45 jets, then I sailed across the Pacific as his guest aboard the *Nimitz*, watching him become a respected junior officer and fleet aviator. The next time we met, he had taken yet another step in his career and completed the Strike Fighter Tactics Instructor course and graduated from TOPGUN himself. As a graduate, he ranked among the navy's most capable aviators. And just like his boyhood hero Pete "Maverick" Mitchell, Lee had returned to help good pilots become great.

The sun was just beginning to light the Nevada sky as Lee and I left his driveway outside Reno, Nevada. Thirty minutes later, it crested the mountains and rapidly climbed into the sky. Lee and I flipped the visors down to keep the rising sun from blinding us as we continued our drive eastward across the desert toward NAS Fallon. He had drawn a 7 A.M. brief, so our day had begun well before sunup.

Lee didn't need coffee to keep him awake during the drive. He had already been abuzz when we met in his kitchen to scarf down cereal, and I'm not sure whether he slept the previous night. He hadn't been this excited about flying in months—and he had one of the most sought-after flying assignments in the navy: serving as an instructor at the Naval Strike and Air Warfare Center (NSAWC—pronounced *N-Sock*). NSAWC unifies several programs that together sharpen the skills of already well-trained aviators to a knifepoint. In 1996, three training programs were consolidated under the NSAWC command at NAS Fallon: the Strike Fighter Tactics Instructor program, formerly called Navy Fighter Weapons School and widely known as TOPGUN; the carrier air wing training department, or STRIKE; and the Carrier Airborne Early Warning Weapons School for E-2C Hawkeye aircraft and crews, often called TOPDOME. Since then, NSAWC has added the SEAWOLF Rotary Wing Weapons School for H-60 helicopter crews, a program to help Navy SEALs learn how to direct and coordinate with attack aircraft from positions on the ground, and a school for electronic attack EA-18G Growlers.

At 8 A.M. that morning, Lee would take a final step toward being a full instructor, able to fly the adversary role so critical to NSAWC training. He would at last fly the General Dynamics F-16 Fighting Falcon, the single-engine jet fighter flown by the U.S. Air Force and NSAWC instructors. It was commonly called the "Viper." Lee had logged hundreds of hours aloft in the F/A-18, but had recently spent nearly as many hours in a dark room, flying a computer-simulated Viper, preparing for this day. He was beyond ready for his first flight.

"From the day you arrive for API [Aviation Preflight Indoctrination] in Pensacola, you're training," he said. "And it never stops. It's almost unbelievable how much training it takes to fly and you *can't* stop. Not only do the technologies and aircraft change, flying itself is a perishable skill—the feel of a jet, being aware of procedures, remembering what to check at what time to keep yourself safe. We never stop improving our skills."

Four years ago, Lee had honed his flying skills at the F/A-18 Fleet Replacement Squadron—the Super Hornet training squadron still often referred to by its former acronym, the RAG (Replacement Air Group)—where he first learned to pilot his new jet. Then he'd flown the Super Hornet almost daily during two deployments to the Middle East and Western Pacific aboard *Nimitz*. He followed that with more time in the jet as a student at TOPGUN. Now, he was tackling the entirely new challenge of the F-16 Viper. By stepping into the cockpit of the F-16, he joined a small group of naval aviators qualified to fly one of the world's finest air-to-air fighters. At any one time, fewer than twenty naval aviators are qualified to fly the Viper. That's one of the reasons Lee chose to instruct at NSAWC, where the instructors fly the agile F-16 Vipers against fleet pilots in traditional Super Hornets. The instructors play the role of adversary, mimicking enemy tactics and capabilities as they train students attending NSAWC courses. They show the navy's aviators what they could face in combat overseas.

The Viper name came from Air Force pilots who thought the plane looked like a cobra when seen at the end of a runway, and while the official Air Force name became Fighting Falcon, Viper remained a popular alternative. The pilots at NSAWC use the term with special pride since it pays homage to the most famous adversary pilot of all time, albeit a fictional one: Commander Mike "Viper" Metcalf, the crack pilot and fatherly commanding officer in the film *Top Gun*. It was Viper who reminded his students, "Gentlemen, you are the top one percent of all naval aviators. The elite. The best of the best. We'll make you better."

Like Commander Metcalf, today's instructors push their students—who are exceptionally talented aviators themselves—to fly smarter, safer, and more effectively. Of course with their own rich experience and the F-16's maneuverability, the instructors have a leg up. Thanks to the instruction they received at TOPGUN and STRIKE, navy pilots have reigned supreme in dogfighting and air attack skills for decades.

TOPGUN's premise has remained unchanged since its inception in 1968. As Metcalf said, they make the best even better.

Selected students come from squadrons around the fleet to train, improve, and learn how to teach others. Most TOPGUN students are junior officers (lieutenants junior grade and lieutenants) between twenty-five and thirty years of age. During Lee's four years as a junior officer in VFA-14, only three out of twenty eligible aviators were selected for the program. TOPGUN students are an elite group. The designers of the TOPGUN program planned for graduates to carry their knowledge of tactics back to their fleet squadrons and train others. Thus, TOPGUN creates a far-reaching training web that keeps the swords of naval aviation razor sharp.

Every TOPGUN graduate receives the Strike Fighter Tactics Instructor shoulder patch, an instantly recognized circular patch with concentric black and red bands around an enemy fighter on a blue field—overlaid with the crosshairs of a gun sight. Graduates become Strike Fighter Tactics Instructors for the duration of their next fleet tour, when their skills are at their peak. They are forever known as "patch-wearers." A select group of graduates get to return to Fallon as instructors.

Lee left the *Nimitz* and the VFA-14 Tophatters to earn his patch and then began a tour as an instructor at STRIKE, the original component of NSAWC. STRIKE involves the entire carrier air wing, and the program's participants regularly shake the desolate mountainsides as more than forty aircraft conduct exercises with or against each other.

For STRIKE, pilots, NFOs, and maintainers all leave their home base to spend five weeks training and operating at Fallon as a complete air wing. Hornets, Super Hornets, early warning E-2C Hawkeye radar platforms, electronic attack EA-18G Growlers or EA-6B Prowlers, and H-60 helicopters and their crews all descend on this corner of Nevada, which provides the navy with endless acres of uninhabited terrain and open sky—civilian flights are routed around Fallon's ten thousand square miles of airspace.

"NSAWC tries to build air wing integration," said Lee. "We teach them to function together. We're fine-tuning their skills so when they leave, they're at the top of their game and ready for deployment. They've already done a cycle of technical training and when they get to us, they learn game-time execution. It's no longer tactics in a vacuum. Air Wing Fallon puts you in the real world."

To add an additional element of the real world, Lee attacks the air wing in his F-16. It's called "flying red."

"When I suit up as Red Air," Lee said, "it's me against them. I'm going to fly my assigned mission using our assigned tactics and if they execute perfectly, I shouldn't be a factor. However, if they don't execute perfectly, I'm looking for that opportunity to drop in on them so I can drive home the learning point. I'm looking to get in there and show the guys the capabilities of the forces they may come up against out there."

Fallon provides reality in another way. The terrain outside Fallon looks a lot like the terrain in Afghanistan.

"I've flown over both places," said Lee, "and Fallon is about as close to Afghanistan as it gets. That makes for great training."

Navy SEALs come to Fallon for JTAC (Joint Terminal Attack Controller) training to help them direct air strikes from forward positions on the ground in hostile territory. Since both the SEALs and the air wing will likely see duty in Afghanistan—possibly at the same time—they have an opportunity to practice as a real team in very real conditions. Participants integrate as an entire combat unit with JTACs guiding aircraft on strikes through rocky valleys and on high ridgelines. Closer to town, convoys representing hostiles will wind through the streets and buildings of Fallon itself, further testing pilots' ability to wait patiently for a safe shot or to attack with pinpoint accuracy. Helicopters conduct search and rescue operations and pluck survivors from high rocky landing zones. Combat pressures are constantly provided by Red Air and NAS Fallon's artillery battery.

"Flying requires such a high level of currency," Lee said. "And we do a superb job of teaching that out on the range. But these schools also teach you how to approach the business of naval aviation: how to brief, how to debrief, how to communicate learning points to other people. Those are not perishable skills. So NSAWC is not just stick and rudder. There's a lot of time spent in the classroom as well."

By 7 A.M., Lee had donned his olive flight suit and royal blue STRIKE undershirt—pilots in each fleet squadron and each NSAWC school wear specifically colored T-shirts beneath their flight suits. Then Lee laced up his polished brown aviator's boots.

He spent half an hour planning his flight at an office table: checking his route and airspace boundaries, confirming his objectives, and reviewing the ways he'd push the limits of his new airplane. He did his best to remain stone-faced and conceal the excitement that came with testing his new skills in one of the world's finest jet fighters.

Soon, we walked from the classroom building into the hangar together, past the wall commemorating the air-to-air kills made by navy and Marine Corps pilots who've graduated TOPGUN or STRIKE. The wall reminds every student of the TOPGUN program's ultimate purpose.

Inside the hangar's equipment room, Lee pulled his helmet, oxygen mask, and g-suit from its spot among at least forty others. He strapped, snapped, and buckled his armor into place and we proceeded to the maintenance shop where he checked over the latest report on the particular jet he would fly that morning. Satisfied his jet was ready, he and the maintenance officer signed the appropriate form and the Viper was Lee's.

He tossed me a set of ear plugs and we walked through the hangar and onto the tarmac where the sunlight bathed a section of F-16 Vipers and glinted off their domed canopies. The planes were painted with tan/brown or blue/gray camouflage schemes and the tail of each bore the circular symbol of the Strike Fighter Tactics Instructor program superimposed over a black lightning bolt, the symbol for STRIKE.

The ground crew had a ladder waiting for Lee to climb, but first, he meticulously inspected the entire jet, walking around and beneath the plane, shaking the flaps, tugging on the weapons pylons, making sure everything was as it should be. When he climbed into the cockpit, he carefully checked every gauge and switch, then waited for the ground crew to supply power for engine ignition. With everything ready, he closed the canopy and the Pratt & Whitney turbofan began to turn. He guided the plane toward Fallon's long desert runway. At the strip's end, I watched him swing the aircraft around so it faced down the runway. Even from afar it was a menacing airplane, and looked just like a cobra poised to strike. Its pointed nose stuck out over its large air intake and its body flared away from the prominent canopy that sat atop its spine. I heard the engine roar and watched the wheels roll forward, slowly at first. Then the jet accelerated down the runway and jumped lightly into the chilly morning sky. It rose quickly above the surrounding mountains. Lee pushed the throttle forward and disappeared.

Not all navy aircraft can vanish from sight as quickly as a Viper or Super Hornet. The E-2C Hawkeye's twin props can only push through the sky at 375 miles per hour. Compare that to 1,190+ miles per hour for the Super Hornet. Yet the Hawkeye plays a critical role in naval aviation and each carrier deploys with four of the large, gray and white, radar-carrying planes. Atop their fifty-seven-foot fuselage sits a twenty-four-foot-wide rotating disc that gives the plane radar purview over more than 100,000 miles of ocean. Its systems can simultaneously track more than 600 targets. What radars on carriers and jets can't detect, the Hawkeye can. It serves as an early-warning sentry and as a battlefield coordinator.

Hawkeye squadrons—tactical airborne early warning squadrons in navy terminology (abbreviated VAW for Fixed-wing, Airborne Warning)—don't fly planes as sleek or fast as fighters nor do they roll in to attack targets with guns, bombs, and missiles. Consequently, their background role often goes underappreciated. Particularly in high-traffic airspaces like those over Iraq and Afghanistan, however, their abilities become clearly important. The Hawkeyes communicate with attack aircraft—the very tip of the naval aviation spear—and pass along information regarding the whereabouts and strength of the enemy. They serve as command platforms for the entire air wing or even the entire theater.

After Lee had left for his morning flight, I met Lieutenant Andrew Hayes, a Naval Flight Officer who flew in the E-2C. He had served in the numerous NFO positions aboard the plane, from mission commander to radar officer to combat information center director; Hawkeyes fly with a crew of five. At NSAWC, Andrew served as a subject matter expert in airborne battlefield command and control, as well as a weapons tactics instructor for the Carrier Airborne Early Warning Weapons School—CAEWWS, or TOPDOME.

As an instructor, he saw a continuous stream of capable pilots and

NFOs pass through his program. "For CAEWWS or AMCC [Advanced Mission Commander Course], you've extracted the more highly motivated and capable out of that already motivated and capable group," he said. "In the [AMCC] we take mission commanders at Level Three and bring them to Level Four. Motivation is never a problem. What we do is fine-tune their capabilities. We teach them to provide good ISR [Intelligence, Surveillance, and Reconnaissance]. We also teach them how to impart that knowledge to others back in the fleet."

Andrew and I walked along the runway and heard the distinctive eight-blade propellers of a Hawkeye change pitch as they pulled harder on the desert air and the plane began its takeoff run. Soon we saw it rise into the sky and bank toward the mountains. Several E-2Cs were always flying from Fallon as part of an air wing detachment or as part of the Advanced Mission Commanders Course, Andrew explained. Hawkeye crews don't always fly together or even with their own air wing, but above the Nevada desert, they learn to coordinate complex operations involving more than forty aircraft—skills they'll eventually employ over oceans, the Middle East, and other war zones.

"In the movies," Andrew said, beginning to lament the Hawkeye's typically low profile and sometimes underappreciated services, "you never see what the E-2s are doing. The navy is moving toward network-centric warfare. Command and control aircraft—the E-2 platform—are the backbone of that network. In order to fight this way, we need the E-2. Nobody's making a movie about command and control; they just show the tip of the spear: guys shooting rifles, airplanes dropping bombs. That's important but most of the weapon is not the tip. It's the rest of the spearhead and the shaft."

All the schools at Fallon have proud histories—although some are longer than others, as SEAL and Growler schools are much newer. But none have quite the special history of TOPGUN. More than any other program, the navy's Fighter Weapons School was born from the aviator's spirit. Pilots wanted it, the government seemed indifferent, and nobody had a budget. But the aviators made it happen anyway.

It started with the no-holds-barred Ault Report, made by carrier commander Frank Ault in 1968. Ault identified numerous problems with aviator training and tactics and suggested forming a fighter weapons school that would teach dogfighting skills. The navy decided it should be formed by Fighter Squadron 121 (VF-121), the F-4 Phantom training squadron (the RAG) at NAS Miramar. Thirty-three-year-old Lt. Commander Dan "Yank" Pedersen of VF-121 received the job of forming the school and together with eight other pilots and NFOs, he made it happen. The squadron had no room and little extra money, so the founders located a portable metal building they wanted as their office and classroom. One of the original nine, NFO J. C. Smith, convinced a construction crew to move the building into place with their crane—for a small payment of beer and scotch. That set the tone for TOPGUN's early days in more ways than one; the original instructors were notorious for living fast and hard in the bars and environs of San Diego. But they were always ready to fly when their time came.

Soon the group of nine secretly flew Soviet MiGs that the government had obtained and they began developing the tactics that would make their nascent program so effective, popular, and respected. Classes started in March 1969, a year after the U.S. had halted bombing missions over North Vietnam.

"The rest of the Navy didn't know we existed," Pedersen recalled. "These skippers and their pilots and RIOs [Radar Intercept Officers] are saying, 'Who the hell do you think you are? We're gonna stop our operations and just come out there?'"[1]

When full air combat resumed in 1972, kill ratios improved dramatically from 1968 and TOPGUN graduates were behind almost every downed enemy aircraft. Their squadron mates recognized their heightened level of skill and Navy Fighter Weapons School suddenly became one of the hottest tickets in the fleet, and so it has remained.

Most of the American public knew nothing about the TOPGUN program until it caught the eye of writer Ehud Yonay, who traveled to Miramar to produce an article for *California Magazine*, entitled "Top Guns." The article also included photography by TOPGUN instructor C. J. "Heater" Heatley. The "Top Guns" article caught the attention of Hollywood producer Jerry Bruckheimer and he tossed it on the desk of his partner Don Simpson. "This is *Star Wars* on Earth," Jerry said. "We should make it."[2]

Don agreed and they brought Paramount Studios in on the scheme. Soon Don and Jerry found themselves in the Pentagon, convincing the Chief of

Naval Operations to support the concept with his carriers, pilots, and aircraft. Without the navy's hardware, there would be no film. After carefully considering the proposition and setting down its ground rules, the navy agreed and the writing team of Jim Cash and Jack Epps Jr. immediately began turning "Top Guns" into a screenplay.

After visiting Miramar and experiencing Air Combat Maneuvering (ACM) in the backseat of an F-14 Tomcat, Jack discovered exactly how to write the film. The flight showed him the intensely physical nature of TOP-GUN. Fighting Gs during high-speed turns, banks, and climbs proved one of the most strenuous workouts he'd ever had. He was sweaty and exhausted when he returned to solid ground.

"This was not just flying," Jack realized. "This was a sporting event! This was one of the greatest athletic things I'd ever been involved with in my life. I came out of that flight feeling that the key to this movie is how athletic these guys are. This is really about sports. From my point of view as a writer, *Top Gun* is a sports movie. The sport is ACM—air combat maneuvering—and any athlete knows you're always trying to see who's the best in any situation."[3]

Jack and Jim Cash produced a screenplay that Don Simpson and Jerry Bruckheimer absolutely loved, but Paramount Studio's executives did not share that sentiment. The film died. Fortunately, Paramount's management team changed and the new president, Ned Tannen, asked Don and Jerry for a film to make. They pitched *Top Gun*, and Ned said, "Go make it."

The revived team recruited director Tony Scott, actors Tom Cruise and Val Kilmer, and some of Hollywood's most promising young actors. They also used the navy's best pilots as advisors and actors. Photographer "Heater" Heatly made an appearance during the film's opening O-Club scene along with future rear admiral Kevin Delaney and Pete "Viper" Pettigrew, a former TOPGUN instructor and technical advisor to the film. Tom "Killer" Kilcline famously buzzed the bridge of the USS *Enterprise* and landed Iceman's jet in the film's closing scenes; in 2010 he was commanding all U.S. naval air forces. Current Pacific Fleet commander Admiral Robert "Rat" Willard played the role of a Soviet MiG pilot and served as lead flight choreographer. Soon this team of civilians and aviators was making one of history's best-known films, one that would define naval aviation for more than twenty-five years—and perhaps forever.

A quarter-century after *Top Gun*'s release, George "Elwood" Dom counts himself as one of the film's millions of fans—and one of the relative few who have that special insider's understanding. He'd been there. George was one of the better-known instructors to teach at Navy Fighter Weapons School. He went on to command the Blue Angels, Strike Fighter Squadron Thirty-Seven—the Ragin' Bulls—and Carrier Air Wing Seven aboard the now-retired USS *John F. Kennedy*, but he always treasured his time at Miramar. Given naval aviation's penchant for nicknames, it's not surprising that even the air station had one: Fightertown USA.

George began his instructor's tour there just three months after *Top Gun*'s May 16, 1986 release. Heady times to be a TOPGUN instructor, he recalled. Suddenly, his post was the most famous navy program in the entire world.

Like most aviators, he noticed the dramatic license the writers and director took to make the film successful, but he understood. Since it was seen as a sports movie, the writers injected a degree of extreme competition not present on the flight line. The actual program specifically tries *not* to fuel such a highly competitive atmosphere; that would have ensured air-to-air collisions as aggressive pilots aimed for the same space in the sky. Nor did the TOPGUN trophy ever exist. George explained that in reality, the program fosters teamwork and kinship; it favors smart tactics over raw skills. As for the locker room scene, well, the director needed to create an environment where rank didn't exist for a moment—and they of course needed to show off their well-paid actors. Otherwise, the film at heart told an authentic story and George and most of naval aviation deeply admired the final product. The truth was better than Hollywood anyway.

"Above all, the flying scenes capture pretty darn well the dynamics of high-speed air combat," George said. "It was the first movie that showed pilots looking everywhere, not just in front of them. And I think it captured the aggressiveness and tenacity that students show in wanting to defeat the instructors. That desire is tactical, not personal—usually. I'm not saying there aren't some instructors students have a real itch to get!

"Before the film, most Americans who thought about flying only thought about the air force. *Top Gun* was a wonderful way to show the country and the world that the navy and Marine Corps have a very capable aviation arm. It brought the notoriety the organization really deserves, was wonderful for recruiting, and gave our aviators a better connection with their civilian friends.

"Like everyone else, I loved the first ten minutes of the movie—the scenes from the *Enterprise*'s flight deck. It was wonderful for our young sailors—who work really, really hard in all conditions—to have the opportunity to go home, point to that first scene, and tell their buddies and families, 'That's my office. That's what I do.' "

After the film opened, the navy experienced its largest jump in recruitment since World War II. Still today, the thrill of *Top Gun* leads many young men and women down the path of military service and naval aviation.

Beyond Hollywood, George also loved the entire concept behind the TOPGUN program. The organization aspires to be the very best in its field, and it generally succeeds. The instructors help their students develop unrivaled skills and the students in turn take those skills out to the fleet to train others. The results enhance the performance of the entire Naval Air Force.

"Both TOPGUN and the Blue Angels—because of their uncompromising commitment to excellence and continual improvement—have a transformative impact on naval aviation, and the navy and Marine Corps in general, by having that attitude and sharing it when pilots return to the fleet," he said. "TOPGUN began the notion of a center of excellence—the idea that you put together a group of people who are selected in order to have an uncompromising level of performance and execution. They set the example for everyone else in the broader organization to follow. In them, you can see how good you can be if you're totally dedicated to mission accomplishment. And TOPGUN graduates go back to the fleet and share those tactics and that mentality with their boat squadrons.

"The way to drive continuous improvement is through the discipline of flight planning, flight briefing, and post-flight debriefs. We do it in the Blue Angels; we do it at TOPGUN and STRIKE; it should be done in every squadron. It's sacred but it doesn't come naturally to humans. Based on our precious self-esteem and ego, it's not natural to sit down and talk with everyone else about how we can do better. But that's *the* significant driver for constant improvement."

Just as they aim never to stop improving the fleet's aviators, TOPGUN commanders aggressively improve their own programs. When George was flying missions in F/A-18 Hornets against Iraq in the first Gulf War, he began noticing navy aircraft weren't delivering their bombs on target on time as regularly as they should be. Others noticed the same problem, and the TOPGUN syllabus expanded to include air-to-ground tactics. The training shift paid dividends as more recent missions in hot zones—Iraq and Afghanistan most notably—have required little air-to-air combat, but lots of ground attack.

The programs at NSAWC have changed along with the navy's aircraft and battlefields, but their mission has remained the same: to maintain the razor-sharp edge of naval aviators, naval flight officers, and aircrew. TOPGUN in particular has created a fleet-wide reputation—and not just because of the film. Throughout the years, many of the fleet's most respected commanding officers have worn the Strike Fighter Tactics Instructor patch. Likewise, graduates of Fallon's other programs take cutting-edge tactics and unequaled abilities back to the fleet where they elevate the entire navy's level of performance. They do so by lessons and through example, and have spread the culture of excellence. It's all part of the concept of continuous improvement that seems so ingrained in the navy community.

5

ESPRIT DE L'AVIATEUR

FOR MANY YEARS I THOUGHT that call signs endowed a naval aviator with extra swagger and some positive notoriety. Viper, Maverick, Iceman, Hollywood, Cougar—the call signs from *Top Gun*—certainly sounded appropriate for fighter jocks. Iceman flew "ice cold," no mistakes. Maverick did things his own way.

I've since learned that call signs don't quite work that way.

In previous eras, nicknames helped aviators identify themselves easily and quickly while communicating via radio. But even as official flight designations like "Eagle Two-Six" replaced personal names in radio protocol, the call signs stayed. They just developed new purposes. While I was with the Blue Angels in Pensacola, Frank Weisser had helped enlighten me about this evolution, saying, "The purpose of a call sign is to humiliate and embarrass you. You have a personal flaw? Bad last name? Done something stupid? A good call sign makes sure everyone knows it and you never forget it. If at first you get an innocuous one, just wait until your first deployment."

I now understand that in reality, a nickname like "Iceman" would have had little to do with its owner's mistake-free flying and more to do with some incident involving several drinks and a snow bank. Especially in modern times, every nickname is a dig. Ones that sound harmless almost always hide a double meaning—rarely positive.

Call signs are incredibly varied and help forge the unique bonds that exist in the carrier aviation community. During deployments, many pilots are only known by their call signs. The entire air wing might know Anne, Bucket-head, Cricket, Duck, Easy, Frick (and a corresponding Frack), Grinch, Hand-some, Intake, Jugs, Kmart, Lunchbox, Moses, Nasty, Opie, Pampers, Q-Tip, Rabbit, Spooky, Tonto, UTAH, Vixen, Werewolf, XX, Yoda, or Zorro, but most couldn't tell you the owner's real name.

Byron "Oggie" Ogden, executive officer of the Helicopter Antisubma-rine Squadron Five (HS-5) Nightdippers, took an academic approach to the subject, explaining the three variations of call signs: earned, given, and un-avoidable.

Unavoidables who have walked across carrier flight decks of the past include "Calvin" Klein, "Pink" Floyd, "Numb" Schull, "Irish" Coffee, "Ra-ven" Poe, "Corn" Field, "Dingle" Berry, "Wilt" Chamberlin, "Missing" Lynk, "Grace" Kelly, "Undra" Cheever, "Wasted" Tallant, "Fidel" Castro, "Vanna" White, and "Rebel" Yelle, among hundreds of equally amusing others that may appear obvious, but usually hide a good story and some reflection of character as well.

"The 'given' category is a strange one," Oggie said, "and difficult to ex-plain. Some squadrons have call signs given to them much like fraternity names were given to pledges. One of my good friends has the call sign 'Pookie' because our CO looked at him and said, 'Kevin, I bet you had a girlfriend in high school that called you 'Pookie,' didn't you?'

"Kevin responded, 'No, sir.'

"The CO said, 'I don't care, you look like a 'Pookie' so your call sign will be 'Pookie.' He still goes by that call sign."

But the most entertaining variety that Oggie described was the "earned" call sign.

One pilot, measuring around five foot six and tipping the scales at 145 lbs., proved a fiery competitor in sports and would often become con-frontational with his typically larger opponents. The pilot earned the call sign "Chickenhawk," from the tiny yet pugnacious Foghorn Leghorn cartoon character.

"Mousse" Clark, who matched "Chickenhawk" in stature, received his nickname for being decidedly un-moose-like in size *and* using prodigious amounts of the hair product. One junior officer overheard a pilot's wife call

him by his pet name and "Bun-Bun" was thus born. A pilot with a pronounced Southern drawl earned "Rat Face" since that's what others heard
every time he said "right face" (his looks may have also been a factor).
"Robin" was small but spirited—quite the boy wonder. One squadron's
commanding officer handed out "Flush" to a junior officer who seemed to
flush his career down the toilet every time he spoke. "Flipper" had an un-
fortunate mishap in a rental van, "Semi-colon" had part of his large intes-
tine removed, someone discovered "Smooth Money" ironing dollar bills in his
stateroom, and "Groundhog" waved off his helo landing three times because he spied the shadow of a helicopter converging on his landing site. He
was seeing his own shadow.

A colorful array of politically incorrect acronyms falls into the "earned"
category as well. Their meanings are neither kind nor PC, and their use has
increased rapidly in recent years—in large part to avoid reprimands from
perception-conscious squadron leaders. Typically, they are cruel and crude
and often quite funny as long as it isn't your own sign. ALF, CHEX, FUN-
GUS, IADS, LAMB, STAP, or TUFI shouldn't be translated, nor should
LAMPSHADE, the longest acronym I uncovered. A small sample is fit
to reveal publicly. For example, IKE stood for I Know Everything, The
Ugly Big American (TUBA) did a particularly poor job of representing his
country at drinking establishments around the world, SAGE was a Self-
Appointed Guru of Everything, ORAL Over-Rotated his jet After Landing,
and FLOYD was "Found Lying On Yard, Debilitated"—you can guess the
story. From the cockpit, COTR mistakenly called "Clear on the right." He
wasn't. COTL made the same mistake on the left. Most others are far worse.
I promise, "IPOD" isn't what you think.

For additional call signs, you can peruse the countless ceramic mugs
hanging from the ceiling of the World Famous I-Bar at NAS North Island
in Coronado, just across the bay from downtown San Diego. The low building's nondescript exterior hides a warmly decorated room with low-beamed
ceilings and a small number of high-tops and tables, reminiscent of the officers' clubs that once hosted the most spirited of naval aviation gatherings
around the world, like Cubi Point in the Philippines and Top O' The Mar in
Guam; many have since been tamed or closed. Over the I-Bar's horseshoe-
shaped bar and its drink well hang an almost countless number of model
planes, reminding everyone of aviation's long history. Squadron memora-

bilia from all phases of that history cover the walls. And when pilots from North Island–based squadrons walk in the door, they can reach up and pull their personal beer mugs from the myriad hanging from the ceiling.

Just remove your cover—or hat—before you enter and don't touch the model airplanes. Break either of those house rules and Diane or Debbie, the ever-gracious and vigilant bartenders, will ring the bell and you'll earn everyone's friendship by buying a round of drinks. For that reason, uninitiated civilians are always encouraged to drop by.

Some of the call signs found on these mugs border on mean, others are crude, and many wouldn't be printable if their true meanings were known. To the men and women in the squadrons, however, they are part of the spirit that distinguishes the naval aviation fraternity (or "fra-rority" as one commander suggested, acknowledging the female members). For men and women who work under great pressure, risk so much, and spend extended lengths of time confined to a ship, call signs provide needed levity and build the camaraderie that makes their teams perform like few others.

Few call signs have echoed through the years like "Hoser," and few pilots have earned notoriety equal to that of its owner. Other pilots have scored more kills, held higher ranks or more prestigious commands, but few living aviators embody the untamed nature of aviation like the one-of-a-kind legend known to decades of F-8 Crusader and F-14 Tomcat pilots: Joe "Hoser" Satrapa.

When he first began flying the Vought F-8 Crusader fresh from flight school in 1966, Satrapa Joe, as he was originally called, had a terrible time with the plane's four 20 mm cannons. In time, nobody could shoot them better, but in his first exercise on the gunnery range, the new pilot went two straight days without hitting the target. On the third day, his frustration reached the boiling point.

He was flying in the tail position in a pattern of four Crusaders when he lost his patience. He cut off Aircraft Three as they approached the target and started shooting from two thousand feet up, one and a half miles out. He hosed off all his bullets in one pass.

J. P. O'Neill, the flight leader, came over the radio and pointedly told the renegade rookie to return to the airfield at El Centro.

"So I'm spanked," said Hoser with an exaggerated sigh. "J.P. comes back and I meet him at his airplane and he says, 'What the hell were you thinking?'

"I had my hat in my hand, pigeon-toed. 'It just got to me,' I said."

O'Neill had the final say on the incident that night, taking care of it in typical aviator fashion. Every evening, the pilots met at the Officers' Club for pizza and beer. Whenever the opportunity arose, the squadron leaders would convene a kangaroo court and anyone who committed a mistake or made a gaffe that day would appear and receive punishment, which usually included funds to pay for everyone else's beer. When Hoser came before the court, J.P. nailed him: "Lieutenant junior grade Satrapa, for hosing off all his bullets in one pass, will hence forth be known as Hoser. That'll be five bucks!'"

A fighter pilot's fighter pilot, Hoser experienced combat over Vietnam, flew at TOPGUN and STRIKE, possessed a widely known talent for guns and ACM, and had more colorful flying stories than just about anyone.

I'd been searching for the true character of the people involved in naval aviation and I thought Hoser might help me find some answers. So after my visit to NAS Fallon, I paid a visit to the legendary and eccentric pilot at his home in the Sierra Nevada Mountains, two hours west of NSAWC. There, I found the raw, unpolished essence of the naval aviator.

When I arrived at Hoser's hunting lodge—as he calls his secluded mountain outpost—I found him standing in the doorway, smiling beneath his thin gray mustache. His square shoulders carried a strong six-foot-three-inch body that had thus far escaped the extra belly weight worn by many of his fellow sixty-eight-year-olds—perhaps because he still has to fit into a small cockpit on a regular basis since he flies "guts-balls, down-in-the-mud-and-smoke" wilderness firefighting missions for CAL FIRE. It's as close to combat as he can get.

At the threshold he shook my hand and I felt—literally—the experience he'd gained from his fascination with ordnance. Hoser had tinkered with ammunition throughout his whole career and he conceded that he knew his toys would eventually bite him. So it was no surprise to him when he was tinkering with a 20mm shell in 1989—trying to increase its muzzle velocity and improve his ability to kill an opponent with the F-14 Tomcat's Vulcan cannon—and it blew up, punching a hole through his hand and tearing off his thumb. The surgeons fixed the hand well enough, but the thumb was more difficult. The navy wouldn't allow Hoser to fly without a right thumb, so the doctors offered to attach his big toe to his hand as a substitute. He wouldn't stand for the idea—until he talked with his friend F-14 and air show legend Dale "Snort" Snodgrass.

"Come on Hoser, you don't want to end your career not flying, do you," Snort asked his fiery old friend. "Besides, every big toe's dream is to be a thumb. It'll get out of your smelly boot, see daylight, and be able to grab things."

"Snort," Hoser exclaimed, "you're right! I never thought of it like that. I'll do it!"

He ordered his doctors to attach his big toe to his right hand.

"Looks like a thumb," he said, admiring the surgeon's handiwork, "but smells like a toe."

He laughed in his slightly raspy way and I realized I was a long way from the procedure-bound world of NAS Fallon. Hoser was not exactly of the modern breed of naval aviators. He had an untamed spirit that the instructors at TOPGUN and STRIKE couldn't quite match—too many rules these days, Hoser complained. He'd flourished in a navy that tolerated eccentricities more than today's. Despite having equally fine skills, a modern-day Hoser would likely lose his wings for pulling stunts like those that dotted Satrapa's career.

The first stunt of note came during his first-class year at the U.S. Naval Academy, where he'd accumulated enough demerits to put his scheduled 1964 graduation in jeopardy. Just ten demerits away from being booted, he appeared before the Academy's aptitude board and they asked for his explanation.

Twenty-two-year-old Midshipman Satrapa said, "Sir, being here at Annapolis is like sitting on the bench waiting to get into a football game. I want to get to flight training, get in fighters, and get over to the war before it's over.

"I told them I'd be the best damn fighter pilot they'd ever seen," he said as he recalled the scene.

The aptitude panel listened and Hoser noticed one member peer beneath the table to see that his shoes were shined properly. They were. But on a dare, he'd worn red socks.

The panel dismissed Hoser without kicking him out of Annapolis, but as he put his hand on the doorknob to leave, one of the officers said, "Midshipman Satrapa, put yourself on report for being out of uniform."

Hoser acknowledged with a "Yes, sir," and left the room. As he walked down the corridor, he heard a roar of laughter from inside.

"I guess they liked that kind of panache," Hoser said. "They kept me, and when I got to flight training, I sparkled like a diamond in a goat's ass."

In 1966, Hoser graduated at the top of his flight school class and had a choice between F-4 Phantoms or F-8 Crusaders. The Phantom had an NFO in the rear seat and, more disturbingly, no guns.

Hoser thought, "No guns? What kind of airplane is this with no guns?"

The officer helping him decide said that guns were history; missiles were the future.

Hoser immediately chose the gun-slinging, single-seat F-8 and began creating his legend by outdueling instructors even before he deployed—that is, after he earned his call sign and got the hang of the F-8's cannons.

Reborn as Hoser, Satrapa made his name with his stunts and unabashed eccentricity. There are endless volumes of Hoser legends—some portion of which have a strong factual basis. Among them are accounts of Hoser fishing with hand grenades (true), flying under highway bridges at breakneck speeds (true), ringing the bells of a church in Vietnam with his cannon (doubtful), and flying into combat with enough guns, knives, and ammunition squirreled into his flight suit to tackle an entire platoon of North Vietnamese Army regulars (also true).

One dark night over Vietnam, he thundered toward a pair of A-7 Corsairs with his lights off and afterburners on—so a white streak of fire spewed from his engine. At the same time, he craftily improvised a surface-to-air missile warning tone which he broadcast to the A-7s. They heard the tone in their headsets and saw what they thought was a North Vietnamese missile streaking towards them. Hoser got the results he wanted: they were terrified; he was supremely entertained.

Another night, he buzzed the Southern California coast in his twin-engine F-14—which was, of course, against all regulations. He only lit one afterburner, however, so when calls from upset homeowners reached the base, they fingered a single-engine plane as the culprit. To Hoser's delight, the single-engine F-8 pilots found themselves in trouble.

On another occasion, Hoser was set to duel two versus two with a pair of U.S. Air Force F-15 Eagles. On the tarmac, Hoser's wingman had mechanical trouble and couldn't fly, but Hoser decided to fly anyway and turn the situation to his advantage. Hoser and his Tomcat NFO (a backseat Radar Intercept Officer, or RIO, as they were known in the F-14 community) took off. They began impersonating two airplanes on the radio. The F-15 Eagles, who expected two adversaries, became distracted as they searched for the "other" navy jet on their radar screens. Hoser quickly bagged two guns kills, maneuvering through missile ranges until he was close enough to trigger his 20 mm cannons. In round two, he flat outmaneuvered the air force pilots for two more guns kills. And as he always said, "There's no kill like a guns kill."

To add a little more insult to his adversaries' loss, Lt. Commander Satrapa impersonated a junior grade lieutenant during the mission debrief, which was done over the telephone. The air force pilots thought they'd been whipped by a student pilot.

The story that Hoser himself seems to like the most began when he and an F-5 adversary went at each other during the Air Combat Evaluation/Air Intercept Missile Evaluation exercises (ACEVAL/AIMVAL)—which pitted the military's best pilots against one another as they tested new weapons and tactics. Most flights were four versus four affairs and Hoser complained it was "hard to have any fun up there.

"If you get in a four v. four, you have to kill three other guys before you can get down to a guts-balls, in the phone booth, goddamn dogfight and go guns only, and have some fun, for Christsake."

One day, he rolled toward the runway in his F-14—alone—and saw his adversary for the day, Joe "Joe Dog" Daughtry, taxiing out solo in his dart-like F-5.

The two pilots looked at each other across the runway at Nellis Air Force Base. Hoser made a motion like he was cocking an old machine gun. Joe Dog returned the gesture: guns only. No missiles. The dogfight was on.

Hoser and his RIO, Billy "Hillbilly" Hill, left first but when the planes began their engagement, Hillbilly couldn't tell whether they faced one F-5 or two. They were in a race for the top spot in the ACEVAL/AIMVAL competition—the closest thing the navy had to Paramount Studios' TOP-GUN trophy. Hoser couldn't take any chances.

"We'd hopefully kill one of them with a Sparrow [air-to-air missile] and shoot the other son of a gun," Hoser explained of his original plan. "But Hillbilly couldn't tell if there were one or two. We can't take a chance so we pop them in the snothole with a Sparrow."

His simulated missile attack scored a hit on Joe Dog before the two friends could even see each other's aircraft.

"Good kill," came Joe Dog's obligatory confirmation. "Knock it off [end the fight], Hoser."

The two planes separated and then circled back for another engagement. Guns only, Hoser had promised. "Fight's on."

Again, before the two jets had each other in sight, Hillbilly and Hoser "launched" another virtual Sparrow. Splash one Joe Dog.

If Joe Dog hadn't been strapped to his seat, he would have gone through his canopy. He'd been fooled twice and was furious.

"Well, it was a Friday," Hoser recalled with a wheezy sigh. "And when I was done debriefing and filling out our stupid papers, I go over to the O-Club about 1630 and there's Joe Dog. He's pissed. He says, 'Hoser! What the hell happened to credibility?' "

Using the appropriate thumb signals, Hoser replied, "Credibility is *down*; kill ratio is *up!*"

The lesson? In a dogfight, expect anything. All bets are off.

Nobody drove that lesson home more pointedly than David McCampbell, a son of Bessemer, Alabama, who downed more enemy aircraft than any other naval aviator—ever. By the end of World War II, he'd destroyed thirty-four enemy planes in the type of thick, guns-only, air-to-air dogfights Hoser would have given his other thumb to join.

"Dashing Dave" McCampbell's career had started inconspicuously. He graduated the U.S. Naval Academy in 1933, and was discharged into the reserves that same day; the navy had limited its officer commissions. He spent a disappointing year working construction and assembling airplanes in Bessemer before the navy recalled him and he finally earned his wings at Pensacola in 1938. He made his real debut six years later.

When he first tasted aerial combat on May 19, 1944, he was serving as CAG, commander of soon-to-be-legendary Air Group Fifteen, aboard the aircraft carrier USS *Essex*. He didn't down any bogies but his F6F Hellcat, named *Monsoon Maiden*, returned from the day's mission so shredded by enemy bullets that the flight deck crew finished the job the Japanese had started by pushing the propeller-driven Grumman fighter into the sea. McCampbell would go on to fly in *Minsi*, *Minsi II*, and finally *Minsi III*, which finished the war with thirty-four small Japanese flags neatly painted under its canopy, signifying its pilot's victories.

Flying *Minsi II* exactly one month after his first combat flight, the thirty-four-year-old commander became an ace. The title required five confirmed kills and most aces achieved their designation after numerous missions. McCampbell earned it in a single day: June 19, 1944. That morning saw the beginning of a two-day carrier duel that was the largest to date, with more than 1,300 aircraft involved on both sides. The Americans embarked 905 of those aircraft aboard their fifteen flattops. Yet in the day's second raid, the Japanese far outnumbered the Americans. An inbound flight of 109 Japanese Jill torpedo bombers, Judy dive bombers, and Zeke (or Zero) fighters was met by Dashing Dave and only ten other Fighter Squadron Fifteen (VF-15) Hellcats. Undeterred by the numbers, the eleven American fighters pushed over and set upon their quarry.

For six minutes, these *Essex* fighters defended their floating home until forty-three other Hellcats joined the fray. McCampbell made good use of his time. While the remainder of his group handled the Zekes overhead, Dave raked the formation of Judys from one side then the other, alternating approaches until he'd downed five. With his ammunition spent, he returned to *Essex* as the newly arrived Hellcats devoured the remainder of the Japanese strike.

When a fourth wave of Japanese planes attempted to attack the American fleet late that day, McCampbell and VF-15 were airborne again, this time over Guam. Dave quickly downed one Zeke for kill number six. Another maneuvered onto his tail and he radioed for help. He raced toward a rendezvous point where three of his squadron mates took care of the trailing Zeke.

He passed along the favor by doing the same for another Hellcat. That was his seventh kill of the day. At breakfast that morning, he'd had only two to his name.

Dave's fellow Air Group Fifteen aviators destroyed sixty-one additional planes that day, far more than any other air group, and the legend of the Fabled Fifteen was born. The fleet's other carrier air groups chipped in to claim a total of 388 Japanese planes shot down in air-to-air combat (although the real number was likely closer to 275). American combat losses on June 19 were seventeen F6F fighters and eight other aircraft.[1]

While history officially refers to the action as the Battle of the Philippine Sea, the pilots always called it the Marianas Turkey Shoot. And nobody shot more than the air group commander from Alabama. But he wasn't finished. The Fabled Fifteen's leader had one more coup before the air group's seven-month tour de force ended; by the tour's end, they would sink more tonnage and shoot down more enemy aircraft than any other carrier air group in history.

On October 24, 1944, McCampbell had his greatest day. It began when he and his wingman ambushed a flight of some forty Japanese Zeke and Oscar fighters. The fighters were returning to Manila from a mission when McCampbell's group spied them. The ace watched them from on high until they formed into a tight formation. "That's when we went to work on them," McCampbell recalled.

McCampbell and his wingman, Roy Rushing, began ravaging the formation from above, with many of their diving attacks yielding two downed Japanese aircraft apiece. By the time his fuel and ammunition ran low, McCampbell had shot nine planes out of the sky for a single-day record that remains unsurpassed. When he returned to the carrier, his tanks and magazines were virtually empty. "When I tried to [taxi forward after landing], I gave [the throttle] near full gun, and the engine conked out on me. So I ran out of gas on the deck. They had to push me out of the landing area. I found out from the mech who reammunitioned the guns that I had exactly six rounds left in the starboard outboard gun, and they were all jammed. But it worked out all right.[2] For his actions that October day, Commander McCampbell received the Medal of Honor from President Franklin Roosevelt.

Dave McCampbell always respected his Hellcats' guns. And Hoser un-abashedly loved those on his Crusaders and Tomcats. During his twenty-five-year career, Hoser earned a reputation as one of the finest gunslingers in the modern navy. In a dogfight, he relished going "guns only"—like a knife fight in a phone booth, he'd call it. *Almost* nobody had finer-tuned gunnery skills. *Absolutely* nobody loved gun fighting with 20 mm aircraft nose cannons more.

After two Vietnam flying tours on the USS *Intrepid* with Fighter Squad-ron 111 (VF-111), he returned to the United States and taught gunnery and Air Combat Maneuvering to new arrivals in the West Coast F-8 Crusader Fleet Replacement Squadron at NAS Miramar, and helped pilots learn to fly the Crusader before joining the fleet. While he was there, he began to love teaching almost as much as combat. Training and indoctrinating younger aviators would become his passion for the remainder of his career. Hoser began to settle down—slightly.

When the navy began its TOPGUN program, Satrapa began flying in adversary roles. Hoser was there at the inception and then traded his be-loved F-8 for the plane that would make TOPGUN so famous: the new twin-engine Grumman F-14 Tomcat, which entered service in the early 1970s. He logged more than one thousand hours in the "Turkey," as he affection-ately calls it. Like so many other pilots who flew the Tomcat from 1974 to 2006, he absolutely loved that aircraft.

"It still brings water to my eyes," Hoser said, and his eyes indeed began to water. "To think of being in a Tomcat and gunning the daylights out of an F-5 or F-16 or kicking the crap out of an F-15 Eagle and you've got seven Gs on the plane and you look in the mirror and you see what a great big son of a gun is behind you! It's a *gigandous* airplane—sixty-five thousand pounds of metal that's turning better than a [comparatively tiny] A-4. That's why people love the Tomcat. You'd never believe an airplane that big could turn that well. A clean Turkey [a Tomcat with no missiles or external fuel tanks] when flown correctly can kick the crap out of an F-16."

At first, Hoser didn't like flying in the Tomcat, which had a rear-seat NFO—or Radar Intercept Officer (RIO)—who handled radar, communi-cations, and guided missiles. Hoser was accustomed to flying solo in the single-seat F-8, but gradually, he changed his mind about his companion, who helped execute the mission and served as a second pair of eyes.

"I had some really good RIOs," he said, naming several. "And when you have a good RIO, you're a two-hundred-percent fighter instead of a one-hundred-percent fighter. A good RIO is worth his salt."

Hoser became one of the best-known instructors in the F-14 community during his stint with Fighter Squadron 101 (VF-101), the East Coast F-14 Fleet Replacement Squadron at NAS Oceana in Virginia Beach, which lasted from 1986 until 1989. There, he cemented his legend among yet another generation of pilots. To them, he was General George Patton incarnate, and every young pilot or RIO passing through Oceana received a specially delivered indoctrination into their new fighter fraternity. It became known as the Hoser Welcome Aboard Speech.

In a style that mimicked actor George C. Scott's dramatic rendition of hard-charging World War II general George S. Patton, Hoser instilled naval aviation's special esprit de corps among its newest members. His speech became so famous that even the long-since initiated returned to hear it. Hoser told the group that every pilot in the room should think he is the best.

"If you don't think you're the best, you won't perform as the best," Hoser would bellow. "And consequently your stay in a fighter cockpit will be short-lived, whether ended by a smoking hole in the ground or by seeking a way of life that is less demanding amongst the plethora of nondescript dirtbags."

"That's a warrior speech," he said reflectively. "If you don't *think* you are the best, you won't *be* the best." Hoser and those who followed his philosophy weren't just pilots or aviators; they were warriors. And Hoser knew how to lead them.

"With warriors," he said, "you've got to be out at the spearhead and show that you have the wherewithal, the gumption, and the guts to lead. If they don't think you have the balls to do that, you might as well pack your bags."

Knowing his exploits and having heard his speeches, nobody doubted him or the veracity of his words. The newly initiated warriors listened, and Hoser passed along the special flame that aviators have handed down generation through generation since 1911.

Hoser never doubted he was the best. Of course, each of his friends and squadron mates thought the same about themselves. He hoped those who sat in his audience would walk away from his performance with the same confidence. In the end, these aviator-warriors shared a firm belief in their own skills, which helped them accept the inherent risks of their chosen lifestyle. They had to maintain supreme belief in their own ability to reach their objective and return home. They had to *know* they could handle any situation or emergency that arose. And the real legends always knew just how far to push safety boundaries—and sometimes sensibility boundaries—and still come back unscathed and with a good story to tell at the O-Club.

"The sword of destiny is kept sharp by those who live on its edge," Hoser said in defense of his flamboyant style in the cockpit. "If you don't keep testing yourself, how do you know where your limits are?"

He shared that spirit with the other legends of naval aviation—individuals who always pushed the boundaries of their machines and their era: Early pioneers like Eugene Ely and Jack Towers; aces like David McCampbell; explorers like astronauts Alan Shepard and Jim Lovell; and performance flyers like Butch Voris and Dale Snodgrass. Their strong personalities—rather than orders or procedures—drove their accomplishments.

The navy's finest aviators have always had supreme confidence in their ability, their preparation, and their crews. They could push the limits of their aircraft because they were good and because they never thought they'd crash—and they almost never dared bring up the subject. Their confidence and smartly tempered cavalier spirit led them to accomplish missions that others would never attempt. They could make difficult decisions quickly; they'd receive their orders and get the job done, following a long navy tradition that has always relied on strong, daring, and entrepreneurial leaders.

In 1801, President Thomas Jefferson sent the fledgling U.S. Navy to defeat the pirates off the Barbary Coast—those sailing from Tripoli in particular. He gave his commanders an objective and let them do their job. With ships like *Enterprise, Intrepid, Constellation,* and *Constitution*—names that would echo through two centuries of U.S. naval history—the American fleet achieved its aim through battle and arms-backed diplomacy. Ever since, the navy has trusted the judgment and abilities of its people. Navy rules generally list what personnel can't do, not what they can; they're free to innovate within bounds. For that reason, stories of individual leadership and creativity fill naval aviation's annals. That background gave rise to personalities like those naval aviators herein. It endowed them with common values and a deep passion for their high-flying vocation. They were all warriors.

"Naval aviation becomes the essence of your spirit and being," Hoser said, the water welling in his eyes again. "Being able to go into combat and bet your ass that you can rely completely on somebody else—and they can rely on you—in the most extreme situation a human mind can imagine, and know they're not going to fail you? That's trust and integrity like nowhere else. The only fear is getting to the end and not being part of it anymore. Not being around all those vital, healthy, intelligent, alert, talented people anymore. That's what's scary."

That thought was what brought the tears.

Many times, people seek naval aviation's character in its machines—its storied aircraft carriers, famed F6F Hellcats, or venerable F-14 Tomcats. But those contraptions of metal and wire mean very little in themselves. I was beginning to realize how the *people* of naval aviation define this special discipline far more than jets, flight decks, and tailhooks. Seeing the indomitable Hoser Satrapa shed gentle tears as he reflected on this special band, watching pilots and crew chiefs work together in pursuit of the perfect mission, and hearing the shouts of aspiring eighteen-year-old sailors who want to jump into raging seas to save lives reminded me how millions of great and varied personalities have written these chapters of history. Naval aviation draws leaders who want to fight and serve—and who also harbor a slightly untamed spirit. Throughout careers and across decades, their bedrock personal values, along with their insatiable drive to be the best, have defined naval aviation far more than the ships they've sailed and the aircraft they've flown.

6

THE HOMEFRONT

THE SIGHT OF A SINGLE aircraft carrier always inspires awe, no matter how accustomed to these titans someone may become. A *Nimitz*-class carrier, of which there are ten in operation, boasts more firepower than many nations possess in total. The carriers stretch nearly four football fields in length—1,092 feet—and have a 100-yard beam. The four bronze propellers harnessed to the ships' two nuclear reactors can bring 280,000 horsepower to bear as they push 97,000 tons of steel through the high seas at more than thirty knots—and they can do it for twenty-five years without refueling. Keel to mast, the ships tower twenty-four stories—more than 200 feet—dwarfing all but the largest supertankers. Their seventy-plus aircraft could handily destroy the air forces of most countries. They serve as homes for 3,200 crew members and 2,400 air wing personnel as they project American force around the globe. They are the proud flagships of the U.S. Navy and ambassadors of America herself.

The first ship of the class, the USS *Nimitz*, was the sixty-eighth carrier commissioned by the United States and carries the hull number Sixty-Eight. Nine sister ships followed: the USS *Dwight D. Eisenhower* (Sixty-Nine), *Carl Vinson* (Seventy), *Theodore Roosevelt* (Seventy-One), *Abraham Lincoln* (Seventy-Two), *George Washington* (Seventy-Three), *John C. Stennis*

(Seventy-Four), *Harry S. Truman* (Seventy-Five), *Ronald Reagan* (Seventy-Six), and *George H. W. Bush* (Seventy-Seven).

I had never seen three of the giant warships amassed together until I drove onto the pier at Naval Station Norfolk, and I have never been in more awe at America's naval power. When the waterfront first came into view, I saw *Theodore Roosevelt, Harry S. Truman,* and *Dwight D. Eisenhower* moored side by side. Their sleek gray hulls and intricate black masts dominated the surrounding area and I tried to imagine the psychological effect the same gathering would have if seen from a hostile foreign shore.

TR and *Truman* floated quietly, sterns to the windy Chesapeake Bay, decks still and empty. The bow of the *Ike*, however, pointed squarely toward the sea, seeming anxious to plow the waters ahead. Sailors and workmen swarmed over her pier and decks, performing every task imaginable. In just three days, the carrier would cast off her lines and push into the bay with her sailors lining the decks, steeled against the January cold in their blue jackets. Families would gather along the pier, braving the morning's chill to wave good-bye to loved ones. The cold wind would surely draw tears, as would the reality of a fifteen-thousand-mile, seven-month cruise away from home. The great ship would glide farther away from the pier and its huddled families, make a gentle turn to starboard, and disappear from view. As she plied the same waters where Eugene Ely introduced the world to naval aviation, her four nuclear-powered turbines would increase speed and her four thirty-three-ton, twenty-five-foot screws would drive her into the open Atlantic, bound for the Arabian Sea.

Those events were still three days away when Brie Hine and I stepped out of a warm Chevy Tahoe and onto the dock. The chilly wind driving inland from the water tousled Brie's long hair as we leaned forward into the small gale and walked toward *Ike*'s pier. As we approached, I saw two barges tied alongside the carrier, making last-minute repairs and improvements to the hull and decking. Other vehicles off-loaded supplies, which we soon discovered were being stacked in the hangar deck before being stowed in the ship's labyrinth of internal compartments. Those supplies were enough to sustain a small town for half a year—or at least for several weeks until the first re-supply operation. The stores included the food needed for 18,000 meals per day, which required 600 gallons of milk, 180 dozen eggs, 620 pounds of hamburgers, and 1,700 pounds of fruit and vegetables. Beyond food, the carrier offered most every service available in a small town. She had a barber shop, laundry, print shop, legal office, post office, hospital, dentist, convenience store, a television station, several completely outfitted gyms, and most other services sailors might need while under way. As for shops and services they might *want*, well, a carrier couldn't provide everything.

Brie and I crossed the gangplank (or brow, as the navy calls it) to this floating city and walked across the lowered aft elevator, which served as the quarterdeck, where guests boarded the ship. At the security checkpoint, Brie showed her military spouse identification and I produced my Georgia driver's license, which the guard would hold until we left. We then turned to gaze at the rows of stacked crates and boxes filling the aft section of the hangar, realizing what massive resources deploying a carrier requires. We walked through the cavernous space, which would soon be crowded with aircraft instead of provisions. Everywhere, members of the ship's crew worked to ensure all the supplies were received and that everything was squared away for the imminent deployment.

Brie quietly observed the activity, knowing it had one exciting, honorable, and yet infinitely sad purpose: to ready the ship to carry its complement of husbands, wives, fathers, and mothers far from home to serve their country. Among them would be her husband, Lieutenant Ed Hine, who flew with Carrier Air Wing Seven and Strike Fighter Squadron 103 (VFA-103)—the Jolly Rogers.

"It's tough, particularly right now," she confessed as we talked about the deployment. "It's hard to describe. Emptiness. Your heart just feels like it's in the pit of your stomach. Part of me wants to hang on to him and not let him go. I want to spend every second with him. I don't want him to leave my sight. It's suffocating, really. The other part just wants him to leave—rip the Band-Aid off—because good-bye is the hardest part. It's so much easier to count the days until he comes home than count the days until he leaves. Then, one day I wake up and think, 'Good, we're halfway. Three months under my belt. I can do this!'"

From the noisy hangar deck, we climbed several sets of ladders and walked down a relatively quiet portside corridor and into the forward wardroom, where Ed and his squadron mates would eat most of their meals during the cruise. It was nothing like the warm two-bedroom house the couple shared in Norfolk. The *Ike*'s wardroom resembled a fraternity house dining room, albeit with a military flair. Food and drink stations stood along one wall, facing a traditional cafeteria-style serving line. The wardroom also offered a salad bar, cereal, frozen ice cream—basically any type of institutional foodstuff the officers might desire while they were under way. Heavy tablecloths covered tables and framed photographs of the carrier and her air wing adorned the walls, trying to give a touch of elegance to the otherwise Spartan room.

"There's just nothing here to remind him of me," observed Brie as she looked around. She wasn't sad. She just stated a fact. "Out here, the boys eat meals in the *officers'* dining room, fly the *Navy's* jets, and sleep in the *ship's* bunks. They live these separated lives on this ship on the other side of the world. But I still come home to *our* house every day. I walk *our* dog and sleep in *our* bed. Every day—every minute almost—I'm reminded that he's not here."

But that's the way it should be, she observed. "When he's away, I try and support him by taking care of everything I can at home. I don't want him to worry about anything because I want him to stay focused on his job. So, I try and do everything I can to put out any fires on the home front. I tell him about the successes, not the problems."

To help with the problems, Brie and other spouses have a community that unhesitatingly supports one another. The previous day, Brie had driven a fellow navy wife seven hours to North Carolina for a medical treatment—then she drove seven hours back. The wife's husband was on deployment, she needed help, and Brie didn't hesitate. Brie had never even met her before. The separation and the strains of military life are never easy, as Brie emphasized, but the military families at Naval Station Norfolk, nearby Naval Air Station Oceana, and in the surrounding communities support each other in countless ways while husbands or wives are at sea.

"A Navy SEAL lives down the street and I met his wife while we were walking," Brie explained. "When we found out we were both military, we exchanged phone numbers on the spot. The next week, we had a flood and she called to check up on me. That doesn't happen in most communities. You become closer a lot quicker than you would elsewhere. Now, I don't call people crying! When I get worried or lonely, I talk myself through it. I'll drink a glass of wine and hug the dog!"

She laughed. "But I *can't* worry about him. Doing what he does, when would I *not* worry about him? I just have to block it."

She finds her closest friends among the squadron's spouses, a group that grows particularly close during their loved ones' long absences. They plan a full calendar of activities—some of which involve entertaining the aviators on the ship from afar, and others are simply plain fun for themselves. The squadron's ready room had a calendar featuring wives and children. Gifts and reminders of home regularly made their way onto the boat, and the squadron wives were producing a DVD—*The Real Housewives of VFA-103*—to send their boys at the halfway point of the cruise.

"I know Ed is grateful that I have a family with the girls here," she said. "We constantly send them pictures and videos of us laughing and having fun. That lets them see that we're not miserable and pining! They know we have support here and that helps them stay focused on the job."

From the outset, Ed and Brie engaged military life as a pair—each supporting the other through the challenges a navy career brings. Ed has always had a fighter cockpit as his goal, and Brie loves him for having the drive to get there. She supported him all the way, and admitted that from their very first date, she knew the type of duty for which she might be volunteering. The couple, now both twenty-eight, met during college, with Brie at the University of Pittsburgh and Ed at the U.S. Merchant Marine Academy in Kings Point, New York. Their first date began at Louie's Oyster Bar and Grill in Long Island, overlooking Manhasset Bay. The two hit it off immediately. When Ed shared his plan to fly for the navy and Brie just thought, "Okay, here we go. . . ."

Brie and I continued to walk slowly down the forward corridors of the *Eisenhower*, past the staterooms and berthing compartments that sailors, officers, and aviators would soon fill. Occasional crew passed us in the hallway en route to stowing candy, stereos, and anything else you might bring to summer camp. They politely addressed Brie as "ma'am," and quickly stood aside to let her pass through the narrow doorways that divide the long hallway at regular intervals.

As we returned to the hangar, we talked about the thousands of families that were preparing to say good-bye, about to face half a year or longer without a loved one.

I asked her, candidly, why she made the sacrifice. Her friends who married outside the military saw their husbands every night. Ed had been gone more than he'd been home during their time with the squadron, which would total two years at the end of this next deployment. Brie counted six or seven months with him at home during their twenty-four with the Jolly Rogers. He'd been away on a series of workups—the short mini-deployments during which the carrier and air wing hone their skills—for nearly five months and the upcoming cruise would last seven. Their most recent deployment had lasted more than five months—and it just ended six months ago. Now *Ike* was headed to sea again.

Brie patiently—and proudly—explained why she chose to live such a lifestyle. "We live in the greatest, most prosperous country in the world," she explained. "And today more than ever it is important to protect our freedoms. There are so many things threatening our way of life that I'm grateful we're doing what we can to help preserve what has always made this country great. I could go on and on about this, but in short, I'm a patriot and I'm so proud of what Ed and his friends do."

Like Brie, Bethany Weisser recognizes a special duty, and she echoed Brie's thoughts the night before we watched her husband Frank perform in Blue Angel Number Five. The three of us had dinner that evening in their home at NAS Pensacola. Like many other Blue Angel families, the Weissers live in a classic military apartment. The circa 1930 quadraplex houses four families, two of whom are Blue Angel team members. The Weisser apartment's hardwood floors and high ceilings have a gracious charm, though Frank wished the small unit had more room for his growing family, which includes his young daughter Kendall and son Ben. But he conceded the small home helped the family grow close and their location put them near other families that form their vital support network.

As we finished the exceptional dinner Bethany had prepared, the couple talked about how that little apartment played a crucial role in every air show.

"When you meet someone and fall in love, you don't quite know how they'll be as a navy wife," Frank reflected. "But we did talk about it while we were dating: 'If we take that next step and get married, it's not going to be a normal life for you.'"

Bethany had not grown up in a military family and wasn't sure what to expect. "It's the kind of thing that you just have to experience firsthand to really know what you're getting into," she said. "I learned quickly life as a navy wife was going to be very different than the life of my friends married to civilians. Frank barely got the weekend off for our wedding, and then had to report back to work at 6 A.M. Monday morning after the wedding weekend! He was gone for most of our first year of marriage doing workups and then deploying for seven months. That first year was a very steep learning curve for this unseasoned navy wife."

Now that the Weissers have two children, Bethany finds herself often taking on the role of father and mother in Frank's absence. The experience has grounded her.

"The 'it's all about me' mentality is a hard one to maintain here," she said. "You quickly learn the things you used to complain about are petty. You learn everyone in a navy family sacrifices in some way. You learn to toughen up and roll with the punches.

"But there is no doubt my experience as a navy wife—and mother— here with the Blue Angels and in the fleet continues to shape me into a better person. It is not always easy, it is not always hard, and it is never boring. I never expected this role in life. I had no idea my path would lead me here; I am grateful it has. And I would pick the life of a navy wife all over again, knowing what I know now."

Frank picked up the conversation. "Bethany truly believes that her service to the country is to be as supportive and nurturing a wife and mother as she can be so I can have less on my plate when I go to work, so I can be the best at my job. She doesn't want to have anything slowing me down. She takes care of the kids and handles most of the hard stuff . . . and she's absolutely great at it."

Kendall and Ben, ages three and one respectively, added a new dimension to the Weissers' life at home and Frank's service in the fleet. As a single guy, Frank looked forward to his time at sea; out there, he got to fly with his friends and do his job. When he married, the time away became much more difficult. When children entered the picture, he found they brought even more new challenges—as well as new blessings. He lamented missing so many of the exciting firsts in their lives and not being present for the important events. He hoped they would eventually understand why he made the sacrifices he did. But having children also added a renewed purpose to his job. He always had something to look forward to outside of work, and as a parent, he could relate to many of the men and women under his command in a new way. Fatherhood made him a better leader at sea.

Like many of his fellow aviators and crew members, he worries that his time deployed will adversely affect his children. It's a constant struggle for him. Thus far, however, he and Bethany have decided that the benefits of setting an example through service and sacrifice are more important than his being home each night.

"We want Kendall and Ben to know that freedom isn't free and that it requires great sacrifice on the part of many in this country," Frank said. "Hopefully as they get older, they will understand our family's sacrifices and one day believe as we do that its value outweighs its cost.

"Our service to America and the risks that entails are required, in our opinion, to allow for a safe and free country for our children to grow up in. Ultimately and most importantly to me is the fact that our service to our country defines in part who we are as a family and our character. While it's not easy for any family to have a parent gone for weeks or months at a time, we believe the strength in character that comes with that separation will be reflected in our children as they both grow and mature. That is certainly worthwhile to us."

The people in the navy's aviation community—whether they're on the carrier or at home raising kids—are truly living for a cause larger than themselves. That creates a powerfully supportive environment for navy families and sets an important example for children—and for those outside the military. These families are certainly not primarily serving themselves, their pocketbooks, or their quality of life. But they're undoubtedly serving their fellow countrymen.

Bethany and Brie serve and sacrifice like navy wives have for generations. Carolyn Booth remembers arriving home from the hospital in San Diego with her first daughter in 1960, two decades before Bethany and Brie were born.

She and her husband Pete began five happy days together as a new family. Then Pete left for a nine-month deployment aboard the USS *Hancock*.

"We communicated with letters while he was gone," Carolyn recalled. "But there was no timeframe—sometimes it'd take a letter ten days, sometimes three weeks. I'd write just about every day—some little note about what was going on. He might get eight or nine letters at once. There was no two-day delivery, that's for sure!

"We just didn't have the technology they do today. Every Christmas, we'd record a cassette tape that got sent to the ship—that was hi-tech back then! And it was very difficult for children with so little communication from their father. It may seem difficult now, but that was the only lifestyle we knew, so we all just lived that way."

Pete's star rose quickly in the fleet and he soon earned command of Fighter Squadron Eleven (VF-11)—the Red Rippers—which his father had commanded years before. He later commanded the aircraft carrier USS *Forrestal*. When he assumed greater positions of leadership in the fleet, Carolyn stepped into larger roles at home. As the wife of the commanding officer (CO), she would run the wives' clubs and help resolve any problems that squadron families experienced. Important news from the fleet came to her first and she'd disseminate it through a telephone tree; she would dial several wives who would each dial several others, and so on. When unhappy information such as a death reached her, she was responsible for delivering that news as well. Still today, the spouse of a CO or XO (Executive Officer) assumes a special role and duty when their unit deploys. The ship or squadron's families look to them for leadership.

Particularly with longer deployments and the absence of electronic communication in the decades before 2000, Carolyn found the support of the tight-knit military community even more important. As a result, the Booths have close friends everywhere they travel today. And after fifty years of marriage, Carolyn Booth would volunteer for life as a navy wife all over again, just like Bethany and Brie.

After visiting the *Eisenhower* with Brie Hine on that cold winter day, I drove the thirty minutes from Naval Station Norfolk to Naval Air Station

Oceana to see the husband she loved and supported. Oceana's 6,800 acres and four runways provide a land-based home to all East Coast F/A-18 Hornet and Super Hornet fighter squadrons. The base hosts major components of five carrier air wings, one each for the carriers USS *Enterprise, Dwight D. Eisenhower, Theodore Roosevelt, Harry S. Truman*, and *George H. W. Bush*. Nineteen F/A-18 squadrons, which included Ed Hine's Jolly Rogers, were divided among them. The day I arrived, his squadron was making its final preparations for deployment aboard the *Eisenhower*.

Wearing a typical olive flight suit, Ed met me by the Navy Exchange— the base's general store—and drove me to the long row of hangars that house Oceana's fighter aircraft and squadron offices. The long metal structures had spots inside allotted to each squadron—among them the Golden Warriors, Gunslingers, Knighthawks, Fighting Checkmates, Rampagers, Ragin' Bulls, Knighthawks, Tomcatters, Sunliners, Swordsmen, Red Rippers, Blacklions, Blue Blasters, Valions, Wildcats, the World Famous Pukin' Dogs, the Navy Reserve's Fighting Omars, and the East Coast F/A-18 Fleet Replacement Squadron, the Gladiators. Beyond the hangar lay the bleached tarmac, where rows of gray jets waited quietly for their next mission.

Ed showed me around an idle two-seat F/A-18F Super Hornet in the Jolly Rogers' section of the hangar, explaining the complexities of the aircraft, which made Eugene Ely's biplane and the planes that won World War II seem like Stone Age creations. The sleek jet had more wiring than many office buildings and the engine, partly exposed for maintenance, was no less complex. I understood why the jets require such a large supporting cast. The number of systems and parts that must function perfectly overwhelmed me.

Weighing in at nearly fifty thousand pounds fully loaded, the F/A-18E (single seat) and F/A-18F (two-seat) Super Hornets outsize their noticeably smaller F/A-18A/B/C Hornet predecessors, which weigh thirty-seven thousand pounds under a full load. Their two General Electric turbofan engines can push them to fifty thousand feet at speeds of nearly Mach 2—1,522 miles per hour at sea level. The aircraft boast a forty-four-foot wingspan and have sixty feet of length. Their wings and rear stabilators give them five hundred square feet of control surface area, which endows the Super Hornet with maneuverability that would make Hoser Satrapa forsake his beloved Tomcats. Hoser would also approve of the Super Hornet's 20 mm Vulcan cannon and ability to carry a deadly and varied load of missiles and bombs. McDonnell

Douglas and Boeing designed the jet to hold its own with any fighter in the world—and it can. They also designed it to put ordnance on ground targets in all types of weather—and Ed had watched it prove itself on that account during the squadron's previous deployment to the Middle East.

After the tour, Ed and I walked to the simple ground-floor locker room, which had metal cages for each pilot's equipment. The room was neither fancy nor bare-bones. Three aviators and two of Ed's fellow Naval Flight Officers joined us several seconds later. In the F/A-18 community, NFOs are called Weapons Systems Officers—or WSOs (pronounced *wizzos*)—and from their position in the jet's second seat, they operate the complex weapons the Super Hornet deploys in combat. These six young officers—all between the ages of twenty-five and thirty-one—suited up for their last mission before they cruised to the Middle East. After that, their next sortie would end with a trap—an arrested landing—on the Middle East–bound USS *Dwight D. Eisenhower*. They wouldn't see another luxuriously long runway like Oceana's until midsummer. It was, as one said, "Time to stop flying like the Air Force."

Ed pulled on his g-suit and helmet and walked with his pilot to the maintenance office where they reviewed the newly completed maintenance sheet for their assigned aircraft. Satisfied, they signed for Aircraft 203.

On the way to his waiting plane, we talked about the impending cruise and its affect on his life—on Brie, in particular. "It's just plain hard on a marriage," Ed said. "I can't overstate this: her understanding of the requirements of my job is critically important. The thing about this gig is that the decisions I make drastically affect both of us. There is the obvious, 'Do you want to stay in the navy or get out? Or when do you want to have kids?' Two of my roommates on this deployment have pregnant wives right now; one may very well still be on cruise and miss the due date."

Other family strains arise when the squadron returns home and the commanding officers ask for volunteers to attend training courses at other bases. When those classes fall on the short periods between detachments and long deployments, pilots and WSOs find themselves choosing between getting the training they need and spending precious time with their families.

It's on deployments that aviators and crewmen alike most depend on support from the home front. "At sea, Brie's support is huge," Ed said. "One of the biggest things you miss out there is a connection to home and she is by far my biggest connection."

Like most couples on board, they e-mail as often as they can and call whenever a chance arises on the carrier's limited long-distance lines. Oftentimes, the men in the squadron have difficulty relating to loved ones at home. Life almost never changes aboard the boat—the pilots sleep, eat, brief, fly, and debrief. Then they repeat—day in and day out. Nothing changes. They mark the passing of the weeks with Saturday's pizza night or Sunday's call to worship. Otherwise, it's like the film *Groundhog Day*—they live the same day again and again. Sometimes they feel they have little to share. When news from home arrives, they realize how much life changes for those they've left in the States; they are reminded what they're missing. Life at home goes on without them.

"When it comes down to it the personal sacrifices are tough," Ed said, "but for me this is the only thing I've ever wanted to do with my life, and I'm a pretty lucky guy to have a wife who understands that about me and supports me."

By this time, we had arrived at a row of three F/A-18F Super Hornets. Each plane had its maintenance crew in attendance and each had its canopy raised, awaiting its pilot and WSO. I stopped several yards shy of the plane and watched the crews run through the final safety checks on the ground. Once everything checked out, the crews climbed into their cockpits and turned over their engines. Soon, the three planes followed one another toward the long runway and one by one, took off for a final round of practice. After the day's mission ended, Ed would drive home where he and Brie would spend their last three days together before he headed east toward the Arabian Sea with the Jolly Rogers, Carrier Air Wing Seven, and the USS *Eisenhower.*

Visiting with Ed and Brie Hine in Norfolk and the Weisser and Booth families in Pensacola taught me something I should have realized earlier. Particularly being with the Hines so close to a deployment showed me quite clearly that the men and women aboard the ships of the fleet weren't the only people who supported naval aviation. I began to understand how a dedicated family as well as an entire shore-based community sustains each member of the crew and air wing. It takes a family and a community—a true home port—to launch aircraft off those decks.

PART TWO

THE ATLANTIC

7

RESCUERS

THE DAY OF THE *EISENHOWER*'S departure for the Middle East brought freezing cold, rain, and snow. The North Atlantic gave the eastbound carrier strike group the most violently inhospitable welcome it could muster. The seas heaved and heavens poured while icy winds rushed off the mainland with astounding speed and force. Sheets of rain and flurries of snow hid the ships from one another and gradually reduced visibility as the strike group sailed steadily into the storm's heart.

The *Eisenhower* pitched on the rolling swells, but her sheer mass and driving screws held her relatively steady. Still, many of her new sailors had to get their sea legs quickly. *Ike*'s escorts, the Norfolk-based destroyer *Mc-Faul* and the Mayport, Florida-based cruiser *Hue City* and destroyers *Carney* and *Farragut*, were also weathering the storm, but not as comfortably.

The thirty-four-foot *Gloria A Dios*, however, had met her match. Her captain, Dennis Clements, had set sail from Norfolk several days before, bound for the Caribbean. Some two hundred miles east of Cape Hatteras, the storm viciously struck the sailboat. The foaming seas pushed the boat up the sides of mammoth waves, then slid her down the far sides like a toy sled. The sailboat's rolling increased and waves broke violently over its sides and bow.

The seas heeled it to port, then dangerously far to starboard. The winds tore at the mast and canvas sails. Finally, a wave nearly capsized the ship and activated its automatic emergency beacon. The roll also opened the ship to the sea and water poured into the cabin, adding to the seawater that had been accumulating since the storm began. Dennis did his best to patch holes punched by the storm, but fought a losing battle. The steering soon went and the engine began to fail; the seawater shorted the electrical system. Dennis struggled—alone, in a heavy rainstorm, battling winds of more than forty-five knots, in complete blackness. Then he felt another wave strike. The boat heeled hard, but didn't stop when the deck touched the water. The *Gloria A Dios* rolled over completely.

Caught in the rigging, Dennis gasped once then the sea closed around him, cold and rough. Somewhere during the 360-degree roll, Dennis wrenched himself free and fought to the surface. Then he watched his ship—the lone noticeable reference point for any would-be rescuers—wallow away into the darkness. Shortly, the sea would claim it entirely. As an experienced mariner, he fortunately wore a survival suit which would, for the time being, fend off the icy water and keep him afloat. He bobbed in the darkness—alone, helpless, and wondering if he would see the same fate as his sailboat. How would anyone ever find him?

Fortunately, he wasn't entirely alone. The U.S. Coast Guard station in Elizabeth City, North Carolina, had received the distress signal from the *Gloria A Dios* shortly after 5 P.M., and a four-engine Coast Guard C-130 patrol plane reached the struggling craft an hour and a half later. By the time the plane arrived, the oppressive darkness of a stormy winter night had descended over the North Atlantic. Dennis Clements was in the struggle of his life, and the cacophony of the storm robbed him of any comfort he might have derived from the C-130's presence by drowning out the sound of its engines. Even had Dennis heard it, the plane's crew could do little but watch the drama play out on infrared monitors as it circled a thousand feet above the scene.

Earlier that day, and more than 250 miles away from the distressed *Gloria A Dios*, the *Eisenhower* began receiving her air wing, which flew in from NAS Oceana. The planes cut through the rain and wind to land on their home for the next seven months, and did so repeatedly to earn their qualifications for this new cruise. Generally, each pilot had to complete four daytime landings and two night landings, with two of the daylight and both night-time landings being arrested "traps" where the aircraft catches the arresting wire. Before quals were scheduled to end on that first day of deployment, however, the deck had begun pitching so heavily and the weather had deteriorated so drastically that the commanding officer, Captain Dee Mewbourne, cancelled flight operations. Launches stopped, the catapults fell silent, and *Ike* recovered the remaining airborne planes onto her pitching deck.

About the same time flight operations ceased, the carrier received word of the distressed *Gloria A Dios*. *Ike* altered her course and headed toward the floundering ship, planning to serve as a refueling stop for a Coast Guard rescue helicopter. As a backup measure, an SH-60F Seahawk search and rescue crew from Helicopter Anti-Submarine Squadron Five (HS-5) aboard the *Eisenhower* briefed for the mission.

Later in the evening, the Coast Guard radioed that their helicopter had mechanical problems and wasn't ready. The fate of Dennis Clements fell to a four-man crew from the HS-5 Nightdippers: Squadron Executive Officer Byron Ogden, Lt. Commander Scott Pichette, Petty Officer David Brandon, and rescue swimmer Kyle Need.

Ogden, the mission commander, remembers reporting to the admiral's command center on *Ike* and hearing Strike Group Eight Commander Rear Admiral Phil Davidson say, "It looks like the Coast Guard can't go. Can you guys do the mission?' "

The admiral and crew knew the hazards presented by the raging storm and the distance to the scene, which was at the limit of the helicopter's range. Commander Ogden, known as Oggie since age twelve, responded for his crew. "Yes, sir," he said. "We can do this mission. It's what we train for every day.'

"Admiral Davidson asked how soon we could be off the deck and I told him we could be off in half an hour," Oggie recalled. "He said, 'We want you to launch.' "

The crew dressed for the mission, donning dry suits and cold weather gear. Then they rushed topside. Through the bitter cold, dark of night, and driving snow, the four crew members rushed toward their Seahawk—designated

Canvass 612—which was chained to the slick, heaving deck. Beyond the edges of the deck waited complete darkness, howling wind, and angry sea.

At present, however, the winds rushed down the deck from stern to bow too fast to allow the Seahawk to launch from its present orientation, with its nose toward the bow. In tailwinds of that speed, the Seahawk's tail rotor would be useless. The deck crew had to laboriously spin the helicopter around so it could launch.

The crew charged the two turboshaft engines, one by one. Once the engines were online, Oggie illuminated the lights on the rotor head, signaling the nearby Landing Signalman Enlisted (LSE) that he was ready to engage the rotors. The green-coated LSE requested permission from Primary Flight Control atop the island. There, the Air Boss and his staff, who controlled the airspace around *Ike*, granted clearance. The loudspeaker boomed, "Stand well clear, Canvass 612 engaging rotors. Stand well clear."

The LSE stood erect and pointed a glowing wand toward the rotors with his left hand. He held another wand in his right hand, which he began moving in a circular motion above his head. Oggie set their four overhead blades spinning, creating a fifty-three-foot halo above the twenty-thousand-pound aircraft. They still couldn't launch, however. They were outside the maximum range their fuel tanks and regulations allowed: 180 miles. They waited.

When they reached a point 178 miles from the location of the original distress signal, the LSE raised one glowing wand to acknowledge Oggie's request to launch. He relayed the request to Primary Flight Control and the loudspeaker boomed again: "Stand clear for breakdown and launch of Canvass 612." With rain, snow, and wind blowing relentlessly across the deck, however, there were few bystanders to warn.

At the LSE's signal, two maintainers carried away the chains and chocks that had been holding the Seahawk in place. When they were clear of the rotor arc, the LSE crossed two wands over his head and backed away. After several steps he stopped, dropped his arms, and pointed the wands at the deck. Then in a fluid motion, he raised both arms, lowered them, and then raised them again, urging the helicopter upward. The Seahawk responded, floating straight up until the LSE spun a single wand in the air then pointed it sharply toward the deck's end. The Seahawk pitched forward and rode the forty-five-knot tailwind into the suffocating darkness of the storm.

With their night-vision goggles (NVGs) functioning, everything above and below the crew was eerily glowing green. Without the NVGs, every-thing would have been pitch-black except the whitecaps on the breaking waves. The wind became an asset and sped them through snow, hail, and rain, delivering them to the scene in an hour's time.

In the meantime, the original Coast Guard C-130 had left its position above the *Gloria A Dios* to refuel. As it departed, it dropped several life rafts near the ship, hoping a miracle might deliver them to any survivors. Since the rafts had no lights, there was little chance anyone would see them at night amidst the rain and waves. Another C-130 soon arrived on the scene, but in the interim, the sailboat had sunk. All the new Coast Guard pilots could see through their infrared scopes were the several rafts dropped by the first C-130.

By the time the new plane arrived, Dennis had been in the water for close to an hour. He was beginning to wonder how long his survival suit could stave off the cold and keep him afloat. He couldn't see anything. Darkness blanketed the ocean—or what little of it he could see. When he found him-self in a trough, the mountainous waves girded his entire horizon. When he crested a wave—the one point he could hope to expand his view—the spray blinded him and sent him choking and blinking back into another trough.

"There was nothing more to be done," he remembered. "It was all over. So I told the Lord, 'God I'm going to believe in you and hope in you until I take my final breath.' And I didn't expect that to be more than a few more minutes. That's when I kicked off my boots and started to swim. I didn't have a direction picked out, I didn't see anything. I just told God that I was going to believe in him until I took my last breath, and I started swimming. I don't know how long I kept that up and then I saw this dark blob in front of me and I bumped into that capsized life raft and I almost didn't believe it was real. I was going to live another day."[1]

A glimmer of hope crept into Dennis's soul and he climbed into the raft. The wind howled so loudly and the waves crashed with such noise, however, that Dennis didn't hear the navy helicopter approach several minutes later. When he finally saw the Seahawk's lights, he turned on his flashlight and hoped its weak beam would pierce the elements.

On the flight out, Scott Pichette and the Coast Guard accurately calculated the sailboat's drift and the helo arrived at the precise spot where Dennis had floated from his last known position. When Canvass 612 first arrived on the scene, the Coast Guard C-130 directed the crew to the location of the rafts, but the Coast Guard noted that they hadn't seen any signs of life. As the navy team closed on the rafts, Petty Officer Brandon—the crew chief and hoist operator who was peering out of the Seahawk's side door—reported the rafts within sight. Oggie was turning the helo to maintain the visual when he heard Petty Officer Brandon report, "I've got motion! I see a flashlight down there."

Petty Officer Brandon directed Oggie into position—no easy task as the aircraft commander faced unpredictable gusts and ocean swells of twenty-five to thirty feet. Oggie and Scott tried to engage the automatic hover, but they gave up immediately as the conditions and giant waves rendered the feature useless. They switched to manual controls. With his left hand, Oggie gripped the collective pitch lever, which controls the bird's lift and altitude by collectively adjusting the angle of its overhead rotors—the greater the pitch of the blades, the more air they move, and the greater the lift they generate. Oggie's right hand was busy fighting with the cyclic control stick (which controls the roll and pitch) and his feet pumped the rotor pedals (which control the left or right yaw) to maintain the helo's position. And he did it as fierce gusts toyed with the twenty-thousand-pound aircraft as if it were made of paper. Yet he held the bird steady, even though he had no hard points of reference. Swells rose and fell, waves moved toward him and away from him, and the icy winds continued to buffet the Seahawk from different quarters. Oggie couldn't tell whether the helo, the seas, or both were moving. He had to trust the directions coming from Petty Officer Brandon who was keeping the survivor in sight. Oggie held them at seventy feet and then it was up to the guys in back.

Oggie recalled, "I was just making sure I wasn't flying into the water. I was squeezing the collective so hard, and listening to Brandon tell me what to do."

"We had to hover at a higher altitude because the waves were so high," Scott Pichette added. "Looking out the left window and watching these mountainous waves come by, it felt like the next wave would hit the belly of the helo."

Thankfully, the crew was experienced. In total, the four men had nearly ten thousand hours of flight time. Petty Officer Brandon and Commander Ogden both had more than three thousand hours. Lt. Commander Pichette had over two thousand hours and three previous rescues. Young Kyle Need already had one rescue and more than one thousand hours.

Kyle would need every bit of that experience. Now it was up to him.

During the flight out, the crew had discussed what might happen once they arrived. An eternal optimist, Scott was convinced they would rescue the survivor, which necessarily meant that Kyle Need would have to go swimming in the freezing, stormy North Atlantic.

"The entire ride out, that prospect was in back of my head," Kyle said with a laugh as we talked aboard the *Eisenhower* when calmer seas prevailed. "I kept trying to forget about it."

Scott razzed him about his impending swim during the hour flight, keeping the mood as light as possible, but once Oggie established the hover and Kyle slid to the door, it was game time. Everyone knew the stakes. Kyle performed a final check of his gear, including his hood, fins, mask, snorkel, and dry suit—a rubberized waterproof suit used for cold weather diving. "I was as prepared as I could be," he said. Petty Officer Brandon hooked him onto the cable, double-checked the connection, and lowered Kyle into the sea.

Before he had gone ten feet toward the water, snowflakes caked his mask. He had to wipe the glass again and again as he descended into the halo of light the Seahawk was casting on the frigid water. The wind grew stronger still; the rain had long since turned to sleet. A single helicopter hovering in the pitch black, a tiny circle of light on churning waves, and a lone rescue swimmer dangling in the stormy vastness of a North Atlantic night: this was the surreal scene two hundred miles off the North Carolina coast. It fazed neither the men in the helicopter nor Kyle Need.

"Once I hit water, I was surprised at how much I couldn't see," Kyle said. "After a few seconds, a wave dropped and I could see where I needed to go.

"We had prebriefed that I wasn't going to unhook from the cable; if I got off that hook, who knows if I would've been able to get back on. I hit the water, swam over, and on the way got hit by three waves. Two knocked the mask off my face. Luckily I'd tied it on like we're trained to do, so I put it back on and kept swimming. I reached the raft and heard Mr. Clements just yelling at the top of his lungs, just as happy as he could be.

"He was enjoying the conversation a little too much, so I tried to get him quiet and get him into the water—'Let's go.' I didn't want to be out there." Kyle pulled the survivor off the raft and into the water.

"The entire time, waves were crashing over the top of us, just crashing over the top of us. I couldn't even imagine describing how big they were. I was just trying to keep him above water."

Kyle muscled through the waves—fit from the PT regimen that began at Pensacola—and towed the man back to the halo of light beneath the hovering Seahawk. He grabbed the rescue harness and hooked Dennis to it. At Kyle's signal, Petty Officer Brandon hauled in the luckiest man on the Atlantic.

"That guy was so happy to be alive," Scott reflected aboard *Eisenhower*, as I sat with the crew of Canvass 612. "He was fired up like it was a Super Bowl party. He thought he was done. Done. Then he looked up and saw the raft next to him. Then he used the signaling device when we came by. He got religion if he didn't have it before.

"Once he was in, we closed the doors and turned the heat up, trying to keep him warm and from slipping into shock. We all had on waterproof dry suits and were sweating like crazy."

Outside the Seahawk's metal skin, the snow still blew ferociously, assailing the returning helo with freezing gusts. The transit took more than ninety minutes, due to the weather and formidable headwind. At 0100 Sunday morning, Canvass 612 alighted on the still-pitching deck of the *Eisenhower*, which battled eastward through the heavy seas. The mission had ended.

Kyle, who was sitting across from me, added, "During the trip back, I used the knowledge I have of medical care, stripped him down and wrapped him up in blankets. He said he wasn't cold, wasn't thirsty. I knew he didn't know what he was talking about and we gave him plenty of water, gave him blankets, kept him warm. I held his hand the whole time to keep tabs on him. He was physically exhausted but I kept tapping him every few minutes, making him give me a thumbs-up to keep him awake."

Kyle reminded me that the rescue swimmers' motto is "So Others May Live."

"That's the reason I took this job," he said of the motto. "I wanted to be part of something different than the regular go-to-college-get-a-job routine. I wanted to be part of something bigger than myself. I looked into it and saw the SAR [search and rescue] option. I swam in high school and figured it wouldn't be too hard. Found out I was wrong soon as I got out of boot camp and into rescue swimmer school! It was five weeks of pain and torture on the body . . . but at the end, you know you can go past your old boundaries, physically and mentally—like I had to do that night off Cape Hatteras."

"The weather was, without a doubt, the worst weather I have ever flown in," Oggie said; his boundaries had been pushed that night as well. "But the most amazing thing about the environmental conditions is that they really didn't negatively affect the actual rescue—it was executed as if the weather was perfect. The fact that I had to hold a manual hover over swells twenty-five to thirty feet high with wind gusts over fifty knots had no bearing on the timely execution of the actual rescue. The frigidly cold water and enormous swells didn't impede Petty Officer's Need's ability to quickly swim to the survivor, properly hook him up to the hoist, and get him on board—all in six minutes!

"Nor did the extreme conditions seem to bother Petty Officer Brandon as he paid out hoist cable and reeled it in multiple times to keep just the right amount of slack in the line to make things as easy as possible on Petty Officer Need. And his directions to me were so calm that you'd have no idea that his comments were made while looking down at his friend and colleague in the ice-cold water while his own face was being frozen by frigid air and biting wind. I still can't fathom the fact that Petty Officer Need was only in the water for six minutes!

"Every time I think back on that night—those weather conditions and the rescue we performed—I am still amazed at what we were able to do," Oggie said. "The rescue we performed on the night of 2 January 2010 is why we do what we do—we fly to save the lives of others. Every time we fly, search and rescue is a mission we are prepared to perform. While getting a rescue is always a rewarding experience, it is best when we are not called upon. Why? Because if we are called upon to act in that role, it means someone is in distress. Around the carrier it usually means someone is in some serious trouble and we would never wish that on any of our air wing brethren. We take pride in our ability to save lives, and we are always ready to do so, but we hope we are not called upon to execute."

Being on deployment with the Nightdippers of HS-5, I discovered more about the rotary wing aviation community I'd first glimpsed at the SAR swimmer schoolhouse in Pensacola. Even though helicopters comprise nearly half of the navy's stable of aircraft, they rarely receive the same attention as the flashier jets. Admittedly, I had known much less about helos, but I was learning quickly.

SAR swimmers take part in most navy helicopter missions; all helos are prepared for the search and rescue function. Beyond that general mission, the helos have several specialties. Most involve the ubiquitous Sikorsky SH-60/HH-60/MH-60 helicopter, cousin to the U.S. Army's Blackhawk. Several variants of the aircraft exist, designated Bravo, Foxtrot, Hotel, Romeo, and Sierra. Bravo, Foxtrot, and Hotel are phasing out, being replaced by more recent Romeo and Sierra models. Each variant has a specific expertise, but most can engage in surface and antisubmarine warfare, conduct search and rescue, and transport troops and gear. Since the variants have different names and designations, the aircraft are usually just called H-60s or Seahawks to minimize confusion.

In the past, one helo squadron has deployed aboard a carrier and elements from several squadrons have deployed aboard the escorting cruisers, destroyers, and frigates in the strike group. In the future, two helicopter squadrons will deploy with each carrier air wing and together, will service the carrier and all the ships in the strike group. One squadron will operate the MH-60S "Sierras" and focus on troop deployment and vertical replenishment—handling cargo and logistics. The other will fly the MH-60R "Romeo," which specializes in antisubmarine warfare.

The navy also utilizes a variety of Seahawk models for air ambulance missions, primarily flown in Iraq and Afghanistan. The helicopter detachments (parts of squadrons, usually called dets) flying those missions receive medevac orders from a central Tactical Operation Center, and two-ship crews aim to be en route to the victim within fifteen minutes. When hospitals are beyond the range of one pair of helicopters, others are vectored to meet them halfway to take on the patients; exchanges prove quicker than refueling. The aviators that rotate in and out of the Arabian theater aim to have their patients to a medical facility within the "golden hour," the sixty-minute window after a trauma that largely determines a patient's survival and ability to recover. Their dedication has saved thousands of lives during the past decade.

In addition to the Sikorsky H-60s, the navy also employs the giant heavy-lifting Sea Dragon helicopter, which weighs thirty-three thousand pounds empty and can airlift an additional thirty thousand pounds of cargo—including more than fifty soldiers. It typically launches from land or amphibious assault ships for cargo, transport, or mine countermeasure details. Its seven blades, ninety-nine-foot length, and twenty-seven-foot height combine to dwarf the smaller Seahawks. But like the Seahawk, its crew mixes officers and enlisted personnel. That combination helps both platforms develop the special bond among crews that exists within the rotary wing community.

The officers and enlisted aircrewmen train together, fly missions together, and rely on one another. A certain level of respect exists between the men aboard a helicopter since they understand the critical value of each other's job. Each has his or her specific talents, each of which the team needs to accomplish its mission. Most times, nobody wants to trade places, as Scott Pichette noted.

"Thinking back to what Petty Officer Need did that night—I could not have jumped in that water," he said. "I could not have done what he did. I'm honored to have been part of that. Those guys will do that all the time—jump out of a helicopter in the middle of the night to save some man's life who they've never met before, who they couldn't pick out of a lineup."

And the navy's SAR crews will do it more than two hundred times every year.

"We definitely feel the same," said Kyle about the bonds in Canvass 612. "I'm an E-5–level, enlisted second-class petty officer in the navy. If anybody else works with an O-5–level senior officer hand in hand, it's usually not as much of a team concept."

In the navy, enlisted personnel and officers often exist in separate worlds, separated by a chasm in rank and rules that govern interaction between the two groups. Rarely would young enlisted personnel like Kyle interact with senior officers.

"But we value their input as much as anyone else's," confirmed Oggie, an O-5–level commander. "If he says, 'I disagree,' nine times out of ten he's right!"

"Every platform has its own advantages and challenges," Scott added. "None is harder or easier. They're just different. Those single-seat jet guys are out there on their own. Helos flying from destroyers and cruisers have to land on that tiny deck every night. All those teams are just different."

"Yeah," Kyle chimed in, "but our team is the best."

Nobody in a navy aircraft lacks for competitive confidence, and in this case Kyle Need's team proved its mettle.

On missions like the one Canvass 612 flew on the night of January 2, 2010, the preparation pilots and crew receive during training at Pensacola pays off. They realized their aspirations of saving those who think they're lost. The Seahawk crew didn't know Dennis Clements before and they'll likely never see him again, yet they set out into the dark to find him and bring him safely home in the most dangerous and daunting of conditions. By flying out into a snowy night at the very limit of their range, finding the victim, leaping into a stormy sea, and completing the rescue, these four HS-5 Nightdippers clearly showed the skill, courage, and dedication to mission— and to others—that exist within the helicopter community. And in the worst of conditions, they were at their best.

8

FREEDOM SEVEN

O N OCTOBER 4, 1957, A tiny shadow passed across the waters of the Atlantic, dancing across waves and warships alike. Then it crossed over the American coastline and cast a much larger shadow—a specter really—over the United States. The Soviet Union had stunned the West by launching a silver, 184-pound, basketball-sized orb called *Sputnik* into Earth's upper atmosphere. The little satellite spun around and around the world, maddeningly passing over United States airspace every ninety-six minutes; day in, day out. A month later on November 3, the Soviets launched a 1,120-pound satellite that carried a dog named Laika. Everyone knew a man—a *cosmonaut*—would soon follow. Then the bombs would fall.

Then-senator Lyndon Johnson fumed, "The Roman Empire controlled the world because it could build roads. Later—when it moved to sea—the British Empire was dominant because it had ships. In the air age we were powerful because we had airplanes. Now the Communists have established a foothold in outer space!"

The autumn of 1957 saw the world change, and the Cold War's arms race became a duel to conquer space. The Soviets fired the first two shots and America had scarcely loaded its pistol. Politicians like Johnson fueled fires of public sentiment: Communist dominance in the stars portended nuclear holocaust from sea to sea.

To exacerbate the situation, America's hastily organized response—the launch of a Vanguard rocket and a satellite—flopped before an international audience on December 6. The rocket exploded magnificently on the launch pad; the satellite landed in nearby scrub pines. America entered 1958 demoralized, terrified, and in the literal shadow of Soviet technology. Those of us who weren't alive then may never understand the fear and fervor that accompanied this new battle for space.

The nascent National Aeronautics and Space Administration organized an all-out effort to catch the Soviets. They launched Project Mercury with the goal of putting an American in space as soon as possible, and they set out to find the men who would *ride* American rockets into space—they didn't want pilots, who were subject to human errors, actually *flying* their sophisticated spacecraft. NASA planned to recruit candidates who would likely bend to their every wish. President Dwight D. Eisenhower viewed Project Mercury differently. He knew America needed heroes, and so he dashed any hopes NASA had for staffing their Mercury project with docile, accommodating subjects. He charged NASA to find its astronauts among the community of strong-willed and accomplished military test pilots. NASA would get men who would insist on flying their spacecraft and be anything but docile.

In the seven pilots NASA selected, America found its new heroes. The Mercury Seven became known by name and face throughout the world; they carried the hopes of the western nations. Gus Grissom, Deke Slayton, and Gordon Cooper represented the U.S. Air Force. John Glenn carried the Marine Corps banner, and Scott Carpenter, Wally Schirra, and Alan Shepard represented the United States Navy. Each of these men would thunder into the heavens from the sandy spit of Atlantic coastline still called Cape Canaveral, then splash back into earth's waiting oceans.

NASA selected naval aviator Alan Shepard for the first flight.

Charles Lindbergh captured headlines worldwide with his inaugural nonstop transatlantic flight in 1927. His solo journey from New York to Paris in the *Spirit of St. Louis* also captured the imagination of a young boy in New Hampshire. Lindbergh became a hero to Alan Shepard and started the young dreamer on an aviator's path. Alan began building model airplanes and spending time at the local airport. Decades later, Rear Admiral Shepard recalled, "I used to ride my bike every Saturday morning to the nearest airport, ten miles away, and push airplanes in and out of the hangars, clean up the hangar, get a free ride once in a while, get to hold the stick once in a while."

By the time Alan entered high school, his teachers had noticed his intellect and encouraged him to skip sixth and then later eighth grades. So he entered high school at Pinkerton Academy as the youngest and consequently small-est boy in his class. He began struggling with academics and athletics, but soon developed a tenacious underdog attitude that would mark his life. Alan would always work harder than the next guy—he was usually younger and smaller than the next guy, so he had little choice. As one example, the Pinker-ton freshman began regularly harnessing himself to a rowboat when he swam, towing it stroke by stroke across a local pond; whatever it took to grow stron-ger and compete with his classmates.

Alan decided to pursue aviation wholeheartedly and he determined that the U.S. Navy offered the best opportunity to fly the newest and fastest planes, so he broke with the family's army tradition and entered the U.S. Naval Academy at Annapolis, Maryland, in 1941. Four months after Alan endured his plebe indoctrination, Japan attacked Pearl Harbor and Alan's entire class leaped onto a fast-track academic schedule. Alan's own fast-track appeared to be toward failing out of Annapolis. With his opportunity to fly in the balance, he sat before the academic review board in the fall of 1942. He found himself in the bottom third of his class, with seventy demerits, and he didn't seem particularly motivated to better his lot. The luck that would mark his later career showed itself that day, however, and the board surpris-ingly gave him a second chance. As it had also showed in sparing Joe "Hoser" Satrapa, the navy has a soft spot for slightly unrefined characters with real potential.

Over the coming year, Alan pulled himself back into solid standing in his class, and in June of 1944, at the age of twenty, he graduated and imme-diately left for duty. Alan didn't receive orders for the flight schools in Pen-sacola or Corpus Christi. Instead, he found himself assigned to the destroyer USS *Cogswell*, enduring typhoons and fending off kamikaze attacks in the Western Pacific. *Cogswell* survived and less than one month after the Japa-nese surrender, Alan's new orders came through. He was to report for navy flight training at Corpus Christi, Texas.

Along the Texas coast, Alan Shepard began building one of history's most successful aviation careers. Raw talent, hard work, ambition, and uncanny luck formed a foundation that weathered the storms churned up by Alan's self-confidence and propensity for pushing the rules. A navy fighter pilot to the core, he had skills and smarts along with a healthy sense of adventure and mischief.

Initially, Alan struggled at Corpus Christi, partly due to his impatience and aggressive nature. In his solo phase of flight training, his performance began to deteriorate and he amassed poor grades at an alarming pace. He was on the verge of washing out, of being left behind in the race of aviation.

His instructor declared him "unsafe for solo," and at the conclusion of his intermediate instruction, his "good" marks accounted for a scant five out of 336. If he didn't improve—and improve quickly—he would return to shipboard duty and never fly. He would certainly not join the elite cadre of aviators where he felt he belonged. Alan Shepard was not about to wash out of flight school. With new urgency, he secretly enrolled in private lessons and began a march toward excellence that never stopped. His father, in full army uniform, soon watched his reformed son make six near-perfect carrier qualification landings. Colonel Shepard then pinned the aviator's wings of gold to his son's chest.

The more-than-confident twenty-three-year-old aviator soon joined F4U Corsair squadron VF-42—the Green Pawns—aboard the USS *Franklin D. Roosevelt*. The squadron's commanding officer, James "Doc" Abbot, noted Lieutenant Shepard's blossoming skill and selected him as his wingman—quite an honor for a pilot on his first deployment. Their close relationship allowed Alan to become one of the first rookies (or "nuggets") to land the Corsair on a carrier at night. Soon Alan took command of a full division of four planes—almost unheard of for such a junior officer. The rising star set his next goal: the U.S. Naval Test Pilot School at Patuxent River, Maryland. Doc Abbot made sure he achieved it and Alan's star grew brighter still.

He arrived at the navy's testing facility at twenty-six years of age, becoming one of the youngest pilots ever to receive that honored assignment. He always thought his skills were advanced; now he knew it.

Alan quickly developed a reputation as an outstanding pilot. In a time when technical learning procedures were sometimes shunned by headstrong test pilots, several unfamiliar planes might be flown in the same day. Today's

flight simulators were nonexistent, so Pax River pilots just "gripped and ripped." The style suited Alan perfectly. He and his fellow pilots would study a new jet briefly then learn the rest aloft—in part because they had little time with so many new models requiring tests as the defense industry streamed new jets into testing to keep pace with the Soviets. Pilots also had more than healthy egos and considered themselves above the tedium of studying the intricacies of each new aircraft. Give them a stick and rudder and clearance for takeoff. They'd discuss the particulars at the O-Club.

Shepard had the job of pushing experimental planes to their limits in speed, altitude, and aerobatics—which he of course loved. And perhaps more than most, he spent long hours engaging engineers in detailed discussions. He possessed a superb analytical ability and had a talent for memorizing data. But you'd never know it from the relaxed, good-times facade he adopted after work. He soon earned a reputation as one of Pax River's finest pilots.

Since his days at Corpus Christi, Alan had also developed a reputation as a showboat. His natural flying ability tempted him to indulge his sense of danger and fun—and he often chose not to resist. He regularly announced his successful missions—and imminent return home to his wife Louise and their daughters—by making a low-level pass over their house, upsetting neighbors who then complained to the base. Upon completion of the Chesapeake Bay Bridge, Alan promptly flew his F2H Banshee under the new span, then ceremoniously looped the powerful jet fighter over the top and passed beneath it once again. He received a reprimand from his commanding officer, but otherwise emerged unscathed. Shortly thereafter, he completed a sand-shaking pass over the tourist-filled beach at Ocean City, Maryland. A photographer caught his tail number and the admiral commanding Pax River gave him a tongue-lashing of the highest order along with an official letter of reprimand.

Shepard remained undeterred, and after completing another perfect test mission in the Banshee, he celebrated by screaming over a formation of men at Pax River itself. As he rolled his plane while making the pass at 150 feet, the assembled men dove for cover. The admiral in charge wanted him courtmartialed. His commanding officers managed to save him; despite his antics, he was their best pilot. He escaped his tour at Pax River with his career intact, future brighter, and his appetite for fun and aerobatics not sated in the least.

His dual personality—outstanding, focused pilot on one hand and free-wheeler on the other—became part of Alan Shepard's being and lore. Author Tom Wolfe dubbed Alan's two sides "The Icy Commander" and "Smilin' Al," and people needed to know with which personality they were dealing. When it came to many aspects of his highly dangerous job, The Icy Commander could be exacting and dead serious; barking at anyone who wasn't performing his role properly in his estimation. For good times and melting away stress at the local Officers Club, however, Smilin' Al was hard to beat as a wingman.

In January 1959, NASA's Project Mercury selection panel reviewed the file of Alan B. Shepard, Jr., and debated how this test pilot's well-documented propensity for hijinks would affect his ability to serve as one of the nation's first astronauts. The committee reviewed the records of 508 test pilots. They selected 110 as finalists for the Mercury Program. Alan outperformed his competitors on a battery of tests and he made each cut until on April 9, 1959, he stepped into the dazzle of media flashbulbs as one of the elite Mercury Seven astronauts—the men who would catch the Soviets and restore America's hope, pride, and security.

Alan called his parents shortly before the public announcement. "Mother was delighted," he remembered. "But, my father took the attitude, 'Well, *what* is this you're going to do, son?'"

First, the son of retired Army Lt. Col. Bart Shepard was about to swerve off a promising and proven career track, even if it was, his army father lamented, in the navy. Worse, Lt. Col. Shepard thought Alan was sacrificing his career for a left-field, experimental distraction that could get him killed.

Alan recalled, "Even at that age—gosh, I was thirty-five years old then, give or take—when your old man says, 'You're gonna do *what*, son?' there is a little pause for reflection."[1]

Alan—like most of the pilots invited to compete for the Mercury Program—couldn't resist the possibility of leading aviation into an entirely new realm. No longer would breaking Mach 3 stand as an intimidating barrier; no longer would the thin air of high altitudes place a ceiling on his craft. *Space*craft wouldn't even need air. Alan saw the cutting edge of aviation moving from Pax River and California's Edwards Air Force Base to

Cape Canaveral, Florida. He had veered away from the traditional path, just like those pioneering naval aviators who shunned the traditional surface warfare routes to pursue the possibilities offered by the untamed sky.

For two years, the Mercury Seven underwent training more extensive than anything previously given to aviators. The astronauts spent countless hours spinning around and around in the NASA centrifuge, executing command sequences and simulating space maneuvers as gravitational forces up to ten Gs pressed them hard into their seat and rendered their arms almost immovable. They endured survival training in the desert and at sea. They had medical tests of every imaginable variety, then psychologists put them through isolation drills and emotional evaluations. They felt more like laboratory rats than astronauts. In crude simulators, they trained for as many contingencies as possible and could locate buttons and switches blindfolded. They were overprepared, but that's what would allow each astronaut to step so calmly into his spacecraft when the time for launch arrived. Alan Shepard's heart rate would barely rise.

In a statement given shortly before his mission, he explained why. "I think the one thing that strikes me as I look back on the training program is that I've really developed a feeling of confidence," he said to reporters. "A confidence in the people with whom I work, a confidence with the systems with which I'm dealing and will have to deal in flight, and of course a confidence in myself."[2]

The seven astronauts knew the training also had another purpose: to identify the man who would fly first. Who would be the first American in space, the unofficial but very real winner of the competition? By the winter of 1961, NASA had decided.

Project Mercury director Dr. Robert Gilruth called a meeting of the Mercury Seven late one afternoon in February. He walked into the astronauts' office and bluntly announced NASA's decision: "Shepherd gets the first flight, Grissom gets the second flight, and Glenn is the backup for both missions." Then he walked out of the room, leaving the seven astronauts to themselves.

"Well, there I am looking at six faces looking at me," Alan recalled, "feeling . . . of course totally elated because I'd won the competition—but feeling immediately afterward sorry for my buddies; they'd worked just as hard as I had."[3]

One by one, the other astronauts congratulated Shepard, who did his best to conceal his glee; he had gone up against the nation's best pilots and flat-out won. Then, one by one, the other six left to ponder the decision. Each had considered himself the best. As testament to the continuity of that mentality, the wall of one modern squadron ready room bears the warning: "Be the best or don't get in the damn aircraft."

On numerous occasions, Alan asked Dr. Gilruth why NASA chose him for the first flight. "All he'll say," Alan related, "is that, 'well, at the right time you were the right guy.'"[4]

It turned out that "the right time" came several weeks too late for America's national pride. Alan had pushed for an earlier flight, one closely following the successful January 1961 test launch of Ham the chimpanzee. The cautious German-born lead engineer Dr. Wernher von Braun decided to conduct further tests, and inadvertently opened the door for the Soviets. They walked right through it. Twenty-seven-year-old Yuri Gagarin lifted off from the Baikonur Cosmodrome in Kazakhstan aboard *Vostok 1* (*East 1*) on April 12, 1961. He rocketed into space, happily humming "The Motherland Hears, The Motherland Knows," and claimed the coveted twin titles of the first person to reach space and orbit the earth.

Alan quickly put the Russian accomplishment into his perspective as a naval aviator. "We knew that on my flight I was scheduled to actually control, precisely aim, and direct the spacecraft," he explained. "The Soviets, we found out shortly after [Gagarin] flew, were only passengers."

Yuri Gagarin had the honor of being the first man in space, but Alan Shepard would consider himself the first true astronaut—the first true aviator in space. Interestingly, had he and his fellow astronauts not pressed NASA to *pilot* their craft, America's spacemen would have likewise been mere passengers.

On May 5, 1961, all the events that dotted Alan Shepard's path finally led to his crowning achievement. At Patuxent River, he had piloted some of the world's fastest aircraft. Ten years later he would golf on the Moon while commanding Apollo 14, but this day, this event, would always rank highest in his mind.

When Alan emerged from the transfer van and stepped onto the launch pad at Cape Canaveral that morning, he looked like a god in his silver pressure suit. His glassy helmet reflected the brilliant beams from the surrounding floodlights. He looked up toward the predawn sky and surveyed the Redstone rocket that, if everything worked properly, would send him into space. He did not consider the other option; he had long ago reconciled himself to the real possibilities that the rocket could explode beneath him or fly wildly off course, driving his tiny capsule into the sea or sand before he could escape. He knew fire trucks and rescue vehicles surrounded the launch area; NASA still thought there was a healthy chance he might die. He also knew hundreds of thousands of people had converged on the Cape for this event and millions watched on television or listened on the radio. On the morning of May 5, 1961, America stopped and waited.

From the launch pad, Alan watched graceful plumes of vapor from liquid oxygen tanks fall gently down the booster's sides. Floodlights illuminated the white panels and black stripes of the Redstone. Red letters spelling UNITED STATES traced its eighty-three-foot height. Atop the rocket perched the black *Freedom Seven* spacecraft, just ten feet tall and six feet wide. America's first astronaut absorbed every detail; it was a perfectly beautiful sight.

"You know pilots love to go kick the tires," he explained, "and this was like kicking the tires on the Redstone. I looked back and up at this beautiful rocket and I said, 'Okay, Buster, let's go get this job done.'"

An elevator brought Alan level with the *Freedom Seven* spacecraft and there he met his backup pilot, fellow naval aviator and Marine Corps Lieutenant Colonel John Glenn, who had performed a final check on the craft and equipment. John helped his rival into the tiny cone and laid him down into the couch that would cradle his back. As the astronaut looked skyward from his recumbent position, John connected the hoses that fed his pressure suit. Alan laughed at the good-natured placard John had hung on the instrument panel: NO HANDBALL PLAYING IN THIS AREA. Smiling, John removed his sign and closed the hatch. The attending technicians saw it sealed properly. John and Alan exchanged grins and a thumbs-up sign through the tiny window. Then the marine aviator's freckled face withdrew. Alan lay on his back, alone atop a rocket that would carry him higher than any other American.

On the ground, NASA stood by with an assortment of prepared statements that addressed the most likely scenarios for the Mercury-Redstone

Three (MR-3) mission's failure and its astronaut's death—one should the rocket explode on the launch pad, another if it incinerated on the ascent, yet another if Alan didn't survive re-entry into Earth's atmosphere.

"People have said over the years, 'Boy, you really must have been scared,'" he shared later. "Fortunately, I wasn't scared. Nervous, but not frightened to death. . . . You have to be trained to the point where you absolutely are not panicked.

"I think all of us certainly believed the statistics which said that there was probably an eighty-eight-percent chance of mission success and maybe a ninety-six-percent chance of survival. And we were willing to take those odds. But we wanted to be sure that if there *were* any failures in the machine that a man was going to be there to take over and to correct it. And I think that still is true of [the space and test pilot] business—which is basically research and development. You probably spend more time in planning and training and designing for things to go wrong, and how you cope with them, than you do for things to go right."[5]

Of course, this type of danger was nothing new for the Pax River veteran. Once, the engines of an experimental F11F Tiger he was testing flamed out at seventy-five thousand feet. He and the Tiger began a sixty-three-thousand-foot freefall. He was finally able to restart the engine at twelve thousand feet and flew straight in for a textbook landing. Somehow, things just worked out for Alan.

As to his other thoughts that day, the intensely private astronaut left us forever guessing, although he did report thinking about how every part of the government's rocket and spacecraft was built by the lowest bidder.

Alan Shepard was a naval aviator at heart, and knew he had the right stuff, that undefined yet almost tangible quality that sets the best aviators apart from the rest. In a highly public contest with the finest pilots in America, he had won. The thirty-seven-year-old had also won the unspoken contest that lies just beneath the surface of cutting-edge aviation; he would fly *higher* and *faster* than any other American. He had earned—no, he had won—the honor through hard work and a career of unarguably strong performances. Never since has America had a competition like that for the Mercury program. Although NASA billed it as a contest to become one of seven, each man knew one real goal existed: to be first.

While Alan had scored a personal victory that would echo across decades, he also knew that a tremendous cast of astronauts, engineers, and others had brought the Mercury project—and him—to this point of realization. He appreciated all they had done, and he knew they all had their full attention trained on the day's launch. They shared his mission to get *Freedom Seven* into space and back home safely. But once the hatch closed, he became a solitary man in a tiny compartment, poised above thirty-seven thousand pounds of explosive fuel and pointed toward the open sky. He listened as the final countdown began.

A series of delays plagued the launch sequence, and Alan grew increasingly frustrated.

At T-minus two minutes and forty seconds, yet another delay occurred.

The reaction from America's first astronaut was quick, cold, and pointed: "I've been in here for more than three hours and I'm cooler than you are," Alan said over the radio. "Why don't you fix your little problem and *light this candle?*"

Minutes later, they did.

"Five, four, three, two, one, zero," counted Deke Slayton, the Capsule Communicator in Mercury Control. "Liftoff!"

"Don't screw up, Shepard," Alan said to himself, then coolly spoke to Deke: "Ah, roger. Liftoff and the clock has started."

Adding a dose of levity, Deke toggled the mike and said, "Okay, José, you're on your way!"

"Roger, reading you loud and clear." No joking came from *Freedom Seven*. Smilin' Al would greet the adoring public at the flight's successful conclusion, but for now, the Icy Commander devoted his entire focus to piloting his craft into history. The Redstone rocket and its astronaut lifted the nation's spirit upward to the heavens at more than 5,100 miles per hour. The United States Navy had joined the space race.

Alan's fellow naval aviators Wally Schirra and Scott Carpenter tailed the quickening Redstone in F-106 jets as long as they could, but they lost him as the rocket pushed through Mach 1 on a vertical climb. The rocket thundered smoothly above the Atlantic, where flotillas of yet more rescue craft waited should something go wrong. As his altitude and speed increased, Alan's smooth ride ended. Gravitational forces pressed down on his body and turbulence gathered around the nose of the rocket, as he had expected. He described feeling like a rat being shaken by a terrier. He remained silent, not wanting a misunderstood word to lead a touchy Mercury Control to abort the flight. He gritted his teeth and waited it out. Soon, the Redstone broke through the barrier and sailed heavenward.

"Okay, it's a lot smoother now," he radioed Deke, with some relief. "A lot smoother."

Two minutes into the mission, *Freedom Seven* was twenty-five miles high and nearing 3,000 miles per hour. Shepard realized he had just set records for speed and altitude, but made no mention of it since he found it difficult to talk—he suddenly weighed 1,000 pounds. Gravitational forces pressed him into his couch as he neared 5,000 miles per hour at 116 miles above Earth. Then the rocket stopped. The spacecraft separated from the big cylinder that had carried it aloft. Alan floated weightlessly against his harness. He could only hear the soft whirring of *Freedom Seven*'s systems. He was in space. America was in space.

Soon the first astronaut switched the controls to manual and set out to fly his craft—becoming the first true *pilot* in space. His experienced right hand guided *Freedom Seven* through a series of well-executed maneuvers, just as he'd practiced for months. He relished every second. Once the ship reached its zenith minutes later, a long freefall awaited. As the craft began arching back toward earth, retrorockets fired and Alan ensured his ship assumed the proper angle for reentry. Since he was, after all, a test pilot, he test-fired the thrusters that future orbital flights would need to slow their spacecraft to suborbital speeds for re-entry. As he completed the exercises, pressure once again began to build as he plummeted back into the atmosphere.

Soon he had eleven times his own weight pushing against him. He couldn't speak. He just repeatedly grunted "Okay" to Deke in Mercury Control, so everyone would know he was surviving re-entry. The heat shield behind his back held firm and the drogue parachute deployed at twenty-one thousand feet, followed by the orange and white main chute, which floated *Freedom Seven* onto a welcoming sea.

A scant fifteen minutes after liftoff, helicopters from the aircraft carrier USS *Lake Champlain* began safely recovering Alan Shepard and *Freedom Seven* from the gentle swells of the Atlantic, some three hundred miles southeast of Florida. The carrier's ecstatic crew gathered on deck to greet the first

American in space, and Smilin' Al received them warmly. Uncharacteristically, he got choked up as he grasped how important his country perceived his flight. A jubilant President John F. Kennedy called his first astronaut aboard the carrier. The Mercury Seven soon flew to Washington where Kennedy presented Commander Shepard with NASA's Distinguished Service Medal. The man of the hour then met fawning Congressional leaders, and led a ticker-tape parade through crowd-lined streets in Manhattan. Alan Shepard was America's first space age hero.

Twenty days after *Freedom Seven*'s historic spaceflight, President Kennedy addressed a special joint session of Congress. There, he announced an audacious goal that stemmed from the success of Shepard's mission. Emphatically, the president said, "I believe that this nation should commit itself to achieving the goal, before this decade is out, of landing a man on the Moon and returning him safely to the Earth. No single space project in this period will be more impressive to mankind, or more important for the long-range exploration of space."

The young president would not live to see his dream realized. Before his death, however, he had firmly fixed his country on the path Mercury had set, a course that pushed the pace of American technological innovation far beyond that of any other nation—something that would drive the nation's success for decades to come.

Eight years after Kennedy laid down the challenge of landing on the Moon before 1970, Apollo 11 Commander Neil Armstrong—another naval aviator—announced to the world that the Lunar Excursion Module (LEM) *Eagle* had landed on the Moon's Sea of Tranquility. The date was July 21, 1969. On that day, Armstrong made mankind's first footprint in the dusty lunar soil.

Naval aviators wholly composed the lunar teams for the next three Apollo missions—Apollo 12 (Pete Conrad and Alan Bean), Apollo 13 (Jim Lovell and Fred Haise), and Apollo 14 (Alan Shepard and Ed Mitchell). In all, seven of the twelve moonwalkers had earned their wings of gold. Naval aviation had indeed established a foothold in the heavens.

America's first spaceman spoke for his fellow aviator-astronauts when he lightheartedly cracked, "Believe me, it's a lot harder to land a jet on an aircraft carrier than it is to land a LEM on the Moon. That Moon business is a piece of cake!"[6]

Truthfully, the Moon business was not a piece of cake. And the first Mercury missions were among the greatest and most difficult leaps ever taken by American scientists and engineers. The Apollo program, which sent astronauts to the Moon, stretched from 1961 until 1975, and cost the lives of three astronauts and billions of dollars. The mishap aboard Apollo 13 almost doubled the number of lives lost. The challenge of space had attracted the country's finest pilots and despite the proven dangers, naval aviators continued to aspire toward the stars.

When the first space shuttle mission blasted off from Cape Canaveral, only two men were aboard—both naval aviators. John W. Young had piloted Cougars, Crusaders, and Phantoms from carriers and Pax River before walking on the Moon and commanding the shuttle *Columbia* on that inaugural 1981 mission. *Columbia*'s first pilot was Robert Crippen, a former A-4 Skyhawk driver and test pilot who later directed NASA's John F. Kennedy Space Center. Navy helicopter pilots Wendy Lawrence and Sunita Williams, both pioneering female aviators, flew aboard the space shuttles *Atlantis*, *Discovery*, and *Endeavor*; Williams spent more than six months aboard the International Space Station. After three hundred carrier landings in F-8 Crusaders, Richard Truly earned command of the shuttle *Challenger* and later became NASA Administrator under fellow naval aviator President George H. W. Bush.

Navy men like Alan Shepard, Neil Armstrong, and those above brought the spirit of Eugene Ely and Jack Towers to a new endeavor. Like their predecessors, the navy's astronauts had the fire, competitive edge, and audacity to accomplish that which seemed impossible and lead their profession and their country across a new frontier.

9

THE YOUTH OF AMERICA

SEVERAL MONTHS AFTER THE HS-5 Nightdippers and the USS *Dwight D. Eisenhower* had deployed to the Middle East, I flew over the same waters through which Kyle Need dragged Dennis Clements that unforgettable January night. The conditions had improved significantly with the coming of spring, and sunny skies and gentle seas had replaced the wintry North Atlantic that witnessed the *Ike* begin her deployment. I had to take my pilot's word for this, however, since I was quite unglamorously sequestered in the back of an almost-windowless C-2 Greyhound.

At more than fifty thousand pounds fully loaded, the white and gray transport planes are among the largest planes that currently operate from aircraft carriers. Their wings, which span eighty feet, support twin engines that power two eight-blade propellers. Inside the dark tunnel of the plane's interior, nylon rigging hung from the exposed walls and swung lazily as the plane cruised through the air. The Greyhound's crew had configured the cargo bay to hold a small mountain of supplies along with a number of passengers. Our seats faced the plane's rear so our backs could absorb the brunt of the arrested carrier landing. Two small windows provided the only view—but all I could see was sky and sea.

West Coast Fleet Logistics Support Squadrons Thirty (VRC-30) and East Coast–based VRC-40 supply aircraft carriers around the world with the supplies and personnel they need while under way. Greyhound pilots seem roundly envied since they experience the challenge and thrill of carrier-based landings and launches, but spend many of their nights in often posh hotels around the world—on dry land and with civilian perks, such as real restaurants rather than a ship's mess decks or wardroom.

Usually, sailors and aviators simply call the C-2 Greyhounds "CODs," short for Carrier Onboard Delivery. I was this day's package.

Over the din of the twin turboprops, I heard the pilot—a member of the VRC-40 Rawhides—lower the plane's flaps and landing gear. Then I felt a long banked turn; I knew we had crossed the carrier's bow and were now flying down the port side of her flight deck, bleeding off airspeed. Then I felt the plane bank into its final turn toward the carrier's stern. When the pilot leveled the wings and reduced power, I knew we were on glide slope, just several hundred feet above the wake of the USS *Harry S. Truman.*

An air crewman in front of me waved his arms, the signal to brace against the shoulder harness. The plane bumped onto the deck and the pilot pushed our twin engines to full power in case his tailhook missed one of the four arresting cables and we needed to get airborne again. Within three seconds, however, a powerful cable brought us to an incredibly rapid but surprisingly gentle halt.

The rear ramp began to lower as we taxied toward the ship's island, the towering superstructure on the deck's starboard side. From there the captain commands the ship and the Air Boss oversees flight operations from the high perch of Primary Flight Control, better known as Pri-Fly. Including its mast, the island is 150 feet tall, but only twenty feet wide at its base to minimize its footprint.

The noise and exhaust generated by this floating airport seeped into the Greyhound's cabin through the opening ramp. I glimpsed a gray landing strip marked with yellow and white lines. An alien cast of deckhands and plane handlers scurried across the deck, wearing dark goggles, gloves, and long-sleeved shirts of every color. Each color denoted a particular role: yellow directed the aircraft and managed the catapults; green maintained equipment, aircraft, and arresting wires; brown was squadron plane captains assigned to individual aircraft; purple kept the gas flowing; blue moved and chained down aircraft; white monitored quality and safety; and red handled the weapons and ordnance.

Adding to the scene's Martian quality was the headgear each individual wore—a cranial, which is a strange but functional combination of crash helmet and headphones that protects the heads and eardrums of deckhands. The ramp continued to open and I watched more of the flight deck's four and a half acres appear. I saw men and women communicating to each other using a robust dialect of hand signals, some taught in classes, some indigenous to the ship and its squadrons. The COD reached the island and I hopped out of the dark plane onto the sunny deck. I looked around and saw the blue-gray Atlantic stretching to the horizon in every direction. I had been suddenly deposited in the middle of a noisy, crowded, exhaust-covered, floating airport in an otherwise empty ocean.

After I stowed my gear below, I reemerged onto the flight deck. The ship's meteorologist (affectionately known as Black Cloud) placed the day's high in the mid-sixties. The light wind gusting over the *Truman*'s bow would have made the deck seem even cooler had it not been for the jet engines bathing it in hot exhaust. They pushed the temperature well into the nineties.

I walked forward from the island, weaving between several F/A-18s, dodging an E-2C Hawkeye's spinning propellers, and ducking to avoid the jet blasts from several tailpipes. The entire deck hummed with activity and I wondered how so many moving aircraft and people could coexist in such a small space without creating disasters on a regular basis. After running the gauntlet of aircraft and exhaust blasts, I came upon Carrier Air Wing Three's Aircraft 400, an F/A-18E Super Hornet from Strike Fighter Squadron 105 (VFA-105)—the Gunslingers. A refueling and change of pilots was under way and it wasn't hard to discover who ran the show.

Chelsea Pygott, a brown-shirted VFA-105 plane captain, stood looking intently at 400's cockpit. As plane captain, she bore responsibility for everything that happened to 400 on the flight deck. The young enlisted airman appeared entirely unfazed by the noise, heat, or surrounding activity. Dark goggles hid her eyes and she stood with her feet slightly spread, hands clasped smartly behind her back, overseeing a hot-seat. That is, she was in charge of bringing in plane 400, directing refueling and a full safety check, getting one pilot out of the cockpit and strapping a fresh pilot in, then getting the aircraft back into the sky again as quickly as possible. From the ground, she watched two pilots change places. Once the new pilot had settled into his seat, the departing Gunslinger descended the plane's ladder and approached Chelsea.

I saw him smile and mouth the words, "Great job." Even though they were less than ten feet away, the cacophony of noise drowned him out. He then gave her a pat on the back as she purposefully climbed the plane's ladder to perform a final check with the new pilot. A minute later, the pilot closed the canopy. Chelsea climbed down and began her next act.

She squatted on the ground, right leg straight out in front of her. She then began signaling the pilot, walking him through the preflight procedures. She made a sweeping circle with her arms then shook her left hand like she was mimicking a tambourine. Two fingers of her right hand flashed out. The new pilot took the cue and started the Hornet's starboard engine. Her left forearm began circling rhythmically, pointing at the engine at each revolution's end. Her arm circled faster and the engine began to scream. Then her right hand flashed one finger and he started his port engine. Her arm circled as he fed the hungry General Electric turbofans with high-octane JP5 jet fuel. She stood up, feet tight together. Her arm circled faster and both engines screamed louder. Then she quickly pulled both arms to her stomach like she was catching a football. She immediately bent her body to the right, feet still locked together, and pointed both arms toward the engine and her hands began communicating rapidly to the white-shirted safety checkers surrounding the plane. She started rotating her left forearm again and the pilot flexed his control surfaces—rudders, flaps, ailerons, and stabilators—so the safety checkers could ensure all functioned properly. When she received thumbs-up signals from everyone involved, Chelsea moved to the plane's nose and passed her plane and pilot to a yellow-shirted plane director who guided them toward the catapult for launch.

Chelsea—called AD3 Pygott by most of the squadron—held the "rate," or job, of an aircraft mechanic, called an Aviation Machinist's Mate (AD). Petty Officer Third Class was her rank, thus AD3. The navy prides itself on its acronym soup of rates and ranks, which often become substitutes for sailors' first names. Aboard ship, many enlisted servicemen and women simply refer to one another as AD2 Sterling, AO1 Hernandez, PR2 Dixon, or AWR1 Torres. Those names immediately identify their rank and job.

The rated specialties in the naval aviation community include Aviation Boatswain's Mate (AB), Air Traffic Controller (AC), Machinist's Mate (AD), Electrician's Mate (AE), Aerographer's Mate (AG), Structural Mechanic (AM), Ordnanceman (AO), Support Equipment Technician (AS), Electronics Technician (AT), Aircrew (AW), Maintenance Administrationman (AZ), and Aircrew Survival Equipmentman (PR). The airmen in these rates all pass through Aviation School in Pensacola before joining their squadrons.

Once in their squadrons, they work hard to earn the next rank. They want to progress from airman to petty officer third class. Then they aim to earn second class and first class. Many aspire to earn the title of chief. Much like a Scout troop, a department on a carrier rewards proven skills and performance with rank. The system encourages a culture of constant improvement, where sailors work hard to earn their next position—and another stripe for their uniform. As each individual improves and shoulders more responsibility, the entire ship becomes stronger and more capable.

AD3 Pygott, who had quickly progressed from airman apprentice to petty officer third class, had also earned the title and role of plane captain, which she would hold formally for six months to a year; the accompanying knowledge would always remain with her. As a plane captain (a "brownshirt" or PC) she was responsible for every facet of her assigned $50 million F/A-18E Super Hornet. Squadron leaders bestow the plane captain role on their junior enlisted personnel as an honor—and as a way to ensure they become familiar with every part of the jet before they progress in their specialty.

On the flight deck, it was Chelsea who had given the final okay before handing the jet over to the new pilot during the hot-seat. Here's the remarkable thing: Chelsea was just twenty years old.

It was nearly 9 P.M.—2100 in navy terms—when she and I sat down together belowdecks. A casual T-shirt and shorts had replaced her brown longsleeves and fatigue pants. At last free from the cranial, her hair curled slightly and was still wet from a shower that had washed away sixteen hours of engine grime and jet exhaust. Her day had begun shortly after 4 A.M. and she had been at her plane by 5:30, well before dawn. Despite being quite exhausted, she sat down with a disarming smile and twinkling eyes. She looked nothing like the dead-serious plane captain I'd seen directing the hot-seat on deck that afternoon in the middle of what seemed like barely controlled chaos.

"That's what gets me excited: adrenaline," she said. "Today, we had too many jets and not enough PCs—and we were making it work!" She absolutely radiated energy and enthusiasm. "We were running in circles, we had our trainees carrying our chains, we were on the run, and still making it in time to shake the pilot's hand and say, 'You're here, you're safe, I've checked this jet, sir—it's good to go flying.'

"The overall mission is awesome," she continued. "Especially when that last jet finally leaves, you're like oh-my-gosh; we wouldn't have been able to do it if it weren't for that AD. If that AT [Aviation Electronics Technician] doesn't fix that wiring, or if that mechanic doesn't fix that drop tank, it all falls apart. You know you couldn't do it without this person or that person. You can't do anything without that green shirt—even yellow shirts and blue shirts who aren't even part of our squadron. It's amazing to watch and see how it all comes together. It's a really amazing and humbling feeling."

Chelsea became part of the navy team in 2008 and came to the VFA-105 Gunslingers in February of 2009, fresh from Aviation School in Pensacola, Florida. Her journey started in Bath, New York—a small upstate town south of Rochester. She graduated high school in 2007 and soon found that college wasn't for her. She lived at home with her mother, had no income, and wasn't going anywhere fast. Her friends worked fast food or similar jobs, but she resisted that path and sought greater purpose and opportunity. She found both in the navy.

"It was such an accomplishment," she gushed about completing basic training. "I never thought I'd do it. The day they gave me my navy ball cap—one that said 'navy,' not 'recruit'—I started bawling. I'd never accomplished anything that big in my life. Nineteen years old. Then I graduated A-School and walked through the doors to my first squadron.

"Now when I go home, I have nothing in common with my friends. I come home to see my grandparents, my mom, and my sister—and my new baby nephew! My friends are all doing the same thing, working at McDonald's or Burger King. They'll ask, 'What have you been doing?' Well, I work on jets, I launch them off an aircraft carrier, I'm getting ready to go on cruise and sail around the world."

In the navy, Chelsea found new opportunities—possibilities that would have been closed to her had she continued on her original path in life. She aspires to serve her country, and she also recognizes how the navy can help her develop new skills and chart a new course. Few corporations would have given a high school graduate such responsibilities, discipline, and a true family. Like many people who came before her, Chelsea found new hope and purpose on the deck of an aircraft carrier.

Chelsea rarely explained the complete nature of her job to her friends in Bath, New York. They simply could not fathom the responsibility—and excitement—of being a plane captain. During training at A-School, she learned the fundamentals behind carrier aviation and jet operations. Her real job training began when she joined the squadron. Hangars and active flight lines were her classrooms. Her teachers were just slightly older than she. Petty Officers Brinier and Curlew—now twenty-two and twenty-three, respectively—pushed her from her first day. They taught her to prep cockpits and to earn her duct diving qualification—meaning she could climb into a jet intake and fix an engine. They also taught her how to direct a plane, brake in emergencies, chain down a Super Hornet to ride out a storm, and coordinate movements on a crowded deck.

"People will ask me, 'Who did you learn from?' I'll say Brinier and Curlew: two of the best PCs out there.

"Their confidence in themselves gives other people confidence in them. They had confidence in what they were talking about, what they were telling me. Now I'm at the point where I'm a hundred percent confident in what I do and I want my next trainee to say, 'I learned from Pygott,' just like I say, 'I learned from Brinier.'"

As a full plane captain with that level of responsibility, she recognizes another obligation—not to the pilot, but to the next plane captain in the squadron. It falls to her to train the next PC and perpetuate the chain of learning that ensures each squadron can maintain twelve to fourteen active plane captains. Once a stint as plane captain ends, the airman will continue along a specialized path, but he or she will take with them an extensive understanding of the entire jet and its systems.

"You're teaching all the new people coming from A-School," she explained. "As PC, it's your responsibility to train them to be a PC. As PC, it's your responsibility to make sure they get all the qualifications [leading up to plane captain certification]: duct diver, brake rider, move director. A PC makes another PC and that PC trains another PC. That's a cycle. We're always learning something new, every day, and passing on that knowledge."

Clearly, Chelsea had as much confidence as any chief or pilot could possess. She *has* to have that type of confidence because not only does she train others, she has responsibility for the taxpayers' plane and ultimately, the life of its pilot. She oversees the entire preflight process and starts preparing a jet more than two hours before the pilots walk to their aircraft. She checks each system: the ducts, the engines, the landing gear, the seat, the controls. Finally, she puts her signature on a document certifying the aircraft checks out safe.

"Then the pilot takes that, reads it, and he signs it too," she related. "He's accepting the jet and saying he trusts that I did my job. I'm an airman; he's the one who has a college degree. Yet he's flying the plane and he trusts *me*—that's really special."

She brushed back her hair, smiled, and added, "Now, if anything goes wrong with that jet? That's me too."

The squadron recognized Chelsea's good work by painting her name on one of their jets; the door of its front landing gear bore black letters spelling: ADAN PYGOTT, BATH, NY. She had since been promoted from Machinist's Mate Airman (ADAN) to Machinist's Mate Petty Officer Third Class (AD3). Navy planes have always had pilots' names emblazoned just beneath the cockpit, but in more recent years, the names of air crew have appeared as well—most often, plane captains. The pilots and crew share ownership of each plane.

The squadron surprised Chelsea with the honor and she still remembers the first time she saw the jet bearing her name and hometown. Several months later, she launched it from *Truman*. "The first time you see your jet go off the boat and see it land again, it's a really overwhelming feeling," she said.

I still had trouble believing that a nineteen- or twenty-year-old could do what she did that afternoon and every day—conduct such a complex and important operation involving a piece of machinery that costs more than the navy's first aircraft carriers. But I would soon become accustomed to teenagers running the show. The average age on an aircraft carrier hovers around twenty-one years old. Yet these young adults have a level of competency and responsibility seen in precious few places. Navy recruits grow up quickly. They are charged with adult tasks and if they fail, their team fails. People depend on them—a new situation for many. They quickly learn to do their job well for the sake of their fellow sailors. In the crucible of a busy flight deck or crowded hangar bay, young men and women grow up fast and reach levels of performance they never imagined.

To support Chelsea and her young shipmates, the navy ensures a gifted team of experienced leaders supports them in every way. That team includes the navy's respected noncommissioned officers—the chief petty officers— who are the senior enlisted personnel that provide the lion's share of leadership for the thousands of sailors on board.

"The chiefs are going to give you hell day in and day out," Chelsea said. "But in the end, they're always gonna have your back. The guys in the maintenance shop are all like big brothers. They'll always be there for us, even if we're not in the shop. No matter what, everyone's got each other's back.

"It's like one big family. I have more family here than I do back home. I love my family back home, but I love my family here too."

Chelsea ranked among the more junior enlisted personnel on the ship. Command Master Chief (CMC) Loran Bather ranked as the most senior. If chief petty officers are the enlisted father figures aboard, Master Chief Bather serves as the grandfather.

A young Loran Bather immigrated to the United States from Jamaica in 1983 and joined the navy three years later. He arrived at basic training after graduating from Harry S. Truman high school in the Bronx and soon joined the fleet as a disbursing clerk. Much like Chelsea Pygott, he reported for duty with a high school diploma and little real-world experience.

As a nineteen-year-old clerk, he was making sure people got paid. Like almost every job sailors receive when they arrive fresh from basic training, it wasn't a glamorous billet. Many first assignments make sailors question why they joined. They may find themselves doing hard or mundane tasks for long hours belowdeck. They don't fully understand how their job helps send an aircraft off the bow. Eventually, however, they realize how their shipmates rely on their work. They comprehend how they support the ship's mission.

"I was in charge of processing pay and ensuring financial records were accurate," CMC Bather said of his first assignment. "But it wasn't until after my first re-enlistment [four years later] that I had the 'aha' moment of realizing how much responsibility I had. Then I realized how many lives were affected by my actions. I don't think our young sailors always recognize the significance of what they do. It might take years for them to fully understand it."

He explained that placing large amounts of trust on sailors at a young age teaches them to trust their leaders, their peers, and their subordinates too. They also learn to trust themselves as they discover they can, in fact, handle their assignments. All this serves to give them the confidence they'll need to assume greater responsibilities and leadership roles. The well-proven navy process for developing sailors seemed like a multistep personal improvement program.

With help and guidance from his mentors, Loran Bather became a petty officer third class, second class, first class, then finally reached the rank of chief petty officer. Along the way, he learned how a chief can inspire an up-and-coming sailor when one of his first mentors, Disbursing Clerk Chief Petty Officer (DKC) Dickerson, encouraged him to pursue the Enlisted Surface Warfare Specialist (ESWS) program, reserved for the most promising enlisted sailors. The program gives them ship and mission-specific training beyond that of their peers. When Dickerson gave Bather the requisite application, the chief had already completed every section. He wasn't giving his younger protégé a choice; all Bather had to do was sign his name. Bather earned his ESWS pin and later put in more long hours of study to earn his Enlisted Aviation Warfare Specialist (EAWS) designation, also reserved for the most promising enlisted personnel. By earning those twin designations, he gave himself an exceptionally deep knowledge of the navy and proved that he could one day run an aircraft carrier.

Bather's star continued to rise and after becoming a chief himself, he went on to attain the rank of senior chief and then master chief. When we met in his office late one night aboard the *Harry S. Truman*, he was just weeks into his assignment as the carrier's command master chief, the highest-ranking enlisted sailor on board. As CMC, he serves as the liaison between the ship's enlisted personnel and the carrier's commanding officer. He also ranks in the top one percent of *all* enlisted navy personnel.

Bather's office wasn't directly beneath the flight deck, yet the roar of jets still punctuated our conversation; we felt the regular reverberating thud of the catapult shuttle against the bow. After a few days at sea, everyone aboard ship just ignores the noise. Some say they don't even notice it.

Our talk that night led to Chelsea Pygott and the other young sailors I'd met. We began discussing how the navy provides a path and an opportunity for so many of America's youth. Not only did the navy offer a potentially exciting job with a reliable paycheck, it offered the chance to serve their country and improve themselves. The enlisted leadership—namely chief petty officers—sets an example that inspires young sailors to pursue excellence. "Our chiefs sport those anchors on their collars that a lot of our sailors want to wear some day," the command master chief said, referring to the rank insignia sewn or pinned onto uniform collars. "They're inspiring those below them."

Younger sailors and airmen are encouraged through the ranks by their seniors, who inspire them, mentor them, and teach them the skills they'll need to earn more responsibility and higher ranks. They'll push sailors hard along a learning curve steeper than most nineteen-year-olds ever experience. In the process, sailors change as immaturity and laziness are replaced by the initiative and goal-oriented mind-set that come from high expectations. Their latent talents begin to shine.

"It takes a special type of person to join the navy," Master Chief Bather continued. "The young man or woman that joins does so for a variety of reasons. They know and expect that it will be a change in their lifestyle, and they come *wanting* this change. They *want* the responsibility and they *want* to learn. The navy places such responsibility in our young sailors because we know why they come and because we take the time to train them to do their jobs."

As those young men and women seize those chances, they embark on extraordinary lives.

"A young sailor has more responsibility than the average American of the same age," Master Chief Bather said. Referring to the helmsmen who actually steer the *Truman*, he asked, "What company would risk an eighteen-year-old driving a multibillion-dollar ship? We place a lot of responsibility on them, but again, it's a special type of person who joins the navy and they expect that added stress. They'll do whatever it takes to get the job done because they are committed to do so."

Like Chelsea and many of her shipmates, future president George H. W. Bush also joined the navy straight from high school. He enlisted immediately after graduation, at the minimum age of eighteen. He completed flight training the next year and received his wings and an officer's commission three days before his nineteenth birthday, June 9, 1943. He was the youngest aviator in the fleet. He then left to serve his country as a torpedo bomber pilot in the skies over the Pacific where he would add his own chapter to the war's annals and show the value of America's youth.

Aviation Electrician's Mate Third Class (AE3) Christopher Poole shared the commitment of George H. W. Bush, Chelsea Pygott, and Loren Bather; he saw the same opportunity on a flight deck. Chris and I met on the deck of another carrier during a rare window of downtime in the Aviation Electronics shop where he worked as a third-class petty officer. At twenty-one, the soft-spoken Texan was one year Chelsea Pygott's senior and near the average age aboard the carrier.

We walked down a long row of F/A-18 Super Hornets that had been chained down along the port side of the forward flight deck, their noses poised above the silent Number Two catapult track. Chris was talking about a recent repair his shop had completed on Aircraft 205, and the terminology he used to explain the problem quickly outstripped my ability to comprehend. I asked him to show me.

We ducked under the fuselage of the nearest Super Hornet and he directed my attention to the landing gear. Inside the bay that enclosed the gear during flight, I found that the number of multicolored electrical and hydraulic lines confused me as much as Chris's terminology. The wires ran everywhere, and each controlled different functions on the jet: gauges, engines, fuel pumps, weapons, hydraulics, flaps, rudders, lights, display panels. If a single wire shorted or otherwise didn't work, neither would the aircraft. The electrical system touched every aspect of the jet, so the problems Chris fielded almost always involved other maintenance departments.

"A few months ago, Aircraft 212 had a severe wiring problem," he said, offering me an example. "It shorted severely and we actually had wires fry open in several places from the engines up to the avionics on the forward fuselage. That's a lot of area to cover. Every shop in the squadron was involved in the repair. We're not just a team in the electrician's shop. Everybody has to work together to keep the planes running. Our shop helps the other shops figure out their problems. On this jet, they had to pull every component out so we could get to the wiring. We ended up routing a new set of wires all the way through the belly of the jet. Two weeks of day and night work to get that thing fixed. Usually we relieve the next shift in the shop. For those weeks, we relieved each other in the hangar bay where we were working on the jet."

With pride in his voice, Chris concluded, "When 212 came back on deck and flew with no problems, it really felt like something. I contributed to that."

Three years out of high school and, like Chelsea, he was working on $50 million aircraft. Nobody would babysit him or coddle him. His superiors expected him to perform, to do his job correctly the first time. Chris had always risen to the challenge and, he admitted, had already become a very different person than he'd been as a high school senior. He was motivated, focused, and responsible.

We stood up and carefully backed out from under the jet, then walked down the flight deck, heading to the hangar bay to escape the stiff wind that had picked up as the afternoon progressed. On the way, Chris explained how he'd arrived in the navy at such a young age—he'd enlisted at nineteen.

"I watched *Top Gun* when I was three," he said, "and here I am!" He laughed. The truth was more complicated, but also more authentic and representative of many young enlistees.

Chris had entered the University of Arkansas when he graduated high school, but quickly decided he wasn't quite ready for college. One day? Yes. At age eighteen? No. He considered how he could learn about aviation and set himself up to pursue a flying career later in life. So he found himself at a recruiting office, then at Naval Training Center Great Lakes, then Pensacola's Naval Aviation Technical Training Center, and finally in a Super Hornet hangar—all within one year. Months later he sailed to the Arabian Sea. He'd never been more than five hours from home.

"I've always loved aviation and wanted to fly," he said in his soft-spoken manner. "Basically my whole life has been trying to get there—and I've hit a lot of bumps. I seem to be doing it the hardest way possible.

"In Texas, I was used to being a few hours away from home," he said, then looked around the hangar deck and laughed. "Now I've been halfway around the world and back! There's really something to helping out the world. We supported Operation Iraqi Freedom and Operation Enduring Freedom and I played a part in that. Pilots told us stories about helping ground troops and I like to feel I helped support those guys over there. They're a lot braver than I am; I just want to help them out."

Poole enlisted to help our soldiers, but he also aimed to make the navy a career. In two years, he hoped the navy would send him to college. For many, the navy provides access to an otherwise unattainable education. It rewards those who serve by funding college or graduate education for active duty personnel or those who have been honorably discharged. Many sailors who couldn't afford college or graduate tuition suddenly have the means to receive that next level of education. The navy invests in the country's future by helping its hardworking men and women get a leg up and realize their potential.

After Chris completed his college courses, he hoped to re-enter the service as an officer and apply for flight school. He mused, "Hopefully I'll come full circle and instead of standing on the flight deck, I'll be flying *off* the flight deck."

"You'd know a lot more about your aircraft than most pilots in the squadron," I observed.

"I'd fix 'em in midair," he answered.

After witnessing the flight deck crew, in all their multicolored jerseys, running between aircraft, dodging jet exhaust and propellers, hauling chains and hoses, and launching planes off the carrier's bow, I began to understand how carrier aviation forges already capable young men and women into an elite corps. The navy's hot, noisy, crowded flight decks create a highly skilled force that can perform its precise, dangerous, and important mission every day, in every condition imaginable. Chelsea and Chris hone their skills in an environment that offers no room for mistakes. On the flight deck, every day is game day, and nobody wants to lose.

Aboard the USS *Harry S. Truman,* I saw the great opportunity the navy offers America's youth. Throughout one hundred years of naval aviation, young Americans like Chelsea Pygott from upstate New York, and Christopher Poole from central Texas have seized the opportunities offered by the navy to make their lives extraordinary. Their stories showed me that the purpose of naval aviation goes far beyond launching aircraft. It offers opportunity to young people at the most important points in their lives. The choices made by individuals during the transition from high school to life thereafter have a tremendous impact on their future. The wrong decisions can stifle not only their own potential but the potential of their family, community, or even country. Underemployment and low expectations can lead to poor self-esteem, crime, lethargy, lack of direction—all the perils that await our eighteen- and nineteen-year-olds. The navy offers those young men and women something proven and positive. It gives them skills, responsibility, and confidence. Then it forges those qualities together during high-pressure flight operations—an experience they'll find nowhere else. Sailors and airmen emerge better prepared for their lives, whatever course that may take. And through this time-tempered process, naval aviation develops the sailors the navy needs for its mission and the citizens America needs for its future.

10

HAITI

On JANUARY 12, 2010, THE aircraft carrier USS *Carl Vinson* left her pier at Norfolk, Virginia. She sailed out of the Chesapeake Bay and into the wintry Atlantic Ocean, bound for exercises off South America en route to her new homeport of San Diego, California. Within twelve hours of her departure, her mission abruptly changed as the world learned that a 7.0 magnitude earthquake had devastated the impoverished Caribbean nation of Haiti.

The morning of Wednesday, January 13, Commanding Officer Bruce Lindsey received new orders from the Pentagon: take on supplies and helicopters in Jacksonville, Florida, and join the international rescue effort in Haiti. Under the full power of her newly refueled reactors, which had just undergone their twenty-five-year overhaul, the carrier leapt southward at more than thirty knots.

For this mission, the strike fighters and electronic attack aircraft that comprised Carrier Air Wing Seventeen would serve little purpose. Its four Hornet and Super Hornet fighter attack squadrons, E-2C Hawkeye airborne early-warning squadron, and EA-6B Prowler tactical electronic warfare squadron remained at their bases on land. Instead, *Carl Vinson* filled her deck with helicopters that could ferry supplies to the island and rescue the injured; her stores carried water, food rations, and medical supplies. When relief operations commenced, the seventeen helicopters on board would bring those supplies to the victims on shore. In addition, the amphibious assault ships USS *Bataan* and *Nassau* and a number of cruisers, destroyers, and frigates carried even more helicopters into the disaster area.

Commander Edgardo Moreno, the executive officer of Helicopter Antisubmarine Squadron Eleven (HS-11)—the Dragonslayers—received his orders on Wednesday morning, January 13. Commander Moreno—better known as "Cheech"—immediately passed word to the two hundred men and women of Jacksonville-based HS-11: a group of sixty-four maintainers, pilots, and crew would deploy in less than six hours.

"I took the call in the office next door," Cheech said, motioning to a nearby office in the HS-11 hangar at Naval Air Station Jacksonville. "They called at about 10 A.M. and wanted us on the [*Vinson*] by 1700 [5 P.M.]."

Typically, months of planning go into a boat detachment. On this occasion, the Dragonslayers had only six hours to plan and deploy, and that included ferrying air crewmen, maintainers, parts, and four aircraft from shore to the *Vinson*, which had paused off the coast. They also had to make arrangements with their families.

"It was not an easy feat," Cheech said. "But when you get that call, you know that people are suffering. Our mission was to ease human suffering and save lives. In the navy we call it HADR, for Humanitarian Assistance and Disaster Relief, and it's one of our core roles. No one had any doubts we could mobilize in that short time. Everyone rallied and got it done and . . . by 1800 we had all our people, parts, and aircraft on the ship and we were tracking south."

Two days later, the *Carl Vinson* and cruisers *Lake Champlain* and *Bunker Hill* arrived off Port-au-Prince, Haiti, bringing the resources of Carrier Strike Group One to bear on the burgeoning humanitarian crisis.

At dawn on Friday morning, American helicopters lifted off the flight deck and made the short flight into Haiti. Cheech piloted the first HS-11 helicopter to land in the stricken nation. That flight began several days of grueling six-hour missions where pilots had to remain mentally alert every second, entirely focused on their job and the crowded airspace and hazardous ground around them. During their first missions, they would search out villages that needed medical evacuations, food, or water. They'd then report the news back to the logistics hub at Port-au-Prince airport. They might receive clearance to deliver supplies to villages or instead might deliver them to the clearinghouse at the airport. As landing zones (LZs) and villages were identified and secured throughout the country, the Dragonslayers began taking their cargo directly to the people and airlifting severely wounded villagers to medical facilities.

Cheech remembers sitting in the right seat of his SH-60F Seahawk, settling the bird onto an LZ on the outskirts of Port-au-Prince. When his wheels touched the ground, he looked out the window to his right and realized they'd landed near a triage site, where the wounded had gathered to receive initial treatment before being sent on their way or airlifted for more acute care. The site was overflowing with injured Haitians. He saw several people scampering toward the helicopter, bearing a small stretcher with a seven-month-old baby. The mother followed closely behind. Less than a minute later, the two crew members in Cheech's cabin had secured the stretcher inside the helicopter and they were airborne and en route to a hospital where a team of doctors would save the baby's life. He would never forget that flight.

HS-11 pilot Mike Ski and air crewman Scott Hatch landed at a similar LZ where most victims were children. "People were everywhere," Scott recalled. "They were surrounding us. We got out and weren't sure where we were going. People would point over here, over there. We found a team of American doctors and they gave us their worst cases. They had kids inside a structure; no furniture, nothing inside. We didn't have any litters so we put the kids in sheets and carried them back to the helicopter. Most had bandages or an IV going. They'd only had very basic lifesaving procedures done. Some were missing limbs. That's tough. Especially when you have your own kids."

In almost every situation, one of HS-11's biggest concerns was making sure nobody got hurt at the LZ. Wherever their helicopters landed, people would mob them, trying to get food or water, or trying to put an injured child inside. Sometimes they would endanger themselves. Other times, they would surge forward and pin the aircrew against the side of the helicopter.

"Our focus would shift from getting them food to keeping everyone safe," Mike said. "In some of the places that were remote, we'd try to bring some security folks first. You'd hover and see two or three Haitians, then as soon as we landed, hundreds would run out and you wouldn't know whether to give them the food and water or get out of there for everyone's safety."

The danger wasn't just from people on the ground. The crews often encountered tight landing zones, bordered by trees and wires that could snag a spinning rotor and throw a helicopter to the ground. Other times, they would land on dry dirt fields or dry creek beds, stirring up impenetrable clouds of tan dust. They were thankful for their training in the desert outside Fallon, Nevada, as they descended using only their instruments. The aircrew, wearing goggles and peering through the dust to spy the ground, might only be able to help the pilot navigate the last three feet of descent.

Not all flight decks are on carriers, as each frigate, destroyer, and cruiser in the fleet has a very active landing zone near its stern. Helicopters flew from a number of navy ships during the Haitian relief effort, including carrier escorts like the 10,000-ton, 567-foot cruiser *Bunker Hill*. On escorts, which form a key part of every carrier strike group, pilots negotiate decks that are less than fifteen feet above the waves and contend with the imposing metal wall of the hangar bay which adjoins the flight deck. When waves toss the small decks of cruisers, destroyers, or frigates, pilots' pulse rates quicken. At night, their hearts can race even faster. Off Haiti, they fortunately experienced smooth seas, which made landing on the fifty-five-foot-wide decks much easier; the diameter of a Seahawk's rotor arc is fifty-three feet so pilots have little room for error.

Winking to her fixed-wing counterparts, one helicopter pilot said, "It's really easy for me to land on a huge deck like a carrier."

The small boys, as escorts are often called, contributed to the Haiti relief effort just like the *Vinson*. In one instance, an HS-11 helicopter piloted by Shan "Splash" Moore, found an isolated island village off the Haitian coast that ran out of food and water when the quake effectively severed their lifeline to Port-au-Prince. All afternoon, the *Bunker Hill*'s crew loaded water onto the HS-11 helicopter using every container available on the cruiser—including jugs, coolers, and plastic bags. Splash would deliver the water to the islanders then return for more.

"We were flying six-hour missions," he said, "but you wanted to get out there and do more. We never said, 'No,' and we would've stayed out there all night if they hadn't made us come back in."

Reflecting on attitudes such as that, Cheech said, "The people of this squadron are extraordinary. And what makes them extraordinary is their resiliency. They had six hours to go home, pack, say good-bye, and get all our squadron's equipment aboard the carrier. Then off Haiti, we had to get the flight deck ready, get the helicopters ready, and fly into unfamiliar territory to ease human suffering which in many cases was heart-wrenching. And we had to do it within Department of State and Department of Defense parameters. The average flight was about six hours and every minute was hot and you had to have your head on a swivel because there were so many aircraft flying around. Pilots and aircrew had to stay a hundred percent focused on their missions. We executed everything that was asked of us and we did so professionally. I never heard anyone complain, from the lowest E-1 airman apprentice to the upper-level brass. I only heard, 'What can we do to help?' "

Among the HS-11 Dragonslayers who stepped up was Chriset Nau (pronounced No); he had particular reason for doing so. The twenty-eight-year-old petty officer was born in Port-de-Paix, Haiti, in 1982 and immigrated to Miami when he graduated high school. He got married and joined the navy several years later—one only needs to be a resident to enlist. The navy helped him earn his citizenship and on the day of the ceremony, he arrived in uniform. He was asked to lead his fellow new citizens in the Pledge of Allegiance. "When you're in an American uniform, you're a symbol to others," he explained.

Since Chriset knew his deployment schedule would take him away from home for long stints of time, he sent his three-year-old daughter to live with his mother in Haiti. He had visited them during Christmas of 2009, returning home shortly after New Year's Day. When he heard about the January 12 quake, his first thought was of them. He called and the phone just rang, rang, and rang. His mother didn't answer. He stayed up all night, dialing his mother and his friends, hoping for news and praying his daughter was safe.

After making history's first shipboard landing, Eugene Ely prepares to take off in his Curtiss biplane from the USS *Pennsylvania*, San Francisco Bay, January 18, 1911. COURTESY OF THE NAVAL HISTORICAL FOUNDATION

The pioneers of naval aviation, 1911. Glenn Curtiss takes the wheel while the first naval aviators sit below. Future admiral John "Jack" Towers and Theodore "Spuds" Ellyson are seated center and right respectively. COURTESY OF THE NATIONAL MUSEUM OF NAVAL AVIATION

Ed and Brie Hine reunited after his seven-month deployment with Strike Fighter Squadron 103—the Jolly Rogers. COURTESY OF MONICA MARTIN, COCOA BEAN PHOTOGRAPHY, VIRGINIA BEACH

Bethany Weisser points her daughter Kendall toward Blue Angel Number Five, piloted by Kendall's father, Frank. AUTHOR'S COLLECTION

Crew from Helicopter Antisubmarine Squadron Five—the Nightdippers—after a harrowing nighttime winter rescue on the North Atlantic. Crew (L-R) Byron "Oggie" Ogden, Kyle Need, Scott Pichette, and David Brandon. U.S. NAVY PHOTO

Twenty-year-old Plane Captain Chelsea Pygott of Strike Fighter Squadron 105—the Gunslingers—aboard the USS *Harry S. Truman*. The average age aboard aircraft carriers hovers around twenty-one; young sailors and airmen shoulder significant responsibilities. U.S. NAVY PHOTO BY MC2 KILHO PARK

Command Master Chief Loran Mather aboard the USS *Harry S. Truman*. The Command Master Chief leads the 200 chief petty officers who oversee the carrier's more than 4,000 enlisted personnel.
U.S. NAVY PHOTO BY MC2 KILHO PARK

George H. W. Bush (center) and his TBM Avenger crew aboard the USS *San Jacinto,* 1944. When he earned his wings in 1943 at age eighteen, America's future president was the youngest aviator in the U.S. Navy. COURTESY OF THE GEORGE BUSH PRESIDENTIAL LIBRARY AND MUSEUM

Cameron Douglas and Ed Hine of VFA 103—the Jolly Rogers—atop an F/A-18F Super Hornet, shortly before flying a 2010 mission over Afghanistan. COURTESY OF ED HINE

Commanding officers from Carrier Air Wing Seven transiting the Suez Canal aboard the USS *Dwight D. Eisenhower*: (L-R) Mark "Beav" Leavitt (HS-5), Sam "Pappy" Paparo (Deputy Commander, Carrier Air Wing Seven), Scott "Topper" Farr (VAQ-140), Scott "Intake" Kartvedt (VFA-83), Ben "Pizza" Hewlett (VFA-131), John "Jake" Ellzey (VFA-143). COURTESY OF SCOTT KARTVEDT

Vice Admiral Bill Gortney, Director of the Joint Staff and former Commander, U.S. Naval Forces Central Command and U.S. Fifth Fleet. U.S. NAVY PHOTO BY MC1 CHAD J. McNEELEY

Captain Dee Mewbourne, commanding officer of the USS *Dwight D. Eisenhower* and the USS *Enterprise*. U.S. NAVY PHOTO

Pilots and crew from Helicopter Antisubmarine Squadron Eleven—the Dragonslayers—on the deck of the USS *Carl Vinson,* off the coast of Haiti. The squadron began conducting relief missions immediately after the 2010 earthquake. COURTESY OF HS-11

Haitian-born Chief Petty Officer José Joseph addresses sailors in the galley of the USS *Harry S. Truman.* From cooks to engineers to pilots, everyone contributes to launching aircraft off a carrier's deck. U.S. NAVY PHOTO BY MC2 GINA K. WOLLMAN

Freedom 7 commander Alan Shepard, the first American in space, 1961. COURTESY OF NASA

Earthquake victims in Haiti watch an HS-11 helicopter return to the cruiser USS *Bunker Hill* to ferry more supplies to their devastated island. U.S. NAVY PHOTO BY MC2 DANIEL BARKER

Tom Hudner of Fighter Squadron Thirty-Two—the Swordsmen—receiving the Medal of Honor from President Harry S. Truman for his actions on December 4, 1950, in North Korea. COURTESY OF THE NAVAL HISTORICAL CENTER

Ensign Jesse Brown of Hattisburg, Mississippi, the first African American combat naval aviator, 1950. COURTESY OF THE NAVAL HISTORICAL FOUNDATION

The crew of Seawolf 28, including gunner Glen Smithen (at left) and pilot "Hollywood Al" Billings (in sunglasses) celebrate Al's 469th (and final) combat mission in Vietnam. Helicopter Attack Squadron (Light) Three—the Seawolves—amassed an extraordinay record of service and heroism. COURTESY OF AL BILLINGS

Chuck Klusmann puts his arm around fellow escapee Boun Mi after the pair broke out of a Laotian POW camp and trekked through the jungles of Laos to freedom, September 1964. COURTESY OF THE NATIONAL MUSEUM OF NAVAL AVIATION

George Coker just after being released from 2,382 days as a prisoner of war in North Vietnam. COURTESY OF GEORGE COKER

Tony Pastula, Harold Dixon, and Gene Aldrich in 1942, shortly after surviving a thirty-four day, 750-mile ordeal on the open Pacific Ocean after their torpedo bomber ditched 1,900 miles south of Hawaii. Their vessel, a tiny four-by-eight inflatable raft, sits beside them. COURTESY OF THE NATIONAL MUSEUM OF NAVAL AVIATION

While future Medal of Honor recipient Jim Stockdale led American prisoners of war from his isolated cell in Hanoi, his wife Sybil led a global effort to bring them home from North Vietnam. COURTESY OF THE STOCKDALE FAMILY

(L-R) Fred Haise, Jim Lovell, and Jack Swigert are welcomed aboard the USS *Iwo Jima* after their near-disaster aboard *Apollo 13* in April of 1970. CORBIS

Rear Admiral Mark Guadagnini aboard the USS *Abraham Lincoln* with commanding officers of Carrier Strike Group Nine. U.S. NAVY PHOTO BY MC3 ROBERT ROBBINS

(L-R) Chief Petty Officer Rob Palmer, Lieutenant Lee Amerine, Petty Officer Third Class Christopher Poole, and Lieutenant Jack Hathaway of Strike Fighter Squadron Fourteen—the Tophatters— underway aboard the USS *Nimitz*. U.S. NAVY PHOTO BY MC3 JOHN PHILIP WAGNER, JR.

Lieutenant Allison M. Oubre (1981–2009) aboard the USS *Nimitz*. COURTESY OF ANDREA ALVORD

The canopy closes over Lt. Denver Amerine as he readies his EA-18G Growler for carrier qualification trials aboard the USS *Carl Vinson*. AUTHOR'S COLLECTION

Lt. Tom "Killer" Kilcline Jr., with his father, future Vice Admiral Tom Kilcline Sr., 1976. COURTESY THE KILCLINE FAMILY

Lt. Tom Kilcline III with his father, Vice Admiral Tom "Killer" Kilcline Jr., Commander Naval Air Forces, 2010. COURTESY THE KILCLINE FAMILY

The next morning he reported to work at Naval Air Station Jacksonville and approached the squadron's commanding officer to share his situation. Commander Max Clark put a reassuring arm around Petty Officer Nau and told him they would take him to Haiti and find his family.

As the crew watched news reports over the *Vinson*'s televisions while they raced south, they realized the severity of the disaster. Petty Officer Nau learned how badly his mother's area had been damaged.

Carrier Strike Group One arrived off the Haitian coast late on Thursday, January 14. The next day, Petty Officer Nau climbed into one of HS-11's helicopters and lifted off from the flight deck. The helo flew over the crystal waters of the Caribbean, then crossed the shores of the Western hemisphere's poorest nation. Even prior to the quake, Haiti was suffering. Now, Chriset looked down and saw earthquake wreckage adding to his home country's troubles. But he could still see the roads and he guided the helicopter to Port-de-Paix.

They came in low over his mother's house and Chriset almost fell out of the helicopter's door as he began waving at his daughter, who was playing in the driveway. She immediately recognized her father and waved with a squeal of delight. His mother heard the noise and came out of her relatively undamaged house. The helicopter settled down and the family was joyfully but briefly reunited. Chriset explained that he couldn't take them to the *Vinson* and they understood. He made sure they were safe and then guided the helicopter toward more villages in need.

Chriset's knowledge of the island and its Creole language became vitally important as the navy struggled to aid the people of Haiti. On shore, he would help locate hospitals and communicate with their staff to determine what supplies they lacked and which patients needed specialized care.

On the carrier, he staffed the *Vinson*'s sick bay for twelve-hour shifts, tending to his wounded countrymen as best he could. "One lady hurt her leg and had it covered up, but she was still cold," Chriset said. "Nobody could tell what she wanted—nobody spoke Creole. I went over and realized she just needed a blanket. I could comfort people by doing what nobody else could do—just understanding them and speaking to them."

Those were the simple jobs where he could bring a smile to someone. Other jobs proved far more difficult. When the buildings around Port-au-Prince and other cities collapsed, they trapped, killed, or wounded thousands of people. Helicopters airlifted the fortunate ones to triage centers on the island or to the floating medical facilities on the *Vinson* and the hospital ship *Comfort*. Although they were lucky to have been rescued, many still had severe injuries that required every bit of the shipboard surgeons' skills. To make the situation even more traumatic for the Haitians, few medical personnel spoke Creole, their native language.

"When those people came to the ship a couple of days after the earthquake, their infections were very bad and we had to do a lot of amputations," said Chriset. "I had to explain to the patients what the doctors were going to do and how they were going to do it. One guy said, 'I can't lose my leg. I walk on the street every day selling things. If I lose my leg, how am I supposed to do that?'

"I said, 'They have to take your leg or you're going to die.'

"He said, 'Just do it then. Give me my life. Do it.' And he stopped crying."

Chriset had never been inside an operating room before, but for two weeks, he helped the surgeons do their work. Sometimes he helped mop up the blood that flowed from the wounds and amputations. Other times, he comforted women, men, and children who lost an arm or leg as doctors saved them from gangrenous infections. At times, he had to hold patients down when the operating team could only use local anesthesia.

While in Haiti with HS-11, Chriset saw things he'll never forget. He witnessed villagers struggling to survive amidst rubble and ruin; he saw wounded victims suffer, then helped doctors begin healing them; and he watched the people of the U.S. Navy give their all to help his people. When he left, he was proud of the job he did, the job his shipmates did. To his fellow Haitians, he was a hero, and he will always remember the good he accomplished for others.

"In the navy," he said, "I go to work every day, wherever that may be, and I have a purpose. If I was doing something else, how could I have come to Haiti to help?"

The navy has always responded to disasters as readily as it has responded to foreign threats. Navy aircraft rescued people from New Orleans rooftops after Hurricane Katrina struck, they brought aid to decimated Indonesian villages after the 2004 tsunami, and they've helped hurricane-struck residents of the Gulf States on many occasions. Throughout its history, the navy has rendered aid to those in need around the world. They'd even been to Haiti before. Like Chriset Nau, Chief Petty Officer José Joseph had returned to his home island in the uniform of his new country to help restore order amidst political unrest during the 1990s.

When we met aboard the aircraft carrier USS *Harry S. Truman*, José Joseph still carried the thick accent of his Haitian boyhood. But he had all the confidence of a chief petty officer in the United States Navy, even as he oversaw one of the least-sought-after divisions on his ship.

Armies march on their stomachs and carriers sail on theirs, but nobody wants to cook and clean. Culinary specialists—those men and women who work the ship's galleys—have some of the dirtiest jobs on the ship and, on the surface, seem most removed from flight operations. Few individuals receive a permanent assignment to the galley or food service division—it's generally a temporary duty assigned to a sailor, one that is rarely relished. It means being up before dawn to start preparing five thousand breakfasts—scrambling innumerable eggs on electric skillets and making dizzying numbers of pancakes on the same. The job also entails cleaning up after those five thousand breakfasts—mopping floors, cleaning griddles, washing dishes—and then pulling clean pans right back out and using them for the next meal. A second round of cleaning takes place before dinner. Then the process repeats and lasts late into the evening. And people complain about the food—constantly.

"FSA [Food Service Attendant] duty is tough," said *Truman* galley veteran Petty Officer Third Class Jonnie Hobby. "Especially with the air wing embarked. You are working thirteen-hour days under way. It's fast-paced and as soon as you are done cleaning after one meal, you're preparing for the next meal."

But having a positive hands-on leader like José Joseph makes the trying experience bearable and even beneficial. "Chief Joseph is definitely one of the best leaders I've ever encountered," the twenty-one-year-old petty officer observed of the galley boss. "He likes to motivate his sailors, whether it's giving you a morning pep talk or getting down on his hands and knees to show you how he wants something cleaned. He embodies honor, courage, and commitment."

When I first walked into the *Truman*'s enlisted mess, the last shifts of men and women were going through serving lines, carrying trays bearing institutional-style plates, utensils, and cups. The scene reminded me more of a high school cafeteria than something on a warship. People laughed loudly at their seats and stopped at different tables to visit friends. Momentarily, they forgot about work and simply enjoyed each other's company.

Unlike most civilian dining rooms, the low ceilings were covered with piping and ductwork that frequently imperiled the head of anyone over six feet tall. They trapped the noise, creating a healthy din. Also different were the omnipresent camouflage fatigue pants, boots, and rainbow of stenciled turtlenecks and long-sleeve shirts worn by the men and women. But just like any cafeteria in any place, the kitchens were hot and busy, tables constantly needed a wipe-down, and an unending stream of sticky, dirty dinnerware assaulted the dishwashers.

"This is probably the nastiest job, the dirtiest job on the ship," explained Chief Joseph. "You walk around the ship and ask any chief—*anybody*—if they want to work on the mess decks and they say, 'No.'"

José Joseph has never cared about his job's specifics or unpleasantries. For the Haitian-born chief petty officer, the U.S. Navy has always offered opportunity, and he viewed his current assignment as a new chance to make a difference and serve his new country.

It wasn't hard to find Chief Joseph. At six foot two he stood above most personnel on deck and his impeccably pressed camouflage fatigues looked sharp against his dark Caribbean skin. His eyes shone like his polished boots and he radiated energy and presence. We had only talked briefly when he noticed a line building near the tray-return area. He spied the bottleneck and crossed the deck in four long strides. The line of people unconsciously opened for him as he made his way to the two closely spaced refuse cans where sailors and airmen were scraping their leftovers. In a single motion, he grabbed one and swung it several feet away from its twin. "Come on, shipmates," he chided in his distinctive West Indies accent, "two lines, two lines, let's keep things moving."

He knew how to run a mess hall.

Like so many chiefs, Chief Joseph had done the hard thankless work of a junior sailor. He had pulled the tough shifts and done the jobs where dirt, grime, and stench don't shower off easily. Running a carrier necessitates some flat-out nasty jobs, many of which are in the galley, like washing thousands of dishes, cleaning grease traps, and separating recyclables from trash. Others include working the engineering spaces, in the belly of the ship where temperatures rise above 120 degrees and crew members go days without seeing daylight. Chief Joseph began working the steamy galleys as a food service attendant during 1991, when he was assigned to a humanitarian mission in Guantánamo Bay, Cuba. There, he cleaned kitchens, cleared tables, and did hard, dirty work twelve hours a day—all while serving some thirty thousand refugees from his native Haiti who had fled the violent coup against Jean-Bertrand Aristide. Shortly thereafter, Chief Joseph landed on Haiti itself with twenty thousand other troops, sent to restore democracy. He returned to his hometown wearing the uniform and carrying the flag of his new country. He remembers the pride he felt when his parents, cousins, and friends looked at how far he'd come. Not everyone was as welcoming, however.

He was serving as a translator with a detachment of marines when a firefight broke out. "I got shot in my hometown, three blocks from where I'd lived," he said. "I'm a young sailor; I'm not a soldier, not a marine. Now here I am less than a year in the navy in the middle of combat!

"It changed my life to a point where I don't take anything for granted. I take my job very seriously. I enjoy what I do. I take pride in what I do. I know that there are a lot of people that look up to me so I'm doing the right thing at all times."

The bullet had slammed into Joseph's leg, but doctors quickly set him on the path to recovery. After the wound fully healed, the navy offered him the opportunity to leave. But he declined. "I wanted to continue to serve," he said. "I felt like the cause was much bigger than me."

Reflecting on that greater cause and his mission as a U.S. sailor, he said, "Working in Cuba and Haiti was always hard work, but I felt like I was doing something worthwhile. Not only was I helping Haitian people, I was also doing something to help my newly adopted country, the U.S."

Without full stomachs, aviators can't fly, airmen can't haul heavy chains across the deck, and engineers can't stand long watches in the power plant. Without galleys and wardrooms, they have few places to relax and release the inevitable tension that builds during a day at sea. Without Chief Joseph's chefs and dishwashers, the carrier simply can't function. Conversely, the better his division performs, the better the ship runs. He understands that relationship and seizes every opportunity to improve himself, his shipmates, and his ship.

"When you have a tough day at work, the chief's mess or mess decks are where you come and relax," he said. "And that helps the whole ship run better. You can find someone with your same nationality and you can speak your own language. You can relax and have a meal. You're going to go back and work hard again but when you come on the mess decks, this is a relaxed place. We provide much more than food."

I never thought of a United States Navy aircraft carrier as a place where people of different nationalities would congregate, but the experience I had with HS-11, Chief Joseph, and sailors on numerous carriers and bases helped me grasp how our navy mirrors the changing composition and complexion of our country.

The *Truman*'s command master chief came from Jamaica. Cheech Moreno's parents emigrated from El Salvador. Chief Joseph and Petty Officer Nau both came from Haiti. I had met sailors from the Czech Republic, Mexico, the Philippines, and a host of other countries. Whether they hailed from Asia, Latin America, Africa, Europe, North America, or the Middle East, they all found the same opportunity in the U. S. Navy.

"This is a country of opportunity," Chief Joseph told me. "This is a country that offers more opportunity than anywhere in the world. I mean, I'm from Haiti. You always have to know somebody there. Even though you may be the smartest person in that area, you cannot go to school unless you know somebody." By contrast, the navy runs on merit alone. It rarely matters who you know. Your own performance determines your future.

While growing up in Haiti, Chief Joseph never wondered where he would find his next meal, but he knew many people who did. He was determined to avoid their lot and immigrated to the United States. There, he finished high school and joined the navy, taking advantage of its willingness to fund part of his education. When he received his first shore duty, he immediately enrolled in a local college. Many of his peers spent the weekends relaxing or going out; he spent every other weekend in school, eight hours a day. During the week, he attended night classes. With the navy covering his tuition, he had the chance to better himself and he took it.

"This country offers so much opportunity without any charge," he explained. "That's why I feel I'm indebted and I owe so much to the country that no matter what I do, I feel like it's my duty. It is my country."

Back in Jacksonville, the helicopters that served Haiti so well during the 2010 earthquake sat quietly in the Dragonslayers' shady hangar. HS-11's executive officer—who would eventually assume the role of commanding officer—and I talked upstairs about Haiti and the impressions I'd been developing about naval aviation.

Cheech Moreno's family came from El Salvador—where his father worked on F4U Corsairs and P-51 Mustangs in their air force—and he shared his perspectives about how the navy assimilates men and women from so many nationalities.

He echoed Chief Joseph's comments, observing that the navy—like America—provides opportunity and a level playing field. Cheech was born in Los Angeles in the Hispanic enclave of Southgate. Many neighboring families didn't encourage education, but his parents always pushed him to pursue learning as far as possible. His dad took him flying at age six, and from then on, Cheech aimed for a cockpit. He worked hard to get there and went to Norwich University, a private military college in Vermont. His parents likewise worked hard to afford the tuition for his first two years. His mother worked two jobs as a seamstress; his father worked overtime for a sandpaper company.

"The summer before my junior year," Cheech remembered, "my parents leveled with me and said, 'To be honest, we can't afford to send you back.' I didn't know what I'd do. Then I got the letter: a two-year Navy ROTC scholarship. I remember Mom getting home, stepping out of her carpool. She was dead tired and asked, '*Qué pasa, hijo?*' I told her about the scholarship and I'd never seen her cry like that. She was so happy—I'm sure in part because she didn't have to work a second job!"

Even at college in Vermont—where nobody looked or spoke like Cheech—he never found prejudice or special treatment. When he arrived in flight school, he discovered the same. The navy readily accepts people from different nationalities, be they citizens like Cheech or immigrants like José Joseph. Once they become citizens—or simply part of the navy—these new sailors and officers find equal opportunity. If they're pilots, nothing matters besides their ability to complete the mission and put their aircraft on the deck. If they're a maintainer, little ultimately matters but their ability to fix an aircraft and send it off the deck safely.

"And look how that diversity helps us," Cheech said. "In Haiti, where did we turn for translators and knowledge about the country? Petty Officer Nau. Having that diversity in the navy helps achieve our missions."

In 2010, all the countless and diverse pieces of naval aviation came together to aid the Haitian people: servicemen and women from different backgrounds, carriers and escorts, helicopters and transports. In less than twenty-four hours, an entire carrier strike group was retasked to aid a tiny, poor Caribbean nation that needed it.

"When it's time to help, to ease suffering and save lives, the navy will shift gears and help," Cheech said. "And in Haiti, I felt that we were absolutely making a difference—and I mean that from the bottom of my heart. Maybe we just put a Band-Aid on the situation, but if we had just saved a handful of lives—let alone hundreds of lives like we did—it would have been all worthwhile. It was special to be part of something put together so quickly and executed so well. Our squadron was proud. They outdid themselves for those people who needed help. That's naval aviation."

PART THREE

THE ARABIAN SEA

11

THE CHAIN OF COMMAND

THE U.S. NAVY DIVIDES THE world's oceans into six purviews, or fleets, which have dominion over the ships, aircraft, and sailors that change operational control (CHOP) into their area as they transit the world's sea lanes. Navy assets in the North Atlantic are commanded by the U.S. Second Fleet, based in Norfolk. Third Fleet ships and aircraft patrol the Central and Eastern Pacific Ocean and receive orders from Pearl Harbor, Hawaii. Fourth Fleet (Mayport, Florida) oversees the Caribbean and the waters off South America, and assets in Sixth Fleet (Naples, Italy) shoulder responsibility for the Mediterranean. Yokosuka, Japan, hosts the headquarters of Seventh Fleet, which has purview over the Western Pacific. Within each fleet exist numerous task forces and carrier strike groups, comprised of varied combinations of warships—carriers, amphibious assault ships, cruisers, destroyers, frigates, submarines; transports—combat support ships, oilers, hospital ships; and aircraft—F/A-18 Hornets and Super Hornets, EA-18G Growlers and EA-6B Prowlers for electronic warfare, E-2C Hawkeye early-warning platforms, C-2 Greyhound transports, P-3C Orion patrol planes, rotary-winged H-60 Seahawks and MH-53 Sea Dragons, and others.

Today, however, no fleet headquarters hums with quite as much pressing activity as that of Fifth Fleet. From its headquarters in the Kingdom of

Bahrain, Fifth Fleet coordinates the naval assets supporting U.S. forces in the Middle East, Central Asia, and Africa.

Bahrain, a thirty-three-island archipelago, lays nestled in a gulf between Saudi Arabia and Qatar. Manama, the capital, sits on the thirty-five by eighteen-mile main island and hosts the country's constitutional monarchy. Not far from the soaring National Mosque and the financial district's clean streets and glass skyscrapers—several of which rise over fifty stories—sits the low complex of earth-hued buildings that houses Fifth Fleet's operations. Navy personnel transiting to or from Middle East assignments fill the walkways and buildings, giving any observer some idea of the massive U.S. mobilization in the region. With Bahrain and nearby Kuwait serving as the main staging points for U.S. military personnel in the Middle East, Americans fill many of the seats on inbound flights. The strategic directives that result in these troop movements flow from offices in the headquarters building. Above its entrance are three lines of lettering: U.S. Naval Central Command/United States Fifth Fleet/Combined Maritime Forces.

Inside, military attachés from a host of coalition countries—Great Britain, Sweden, Iraq, Australia—filled the lower corridors. After weaving through the attachés, I arrived at the office suite of Vice Admiral Bill Gortney. From there, the seasoned three-star admiral commanded all the U.S. and coalition naval forces in the Middle East and Africa—the purview of U.S. Central Command (CENTCOM).

The son of a naval aviator, Vice Admiral Gortney had flown A-4 Skyhawks and F/A-18 Hornets and Super Hornets while logging 5,300 mishap-free hours and 1,235 carrier landings in his thirty-one years of flying for the Navy. He has commanded two strike fighter squadrons, Carrier Strike Group Ten, and Carrier Air Wing Seven—which at present was just several hundred miles away in the Arabian Sea onboard the USS *Dwight D. Eisenhower*. Clearly, he was a carrier guy. His most recent commands, however, had significantly broadened his view of naval aviation and its chain of command.

Carrier strike groups seem so powerful and widely used that it becomes easy to forget they comprise only one part of America's overall strategy—albeit an important one. Vice Admiral Gortney ensures that the *Eisenhower* works in perfect concert with all other navy assets in the region to execute the foreign policy of the United States.

"Naval aviation is more than just what's on the carrier," the three-star admiral explained in his office, which was decorated with wares from Abdul Abdulla, a local rug merchant known to thousands of visiting American servicemen.

"What's on the aircraft carrier provides thirty percent of the combat air support over Afghanistan. Those planes are protecting those heroes on the ground and that's part of our weapons system. There are also P-3s flying from bases in Iraq and Afghanistan and providing support. We have helicopters all over the AOR [Area of Responsibility]. We have EA-6B Prowlers in Afghanistan, we have H-60 Seahawks in Kuwait and Iraq configured for air ambulance missions. In the first days of OEF [Operation Enduring Freedom], almost all the air support came from three aircraft carriers [*Enterprise*, *Carl Vinson*, and *Theodore Roosevelt*]."

While the support of those three alternating carriers was certainly impressive, it doesn't compare to the armada of six carriers deployed on the Red Sea and the North Arabian Gulf during Operation Desert Storm in 1991. (To minimize Iran's regional influence, the navy rarely uses the term Persian Gulf.) When coalition forces swept Iraqi troops from Kuwait, navy aircraft flew thousands of missions from the carriers *Midway*, *Saratoga*, *Ranger*, *America*, *John F. Kennedy*, and *Theodore Roosevelt*. Only the *TR* remains in service.

Vice Admiral Gortney had served extensively in the Middle East; he had seen Desert Storm and other conflicts simmer, erupt, and subside. He had known war in the region and sensed the beginnings of another—one he hoped his forces could prevent.

"Naval aviation is fighting and winning two wars," he said, "and preventing a third from occurring with Iran." If conflict should erupt with Iran's regime over its alleged pursuit of nuclear weapons, responsibility for action would fall on his shoulders—and on the ships and aircraft he commanded.

Now that Vice Admiral Gortney oversees a range of assets, he understands well how naval aviation supports the U.S. strategy for the entire region. As commander of Fifth Fleet and U.S. Navy Central Command, he oversees four key lines of operation. Overall, the task forces and navy units in CENTCOM provide partnership, strength, and presence in this volatile region, he said. They keep the sea lines of communication open and provide a presence in the area, physically reinforcing the words of America's foreign policy. They "find and finish" Al Qaeda, along with providing maritime security against smugglers and pirates. They support operations in Afghanistan and Iraq, and are on-call in the event of any natural disasters or other crises.

As he explained his role, I began to understand how the actions of carrier strike groups, individual carriers, squadrons, and aircraft fit into a greater picture, dazzling in its complexity but united in its purpose. And while the strategy remains broad and multifaceted, the carrier still plays the central role.

"That carrier deck is four and a half acres of sovereign American territory," he said emphatically. "It allows our nation to project power peacefully or with a hammer without ever having to ask people's permission. It gives our nation physical and political access to project that power. As long as we're in international waters, we can put that ship wherever we want."

Fast fleet aircraft carriers spearheaded America's march across the Pacific during World War II, sending strikes against islands and the Japanese mainland from their seaborne airfields. When the Korean War erupted, carrier aircraft responded from ships stationed in the Yellow Sea, Sea of Japan, and the East China Sea; U.S. aircraft could support our troops without surrounding countries having to provide airbases or permission. The Yankee Station rendezvous point in the Gulf of Tonkin saw American carriers launch thousands of sorties into Vietnam during the 1960s and 1970s. Throughout the Cold War, our carriers stood just miles off the shores of hostile or threatened countries, showing our strength and resolve against an aggressive communist foe. Our aircraft could be over targets on land within minutes, but the Soviet Union and its satellites could do nothing as long as our ships stayed in international waters.

But naval aviation wasn't just about our ships and aircraft projecting power. The vice admiral explained that it's also about the energy and dedication I'd been witnessing since immersing myself in his world.

"That sense of purpose you felt from the crews on *Nimitz, Ike,* and *Truman?* You'll see it on a destroyer or a cruiser or a submarine or in a P-3 squadron. There are people in America who are critical of the youth of America and they should not be. If they come out here and see what our sailors and our marines are doing they'd be very proud of the youth of America.

"One hundred percent of the force here raised their hand to volunteer to serve their nation and put on the cloth of their nation in a time of war. That is another piece people need to remember. They're volunteers and they joined in a time of war. Some of them don't remember peacetime."

When I visited Vice Admiral Gortney, the USS *Dwight D. Eisenhower* served as the carrier-on-duty in the Fifth Fleet. She was stationed off the coast of Pakistan, in the Arabian Sea, seven hundred miles southeast of Bahrain. From the moment I landed aboard her deck on a C-2 Greyhound COD transport crewed by the VRC-40 "Rawhides," I sensed a different atmosphere from what I'd experienced on other carriers. When the back ramp of the plane opened, the heat of the Middle East filled the cabin—accompanied by the smell of heavy jet exhaust, which combined to make the air almost too thick and hot to breathe. I saw that many of the flight deck crew wore bandanas over their mouths and noses to ward off dust and fumes, giving their lungs a fighting chance to process oxygen. I'd never walked onto a hotter flight deck, but that wasn't the main difference I noticed from the decks of *Nimitz* and *Truman.*

It was the bombs.

The aircraft on the *Eisenhower*'s flight deck all carried live bombs, intended for Taliban militia in the mountains of Afghanistan. If they were employed, they would save American troops on the ground who were battling the insurgent terrorists. The bombs were real, these missions were real, and they originated from this very warship. As I emerged from the rear of the plane, I saw a deep seriousness of purpose among the men and women on deck. I stood on the lone aircraft carrier that was supporting the nearly 100,000 U.S. troops engaged in Operation Enduring Freedom. In many instances, those soldiers and marines in-country depended on this aircraft carrier, her planes, and her men and women for their lives—and the crew knew it.

From the ship's bridge high above the flight deck, Captain Dee Mewbourne surveyed this scene and watched me weave through the deck's traffic, walk toward the island, and disappear inside. When I had climbed the seemingly endless series of ladders that led to the upper levels of the superstructure, I found the captain on the port side of the bridge in an elevated leather swivel chair that afforded him a prime view of the entire flight deck. To his right, a twenty-year-old helmsman steered the 97,000-ton ship, making minute adjustments to a nine-inch wheel to maintain the ship's precise heading into the wind. He stared intently at a digital display that showed him the ship's exact course, second by second. His hands were never still as they manipulated the little wheel that directed the twin forty-five-ton, twenty-nine by twenty-two-foot rudders beneath the waterline. Other officers and enlisted personnel tended to the array of radars and navigation equipment that kept the carrier on course and sovereign of the surrounding seas. The final decision about any action sparked by the information flowing into the ship's bridge belonged to Captain Mewbourne, *Ike*'s commanding officer.

Since arriving at the U.S. Naval Academy in 1978, Dee Mewbourne dreamed of commanding an aircraft carrier. With that as his goal, he'd become a naval aviator, completed a tour at Naval Air Station Patuxent River as a test pilot, logged more than one thousand arrested landings, and risen through the ranks to arrive at his present post. He had successfully navigated ten deployments over twenty-eight years of service and twenty-eight years of marriage. "And I give all the credit to my wife," he said with an easy smile.

At present, his carrier was launching yet another sortie toward Afghanistan—something that happens every day, around the clock. From the bridge, we watched color-coded teams from four fighter attack squadrons, an electronic attack squadron, a helicopter antisubmarine squadron, and an early-warning squadron feverishly working to prepare the next aircraft for the catapult and recover those aircraft returning from their missions. Men and women in shirts and cranials of every color—red, green, white, blue, purple, yellow, brown—were rushing across the deck, moving planes and helicopters, pushing ordnance carts, hauling fuel lines, and operating catapults. Sometimes it seemed entirely unorganized, but I knew everything happened exactly as orchestrated by conductors in one of two places.

One was Primary Flight Control—Pri-Fly—which mirrored a civilian airport's air traffic control center, although much smaller. From their perch one level above the bridge, the Air Boss and his second in command—the Mini Boss (so-named for his position, not his stature)—monitored all aircraft aloft and guided them into the recovery pattern for a safe landing on deck. A team of enlisted personnel helped the two directors track the planes, noting positions and figures on windows and glass panels using wipeable markers. Several pilots from the air wing stood by to assist and track their own squadron's aircraft.

When the planes were on the deck, they fell under the purview of Flight Deck Control, which was housed on the first level of the island, just two doors away from the flight deck itself. The Handler, often a lieutenant commander, made sure the cramped office kept every inch of this floating airstrip meticulously organized. Officers and enlisted personnel gathered around a six-foot-long, two-and-a-half-foot-wide model flight deck like Vegas gamblers around a craps table. They called the scale model the "Ouija board" and slid miniature planes and helicopters around it to mirror the situation outside. They placed an assortment of painted bolts, washers, and nuts on the aircraft to indicate which needed maintenance, ordnance, gas, respotting (repositioning), or other attention.

"Some call it a ballet, some call it controlled chaos," Capt. Mewbourne said, seeming to read my thoughts as I looked over the deck. "It still amazes me that it comes together so seamlessly and seemingly effortlessly.

"The work in naval aviation is so great," he said, turning away from scene below. "It *inspires* people to greatness, to achieve great things. You wonder what makes people rise to that level of professionalism we see on deck. What makes them achieve that level of excellence?

"They believe in their mission. They follow their orders. They know it's important and they achieve the standards that are required.

"In naval aviation—carrier aviation in particular—we're able to touch all the missions of our navy, we always have. Being forward deployed, being a deterrent, keeping sea lanes open, relief work, armed combat—we see all those things. People feel that when they're on a carrier, they're at the middle of whatever's going on in the world. They feel valuable. It's very clear when you're working on the flight deck—you feel the rumble and heat and get an adrenaline rush. You feel like you're making a difference. You know those airplanes you're launching are going out and conducting a mission. You feel like your life matters, no matter what role you play. Throughout the ship, everyone feels connected to what we do. They understand the relationship between their job and what we do as a mission. They see their contributions to the total team effort. They're proud."

At that moment, the captain's radio buzzed. It was the ship's second in command, the executive officer: "XO to Captain."

"Captain, go ahead," he responded.

"The cylinder for the Number Three arresting wire blew," the XO reported. A brief discussion ensued, with a third officer giving a quick damage report from the spaces below deck where the arresting gear resided.

"Okay, strip the Three wire, and have the planes target the Two wire when they land," Captain Mewbourne replied calmly. "Take Three offline for service for the next twenty-four hours." As an afterthought, he asked, "Can you fix it in twenty-four hours?"

"Yes sir, I'm confident my guys can do it," came the response.

"Okay, thanks," the captain said, setting the radio back in its place as if nothing out of the ordinary had happened. He turned to me and saw my surprise.

"It doesn't do any good to get excited," he explained. "I worry about everything but try to stay calm. There's an awful lot going on out there— thousands of pieces. If you had to launch one airplane and you had to go through a step-by-step checklist—what it required from starting up the reactors to loading up food to getting flight physicals to getting the jet topside and ready—if you have to list it all, it'd be a million steps or more. I can't worry about every little thing.

"To make it all happen, we have to empower people to do their individual jobs," he said. "We give them the tools they need—things like priorities, tasks, and authority. Then we get all our people pulling together and those launches seem to happen effortlessly every forty-five seconds. It's amazing.

"Our people are the most valuable things we have on board," he added, "and we try hard to let them know that. In turn, people are willing to work a bit harder."

As I stood there, something dawned on me: as commanding officer of the *Dwight D. Eisenhower*, Captain Mewbourne bore ultimate responsibility for every single thing that happened aboard his ship. Any sailor on that ship could end his career. An airman could start a fire, an air traffic control mistake could cause a severe mishap on the flight deck; incidents like that cost lives. They can also end careers for officers in charge. The consequences are very real, and the navy holds people to account.

For example, in 2008, a fire erupted aboard the aircraft carrier USS *George Washington* while the ship was transiting from Norfolk to her new homeport in Yokosuka, Japan. Mistake one: sailors were smoking in a restricted space. Mistake two: 115 gallons of flammable refrigerant compressor oil were improperly stored in an adjoining boiler exhaust and supply space. That's all it took to cause $70 million in damage, injure thirty-seven sailors, and cost the captain and the executive officer their commands. The official investigation found that a series of small lapses in procedure and leadership compounded to lead to the blaze, and all responsibility ultimately resided with the men at the top.

The captain thus has powerful incentive to make sure the sailors on his ship are capably led and trained to the point that they can do their jobs blindfolded. Every commissioned officer or enlisted chief petty officer feels the same responsibility and worry. Up and down the chain of command, leaders are accountable for the men and women under their charge. They share the personal liability of leadership. But since none of those leaders can be with every sailor every minute, they must teach, train, and trust.

The man who bore ultimate responsibility for everything transpiring on this floating city of five thousand people slid out of his chair and motioned for me to follow him off the bridge and down the corridor that led along the port side of the island. He lifted the steel lever on an external door and we stepped into the sunlight. Heat, noise, and jet exhaust rose up from the flight deck three stories below. We hooked our arms over the railing of Vulture's Row, as the catwalks overlooking the flight deck are called. We watched the great pageant unfold in all its chaotic yet precisely orchestrated glory. The captain squinted as the brilliant sunlight reflected off the Arabian Sea, plane canopies, and every other surface aboard ship. The wind whipped around the catwalk. Dee Mewbourne soaked up the entire scene, a satisfied smile on his face.

"You know, from age seventeen 'til today, I've worked to achieve this," he almost sighed.

Another plane roared off Catapult Three, directly in front of us. The deafening sound of its jets faded as it pulled away from the ship to join another Hornet already aloft. White steam released from the catapult drifted over the deck like windblown smoke. A yellow-shirted plane director stepped onto the catapult track to guide the next jet into place. The production continued, as it did every day.

"No one ever achieves their dream at forty-something years of age," the captain continued, with a mixture of gratitude and melancholy—his command would come to an end soon after the cruise ended and he would receive a shore-based position. "But here I am living my dream. I don't like being separated from my family, but I love being captain. One thousand days in command and every single one has been a tremendous blessing."

The work of naval aviation makes it a job like no other. It inspires people to new levels of performance. Throughout my travels, I met men and women who absolutely loved their work. They live an adventure every day—doing their country's business, working a busy flight deck, visiting a foreign port of call. But theirs is not a meaningless, self-serving adventure. Rather, naval aviation is an adventure with a higher purpose. It lends significance to a life.

In the civilian world—as in the military world—people strive to achieve success, however they may define it. They chase that ideal throughout their lives, sometimes quite relentlessly. Many become disenchanted or disappointed, particularly when they achieve those traditional benchmarks—an elegant home, a luxury car, a corner office—and find themselves still unfulfilled. They chased success, not significance.

The navy offers individuals a chance to obtain both. The excitement attracts people from all backgrounds and their shared goals bond them together. They find the satisfaction of success and significance when their team accomplishes its mission and helps achieve their country's aims. People who planned to serve just the minimum term of two to four years regularly reenlist and their careers last for ten, twenty, or thirty years. They can't leave their team and their shipboard family. They love the work, trust the people, relish the adventure, and believe in the purpose.

Later that evening, I sat down with five of Carrier Air Wing Seven's squadron commanders—called skippers, in homage to old seafaring traditions where crews referred to commanding officers as skippers. These seasoned leaders relayed the orders of Vice Admiral Gortney, Captain Mewbourne, and their Air Wing Commander (CAG) to their squadron mates aboard *Ike*, and together, they would take to the sky to execute them.

In his squadron's ready room, Mark "Beav" Leavitt of the HS-5 Nightdippers hosted fellow squadron commanding officers Scott "Topper" Farr of the Electronic Attack Squadron 140 (VAQ-140) Patriots, Scott "Intake" Kartvedt of the VFA-83 Rampagers, Jon "JT" Taylor of the VFA-131 Wildcats, and John "Jake" Ellzey of the VFA-143 World Famous Pukin' Dogs. Jake's squadron earned the name when an aviator's wife observed that the winged black lion on the squadron insignia looked more like a violently ill canine than the mythical Griffin it aspired to depict. The commanders' ages hovered around forty and each had almost twenty years in the navy. They had one of the most coveted capstone assignments a naval aviator can have: command of a squadron.

Men who have been squadron commanding officers—usually called COs or skippers—help select their own replacements, giving them a trial run as squadron executive officer, which usually leads to the CO assignment in the same unit. Once they have the top job, they are responsible for all the aircraft, personnel, and equipment within their squadron—that's more than $500 million in aircraft alone. Then there are more than two hundred people, most of whom are ten to twenty years younger than they—and skippers are ultimately responsible for ensuring each one does his or her job and returns home safely. Many consider squadron command the best leadership training in the navy and most skippers make the rank of captain.

The ready rooms for all Carrier Air Wing Seven squadrons are on the on the oh-three (03) level of the *Eisenhower*, three decks above the hangar and directly beneath the flight deck. And since it occupied a space toward the aft of the ship, the ready room where we met filled with noise every time a jet launched from one of the ship's two rear (or "waist") catapults. We'd hear the engines roar as the catapult held the bucking jet in place, then the engines would fade away as the catapult's piston engaged and accelerated the screaming jet toward the deck's end.

Likewise, the room shuddered each time a jet returned and landed on the deck above us. That night, *Ike*'s aircraft would operate well into the evening. Takeoffs and landings punctuated our conversation. We could also watch the night vision images of aircraft landings coming over the PLAT, the live television feed from the flight deck.

Just as we all sat down at the room's leather and steel desks, another Super Hornet slammed onto the deck and talk momentarily ceased until we heard the plane's engines power down.

"Do you realize what's happening on deck right now?" Scott "Intake"

Kartevdt asked. "The average age up there is around twenty. Our squadron is getting ready to bomb a target that we string behind the ship. Sailors are putting illumination on it and getting ready to release it. There's a plane captain—an eighteen- or nineteen-year-old airman—responsible for preparing that $40 million airplane for flight. And one of our pilots will hand their life to him at the bottom of the ladder and trust that they'll be able to hand it back when the mission is over. Redshirts are loading the strafing rounds, loading the bombs. The catapult crews have the cats ready to go. Plane directors are taxiing aircraft around. Arresting gear teams are ensuring the wires are squared away. The reactor personnel are ensuring we have the power to create wind over the deck and it's all working together.

"Most of those men and women haven't been to college, many come from broken homes or rough backgrounds. But when they join the navy, join our squadron, they inherit a history and have a chance to prove themselves.

"And some of them make only eight hundred dollars every two weeks! Some of them join to support and defend the Constitution of the United States. Some of them raised their hand and took that oath but they really needed the money or needed to get out of their situation. But regardless, when we pull back into Norfolk in July, what they'll have besides money is relevance in their life because what they did was support and defend this country so the three hundred million citizens of our nation can live free and not think about it.

"When our pilots get airborne and point at the ground in Afghanistan and the bullets come out the way they're supposed to and they recover and they land and it's all successful and it's commonplace, I attribute it to the values we all share."

"The navy has its core values of honor, courage, and commitment, and it takes all three of those things," added VAQ-140's skipper, Scott "Topper" Farr.

"And all three of those things are embedded in patriotism," said Jake Ellzey. "Love of country, sacrifice before self. And it's truly mind-boggling they do it day in and day out. And they're from Kentucky, Alaska, Texas, Arizona, California."

"And from Vietnam, Puerto Rico, China," Intake added.

"I have a kid from Ghana," Topper said. "I asked him why he joined. He said 'I love America.'"

Another slam shook the ready room and we heard engines roar above us. Intake and Jake, who sat facing the television that broadcast the landings, immediately yelled, "That was a Prowler!" I turned to see a plane getting airborne again after missing the arresting wires. Everyone in the room except for Topper roared with laughter. Only VAQ-140 flew the antiquated EA-6B Prowler; it was Topper's plane that had boltered—that is, missed the wires.

"No skipper wants to be around other skippers when that happens," Jake said, punching Topper in the arm.

Topper attempted a technical defense based on the age of his Prowlers, but Intake wouldn't have it. "Whatever," he said, grinning. "Your guy missed it." The CO always bears responsibility.

"Anyway," said Topper, moving on, "it's all centralized planning, decentralized execution delegated down to the lowest level." The skippers took orders from above and translated them into actions for the squadron's leaders, who would in turn pass orders to the individuals working under them—trusting everyone would do what needed to be done.

"The way the navy breeds their leadership throughout the command structure empowers each individual to make decisions," elaborated Intake. "Where other services tell their members what they *can* do, the navy tells you what you *can't* do. [As long as] you can get the proper success and justify the decision and do it safely—then you're lauded for it."

"Tell us what to do and we'll get it done," echoed Beav. "And we'll get it done rapidly and won't hem and haw over the structure and formality of it. We get stuff done and get it done right."

"Then everyone is held accountable," Intake said. "For us, on that first night as skipper at sea, you're all of a sudden responsible for these twenty-five-, twenty-six-, and twenty-seven-year-olds who are landing $40 million airplanes on the back of a multibillion-dollar ship and they're only three years out of college. That gets your attention!"

"We're accountable for our squadrons, like the captain is responsible for this ship. And that seems to be a trait that's less and less understood or cared for in this world," Topper added.

"Sailors who join this family are taken care of, but they're also held accountable," said JT, skipper of the VFA-131 Wildcats. "Their entire personal space is less than the size of a coffin. All their worldly goods, their bunk, all their pictures, fit inside the space of a coffin. The only privacy they have is the curtain on their rack. That shared sacrifice creates cohesion in each squadron that's unheard of anywhere else."

"This is serious business done by some amazing people," Topper said. "Unfortunately, most things people know about naval aviation come from *Top Gun*, which is really kind of trite and embarrassing."

"What's your beef with Tom Cruise?" Jake asked.

"Hey, if *Days of Thunder* had come out before *Top Gun*, Topper would be racing NASCAR!" Intake said, eliciting a round of laughter.

Topper smiled quickly then soldiered through, trying to salvage his line of discussion. "Well, that perceived cockiness is a coping mechanism because to do what we do we have to think *it* won't happen to us. Nothing will go wrong. Why? Because we trust that everybody is doing everything right. When something happens that puts a dent in that mental armor, it makes you reflect on what you're doing taking the risk to fly."

Topper's last line of thinking made him momentarily reflective. "I can't believe how fast sixteen years of flying have gone by," he said earnestly and somewhat sadly. "I remember being a youngster and sitting in an orange and white training airplane at Pensacola dreaming about getting my shot. Then you blink and sixteen years go by."

"We're all about to be voted off the island," said Jake, referencing the end of their squadron commands, which would come soon after they returned to Norfolk. Some might retire, others would continue on to higher-ranking shore-based duties where they would almost surely not fly missions so often and enjoy the camaraderie of a squadron on deployment. Unfortunately for aviators, as they attain higher rank they get less time to pursue their passion for flying, a primary reason they joined the navy and something they look forward to each day. At some inevitable and bittersweet point, every naval aviator—no matter how good, no matter how spirited—suits up and climbs into a cockpit one last time. They all fly away from a carrier in their trusted aircraft on one final mission to savor the freedom and exhilaration of the sky.

"That makes us reflective," Jake continued. "This could be our last flying tour; probably will be. But we have reached the pinnacle of our profession.

"We each have responsibility for half a billion dollars' worth of stuff—

and that's just the airplanes alone. We also have two hundred people in each squadron from all different backgrounds, all volunteers. We didn't interview any of these folks, nor did we train them. It takes an all-hands effort to make sure those two hundred people in our squadron are doing what they're supposed to be doing. We're the ones who are responsible for the failures and get the accolades for the success. It's a very stressful job."

"So when we go out on the town," Jake continued with a wry smile, "there's a lot of steam that needs releasing, especially doing this out at sea. If anything goes wrong, it's a big deal. If our people don't do what's right in-country, innocents die and we're ultimately responsible for that."

Intake said, "And we all know our values are aligned because after being at sea for a hundred days and being within a thousand feet of each other, we still end up at the same Irish bar at whatever port we're in!"

"Buying each other drinks," Topper added. Everyone laughed; a legendary camaraderie exists among air groups and within squadrons—and particularly between skippers.

With light hearts, they began talking about the generations of aviators who'd experienced the same thrills of flying, the same boredom at sea, the wild port calls around the world—often at the very same establishments. Every year, the generations collide at Tailhook, a cherished albeit somewhat infamously raucous gathering of naval aviators from past and present. The conference presents a chance to renew old friendships made during long deployments, and it offers opportunities for aviators to connect across decades. The COs in the room with me that evening particularly appreciated meeting the veterans of World War II and hearing the firsthand accounts of Midway, the Marianas Turkey Shoot, and the Pacific island campaigns.

"When those World War II guys see your flight suit, they just want to talk with you," Jake explained. "Sometimes they have to get close to see your wings because their eyesight is so bad. But you grab them and sit down with them—they're part of history. It's unbelievable what these guys did. They'll tell you about their missions at Midway like they were yesterday. You won't find a sharper group of people because they always had that inquisitive nature and they just kept going. Their minds are steel traps and if you look into their eyes, there's a gleam in them. The same gleam we have in ours."

"It's the same brotherhood," Beav said. "They were out on a ship months at a time, going into ports blowing off steam. They were doing the same things sixty years ago that we're doing today so we have that common bond."

Naval aviators are elite and their bonds particularly special. As the skippers explained, there are 335,000 men and women in the United States Navy—one tenth of one percent of the U.S. population. Out of that number, 55,000 are serving on our nation's eleven aircraft carriers. Of those, only 1,000 to 2,000 are active aviators.

"That is truly elite," stated Topper. "And then consider the fact they do it for a pittance when it comes to monetary reward. It humbles each of us in here to be a custodian of a squadron with history and tradition and those types of people. We're part of an enduring institution."

These skippers were smart guys and many of their civilian friends worked for investment banks, businesses, and law firms. While they might indeed work long hours, those friends at least went home to their families on most nights. And their salaries—their monetary rewards, to use Topper's language—far outstripped the salaries these senior officers earned while they were spending months away from their families, overseeing two hundred people and $500 million worth of aircraft, and flying dangerous missions over hostile territory. But here's the thing: the skippers didn't care.

These aviators love what they do. They love *why* they do it, and they love *who* they do it with. They wouldn't even consider trading places with their high-salaried civilian friends. In all the squadrons I visited, among COs, officers, and enlisted crew alike, I found a refreshing breed of people who aren't motivated by money. Instead, they quietly devote themselves to service, each other, and executing the orders of their commander in chief.

"Our junior officers are brilliant," said Jake. "They could get out and go make millions on Wall Street. Maybe they will one day. Until they do, they have the best job in world."

"But we don't talk about that very often," Topper said. "We take humility seriously in all aspects. Intake was just recognized by the American Legion with the Valor Award for a close air support mission he flew that helped out an assault team on the ground. He suppressed enemy fire and allowed the friendly forces to escape without any casualties. But he wouldn't tell you that. I'm his roommate, I will. We're all forty years old and we still have roommates!"

Suddenly, Topper's face dropped when another plane slammed into the deck above us—he was watching on the monitor. The roar of jets again filled the room. Laughter burst from the other COs seated across from me and they pointed to the television screen. I turned just in time to see another EA-6B Prowler from VAQ-140 flying off the deck after missing the arresting cables.

Topper shook his head and Intake mercifully ended his friend's humiliation by turning to me and offering to take me topside to watch his squadron's planes practice strafing runs. I'd learned that aviators and crew members never stop training. Every day of their cruise they are running drills and practicing their skills, getting better each day.

"You're about to see the greatest leveling field of all time," JT said as Intake handed me a pair of night-vision goggles (NVGs). "Regardless of where we went to school, where you got a degree, you get your foot in the door at Pensacola and you're all on the same playing field. From the number one guy at Annapolis to a B student at the University of Florida—Go Gators—they put you in an airplane, tell you how to fly it, and everyone has an equal chance.

"As you rise up through the ranks, if you can't put it on the deck of a carrier at night, when the deck is moving, in bad weather, jet not functioning properly, it doesn't matter where you came from, who your dad is, or who you know. It's just you and your skills. It's the greatest leveling field ever devised."

Intake guided me down the oh-three level port corridor toward the stern, and then we opened a metal door. We stepped outside the ship's skin onto the metal decking that girds much of the carrier. Black water hissed along below us as the hull sliced the smooth sea. The flight deck was directly above us, and was almost completely dark. We waited momentarily for our eyes to adjust and then walked up several steps to the flight deck itself. The absence of moonlight let millions of stars shine in the dark Arabian sky, providing just enough light to see the *Ike*'s bridge in the distance. We were very much alone, hundreds of miles away from land, thousands of miles away from home.

The Landing Signal Officer (LSO) platform hangs over the port side of a carrier, almost at its stern. That night, eight officers in flight suits and reflective float coats crowded it, making sure the deck was ready to recover the aircraft safely. An LSO from each squadron would have their pilots confirm their fuel state as aircraft entered the last two miles of the pattern, and then they stood by to help in case the jet drifted out of the groove on approach. At three-quarters of a mile from the ship, pilots would call the ball, indicating they could see the directional Fresnel lens, which uses a system of bright lights to help inbound pilots hone their final approach. The lens sits on the port side of the ship and has an amber ball of light that floats along a vertical axis, crossed by a row of bright green lamps. If pilots approach too high, the amber ball appears above the row of green lights. If they approach too low, the "meatball" drops below the greens, indicating an aviator needs to apply more power. Aviators block out weather, moving decks, and all else; they focus on keeping the ball aligned with the green lights from the time they call it until they're safely aboard. It's called flying the ball.

Pilots haven't always had the Fresnel lens, and once relied much more on direction from their fellow aviators. Since the early days of aviation, LSOs—often called "paddles"—have helped carriers expeditiously and safely recover their planes. Kenneth Whiting, the executive officer of the navy's first aircraft carrier, the USS *Langley*, began occupying the aft port section of *Langley* during aircraft recovery and used his body language to help pilots land safely. Rumor holds that he snatched a seaman's floppy white cap to use as the first paddle. By World War II, every carrier in the fleet had an officer stationed on their aft port quarter, using his arms, legs, and two hand-held paddles to communicate with inbound pilots—helping them know if they were approaching too fast, too slow, too high, or too low. Often tanned, shirtless, and wearing shorts, many World War II LSOs brought tremendous personality to carrier landing operations with unique routines that involved riotous body language that pilots came to love and trust. Even as telephones and radios have replaced the grand gestures and wooden paddles of earlier generations, the nickname has remained, as have the legends. First among them: the late John "Bug" Roach. Bug served eight tours as an LSO and cared as much for promotion as Hoser Satrapa, his East Coast counterpart in tailhook lore—which is to say he cared very little. He loved flying, his fellow flyers, and recovering aircraft. Returning pilots always took solace in hearing Bug's voice over the radio, and seeing his moustache, steel-toed cowboy boots, and stogie as they flew over the ramp. Still today, aviators widely consider Bug the navy's best LSO ever.

———

That night in the Arabian Sea, Intake and I stood on the *Eisenhower*'s LSO platform, looking into the dark night. He pointed off the port side and asked, "Do you see them?"

I noticed two stars moving across the sky: two inbound Hornets from his squadron, the VFA-83 Rampagers. We both donned the NVGs and the fighters became momentarily lost in the vast, twinkling array of stars that the goggles revealed. The goggles trapped every bit of available light and for the first time, I could see every single star in the sky. I'd never witnessed anything like it.

"Pretty unreal, eh?" Intake asked. "Imagine seeing it when you're alone in a cockpit at forty thousand feet.

"Now here come our guys. See 'em?"

Through the goggles, I watched two Hornets hustle toward the ship's wake then dive at an angle. A bright stream of tracers shot from their 20 mm nose cannons and tore into the wake all around the floating target. A hit. The planes pulled out of their dives and thundered away back into the night to get into the pattern for another round. Jets from Jake's VFA-143 Pukin' Dogs and from the VFA-103 Jolly Rogers followed, one sending a string of bright concussions across the surface as the pilot laid a series of practice bombs into the wake.

In between passes, Intake took off his goggles and turned to me. "You know, we talked a lot downstairs about mission and duty and what we do. As for why we go, there are good men and women on the ground who are trying to uphold the rights of humanity. That's why we do it. That's why we're out here practicing in the pitch-dark in the Arabian Sea. That's why we fly six hours over Pakistan and orbit day in and day out, day and night— because there are some things that are just right."

He paused then said, "And if I'm not willing to lay it on the line to protect the lives of those soldiers and marines—and the lives and way of life of my family back home—then who is?"

With that thought in my mind, I turned back toward the black sea and watched the exercises continue until the LSOs resumed recovering the planes, guiding them through the dark night to the tiny strip of light that was the only refuge for hundreds of miles.

Almost every pilot I'd met mentioned night landings. Most proudly noted that while several nations conduct carrier operations, only the United States conducts them at night. Nothing drives aviators' pulse rates higher than being on final approach over a dark sea, often with no horizon as reference. In that case, instruments alone guide them in for landing. If the instruments malfunction, the task becomes exponentially more difficult and dangerous.

That's exactly what happened to Lt. Nicole "Bad Dog!" Johnson. The VFA-143 aviator's lighted heads-up display (HUD) failed during the exercise. In the dark of night, her other instruments were of little use. It wasn't a catastrophic failure, but it robbed her of the familiar, safe routine so important during a night landing. She had two options: land the plane back on the carrier or eject. There was no alternate place to land.

A squadron mate joined up with her and she flew off his wing, trusting his flying and instruments to set her on the right glide slope. From there, the LSOs coached her toward the ship until she saw the "ball"—the Fresnel lens. She adjusted her throttle and flaps to keep the bright amber light aligned with a horizontal row of green lights. Trusting the ball and her experience, Nicole flew steadily through the last mile of darkness and across the stern. The lights of her jet streaked by the LSO platform at 140 miles per hour. Her wheels found the deck and her hook snagged the number three wire, right on target. Her twin engines roared and their orange eyes burned fiercely as she powered up. Then they quickly faded as the arresting cables pulled her to a stop. She pulled the throttle back to idle and followed the glowing wands of a plane director as he led her away from the landing area.

"Apparently the air crew had bets on me breaking the jet tonight—and somebody won!" Nicole said later that night to our table in the Eisenhower Grill, otherwise known as the forward wardroom. Nicole was unwinding after her flight and sharing a midnight meal—called midrats—with Ed Hine and Cameron "Chappy" Douglas of VFA-103 and me. In the relaxed postflight atmosphere, she could laugh. She'd made it home.

"At night on the flight deck, I'm never comfortable walking around," she said, taking another bite of the breakfast burrito that the galley had cooked to order. "More often than not, it's so dark that you park, you get out, look around, and wonder where you are! And landing like I did tonight is an entirely different story. Night landings are hard enough—the last thing you need is for your equipment to go on the fritz."

That night was just practice. The next day, Ed and Chappy would fly over real targets in Afghanistan. We left our table around 12:30 A.M. so they could get some sleep.

12

ORDERS TO EXECUTION

THE LAST TIME ED HINE AND I had seen each other, he and his wife Brie were together in Norfolk, three days away from this deployment, which was only now nearing its halfway point. We were now halfway around the world from Virginia. In geography and environment, neither of us could get much farther from home. As we left midrats and walked toward the VFA-103 ready room, he told me about the missions his squadron had been flying.

First, they were long. He and his pilot would spend thirty to forty-five minutes on the flight deck, then launch and fly to the coast of Pakistan. They'd proceed up a corridor known as the Boulevard, which would put them into Afghanistan's airspace an hour and a half later. There, they would find a tanker and fight turbulence and winds to maneuver their fuel probe precisely into the small basket at the end of a refueling line. They'd tank, disengage, and begin circling their assigned area, ready to provide support for soldiers and marines on the ground. Perhaps they would identify buried roadside bombs. They might help a unit see beyond the next ridge or they might unleash their cannon or bombs to get friendly forces out of a jam. Maybe their sheer presence would keep American servicemen and women safe. They might be needed; they might not.

Often, Ed explained, their mission would change several times during a flight and they had to provide unplanned types of support for different units. Their missions had a fluidity that demanded flexibility and on the spot judgment. In their business, you have one chance to make the right decision. You can't call a bomb back to your aircraft.

Regardless of how they supported the troops, they'd refuel twice more, then return down the Boulevard, passing high over Pakistan once again. They'd cross the coastline, fly out over the Arabian Sea, and land on their floating base, often in the dark, always physically and mentally drained.

"We're here to support the guys who are pounding it out on the ground," Ed explained as we walked through the hushed corridors. "If it's something as simple as jet noise overhead that keeps terrorist heads down—well, then, job well done. If we're called on to provide something more dynamic then that's what we'll do, but the bottom line is we're out here to be an extension of the marines, sailors, and soldiers on the ground and become a tool for them to use in the best way they see fit.

"Yes, it's tough to fly these missions and be deployed over here away from our families," he added. "But let's be honest, the job we do is not even close to as hard, dangerous, or dirty as the job that's being done in Helmand, or Kandahar, or any other place in Afghanistan by the guys on the ground."

We reached a door marked with a black flag bearing a white skull and crossbones and the phrase: FIGHTIN' 103. When we opened the door and entered the Jolly Rogers' ready room, the squadron's mascot, a set of real skull and crossbones, grinned at us from its perch atop a tall cabinet. Rumor and tradition hold that the bones belonged to Ensign Jack "Bones" Ernie, an aviator from Fighter Squadron Seventeen (VF-17), the World War II squadron to which VFA-103 traces its lineage. True or not, Bones is a part of the squadron.

"There's been very little excitement on this trip," Cameron confirmed when we were inside. "Lots of time in the air and lots of tanking, but not much action. On a mission, you kinda hope that's something is going down, but then again, if we're not dropping bombs, it means they're getting the job done and they're safe.

"But regardless, these flights are important because of the support that we're able to give to the guys on the ground so that they can accomplish their mission of helping the Afghanis to set up a legitimate government without interference from the Taliban. The type of support we give will vary from flight to flight, but the goal is always to protect the lives of both U.S. and coalition forces who are on the ground by preventing insurgents from interfering.

"I'm here to make a difference and to feel like there is something that I am doing that is worthwhile. Supporting Operation Enduring Freedom definitely falls into that category. Whether I'm here or not, those troops on the ground will still be there, and they will still have to do their jobs. So, while I'm here, I'm driven to provide the best support that I can because later in life I know that will be the thing that I look back on to determine if I made a difference. The answer doesn't lie in bombs dropped, but just in the satisfaction of knowing that the JTACs [forward air controllers on the ground] are appreciative of any help that we're able to give them when we fly overhead."

The day had worn all of us out by this point and the ready room had mostly emptied of other pilots. The passage of footsteps in the hallway outside had slowed to a sporadic trickle as much of the *Ike*'s crew was asleep, trying to get a full night's rest before operations began at a typically early navy hour. We pulled ourselves out of the leather seats and headed for our racks, where the gentle roll of the ship lulled us to sleep.

Nine hours later, I watched the squadron come together to execute American foreign policy. The government's goals resulted in a long chain of orders that had cascaded down through ranks and commands and culminated—as most things in naval aviation do—in launching an aircraft on a mission.

With morning sunshine lighting the deck, I watched three ordnance personnel push a load of bombs from the ordnance elevator near the island toward Aircraft 207—or "Side 207," as jets are often called. The Super Hornet was chained down with its tail hanging over the aft end of the carrier, casting a shadow on the white wake below. The ordies expertly wove their bomb cart through the aircraft moving across the ship's deck. One redshirt pushed from behind while two others—their eyes hidden behind dark goggles—pushed from each side, ensuring the cart rolled straight and the bombs stayed put. Detonators and guidance heads were affixed to each bomb being carried by the team. The bombs were ready for war. Everyone was dead serious.

The redshirts all wore red cranials, dark goggles, dark pants, and gloves. They sweated beneath the heavy clothing and the already blazing Arabian sun. Their long-sleeved red shirts—faded in varying degrees—bore stenciled black letters spelling out an assortment of last names, nicknames, rates, and ranks. In addition, each shirt was marked "VFA-103." They were all part of Fightin' 103, the Jolly Rogers. Aircraft 207 was their jet.

Cameron and Ed would launch for their six-hour mission around 1100 and a rainbow of shirts had converged on the F/A-18F as the squadron's assorted departments each lent their expertise to the preflight process. White-shirted quality control personnel looked over the jet's every surface. Green-shirted airframers were double-checking the repairs they'd been ordered to make to the plane after its last mission. And a young brown-shirted plane captain was overseeing it all.

The ordies rolled their volatile cargo toward the empty pylons beneath the wings of the jet. At the left wing, five redshirts surrounded the bomb cart. Two gripped each side of a Paveway Laser Guided Bomb; a fifth red-shirt gripped the rear. One screamed out a count so his voice would carry over the deck's incessant jet noise: "On three! Raise the weapon!" Then in unison, the crew heaved the weapon onto the jet and secured it to the pylon. Then they added two more bombs to the pylons in the same manner.

Cameron and Ed, the plane's pilot and weapons systems officer, arrived planeside and added the olive and tan of their flight suits to the colors surrounding 207. In their right hands, they each carried green flight bags containing notes, charts, and other articles they'd need during their long flight. Their white helmets, emblazoned with the skull and crossbones insignia of VFA-103, shone in the sun; dark visors hid their eyes.

They spoke with the plane captain and began walking around the aircraft, inspecting both sides and shaking the bombs hanging beneath the wings to ensure they held fast. Cameron checked the 20mm M61 Vulcan cannon in the nose, then climbed up the ladder into the open cockpit. Ed followed, taking his seat in the rear. The aviators strapped themselves in and received a final check from the plane captain. Then the plane captain dismounted and the canopy slowly closed.

The same pageant I'd witnessed AD3 Chelsea Pygott conduct aboard the USS *Harry S. Truman* now commenced on the *Ike*. The plane captain flashed a series of hand signals to the pilot and surrounding personnel. Cameron fired up his jets, one by one at the PC's direction. The plane's control sur-faces flexed until PC and pilot were satisfied that the jet was ready to fly.

The PC handed his plane off to a team of yellow-shirted plane directors who guided the 207 jet from the very stern of the flight deck to Catapult Four amidship, handing guidance from one yellow-shirt to another as the plane rolled forward. When 207 reached the catapult, the last yellow-shirt in the chain expertly guided the Super Hornet's front wheel onto the cata-pult track and coaxed it forward until the tire almost touched the small shuttle that would soon sling the jet down the deck as if it weighed almost nothing. A metal bar protruding from the front landing gear slid over the shuttle and fell into position. The officer in charge of the catapult—the shooter—began his performance, and signaled his men to engage the cata-pult. He stood erect, hands clasped on his chest. Then he smoothly extended his right arm out to his side, palm out toward the stern. At that, the shuttle inched forward and pulled the launch bar tight. An ordnanceman raced to the side of the fuselage to arm the bombs, then scurried out of the way.

The yellow-jacketed shooter spun two gloved fingers in the air, calling for full military power. Cameron complied and pushed forward on the jet's throttle. The engines screamed, drowning out all other noise. The plane bucked against the holdback bar and the catapult's locked piston, which kept it from thundering forward. Final checkers watched the Super Hor-net's flaps, rudders, stabilators, and ailerons flex one last time. When each was satisfied the jet was ready, they crouched on the deck and raised their arm high and held out a thumbs-up sign. From the cockpit, Cameron snapped a salute to the shooter, who promptly brought his heels together and returned the salute smartly. Cameron and Ed held on to the canopy's metal framing and braced for naval aviation's greatest ride. The shooter dropped to one knee and extended his right arm across his body and to the left, toward the stern. Then he moved it gracefully from left to right like he was opening a gate. As his arm completed its sweep, his top two fingers pointed directly toward the bow of the *Eisenhower*. He stopped and raised his forearm slightly, as though he'd just fired a pistol.

At that signal, a crew member opened a valve and scalding steam from the ship's reactors rushed into the space behind the catapult's piston. The pressurized steam—precisely measured for each plane and its load—hurtled the catapult shuttle down its track with incredible force and speed, dragging the bomb-laden Super Hornet along with it. Pilot and WSO were slammed back into their seats as they accelerated along with their jet. Less than three seconds after the catapult engaged, Cameron, Ed, 2,000 pounds of arms, 17,000 pounds of gas, and 33,000 pounds of airplane leapt off the deck at 160 knots and began rising over the ocean, bound for the war in Afghanistan.

Since the days of Operation Desert Storm—now usually called the first Gulf War—thousands of naval aviators like Ed and Cameron have launched off American carriers to follow their orders and execute missions over the Middle East. They've enforced no-fly zones, supported multinational forces, and kept both Iraq and Iran in line. Ten years after coalition forces expelled Iraqi troops from Kuwait, masses of American aircraft once again darkened the sky over the Middle East.

Just eight days after Al Qaeda terrorists hijacked four airliners and attacked the Pentagon and World Trade Center on September 11, 2001, then-Captain Rich O'Hanlon stood on the bridge of the aircraft carrier *Theodore Roosevelt* as she and Carrier Air Wing One were pushed away from the pier at Naval Station Norfolk. The entire world watched his departure, knowing his carrier and her strike group were sailing to war. His sailors manned the rails with expressions more serious than usual as the ship left Norfolk, passed through the mouth of the Chesapeake Bay, and cruised into the open Atlantic. As his flight deck began receiving the aircraft of Air Wing One off the Virginia coast, Captain O'Hanlon watched his crew work with a sense of purpose greater than he'd never seen. *TR* had pushed up her deployment and was rushing to Afghanistan to avenge the September 11 attacks and destroy Al Qaeda's nesting grounds.

As the carrier strike group transited the Mediterranean, the captain heard about a Yankee Stadium rally held by New York City mayor Rudy Giuliani and New York State governor George Pataki. At the rally, the pair unveiled an American flag that FDNY firefighters had raised over the smoldering ruins of the World Trade Center—a moment captured in one of the decade's most famous photographs. They promised the gathered New Yorkers that they would send the flag to the U.S. Navy.

"Well, the flag wound up on the *Theodore Roosevelt*," said Rich O'Hanlon nearly ten years later; he had earned the rank of rear admiral and presently commanded all naval air forces in the Atlantic. "We were in the Mediterranean at the time, doing warp speed to the Suez Canal. We knew the flag was coming. It came aboard on the COD and the package came down to me in the captain's port cabin. When we opened it, I remember the smoky smell coming from the flag. The flag then made the rounds to all the ready rooms and spaces on the ship so people could see it."

The next day, the captain arranged a rally on the flight deck. The climax came as the *TR*'s firefighters passed the World Trade Center flag from the flight deck, up the ladders inside the island, to the mast. There, firefighters attached it to the halyards and began raising it. As the *TR*'s firefighters ran the flag high up the ropes, the captain heard singing from the crew. It grew louder. Spontaneously, the men and women of his crew had begun to sing the national anthem, "The Star-Spangled Banner." For captain and crew alike, it was an amazing and unforgettable moment.

A week later, *TR* launched her first combat sorties against the Taliban. The ship began flight operations at 10 P.M., under the dark sky. As pilots and crew maneuvered bomb-laden jets onto the catapults for launch, they looked up at the mast where a spotlight shone on the World Trade Center flag, reminding each man and woman of their purpose that night.

Since aircraft from the *Enterprise, Carl Vinson*, and *Theodore Roosevelt* began launching strikes against Afghanistan in 2001, and since *Abraham Lincoln* (on a record 290-day deployment) launched the early strikes against Iraq in 2003, navy aircraft have flown tens of thousands of missions in support of U.S. or coalition forces on the ground in those two theaters. The *Lincoln* alone launched more than sixteen thousand sorties during her long deployment, mostly over Iraq. Carriers based on both the East and West coast of the United States have made the long voyage to the Arabian Sea to take their turn fighting the war on terror, and most carrier aviators on active duty today have either flown over one of those two countries or supported those who have. The dogfights promised by *Top Gun* never materialized for these aviators, but their missions have helped countless servicemen and women live to fight another day—and live to see their families once again. Regardless of the sometimes contentious politics of the two wars, every person aboard the ship wants to protect their brothers and sisters in arms.

It wasn't just men and women supporting our troops, however. In a time-honored tradition of passing time and building morale at sea, the Pukin' Dogs of VFA-143 flew with one of history's most versatile aviators, call sign "Fighting Fish," or simply "Fish." The brilliantly blue Siamese fighting fish (betta splendens) logged hundreds of hours in Ziploc bags and plastic jars during the USS *John F. Kennedy*'s 2001–2002 Arabian Gulf deployment, and helped provide battle-weary aviators with the relief and levity so necessary in their high-stress occupation.

F-14 veteran Captain Calvin "Goose" Craig was skipper of the Pukin' Dogs during the deployment and he remembered first discovering the fish as it swam leisurely in a plastic jar on the duty desk in the VFA-143 ready room.

"What the hell is a fish doing out here?" he asked the junior officers, the energetic under-thirty lieutenants and lieutenants (junior grade) who were behind the stunt.

The JOs informed the skipper that the fish had become the squadron's new mascot; its blue color matched 143's colors perfectly. Craig considered his JOs an extremely tight and spirited group, so he let it go. Then the fish began appearing at various squadron and air wing meetings.

"I said, 'There's no way that's the same damn fish! Are you guys mailing them in? How are you getting them aboard ship?'"

"No sir," the JOs replied to then-Commander Craig. "It's the same fish."

"Then one day I go into the ready room and there's the fish," Craig said. "And they have a log book for him! I asked, why does the fish have a log book."

"He's got flights."

"The fish has flights?"

"Of course."

"Who takes the fish flying?"

"Everybody takes the fish flying!"

"Well, the fish is not supposed to be flying. Keep that fish out of the aircraft!"

"Roger that, skipper."

"I might as well have ordered them to fly it every single hop because next thing I know, the JOs say, 'Skipper, come on down to ready room—there's cake and ice cream.'

"What for?"

"It's the fish's hundredth trap!"

"That fish is *still* flying? I thought I told you guys to knock it off."

"Well, skipper, everybody really likes the fish . . ."

Indeed they did. The fish went flying with every squadron in the air wing. It flew in F-14 Tomcats, it flew in E-2C Hawkeyes and EA-6B Prowlers; it flew in now-retired S-3 Vikings, it flew in the Seahawk helicopters, and it flew in F/A-18 Hornets. And the fish's flights were well documented. A video tribute to this smallest of aviators was screened to tremendous laughs at Foc'sle Follies, the carrier's comedy show. The fish became *JFK*'s biggest celebrity. The Fighting Fish remains a legend to this day, and it symbolizes the fun-loving spirit that infects young aviators when they're at war, at sea, and far from home. That spirit builds the camaraderie they need to function as a team and manage the weighty stress of combat.

War is a serious business, often brought about by leaders of an older generation, yet always fought by warriors of a younger one. Among the many warriors who have executed the orders of their commander in chief in combat is Jay Consalvi.

As long as he can remember, Jay wanted to fly jets—specifically the Grumman F-14 Tomcat. He now ranks among those fortunate few who have achieved that dream—and lots have dreamt it. But Jay should never have made it into a Tomcat cockpit at all. He wasn't supposed to be alive. A week before he turned seventeen, July 4, 1997, a friend accidentally shot him in the face. The .40 caliber hollow-point bullet smashed through his teeth, mouth, and throat, slicing through an artery on its way. At first the doctors didn't expect Jay to survive, but he fought back and recovered fully, his dream of naval aviation driving him. His progress amazed the doctors but they refused to endorse the flight physical he needed to attend the Naval Academy and fly. Again, Jay didn't give up and he found a physician who shared his optimism. Jay was cleared to apply to the Academy and pursue aviation.

He graduated in 2002, excelled in flight school, and joined the second-to-last class of aviators to train on the F-14 Tomcat, which was retired in 2006. When he arrived in the fleet, his squadron mates learned about his harrowing gunshot experience. Naturally, they immediately assigned him the call sign "Faceshot."

The USS *Harry S. Truman* took her turn as the carrier supporting Operation Iraqi Freedom in the late fall of 2004, and her strike group arrived in the Northern Arabian Gulf on November 20. The Swordsmen of Fighter Squadron Thirty-Two (VF-32) had embarked aboard the ship with their complement of aviators, maintainers, and twelve F-14 Tomcats. Jay joined them for his first combat cruise, along with a film crew that recorded his story in the acclaimed documentary *Speed and Angels*.

He flew routine support missions over the oil rigs, streets, and deserts of Iraq for his first month on station, gaining experience, getting comfortable in his jet, and becoming accustomed to the routine. On December 29, 2004, the daily drill began as usual. The same plane directors guided his Tomcat—designated Vicious 4-6—into position. The same ordnanceman armed Jay's bombs and guns, and the same shooter signaled him to burn the big engines at full military power. At the shooter's direction, the catapult slung his jet down the deck and tossed him into the sky just as it had on every other mission.

Then as they patrolled northern Iraq, Jay and his RIO—Dean "Demo" Castillo—received a call from an air controller who redirected Vicious 4-6 to the city of Mosul. Americans were in trouble.

Jay and his wingman arrived over a street in Mosul where roadside bombs had pinned an Army Stryker Brigade convoy. Bombs had destroyed the first and last vehicles in their column of rolling armor, effectively blockading the roadway. The remaining trucks had stopped, the men were taking blistering fire from all sides, and they had no escape route. The Strykers returned fire as they tended to the wounded and established what defenses they could. Their radioman called in friendly and hostile positions to the inbound Tomcats, and Jay and Demo looked down at the muzzle flashes when they arrived overhead. The aviator and RIO had to make sure they knew which were friendly. Some they could identify easily enough—hostiles were the ones firing at them from rooftops; tracers from their weapons flashed by the Tomcat's canopy. Luckily the Tomcat crews didn't see any shoulder-launched surface-to-air missiles, which are far deadlier than AK-47 rifles.

The Strykers were embedded in an urban environment with buildings all around them; some likely had civilians inside. Jay listened to the frantic calls and directions coming over his radio and did his best to evaluate the situation. It was a scenario that would challenge even an experienced pilot. Jay had only a month of combat experience, and now he would have to make a low attack, under fire, in tight quarters where an imprecise string of bullets from his 20mm cannon could kill his fellow Americans or innocent civilians, including children. But he knew that if he didn't help the soldiers on the ground, nobody would. He took a deep breath and rolled in, cleared hot, cleared to drop ordnance.

At three thousand feet, Jay pulled up without shooting. He didn't like the lineup. More precisely, he couldn't stop thinking about how close the friendlies were to the insurgents—and he would be shooting a cannon from 3,000 feet while flying at nearly 500 knots. Calmly, Demo focused him: "Dude, we gotta make it happen."

Vicious 4-6 rolled in again and began his strafing run, coming in at "angels three"—3,000 feet.

"I pulled the trigger," Jay said, "and there's absolute silence on the radio. My heart just absolutely sinks. I just killed the good guys. I'm thinking, 'What did I just do?'

"Then the guy on the ground screams, 'Good guns, sir! Good guns! We need an immediate re-attack, they're still firing!' "[1]

With renewed confidence, Jay brought the big fighter into a tight turn and lined up for another run. He unleashed a stream of bullets then pulled out.

Suddenly, Demo shouted into the radio: "Break left!"

"I pulled the stick and let go and at the same time I dumped out a bunch of [decoy] flares from the back of the airplane," Jay said. "They had shot a surface-to-air missile at us that I never even saw.

"I looked back and it blew up about a quarter mile behind the airplane. You could see this spiral smoke trail that went up. I'm convinced that if Demo hadn't called 'Break left,' I wouldn't have put the flares out and I think that missile probably would have hit us."[2]

After recovering from the shock of the SAM attack, Jay and his wingman made four more strafing runs, but the insurgents hadn't stopped attacking the Strykers. Most of the fire came from one building on the west side of the street. The Strykers requested help and Jay suggested using a laser-guided bomb. The men on the ground agreed and took cover. Demo lit the targeted building with a laser from their F-14 while their wingman began his attack run. The second F-14's laser-guided bomb picked up Demo's laser, the pilot released it, and it flew true.

"There wasn't any more gunfire that came from that building that day," Jay said. His voice held a touch of sadness. Taking life wasn't easy.

But the Americans on the ground were safe. They could continue their mission of securing Mosul and restoring order to Iraq. The navy had played its part and the orders that had transited the long chain of command had been executed on the battlefield by a young pilot who stepped up under pressure to perform his duty.

When the time arrived for me to leave the USS *Dwight D. Eisenhower*, a petty officer ushered me out onto the flight deck and toward a COD that was waiting with its propellers already spinning—I was running late. I jumped onto the back ramp and it immediately began to close. Once in my rear-facing seat, I fastened my shoulder straps and felt the plane taxi to one of the forward catapults. Minutes later, the turbines powered up, the propellers increased their pitch, and the plane shook with vibration. I knew the shooter was directing the pilot to flex his control surfaces and gun his engines. I imagined the salute between pilot and shooter that was taking place. I imagined the shooter pointing his arm toward the bow like he was aiming a pistol. Suddenly, I lurched forward harshly, the nylon straps digging into my shoulders. About two and a half seconds later, I was thrown back into my seat as the catapult shuttle slammed into the bow and slung us off the *Eisenhower* at more than 140 knots. Through the small window on the plane's right side, I saw a clear sky and a blinding expanse of the Arabian Sea stretch out below us.

As we flew back to Bahrain from the *Eisenhower*, I thought about what I'd found in the Middle East—and the other visits I'd had with the people of naval aviation. Whether they were just starting their careers in Pensacola, working flight decks in a combat zone, or leading squadrons and fleets, these men and women understand something far deeper than a set of orders. They understand the pure ideal of citizenship that many have forgotten. They are making sacrifices on behalf of their country. They are serving their fellow citizens—even though many of those citizens at home will never fully understand the sacrifices being made on their behalf.

I remembered a radio interview with a former presidential cabinet secretary that I'd heard. "We don't really know what to do as citizens," the former secretary said flatly, speaking about Americans. "Our sense of efficacy as citizens and the practice of citizenship is almost completely gone."[3]

I wondered where he'd been—apparently not the same places as I had. He must not have seen Chelsea Pygott or Chief José Joseph at work aboard the *Truman*. He clearly hadn't seen sailors loading bombs onto planes in the thick, hot air of the *Eisenhower*'s flight deck. I hoped he wouldn't share his opinions with the thousands of young men and women who volunteer to put on a navy uniform and lay their life on the line for their country.

With every new person I met and with every post I visited, I grew more impressed by the school of citizenship run by the United States Navy. When he made his nineteenth-century observations about America's young republic, the French philosopher Alexis de Tocqueville wrote about the associations and "schools of democracy" that developed the citizens our form of government required. To function well, the American republic needs individuals who willingly serve one another and sacrifice for the greater good. I'm sure Tocqueville never imagined the U.S. Navy as a school of democracy, and perhaps it wasn't in the early 1800s. Today, however, he would see that our naval servicemen and women protect our freedoms while also developing skills and values that serve America well—while they're in the military and, perhaps even more important, when they leave the service. They carry those virtues back to thousands of communities across the country and become living examples of citizenship.

PART FOUR

THE EASTERN SEAS

13

BROTHERS IN ARMS

A VIOLENT WAVE OF WHITE snow curled over Ensign Jesse Brown's F4U Corsair as the blue plane's long fuselage slammed into the mountainside and plowed through the deep snow that covered the barren, windswept peaks near Somong-ni, North Korea. Ice and frozen ground beneath the powdery snow quickly stopped the plane's big thirteen-foot propeller, then wrenched it from the engine in a cacophony of ripping metal. As the propeller flipped away from the charging plane, the ground caught the Corsair's skidding nose and bent its body thirty-five degrees to the right. Inside, the twenty-three-year-old pilot took the jarring blows like a rodeo rider who was strapped to a champion bull. When the ride finally stopped, a swath of plowed snow and scarred ground lay in the plane's wake. Quiet fell over the snowfield.

Peace lingered for a moment as Jesse realized he had survived the impact. He was grateful. He took stock of his situation, item by item. He immediately smelled smoke from a fire somewhere in the cylinders, tubes, and wires of the mangled engine—although he couldn't say how near the flames were to his 237-gallon fuel tank.

Then he discovered the crash had crushed the space between the seat, instrument panel, and rudder pedals, pinning his legs. He tried to move them, but only received jolts of pain. He removed his helmet and gloves and attempted to unbuckle the parachute harness that kept him strapped to his seat, hoping to get more leverage to free his legs. The buckles jammed and his gloves and helmet fell into the empty space beneath the platform on which the pilot sat. Those precious accessories now lay out of reach.

Jesse looked up through the cockpit canopy that had slammed shut on impact. He saw his squadron mates circling overhead. He slid back the glass. The comforting sound of friendly propellers overhead poured into the cockpit, followed shortly by subfreezing mountain air. Frigid cold enveloped Jesse like the smoke that seeped up from the smoldering engine. The cold bit his face, numbed his exposed hands, and burrowed toward his body's core though his parka, rubberized immersion suit, sweater, wool shirt, and long underwear. America's first African-American combat naval aviator realized that either his friends would rescue him or he would soon die from fire or frost.

That day on a North Korean mountainside—December 4, 1950—found Jesse Brown thousands of miles and many years removed from his hometown of Hattiesburg, Mississippi. He had grown up in the midsize southern town with his hardworking father and strong-willed mother, who had six children together. Their small shotgun house had neither electricity nor running water. Jesse took his weekly bath in a tin tub, set on the wooden floor. The Great Depression hit when Jesse was five years old. The shock waves of the Wall Street crash found their way to the deep South and cost Jesse's father his warehouse job. Soon the Browns were living as sharecroppers twelve miles outside Hattiesburg. Jesse often helped in the fields. The children walked three miles to school.

Like many African Americans in rural Mississippi, Jesse endured the prejudice that pervaded much of the South in that era. Yet he never let Mississippi stifle his dreams, which included an enduring aspiration to fly. Few people, even within his own family, believed he would ever find his way to a pilot's cockpit. But Jesse never doubted, never became discouraged to the point of surrendering. He worked his way to the top of his high school class then followed the example of his hero, Jesse Owens—a fellow track athlete—and attended Ohio State University. Blacks comprised less than 1 percent of the student body in Columbus and the university had never admitted a black student from Hattiesburg. Undaunted, Jesse applied and earned an acceptance. He packed his bags, headed north, and arrived for classes in 1944.

After completing nearly two years at Ohio State, Jesse learned about the navy's new postwar aviation program and approached a recruiter. First, the recruiting officer told Jesse that flying would prove too difficult, too far above his abilities. When that didn't deter the potential recruit, the officer let Jesse know quite pointedly that the flight training program had never received a black student. As a final obstacle, the recruiter pointed out that Jesse hadn't completed the requisite two years of college. Several weeks later, Jesse traveled to Cincinnati and passed all the required tests, including one that proved he had the knowledge of a college junior.

After that rough beginning, Jesse remained on guard for racism during his navy training; he'd grown up expecting the worst from whites—and often received it. He wondered if instructors would fail him—wash him out—just because his skin was darker than theirs. He knew many midshipmen had never met a black person, particularly one from Mississippi. What would they think of him? What would they say to this sharecropper's son?

When he walked onto the bus that would take him to preflight screening, the driver almost didn't let him board; he thought no black could possibly be reporting for aviation training. The bus eventually deposited Jesse in Glenview, Illinois, and on March 17, 1947, he took his first flight with an instructor. He quickly realized the facility aimed to weed out a good portion of each class, and by that evening, one of his only friends—a white student—had already been dismissed for getting airsick.

On that initial day, Jesse had endured a few snide comments and a good many stares. But his instructor, a Nebraskan named Roland "Chris" Christensen, had gently coached him through it all, both aloft and on the ground. Lieutenant Christensen made a special point of helping the young aviator and on April 1, Jesse made his first solo flight. He qualified on his final check ride at Glenville and by April 10, he had reported to Navy Pre-Flight School in Ottumwa, Iowa.

There, he met his veteran drill instructor, Chief Aviation Ordnanceman C. F. Shaw. AOC Shaw summoned Jesse to his office soon after he reported.

"Brown, I want to tell you that you're not going to get any special treatment here—from me or anyone else," the chief said. "I don't know how you managed to get here and I don't give a damn, though I am surprised. Far as I'm concerned, performance is the only thing that counts whether your skin is black, white, or polka-dot. My job is to test you to the limit."[1]

Jesse understood. And he watched five or six of his white classmates leave each day because they failed the chief's tests. The next weeks saw Jesse learn to swim and meet every challenge thrown at him. By the end of May, he had graduated from preflight training—the first African American to do so. His next stop in the whirlwind tour that seemed to be navy flight training was Pensacola, Florida. He'd been to Pensacola once, with the Glenville basketball team; the all-white team in Pensacola hadn't let him play. Now, he'd be flying navy aircraft and they couldn't stop him.

In the fall of 1947, Jesse began basic flight training along the Gulf Coast, still conscious of his skin and the reactions and looks it occasionally drew. But as Jesse's flights became more demanding, his grades began to falter. Each flight seemed worse than the one before, as his instructor reports showed.

October 8: "Does not use enough right rudder in climbs. Could not line up with runway for takeoff."

October 13: "Makes large corrections in nose attitude during steep turns—chasing the altimeter."

October 15: "Does not apply enough left rudder in approach turn."

October 17: "Made a good takeoff from Corry [Field] but shoved forward on the stick when picking up wheels. Couldn't hold ninety-five knot climb-out. Doesn't use trim tabs enough."

His frustrated instructor, William Zastri, assigned him a new teacher. His slide continued. "Lost excessive altitude in recovery from power-on stall," his new instructor reported. "Poor drift correction . . . Doesn't bank up steep enough in downwind turns . . . Forgot prop pitch in precision landings and hi and lo [sic.] altitude emergencies."[2] For some reason, Jesse's performance continued to decline.

Was the navy intentionally trying to bar him from its select cadre of aviators?

In a letter to his wife Daisy—he kept his wife a secret from the navy since marriage was against regulations for yet-to-be-commissioned ensigns—he leveled with himself and wrote, "I realize I was more worried about being black in a sea of white than I was about flying an aircraft. Every flight I take I discover that my main enemy at this point isn't human; isn't white. It has an engine and wings and rudder pedals and a control stick. It is neutral and waits out there every day for me to handle it properly."

He began realizing that he was making mistakes; nobody was conspiring against him. He tried to focus, tried to improve his marks, but it was almost too late. He received a letter from the training wing's personnel review board on December 4. It was the dreaded summons that often heralded the end of an aspiring aviator's flying career.

"To the Student," the letter began. "In view of your difficulties in flight training to date, you are herewith handed your flight record in order that you may answer the following questions . . ."

The first was, "Have you any complaint or criticism to make concerning your treatment or training?"[3]

Jesse thought back on his training, remembering a handful of bad encounters with narrow-minded people. He'd let those incidents distract him. Then he considered his flights and the sophomoric errors he'd made. He began to realize that his instructors and classmates had accepted his color— the *navy* had accepted his color. They just weren't accepting his poor flying. This was his fault, he finally understood. The navy had been fair.

"No," he wrote in response to the question.

When he appeared before the review board, Jesse tried to explain his mistakes but the presiding officer seemed ready to end his short aviation career that night. Then William Zastri spoke up. The instructor who'd given Jesse so many down marks testified that he saw promise in his former student. He urged the board to give Jesse more time—and mercifully, they did. Jesse responded with renewed focus. An instructor soon wrote, "Good hop. This student has the makings of a fine pilot."[4]

Jesse progressed into the later phases of flight training and continued redeeming his low marks with solid performances. In June, he earned his carrier qualification. He was ecstatic. His confidence and focus had returned. A reinvigorated Jesse Brown received his wings of gold on October 21, 1948—becoming the first African American to complete the navy's pilot training program. Most of his life—all twenty-two years of it—had been dedicated to reaching this moment, achieving this dream. He savored it with his friends and (secretly) with his bride, Daisy.

The following year, 1949, he reported to Fighter Squadron Thirty-Two (VF-32)—the Swordsmen—in Quonset, Rhode Island. He was sworn in as an ensign that April and at last, he and Daisy could lead an open life as a married couple. He began flying the Grumman F8F Bearcat, the newest and fastest fighter in the fleet, and became part of this new family of men who accepted Jesse as readily as their wives welcomed Daisy. In November, a young, handsome pilot named Tom Hudner joined the squadron and Jesse welcomed him aboard. The two could have hardly been more different.

The path Tom followed to VF-32 did not resemble the gauntlet Jesse Brown endured to reach the same place. Tom's father had graduated from Harvard University and Tom himself had attended the prestigious prep school Phillips Academy at Andover, Massachusetts. He spent his summers on the Rhode Island seashore, learning to sail and watching the navy's newest ships cruise in and out of the naval base near Newport. He graduated from the U.S. Naval Academy in 1946 and had known little but boundless opportunity. During their first Mediterranean deployment aboard the USS *Leyte*, the two aviators came to know each other as the squadron shifted from the Grumman F8F Bearcat to the Vought F4U Corsair, but were never the closest of friends. Yet Fate would bring them together in an event that would echo through history.

While the *Leyte* was deployed in the Mediterranean, war broke out in the Far East and the carrier received new orders: return to Norfolk, spend ten days in port, and depart for Korea via the Panama Canal. So in September of 1950, Jesse left his wife Daisy and new baby Pam to sail with the Swordsmen and the *Leyte*, bound for Korea, where North Korean communists had invaded the Republic of South Korea on June 25, 1950. The United States and the United Nations had quickly intervened to help the South. By the time the *Leyte* left for Korea, the North Koreans had almost pushed the United Nations forces into the sea. As Jesse steamed west, however, General Douglas MacArthur executed a daring amphibious landing at Inchon and began herding the communists back into the North, utilizing air cover provided by American carrier-based aircraft.

The Swordsmen of VF-32 and the USS *Leyte* arrived off the Korean peninsula in October of 1950 and took up their watch. Combat missions supporting U.S. and U.N. forces were brutal and cold but routine. The pilots bundled themselves against the frigid cold and often launched before dawn for missions that would end over strategic targets or advancing Chinese and North Korean troops. F4U Corsairs and AD Skyraiders handled much of the close support work, helping ground troops on a scale not previously seen. By the conflict's end, American carriers would launch 346,487 sorties and lose 559 aircraft. Enemy aircraft downed four navy planes while navy aircraft downed thirty-seven of theirs. More than half of the aviators flying in the war were reservists recalled to active duty.

During the conflict only one U.S. Navy aviator became an ace: Lieutenant Guy Bordelon, who flew the F4U Corsair like Jesse Brown. Guy flew from the USS *Princeton* and between June 29 and July 16, 1953, he downed five enemy aircraft, all at night. He split his first four kills evenly between the nights of June 29 and June 30. He flamed Kills Three and Four in such rapid succession that he remembered thinking, "Over so fast?"[5]

Interestingly, Guy almost never graduated flight school. Also like Jesse Brown, he'd struggled. Instead of being shipped to a fleet squadron upon receiving his wings, Guy immediately began instructing new students, which gave him more time to practice and sharpen his aerial skills. In the end, his "plowback" assignment (as in, being plowed back into the training command) paid off.

On October 28, 1950, the *Leyte* sailed to Japan to give her men a well-deserved rest. The respite would be brief however, and on November 4, 1950, navy shore patrolmen rounded up *Leyte*'s crew throughout the port. Liberty had been cancelled.

Chinese troops were massing at the North Korean border, threatening America's foothold on the peninsula. The *Leyte* was sailing back to Korea immediately to help. On Thanksgiving Day, more than 150,000 Chinese troops stormed into North Korea and pushed back the 8th U.S. Army and surrounded some 10,000 marines at the Chosin Reservoir. By the end of November, Chinese armies were pushing American and United Nations forces south along a narrow, frozen road toward the sea. On one side of the road were steep mountains. On the other side were drop-offs and the frozen Chosin Reservoir. The weather and fighting proved equally bitter. Thermometers gave readings of more than thirty degrees below zero. More Chinese died from exposure than from American munitions. Likewise more than half of the U.N. casualties were weather-related. By the campaign's end, more than twelve thousand U.S. and U.N. troops were killed or injured. Chinese casualties were estimated at more than sixty-five thousand.[6] The long retreat was literally marked by bodies, frozen where they fell. For U.S. troops, the only salvation came from above.

Continuing their now-well-practiced role, Skyraiders and Corsairs, including those of VF-32, fended off Chinese ground forces so the retreating column of marines and refugees could reach the safety of the sea.

Around 1:30 P.M. on December 4, 1950, a group of VF-32 fighters launched from the *Leyte* and winged toward the Chosin for another support mission. They flew over the high, rugged mountains and began their armed reconnaissance patrol deep inside North Korea, some seventy miles south of the Chinese border. The Swordsmen flew their Corsairs in four-plane groups, and Jesse flew the third plane in the section leader position. Even though Lieutenant Hudner outranked Ensign Brown, he flew on Jesse's wing as "tail end Charlie." Flight time and experience counted more than anything else among Jesse's fellow aviators.

Tom received a radio call from Jesse halfway into their three-hour mission. A bullet fired from a lucky North Korean sniper below must have found its mark; Jesse's plane was losing oil—far too rapidly for him to reach the carrier. Tom and others confirmed: a trail of vapor streamed from Jesse's plane. His engine wouldn't last long enough to return to the *Leyte* or a land base, so he had one option: a wheels-up crash landing in the snow. Tom helped Jesse find a clearing among the peaks and scrub pines below. Jesse's plane was losing power rapidly and he did his best to aim it toward the field. Tom descended alongside his wingman.

"So he could concentrate on his flying, I called his check-off list," Tom recounted. "Reminding him to open his canopy, which he did, and then to make sure his shoulder harness was locked; if his engine had definitely quit, to shut his magnetos off so if he hit the ground, it'd minimize the chance of it catching fire."[7]

Even with those precautions, Jesse had only a small chance of surviving a crash landing without power and both he and everyone in the squadron knew it.

"When [Jesse] hit the ground, he hit it with such force that the aircraft actually buckled at the cockpit," Tom recalled. "And there was no question in the minds of any of us that he perished in the airplane."[8]

Jesse's squadron mates circled the crash site while their flight leader flew to higher altitude to radio for a rescue helicopter. While he was gone, the other pilots saw Jesse wave from the cockpit; they were all surprised he had survived.

Then Tom spied smoke seeping out from his engine. Despite the fire that had started in his Corsair, however, Jesse still didn't get out. He just waved. Tom quickly deduced that his wingman was trapped inside the cockpit.

Tom knew several things: the rescue helicopter wouldn't arrive for thirty minutes at best, the fire could reach Jesse long before that, and it was strictly against policy to land for a rescue attempt. He didn't think long about his decision. A fellow pilot and squadron mate was on the ground and needed help. He decided to land near Jesse and rescue him. He announced his decision to break policy over the radio and peeled off from the group; he was going after his wingman.

He jettisoned his rockets and ammunition and circled his landing site before bringing his Corsair in for a wheels-up landing. The twenty-six-year-old aviator flew the plane up the hillside's slope with his flaps down. He peered along the side of the Corsair's long fuselage to gauge the rapidly closing distance to the ground, and he tried his best to ease the twelve-thousand-pound plane into the icy snowfield, which was racing beneath him, coming ever closer.

In his smoldering, frigid prison on that North Korea mountainside, Jesse Brown looked up as he heard the roar of a Pratt & Whitney engine close by and overhead. Then he heard his wingman's Corsair strike the mountainside. He listened to the metallic rumbles, groans, and shrieks he had experienced minutes earlier when his own plane struck the ground. Then that awful silence fell again. The only sound came from the still-circling aircraft who would keep the enemy at bay should North Korean troops show up.

Several minutes later, Jesse heard boots slogging through the snow. Then he saw his friend, Tom Hudner. "Tom, we've got to do something to get out of here," he stated matter-of-factly.

"I couldn't believe how calm he was," recalled Tom.

Even with the Corsair lying on its belly, the cockpit remained several feet above Tom's head. He struggled to climb up to Jesse's level, but his boots were caked with ice. The icy gull-shaped wings, which dipped gracefully from the plane's body before rising upward, compounded his challenge; he kept sliding as he stretched for the cockpit. He couldn't find stable footing. Once he finally peered inside the cockpit, hanging on with one arm, he discovered a hornets' nest of problems.

"I could see that his knee was pinned into the side of the fuselage where the fuselage had buckled and slammed his leg into the control panel that we used to straddle," he explained. "He couldn't move it; that's why he didn't get out. He was bareheaded when I got to him because he'd taken his helmet off and he was bare-handed as well . . . By the time I got to him, his fingers were already frozen—just frozen stiff."[9]

Tom quickly placed a wool cap on his friend's head and wrapped a scarf around his freezing hands; it was all he could do. Then Tom turned to the other problems: Jesse's legs and the fire in the engine. He shoveled handfuls of snow on those flames he could reach, thankful the high altitude had slowed the fire's progress. He tried his best to pry Jesse's legs out of the crushed cockpit, but with snow packed onto his boot soles and one arm occupied with just holding onto the cockpit, his efforts were futile. He ran back to his airplane and requested the rescue helo bring a fire extinguisher and an axe.

Overhead, the Corsairs of VF-32 had settled into a pattern, guarding their fellow pilots against Chinese or North Korean troops and simply demonstrating that they wouldn't leave Tom and Jesse. The pair of aviators waited for the helicopter on the mountainside below with Jesse beginning to drift in and out of consciousness. Tom suspected that in addition to the frigid cold, serious internal injuries were also sapping life from the downed aviator. Tom recalled, "During the time—we both knew it was a pretty desperate situation—he said, 'If anything happens, tell Daisy how much I love her.'" Otherwise they said little.

Forty-five minutes after Jesse crashed on the mountain, Marine Corps Lt. Charlie Ward approached the snowy slope in an HO3S Sikorsky helicopter, an ungainly early-generation model that looked more like a bug than an aircraft and had barely enough power for the job. The mission was not without risk. His fellow aviators knew Charlie as an accomplished and respected rescue pilot with extraordinary courage, although he would modestly say in his deep southern drawl, "Ah don't know the meaning of the word 'fear,' not because Ah'm brave, I just don't understand big words."[10]

Bravery aside, he had to cope with his given equipment. The helicopter was designed to carry two people; it would need to carry three. Charlie told his crew chief to stay at the base, knowing the extra weight would certainly stop him from airlifting the two downed aviators. To compound the danger, Charlie knew that this particular helo had a notoriously unreliable engine and if it stopped in the frigid air and high altitude, he doubted it would restart.

The HO3S also lacked working brakes and when he arrived on scene and settled his craft onto the slope, Lt. Ward left the rotor spinning, hoping the force from its rotors would stop the Sikorsky from sliding down the hill, leaving all three men stranded well behind enemy lines as night approached. And Charlie still worried about the Sikorsky's ability to lift three men in the thin mountain air.

He put those worries aside and brought Tom the axe and fire extinguisher he had requested; neither accomplished much good. The axe bounced off the aluminum surfaces and wasn't strong enough to use as an effective crowbar. The small extinguisher only doused the flames that crept closer to the gas tank. Try as they might, they couldn't budge Jesse's legs. Tom considered using his survival knife to amputate the leg, but realized their position and Jesse's rapidly deteriorating condition would make that a useless and needlessly brutal exercise. When they decided against that drastic step, they arrived at the end of their options.

"Even between the two of us there was nothing we could do," Tom said.

Above the scene, Corsairs began peeling off, two by two, having no choice but to return to the carrier before night fell and their gas tanks ran dry. Ward and Hudner watched the fighters depart and huddled out of Jesse's earshot. They simply didn't have the tools they needed. Jesse was beginning to slip away, just like the daylight.

The helicopter wasn't equipped to fly at night. Lt. Ward would have to leave, and Tom knew that neither he nor Jesse could survive the night in those conditions. With the temperatures just five degrees above zero, night descending in hostile territory, and Jesse unconscious and hopelessly pinned inside the plane, Tom had no real choice.

He told Jesse he was leaving to get more equipment, but to this day, remains unsure if Jesse even heard his words. America's first African-American combat naval aviator had fallen unconscious in freezing temperatures. Tom knew he would never wake up.

"We finally had to leave Jesse there," Tom explained. "Both knowing as much as we wanted to, there was no other way to help him out; there was just no other way to do it."[11]

With darkness falling quickly, the helicopter struggled into the thin air and carried a cold, exhausted, and deeply saddened Tom Hudner away from his wingman. He had done his duty and done his best; he could not have done more.

In the last of countless letters he penned to Daisy prior to the crash, Jesse had written, "Knowing that he's helping the poor guys on the ground, I think every pilot here would fly until he dropped in his tracks."[12]

Following the brave example of many pilots before and after him, Jesse had done just that.

On April 13, 1951—four months after that day in North Korea—Thomas Hudner walked into the Rose Garden of the White House, accompanied by his mother. He stood alongside Jesse Brown's wife Daisy as President Harry Truman hung the light blue ribbon and bronze star medallion of the Medal of Honor around his neck.

"I'll never forget it," Tom said, reflecting on that frigid day above the Chosin. "It was one of those things that could have happened to anybody at any time. I've always been very grateful I was able to do what I could at the time. What I think of often is that this was a time [when] we were having a lot of problems integrating the services—and Jesse Brown was going to be the real leader. He went through almost unimaginable hardships going through school, but especially when he got into the navy. We always wondered what he would have turned out to be. So my association with Jesse is something I've always been proud of; to have known a person like that.

"I look back on it now and I feel very proud that I served my country honorably and I like to use my resources any way I can to let people realize what a great organization the navy is and what a wonderful country ours is. Not enough people realize how lucky we are to be Americans."[13]

One man who always seemed to realize his fortunate birthright was

Ronald Reagan. In his forever distinctive voice, the fortieth President of the United States invoked Tom Hudner and Jesse Brown on the campus of Tuskegee University in Alabama during a 1987 speech.

"Now, I would like to tell you that they both made it and that, over the years, [Tom and Jesse] have been best of friends, sharing family outings, caring about one another," President Reagan said as he concluded his address to new graduates. "But that was not to be. Ensign Jesse Brown died on that slope in Korea. When he risked his life for those besieged marines, Jesse Brown didn't consider the race of those he sought to protect. And when his fellow pilots saw him in danger, they did not think of the color of his skin. They only knew that Americans were in trouble."[14]

The following decade, more American warriors—black and white alike—would land in Asia and find themselves in trouble. They too would look to the skies for salvation.

On the night of October 10, 1968, a group of U.S. Navy SEALs walked into a hooch at Nha Be Naval Support Activity Base, a tropical compound crammed onto a tiny point of cleared land along the main shipping channel in the Mekong River Delta. They were in the rich delta farmland of South Vietnam, less than fifteen miles south of Saigon and twenty-five miles from the South China Sea. It was hot; nothing like the frigid cold of North Korea. Even though the sun had gone down, the SEALs still sweated in the thick tropical air. They sat down with one of the naval aviators who shared the base with them: Lieutenant Al Billings of Detachment Two, Helicopter Attack (Light) Squadron Three (HAL-3)—the Seawolves. Nothing about the deadly "Huey" gunships of HAL-3 resembled the rickety and underpowered Sikorsky HO3S Charlie Ward had flown during the previous decade, but they had a similar mission: to save fellow warriors in danger.

Navy SEALs, patrol boat river crews (PBRs were armed thirty-one-foot speedboats that were key parts of the "brown-water navy" that patrolled the Mekong), and Seawolves shared the small beachhead of a base, and they had become a family; to the SEALs and PBR crews, Al was just "Hollywood." He had maverick style, but always had their back. Their units would venture into the Vietcong-infested islands, jungles, bogs, channels, and peninsulas to find Charlie, as everyone called the communist insurgents attempting to take over South Vietnam. ("Charlie" was singular or plural; short for the phonetic Victor Charlie.) Charlie operated among the villages, trees, and fields of the delta and when PBRs and SEAL teams found him, the Seawolves would cover their brethren, rolling in riding Bell UH-1 Iroquois gunships like the cavalry rode horses.

That particular October night, the SEALs brought Al a map and pointed out their next insertion point. They asked Al if he could cover them. One of Seawolf Detachment Two's two helicopters was down for repairs, and Al explained that squadron policy dictated that aircraft couldn't fly alone. And even if he launched single-ship, he'd only have half the firepower of a typical two-ship fire team. The SEALs in turn explained the tides and moon were just right for their operation; they had to go that night. Al promised he'd cover them, as he always did. He would be overhead within ten minutes of their call.

When he called the officer in charge (OINC) to explain the situation, the OINC responded that single-aircraft missions were forbidden without exception. When their discussion ended, however, both men held an unsaid and quite unfriendly understanding that Al would go if called. He was that kind of guy; he always did right by the troops, despite policies if necessary. The OINC despised him for that reason; his men loved him for it.

Before Taps sounded that night, Al gathered his seven-man crew. He explained the situation: "Here's the way it is: squadron policy is not to go out single-aircraft, but if the SEALs get in trouble, I said I'd come get them. I need three other crewmen."

All seven volunteered to go.

The gunners were all enlisted personnel. They had started their careers like Al, and he always had a special love for the young, hardworking petty officers and airmen who flew with him. Al had enlisted at age nineteen and entered the navy's enlisted flight training program. He received his wings of gold and his officer's commission on the same day: June 17, 1966, at age twenty-one.

"I always had an affinity for the enlisted guys because I felt they made me who I was," he said. "As long as I took care of them and they believed in me, they busted their butts. They'd work twenty-four hours a day if they believed in you. They did the field maintenance on all the aircraft, all the maintenance on the guns, did all the logistics loading, ordnance loading.

They'd work around the clock to fix an engine, then they strapped on their armor, hopped in the back seats, and flew with us.

"I took on COs, I took on CAGs, I took on admirals and we always won because of those enlisted guys," he said, referring to his headstrong leadership style, which won him love from his men but earned flack from his superiors. "I challenged them, but my guys backed me up. Just like they did when the SEALs called."

The SEAL team radioed for help around 2:30 A.M. Three team members had sustained severe wounds and Charlie had cut off the return route to their boat. They were in deep trouble. Gunfire and screams punctuated the SEALs' call for help.

Seawolf alert crews slept in their uniforms and boots, and within seconds of the distress call they were rushing through the darkness and heat to their waiting gunship. They were more than awake by the time they leapt into the green Iroquois and started its rotor spinning.

"I loved this kind of shit," said Al. "It was better than sex. Everything was multiplied tenfold. Your hearing, your sense of touch, your smell, everything was heightened. . . . I never felt so alive as when I was scrambled in support of someone in trouble, on a moonless night where you couldn't see your hand in front of your face."

Seawolf Two-Eight slowly lifted off the runway and nosed forward trying to generate enough lift to get its heavy cargo of weapons and ordnance airborne. The modified Huey carried two rocket pods with seven rockets each, twin 30 caliber mini-guns, a lethal 50 caliber cannon, boxes of grenades, and hordes of ammunition. Al packed a 45 caliber pistol for good measure. The gunship cut through the thick, pitch-black night, coordinating with inbound army DUSTOFF rescue helicopters as they went.

"It was like being in a dark closet with no lights," Al described the night. "You couldn't see anything."

Within the promised ten minutes, they were over the SEALs. Al saw the red lights the SEALs were shining straight into the sky so the Seawolves could see their position but Charlie could not. The men on the ground directed Al to a spot two hundred yards away from their lights and he rolled in.

"It was a dark moonless night," Al recalled later. "With our running lights off, all Charlie had to shoot at were our muzzle flashes and the sound of the helicopter. We were maneuvering at 85–95 knots at a thousand feet above the ground. All Charlie did when he fired at us was give away his positions to the door gunners."

The SEALs crackled over the radio, warning Al of the fire the Vietcong were directing at the helicopter.

"It was typical of them," he said. "Pinned down with three wounded and after everything they had just gone through, they were concerned about the Seawolves. It said a lot about the caliber of people they were."

After his passes, the tree line grew quiet and Al turned his attention to a nearby jungle compound where the SEALs suspected the guerillas were based. Again he rolled in, lights off and guns blazing. Tracers began streaking upward from the buildings, painting red lines that crisscrossed the sky; for each tracer the crew could see, there were four bullets they could not. Al doggedly flew through the flack as his gunners bravely stood in the helo's open doors returning fire. Not that it mattered whether a crewman was standing in an open doorway or behind the aircraft's aluminum skin. The skin was so thin, it might as well not have been there. Bullets could pass through as if the metal was paper.

"Every time a bullet hit," Al remembered, "it sounded like a BB puncturing a Coke can." Imagine that happening every few seconds. It wore on the nerves of the crew and pilots. Everyone in the helo had armor plates on their seat bottoms, otherwise they were completely vulnerable. Every time they heard the "pop," they wondered if someone onboard had been hit.

By the time Seawolf Two-Eight had exhausted its fuel and ammunition, the army rescue helicopters were still thirty minutes out. That gave Al's bird time to return to Nha Be for the quickest refuel and rearm he ever had. His rotors never stopped spinning and he was sure he would have been in deep trouble had the safety officer been awake at 3:30 A.M.

When the helicopter returned to the SEALs' position, two army medevac helos were also arriving. All was quiet below until the two army slicks began descending toward the landing zone (LZ). The Vietcong had been waiting for the extraction and suddenly tracers poured out of the woods. The two rescue slicks pulled up and Al dove toward the tree line, with his gunners hammering away. The woods became considerably quieter. On the next go-round, Al proposed leading the slicks into the LZ.

"They seemed to like the idea and rolled in behind me as they made their approach," he said. "I led the slicks in and as soon as Charlie fired his first round, I dumped several more rockets into their position . . . I had time to come around and lay down a few more rockets as the slicks picked up [the SEALs] out of the LZ and departed. They were able to get out of the LZ without taking any hits."

Back at the base, the OINC was nowhere to be found, which was fine with Seawolf Two-Eight. Al knew he'd take heat from the ornery OINC for breaking the squadron's rules and launching single-aircraft. Fortunately, the next day, the SEAL commander paid a visit to the Seawolves' skipper and thanked him for saving his team; this happened before the OINC was able to reprimand Al for disobeying policy and orders. The skipper of HAL-3 instead ordered the OINC to nominate "Hollywood Al" Billings for the Distinguished Flying Cross.

The Distinguished Flying Cross, slightly tarnished with the passing of years, hangs inside a glass case in Al Billings's study. Glints of sunlight from Lake Murray danced across its casing as we sat on his porch watching the autumn sun settle toward the South Carolina pines across the sparkling blue lake. Al's wife Trish had joined us as he finished smoking his daily cigar—a trademark habit he'd had since he first set foot in Vietnam more than forty years ago.

About those first days in-country, he recalled, "I remember reporting for duty and a maintenance officer said HAL-3 had more Purple Hearts [medals for wounds suffered in combat] than any other squadron in the navy!" Al laughed. "I wasn't sure if that was something to brag about! And I wasn't sure what I was getting into."

He was joining what would become one of the most storied units of the Vietnam era. The HAL-3 Seawolves were formed in South Vietnam during 1967 to support operations in the Mekong River Delta. They would be the navy's only attack helicopter squadron to fly in Southeast Asia and they did every job imaginable in the delta—inserting SEAL teams, rescuing wounded or patrols under attack, providing air cover for PBRs—all with the common goal of leaving no man behind. The unit's first leaders had no real models and few resources as they created the squadron. Their first helicopters were secondhand army aircraft with thousands of hours' wear and tear. In the great navy tradition, the Seawolves winged it and during the unit's five years of service, HAL-3 became one of the most decorated navy squadrons of the entire war. Sadly, it also sustained the most casualties: forty-four men died on Seawolf missions into the viper pit that was the Mekong Delta. More than two hundred HAL-3 pilots and aircrew were wounded during their 120,000 combat sorties.

"Our job—the Seawolves' job—was to protect and save lives," Al said as we sat on his porch in South Carolina. "It was more than a job; that's what the Seawolves lived for—to help protect the lives of people who were in trouble. We were a quick reaction force and our main mission was to protect the PBRs or anyone else on the delta if they got in trouble. Usually when a gunship came in with guns blazing, Charlie hauled ass because he knew it was a losing battle. We were the guys who rode in on the white horse. We were the cavalry."

"Now the PBR guys," he segued. "Talk about a bunch of heroes and guys with guts. They'd go out in fiberglass PBRs and they would go up these narrow rivers and tributaries. The rivers would be so narrow that Charlie could just toss a grenade into the boat."

Al knew about the bravery of the PBR crews, and next to the Distinguished Flying Cross in Al's study hung the Silver Star, the third-highest decoration given by the navy. Only the Navy Cross and Medal of Honor rank higher. He took a puff on his cigar and began to tell me the story behind the award. He looked out across Lake Murray, and pointed to a spot in the middle of the channel: "That's about seventy-five yards. That's how wide the river was in the spot where it took place."

"It" was one of the most impressive combat rescue missions flown during the entire war.

On November 8, 1968, one month after his SEAL rescue, Al had one week left on his tour; he had run almost the entire gauntlet of a Mekong Delta deployment and survived. He suited up for a patrol mission that night, and even volunteered to take the nugget seat—the most junior officer's position on a two-ship fire team, which was the left copilot seat of the trail aircraft. He knew the other pilots wanted aircraft command time; he'd trained them and was happy to let them have the controls. He was coasting home.

Upriver, deeper into the always treacherous Rung Sat Special Zone, two

PBRs from River Division 593—the Iron Butterfly—were returning from an operation with a team of commandos and marines. Suddenly, from the dense undergrowth on both riverbanks, Vietcong guerillas sprung an ambush. Rockets slammed into both boats then AK-47 rifle fire erupted. The first rocket injured all five people aboard PBR 755. Seaman Jim Lonsford had taken shrapnel in his throat and after a less wounded Petty Officer Dave White put gauze on the wound, Lonsford laid on the bow pinching his severed artery to stop the blood loss. He couldn't last long. Nor could Seaman Molodow, who had suffered a serious head wound. White applied pressure to keep Molodow's cerebrum inside his skull, then put a bandage around his head. White also gave Molodow his helmet and flack jacket.

The crew of PBR 841 was still functioning after the initial barrage and their radio was intact. They called the base at Nha Be, screaming for help, but they also realized their predicament. They were under extremely heavy fire—too hot for an extraction—and had no nearby LZ. They didn't think anyone could or would save their two dying teammates or their own lives for that matter. They battled back valiantly, hoping for someone to respond.

Al's fire team had lifted off for a routine patrol shortly before the ambush occurred and the radio operator at Nha Be redirected the two HAL-3 gunships to the PBRs' position on the Nga Ba River. When the Seawolves arrived high over the scene, they saw the two PBRs taking heavy fire from both sides of the river.

From the nugget seat in Seawolf Two-Eight, Al radioed the fire team leader in the first helicopter: "We've got to get down there. These guys are bleeding to death."

The team leader responded that the jungles on both sides of the river had no clearings and Charlie controlled them anyway. Nor did the thirty-one-foot PBRs offer any landing options for the much larger helicopters. But the pleas for help continued coming over the radio from the desperate men under fire.

Al turned to his aircraft commander, a higher-ranking officer he had trained. Al calmly said, "I have the aircraft." There was no discussion. Al took over the collective and cyclic controls and nosed the helicopter toward the firefight below. He radioed his fire team leader and told him he was going in. The leader forbade it, but his response was lost on Al. Hollywood was already committed and entirely focused on the job at hand.

Al flew along the right riverbank and unleashed seven rockets, all the while talking with the one functioning PBR, encouraging them to lay down fire. He told the Seawolf fire team leader to do the same. He had ceased to argue by this point and covered Al, bringing his Huey's 50 caliber to bear on the Vietcong. When Seawolf Two-Eight reached the end of its rocket run, Al pulled up and executed a rotor over, a high-banked 180-degree turn that positioned him for a run down the river's other side. He put seven more rockets into the opposing bank.

Then he turned his attention to the disabled PBR where the two most wounded men lay on the deck, their lives slowly ebbing away. From nose to tail the Huey was fifty-four feet long; forty-two of that was the fuselage. With no other options, Al radioed that he was going to land his left skid on the bow of the much smaller PBR. As he settled the helo toward PBR 755, which was adrift with no power, the eighty-knot rotor downwash pushed the boat this way and that until Al could trap it with his skid. Now his challenge was maintaining enough weight on the bow to keep the boat steady and the Huey attached, but not so much that he'd swamp it. Had he been less focused, he would have noticed the noise of bullets pinging off the armor of the PBR and popping through the skin of his aircraft. It sounded like a line of aluminum cans being peppered on a summer camp rifle range. Add to that the sounds of the Huey's thwapping blade, the engines of the other PBR as it raced back and forth providing cover, and the cacophony of weapons fire. It was a perfect nightmare.

Years later, Al reflected, "I don't know how I did it. Don't know how long it was. You just don't know in combat. That's why it's so important that the navy stresses training. When everything else shuts down, the training kicks in and you function like you're supposed to.

"I was totally focused. I'd assessed the positions. I dumped seven rockets where they were firing on one side and put seven down the other side. [Crew chief Petty Officer George] Heddy was keeping the twin 30 cals going and loading cans of ammo one box after another into both guns without letting up on the right bank. I knew there were a lot of bullets flying around but I had to be so focused on my mission. I didn't think about it.

"[Gunner Airman Glen] Smithen, the kid climbing down into the boat to rescue the PBR guys with the bullets flying everywhere, he commented that he drank himself to sleep that night and for two weeks after. That's what I consider a real hero because he was petrified but overcame the fear and did the job anyway."

Glen Smithen was indeed terrified, but resigned himself to his duty. "My biggest fear was that Mr. Billings was going to use my side to pull [the wounded] into the chopper," Smithen recalled later, "and I was correct. At this point I was completely terrified and just knew we weren't going to survive the mission. I was only twenty years old at the time and didn't want to die in Vietnam. In our favor was our pilot, Hollywood Al Billings. If I had to do it, I wouldn't want to attempt it with any other pilot. He was amazing at his job and I always had the utmost confidence in his abilities and judgment.

"As we approached the PBR, the gunfire started increasing in intensity but we all stayed focused on our task. Mr. Billings steadied the chopper next to the boat and placed the skid on the deck. At that point, I jumped out and grabbed the first wounded and literally tossed him into the chopper. Bullets were hitting all around us as I grabbed the second wounded soldier and tossed him into the helo. My guess was they both weighed between 180 to 200 pounds, but my adrenaline was so charged it was like lifting a small child. I jumped back into the chopper with gunfire still ringing around us and we flew off.

"The first wounded sailor was wounded in the neck with blood pumping out at a steady flow. I applied pressure to stop the flow. The second sailor was wounded in the head and I honestly thought neither was going to survive."[15]

The heavily armed Seawolf gunships flew at more than one thousand pounds above weight limits, so when Smithen had recovered the wounded and Al disengaged from the PBR, he didn't have enough power to get the bird airborne, especially with four hundred extra pounds of body weight. The Huey lifted off the bow, then settled its nose into the water as Al dipped forward to gain power and get away. Water began collecting in the chin bubble, adding even more weight to the problem.

"I didn't have enough power to really get airborne," he said, "but I wasn't staying there because Charlie was trying to get us! So I headed off downstream like a motorboat . . . The skids were in the water, the chin bubble was pushing water around like a boat. I was pulling power trying to get the water to drain out of the chin bubble. I finally got airborne, drained the water out, held it level, and we were able to get back."

En route to the Army Third Field Hospital in Saigon, Heady and Smithen rendered aid to Lonsford and Molodow, both of whom were still bleeding and fading rapidly. Al radioed ahead to the hospital and told them what to expect. When Seawolf Two-Eight landed, yet another set of men was ready to do their best to save the PBR sailors. Many elements, many heroes, and a few broken rules had combined to pull off the rescue, but as Al put it, "Both the guys lived, which is the bottom line."

That wasn't the bottom line for the officer in charge, whose direct orders Al had disobeyed by attempting the rescue. When he returned to Nha Be, Al suffered quietly through a berating diatribe. He left the OINC's office thinking he'd lose his wings. The *Navy Times* picked up the rescue story, however, and two days later, the squadron's commanding officer ordered the still-fuming OINC to nominate Lieutenant Al Billings for the Silver Star.

"River Division 593 and the river patrol force recognize Glen and Al and the Seawolves as warriors and heroes for what they did for us," said PBR veteran Ralph Christopher. "Patrolling the Rung Sat Special Zone—Forest of Assassins—was very dangerous and many sailors were lost fighting there protecting ships carrying important cargoes to Saigon, and the number would have been much higher if not for the Seawolves overhead and men like Glen and Al that braved the many dangers and were not afraid to come to our aid and support us, even under fire. We commonly called them the cavalry of the sky and they were some of the heroes of my youth."

Wars and military service may begin with high aspirations and strategic goals, but often, they become about brothers in arms. Those in the field fight and bleed for one another. Al couldn't care less about his commendations; in fact, he told the OINC as much. Nor did Tom Hudner break protocol to rescue Jesse Brown because he wanted a medal or thought the rescue would advance a strategic objective; he wasn't sacrificing himself and his Corsair to take out a fortress or vital target. Tom and Al became heroes because they did their best to take care of their fellow warriors; from loyalty came bravery. When bullets fly and lives are in jeopardy, the people of naval aviation have always put others first—be they squadron mates, shipmates, or other Americans whom they've never even met.

14

RETURNING WITH HONOR

FROM THE VANTAGE POINT OF his parachute, Lt. Chuck Klusmann watched his mortally wounded RF-8 Crusader barrel into the Laotian countryside and disappear into a cloud of fire, smoke, and trees. He'd heard of the peaceful period of silence that often accompanies a bailout: the fiery, jarring ejection followed by the arc of the pilot and his seat, the jerk as the chute deploys, the soft wind that muffles the sounds on the ground below. But in this instance, gunfire spoiled any serenity he may have found in drifting over the green fields and forests of Laos.

"It dawned on me that there was only one target to shoot at, and that was me," Chuck recalled several decades after his 1963 mission over Laos, just west of Vietnam. "I could hear bullets whizzing by but none seemed too close. I guess it was about this time that I realized that I was about to fall into really deep trouble."

The wind was carrying him toward a lone tree in a small field and he smashed right into it, badly twisting his right leg, knee, and foot. He crashed through limbs and leaves before reaching the hard ground. Once there, he set about fixing his leg by wedging his foot into a bush and pulling his leg until several joints popped back into place and the pain subsided. Soon he heard a U.S. Helio Courier, a single engine prop plane circling overhead. He hobbled out from beneath the tree and signaled it with a mirror from his survival kit. A quick rock of the little plane's wings told him that help would be inbound.

Indeed, a big Sikorsky H-34 helicopter soon arrived and began its approach, but the surrounding hills erupted with gunfire. The barrage wounded the helicopter's copilot and put eighty holes in the aircraft before it withdrew. A gunship arrived on the scene and strafed the area, hoping to suppress the communist fire so a second H-34 could begin its approach.

"As he got near," Chuck said, "it was clear that there was no chance for a pickup and that a further attempt would result in more people in the same boat as me or possibly worse. I waved off the second H-34. It just seemed like the right thing to do at the time, and there were never any regrets. There was also not a doubt in my mind that these guys had pulled out all the stops and made every possible effort to rescue me. It was a great effort but it just wasn't in the cards that day."

Troops of the Laotian communist movement—the Pathet Lao—closed in on their prize and Chuck weighed his options. "They were all heavily armed with automatic weapons like BARs and Kalashnikovs," he said. "I had my trusty .38 with five tracer bullets. Not great odds! Needless to say I became their guest for a while." The Pathet Lao escorted their captive to a nearby village, a loose noose around his neck and his injured gait assisted by a crude crutch. Chuck Klusmann had begun his ordeal as a prisoner of war.

As he regained his strength over the coming weeks, Chuck naturally began thinking of escape. He first tried digging under the walls of his small hut, but discovered his captors had anticipated this and had driven long bamboo stakes into the ground all around the shack's exterior walls. He didn't have long to develop other ideas since the Pathet Lao soon moved him to a complex deeper in Laos. En route, he recognized several structures from reconnaissance photographs, and thought he might have the information he needed to plot another escape.

He found his new jail surrounded by two concentric barbwire fences that rose from the ground to a height equal to the eaves of the crude one-story building. The Pathet Lao had constructed the first barbwire fence three feet from the mud-plastered hut that held Chuck, covered the next five feet of ground with razor-sharp concertina wire, and then raised another barbwire fence. A single gate served as the only entrance or exit. Through that gate on the next day came thirty-five Laotian prisoners. One prisoner named Boun Mi spoke passable English and soon approached Chuck about escaping. He drew him a map of the surrounding area. Chuck thought the map accurate and the cartographer trustworthy, so the two began plotting.

They started working the nails that fastened the lower strands of barb-wire to the posts of the interior fence. Over the next few weeks, they loos-ened the nails enough to pull them out, which would allow the prisoners to lift the barbwire and crawl under it. With the interior fence ready, they left the loosened nails in their holes and began work on the outer fence, which required considerably more finesse.

The guards permitted the prisoners to wash their clothes in a nearby creek, and Chuck made a point of drying them on the outer fence. "When we did that," he explained, "we managed to work on the nails of the outer fence. We could be very slow and deliberate about exactly how we hung our clothes, to the frustration of the guards. Eventually, we thought that we were ready to give it a try." After three months of being caged, Chuck was more than ready to leave.

He and six Laotians, including Boun Mi, chose a dark, rainy night for their attempt. Chuck changed out of his flight suit and into the dark pajamas his captors had provided. Then he put on his flight boots, the slick-bottomed soles of which he'd smartly laced with grooves to provide traction. Between the dark clothes and the improved boots, he was ready for the jungle.

Chuck had also taken care to buy himself time by fooling his guards into thinking he was still in his appointed place. He spent the day walking around in his flight suit and tennis shoes and that night, prominently hung those at the foot of his bed and put up his mosquito net. Then he bent sev-eral pieces of bamboo and put them under his blanket. "This way," he said, "at night they'd come by and shine a light in from outside the wire and it'd look like my clothes were still hung and I was asleep.

"The farther we could get before they discovered we were gone, the big-ger the circle would be that they had to search, so we wanted to get as far away as possible before they discovered us. But boy, I would have loved to have been a mouse in the corner watching what went on when they discov-ered we were gone!"

———

During the night, the rain grew heavy and the darkness thickened; it was time. As soon as a fellow prisoner had distracted the night guard, Chuck slipped around to the building's rear and on Boun Mi's signal, pulled the nails from the inner fence, lifted the wire, and wiggled underneath the strands. He delicately picked his way through the coils of razor wire, then removed the nails from the exterior fence. He wiggled under the last strands of barbwire and streaked across two hundred yards of open space to cover. Boun Mi and two others soon joined him, but two other conspirators did not. One Laotian stayed behind to wait for the last two prisoners; they never saw him or the others again.

Chuck, Boun Mi, and one other Laotian headed for the hills. Chuck pushed their little band hard across one last open expanse of ground and then they entered the jungle. Once inside the dense foliage, Chuck's familiarity with the American outdoors took over.

"In the jungle, the odds were on my side," he said. "I was used to being outside—I'd hunted, fished, hiked—I was at home out there. The only time I was really scared was actually going under the wire and getting out. I just knew they were going to start shooting at us! But it was a rainy night and their guards don't like to stand out in the rain any more than ours do. They were down to just one guard standing under a lean-to and it was raining pretty hard, so that was in our favor."

Moving quickly along game trails, they tried to put distance between themselves and their captors before daybreak, when the guards would discover their escape. They headed south toward a village Boun Mi knew would help them.

"There was a road on the other side of a ridge, and we had to get across it before daylight," Chuck said. "As we were coming up on the road, I looked up and there was a farmer out there planting rice. Here I am about a good head taller than the rest of them with the big beard I'd grown during the last three months. I squatted down as far as I could and tried to blend in. He didn't pay any attention to us."

They crossed the road just before dawn and pushed onward. Later the following day, the third member of their group insisted on finding food in a local dwelling, against the advice of Chuck and Boun Mi. Chuck watched from afar as the Laotian entered a small farmhouse and recalled, "About ten minutes after entering the house, he emerged with his hands tied and a rifle at his back. He had walked into a guerrilla outpost. The group holding him was met by a group of soldiers coming up the road. They talked with them briefly and then took off after us.

"We had a pretty hectic four or four and a half hours. We could hear gunshots and people shouting, but I don't think they ever actually saw us. We later learned the guy who waited at the camp and the guy who got captured both got shot, which was what we figured would happen to us if we got caught."

Chuck remembered moving faster than ever, pushing through the hills of Laos. Recounting the tale years later, Chuck laughed and said, "The remainder of our trek was just pure drudgery; going up over one mountain and down the next! The terrain was very rugged and steep so it was fairly slow going. We did manage to eat some bamboo shoots, corn stalks, and sweet potatoes from abandoned slash-and-burn farms, and some wild berries and fruit. Water was not a problem since this was still the rainy season."

Leeches, however, proved a ubiquitous problem. The twosome used animal trails where possible, since that made the travel easier, but the leeches were particularly thick there. "We stopped occasionally to remove them just to keep from losing too much blood," Chuck said. "They always go back to the same spots on you, though, so some places were getting pretty bad. We kept going, however, because our motivation remained high even though our capabilities were lagging."

After three and a half days of hard travel and constant worry about recapture, the pair heard voices. Boun Mi recognized them as friendly; they had reached an outpost of Baum Long, their intended destination and a safe haven from the communist forces. Still limping, Chuck walked the remaining two kilometers to the village where he found a warm welcome, food, and treatment for his countless cuts, scrapes, and leech bites. The villagers used a radio to contact American forces and within the hour, a small turboprop plane appeared and Chuck watched it land in a nearby field.

He had taken off his boots—which he'd worn for three straight days—and without the boots to compress them, his feet had begun to swell. He couldn't get his boots back on so the villagers gave him sandals and he struck out up the hill to the airstrip as best he could.

"As I was hobbling up the ridge I heard an American voice calling 'Lieutenant Klusmann, Lieutenant Klusmann!'"

He shouted back, "Here I am!" His three-month ordeal had ended.

"That was the point I think I realized I was finally really free," he said. "I was getting out of there.

"Mine is the *Reader's Digest* version of being a prisoner of war in Southeast Asia," Chuck said forty-seven years later. "I was only there for three months. So many of those guys were there for six, seven, or eight years."

One of those long-serving prisoners was George Coker.

Lieutenant George Coker served as a bombardier-navigator aboard an A-6 Intruder attached to Attack Squadron Sixty-five (VA-65)—the World Famous Fighting Tigers—aboard the aircraft carrier *Constellation*. He had logged fifty-five successful missions over North Vietnam from the *"Connie"* before a missile ripped through the wing of his Intruder. The plane went out of control and fell toward the fields below. George ejected at 1,500 feet. When he landed, North Vietnamese Army troops descended upon him before he could even take off his parachute. Thus in August of 1966—less than one month after his twenty-third birthday—George Coker began 2,382 days of captivity where on average, he spent just 15 minutes per day outside his various cells in Hanoi, North Vietnam. He would not return home until March of 1973. But not for lack of trying.

Unlike the primitive prison camps Chuck Klusmann found in Laos, the North Vietnamese confined their POWs to French-built prisons. American inmates dubbed their jails Alcatraz, Dirty Bird, Heartbreak Hotel, New Guy Village, and Las Vegas. Las Vegas included cell blocks named after various casinos; the men did their best to keep a sense of humor. From their own experiences as prisoners under French rule, which had only ended in 1954, the North Vietnamese understood the value of keeping their captives isolated. The Americans rarely saw one another before 1970 and an elaborate code system became their only means of communication and moral support. The system related letters to taps they would knock on walls, bars, and doors. Some swept floors in code; others brushed out their chamber pots in code. In the Alcatraz prison, men coughed, sneezed, and sniffed in code. One of the highest-ranking POWs, Commander James Stockdale, passed code with hand signals when he could and even tied strings of code: he tied knots corresponding to letters into long threads from his pajamas then left the knotted strings in designated locations. Despite full-scale campaigns by the captors to prevent communication, information hummed back and forth among prisoners. They called their language the Smitty Harris tap code, named after an officer who'd remembered it from survival school.

	1	2	3	4	5
1	A	B	C	D	E
2	F	G	H	I	J
3	L	M	N	O	P
4	Q	R	S	T	U
5	V	W	X	Y	Z

To communicate the word "by," for example, Coker or a fellow prisoner would tap once, then twice. He followed with five taps, then four more. Abbreviations like GNGBU (Good night, God bless you) became well-used, as did abbreviations for words, like TN for *then*, U for *you*—shorthand these veterans now see their grandchildren using in text messages.

Often, two prisoners would spend months or years tapping in code to each other through their cell walls without ever seeing each other's faces. By pressing their ears to cups placed against the walls, the prisoners could amplify soft taps and help hide the communication from the guards. Conversations in tap code often became the only personal exchanges prisoners would have for months on end—aside from sessions with interrogators which could begin at any time. The prisoners lived in constant fear of tormentors like Rabbit, Pigeye, Cat, and a host of other similarly nicknamed guards and communist officials.

For sustenance, Coker and the others had only rice and an assortment of watery vegetable soups. To this day, he can't eat anything made with pumpkins. And while others his age married and started families, he spent his twenties languishing in solitary confinement cells, often in leg irons, enduring excruciating torture and unfathomable loneliness.

Decades later, those wartime experiences put the Coker children at a distinct disadvantage; they never have license to complain. "It's always his trump card," Coker's daughter Teresa told me as we ate lunch with her parents at their home in Virginia Beach, which has become a prime retirement location for naval aviators along with Pensacola, Jacksonville, and San Diego; many retired servicemen choose never to leave the tight-knit communities that surround naval air stations. "If we ever complain about our food, there's a good chance Dad will say, 'I've had worse!'" Teresa giggled. Her father shrugged defensively and grinned.

Shortly after becoming POW #123 of the Vietnam War, Lt. Coker began learning about the treatment he would receive during the remainder of his twenties. The Vietnamese realized they couldn't win an outright military victory. They instead hoped to sway public opinion. To fuel sentiment against the U.S. presence in Vietnam, North Vietnamese officers tried to extract propaganda statements from the 766 Americans they captured during the course of the conflict. To those ends, they employed brutal techniques of torture.

In a detached voice marked only by the traces of a New Jersey accent, Commander Coker explained what he endured for refusing to acquiesce to his captors' demands. He told me about the ropes.

"They would strap your arms behind your back and they would 'figure eight' a rope around your arms and put their foot in your back and pull on it until basically your arms were touching from your elbows to about here," he said, pointing to his upper arms. "Your shoulders were almost touching in the back. They'd just put their foot against you and keep pulling—an inch at a time while you're screaming your head off. The thing that stopped them would be when your shoulders touched and your elbows are touching; the ropes had tightened up and you just couldn't pull them any closer together.

"Then what they'd often do was they'd pull your arms up over your head and so now you're really getting pulled out of your shoulder sockets. And they could either hang you like that from a hook in the ceiling or they'd bring the rope over and double up your legs and pull you up so you're being twisted up like a pretzel—and it hurt like hell, that's all there is to it. Just unbelievable pain. Every joint in your body was screaming pain."

Nobody could hold out forever, and eventually every man reached a point where he'd cry, "I submit." But die-hard prisoners like Coker resolved never to make anything easy.

The men needed a common code to unite them and a set of standards to which they could aspire, even under duress. Their commanding officer gave them one, spread throughout the prison system by tap code. The POWs as well as the Vietnamese recognized Navy Commander Jim Stockdale's rank and leadership and he assumed de facto command of the American servicemen in Hanoi, navy and air force alike. He made it his mission to unite them against the North Vietnamese. Stockdale had led the first air raid of the Vietnam conflict—shortly after the Gulf of Tonkin incident—and he vowed to press the fight from his tiny isolated cell, which he began occupying thirteen months after those first shots. In the process, he confounded, undermined, and enraged the North Vietnamese guards more than any other prisoner. Despite their attempts to prevent communication, he organized resistance. Once, he nearly beat himself to death, disfiguring his face so the Vietnamese couldn't use his image for publicity. All along, he never forgot that realism and unity presented the prisoners' best hope.

He never deluded himself. He always remained realistic about his circumstances—they were brutal, harsh, and utterly demoralizing. But he said, "I never lost faith in the end of the story."

He knew he would return home to America eventually and never surrendered that hope, even in his darkest moments; it's what sustained him. Even so, he always retained the discipline to face the physical and mental anguish of his daily existence—"the brutal facts of your current reality," he called it.[1]

As for the unity, he said, "[The men] demanded to be told exactly what to take torture for. They saw that it was only on that basis that life for them could be made to make sense, that their self-esteem could be maintained, and that they could sleep with a clear conscience at night."[2]

Stockdale spread his set of rules throughout the POW community. BACK US became the acronym:

Bow (Don't bow to captors in public)

Air (Refuse to read propaganda over the air—on radio, television, or over the prison loudspeaker)

Crime (Admit no crimes)

Kiss (Don't kiss the captors good-bye—or be at all amicable—upon release)

Unity over Self (Prisoner unity was paramount; shared sacrifice was the rule).

As the commanding officer, Stockdale also issued two additional rules: 1) we all go home together, and 2) no repent, no repay. Nobody should leave early, even if they were given the opportunity, and no prisoner should apologize or in any way do penance for their actions.

Prisoners went to extraordinary lengths—to the exasperation of their captors—to follow these rules and not submit to the demands of their interrogators.

The ropes that George Coker described proved the most common instrument of submission used by the guards, but the worst ordeal Coker experienced involved less intense pain—but over time, brought even greater agony. For two months, George refused the guards' demands for propaganda statements and held fast to Stockdale's rules. So for two months, the guards awakened him around 5 A.M. and stood him against a concrete wall with his hands raised above his head. He remained standing until 6 P.M. with his arms raised. Thirteen hours a day, every day, for two months. If his arms dropped, they beat him.

"For one day it becomes a monumental effort," George explained. "At two months, it kinda becomes unbelievable. I just don't know how you do it physically—you do strange things under duress—but the real battle wasn't physical, it was mental. You're not willing to say what they want you to say, so you have to convince yourself that it's worth taking the pain versus doing what they want you to do.

"Part of you drifts away, thinks about something else to buy you time, but no matter how good you get, when your mind came back to the present it would hurt like hell."

He trained himself to focus on prayers, family, memories, anything to help him escape the pain, loneliness, exhaustion, and hopelessness of torture. As the weeks progressed, he continued to refuse writing statements against the United States, but long hours on the wall taxed his brain and body heavily. He felt his mind slipping away and knew that keeping some positive memory offered the only hope for escaping—although only temporarily—the pain and sheer longevity of days on the wall. Toward the last weeks, he felt as if he'd completed a marathon, but was forced to run another block, then another, and yet another with no end in sight.

"As time goes on, it gets more and more difficult to do this," he explained. "You're having to make the decision to keep standing more and more often. It becomes a vicious cycle because you can't get away for five or ten minutes, much less an hour. At the end I was living second by second. Sometimes you try to pass time by counting—you'd count to 120. At the end I couldn't count to sixty. I couldn't get there. I could barely remember who I was. I could barely remember my family—if you'd asked me family names I couldn't have told you. The brain was shutting down, it wasn't functioning." In the end, he held on to this faith, his memories of sports, and Scouting.

"The very last thing I could consciously hold on to was the Scout Oath. By the end, I could only get out that first verse: 'On my honor I will do my best.' That forced my brain to function and say, 'I *will* do this again. I *will not* do what they want me to do.'

"At the end I was at the brink of total mental and physical collapse. Then two days before Christmas they called a truce and let me off the wall."

In a battle of wills and character, this American prevailed.

Like Chuck Klusmann, George Coker never stopped thinking of escape and after spending one year in captivity, he decided the time had come to go home. He had endured two weeks of particularly rough torture sessions and he had nothing to lose. Coker's fellow prisoner, Air Force Captain George McKnight, had been assigned outdoor duty at the Dirty Bird prison—an exceedingly rare occurrence, with good reason: being outside could allow prisoners to observe local landmarks that were visible over the compound's walls. McKnight did not miss his opportunity. He recounted his observations to Coker and together they calculated their location based on maps they recalled from numerous mission briefings. They fixed their exact position in Hanoi and began plotting their escape.

"It was maybe the only time that we were there that a POW knew where he was," Coker recalled. "At no other time did a guy know where he was. You might be climbing out of your compound into a cage of circus lions for all you knew or the Ministry of Defense. You'd have no idea if you'd be climbing into a cage that was harder to get out of. I don't think anybody ever knew what was outside of that big wall they wanted to climb over." But at last, McKnight and Coker did.

Five nights after they hatched their plan, they were ready. Chip by chip, they had slowly and methodically whittled away the soft wood surrounding the hinges of their cell doors and now, the doors were hanging precariously in their frames, although their captors never noticed. Nor did their captors realize these two American aviators had learned to unlock their handcuffs and leg shackles. The worst oversight the North Vietnamese guards made was underestimating the ingenuity and audacity of George Coker.

Minutes after the guards completed their evening round on October 12, 1967, Coker and McKnight pushed the cell doors open, stepped outside, and carefully returned the doors to their frame. "Fifteen minutes later, the guards came back, the door was firm, and it looked like we were asleep under the mosquito net in the corner. We had moved our stuff to the far corner so it'd be as dark as possible and as far away as possible, so when we rolled up our trash under the mosquito netting, it looked like a body was there."

Together, the Americans crept through the dim hallways of the prison and climbed onto the rooftop where they moved stealthily toward the wall separating the POW compound from the deserted streets of northern Hanoi and, more important, the Red River. After creeping through darkened roads to the riverbank near the Tanwa Bridge, the pilots rushed across the low-lying marshes at the river's edge, tied their wrists together, and became two small heads bobbing south with the main current toward the Gulf of Tonkin and the American fleet.

"The idea," Coker said, "was to get into the river. Then we were going to go downriver to the Gulf of Tonkin . . . and there, the game plan was to steal a little sailboat—they have a bunch of little fishing sailboats all over the delta—and the idea was to steal one of those and sail it to the fleet. It seemed like a plausible idea. It might have been far-fetched but what the heck. I think I was looking at forty or fifty miles . . . and the first day we got about fifteen, and we didn't get into the water until midnight."

Dawn began to break around 5 A.M. and McKnight and Coker swam to shore to find a hiding place to spend the day, safe from the eyes of the thousands of Vietnamese who traveled the river. They found a suitable spot in the muddy riverbank, where only someone looking directly down into their hiding place could have seen them. Unfortunately, someone looked.

"I'm guessing about nine o'clock a little old fisherman with a cane pole was going down the bank," he said. "And he happened to stop right above us and he looked down and there were two white guys down there. And that was the beginning of the end. He was more frightened than we were. He ran away and within two or three minutes, hundreds of people were running toward the bank. The great escape was over."

The concluding chuckle he gave decades later belied the emotions he felt in 1967. The two fugitives were returning to life as POWs. Coker would spend the next two years confined alone to a three-foot by nine-foot cell with a constantly burning lightbulb. Beatings and torture sessions were commonplace, yet Coker remained among the most defiant captives the North Vietnamese faced. Jim Stockdale likened him to the fiery actor James Cagney and even decades later, it's not difficult to imagine him fighting his captors with all his might. Consequently, George served a long stint of time in the Alcatraz prison, located behind the Ministry of Defense in Hanoi, one mile away from the main Hoa Lo prison where most POWs were held. Stockdale came to Alcatraz with ten other U.S. airmen who all earned solitary confinement in this special facility due to their fierce resistance. Representing the navy in the eleven-man Alcatraz Gang were George Coker (the youngest of the group, who was born the year Jim Stockdale graduated from the Naval Academy), Jerry Denton, Harry Jenkins, Jim Mulligan, Howie Rutledge, Bob Shumaker, Jim Stockdale, and Nels Tanner—all of whom have stories of courage and perseverance worthy of their own book.

Showing a defiant spirit akin to Coker's, Denton became famous for a 1966 televised interview hosted by a Japanese journalist. Instead of reciting rehearsed answers during the interview as the North Vietnamese had

planned, Denton responded to a question about American atrocities by saying, "I don't know what is happening now in Vietnam, because the only
news sources I have are North Vietnamese, but whatever the position of my
government is, I believe in it, I support it, and I will support it as long as
I live."

As a reprisal for his boldfaced answer, the future U.S. senator from Alabama endured the most ferocious torture session of his captivity. He reported that the soldiers standing guard silently shed tears for his pain
and unbreakable spirit. But his statement wasn't his greatest coup. After
the Japanese host smuggled a copy of the video out of North Vietnam,
American intelligence officers discovered an ingeniously hidden message
that neither the host nor the North Vietnamese noticed. During the interview, Denton blinks his eyes unusually often, something most viewers
attributed to the bright studio lighting. In fact, he blinked in Morse code,
"_ ___ ._. _ .._ ._. .," translated "T-O-R-T-U-R-E."

What inspired me as much as the courage shown by America's POWs was
the strength shown by their families at home. These military spouses and
parents resolutely held their families together until their husbands and sons
returned home from an ordeal that had no predetermined end; often, they
didn't even know if their loved ones were alive. I had learned that it takes
a family to launch a navy aircraft, and for the men held in Southeast Asia, it
took a family to bring them home.

Doyen Salsig delivered the bad news to the Stockdales late in the
evening of September 9, 1965. Fourteen-year-old Jimmy Stockdale let his
mother's best friend into his family's Coronado, California, home. Doyen
met Jimmy's mother Sybil as she came down the stairs. Doyen rushed toward Sybil and wrapped her arms tightly around her friend as she delivered
the news that Sybil's husband, Commander Jim Stockdale, Carrier Air Wing
Sixteen's commander, was missing over Vietnam. Sybil Stockdale wondered
how her husband could be *missing*; surely someone knew where he was.

Doyen explained gently that Jim's A-4 Skyhawk had been shot down
over North Vietnam. His wingmen had seen a parachute, but didn't know if
Jim had survived the local reception.

The base chaplain, a young lieutenant, arrived shortly thereafter and repeated the little information the navy had. Sybil neither cried nor screamed; she began to shake. After the chaplain and Doyen left, Sybil walked slowly to Jimmy's room, where he lay on his bed, listening to the radio. He looked to her for answers, but she had none to give. She had no idea if Jim were alive or dead. Jimmy was fourteen and old enough to understand. She rubbed his back softly and began thinking about how she would tell her three younger sons, Sid, Stan, and Taylor.

The next morning her boys cried together then went to school and Sybil confronted her life, which had changed so drastically since the previous day. She could fret and slip into a listless state of self-pity or resolve to handle the ordeal and all its unknowns like a U.S. Navy wife.

She immediately ensured the navy would send her Jim's paycheck directly so she could pay the family's mortgage, which they agreed to do after she threatened to phone an admiral in the Pentagon. She also devoured every scrap of news and history about Vietnam and the escalating conflict there. While many Americans expected a brief and easy war, she realized years could pass until it ended. She steeled herself to endure five years of separation from her husband—if he were, in fact, alive.

That fall, she suffered through his birthday and hers, and the family celebrated Christmas still not knowing Jim's fate. She and her boys soldiered on, month after month, never knowing. She did everything imaginable to distract her mind from the unanswerable questions that constantly plagued her and a growing number of other families with husbands and fathers listed as missing in action. Contrary to the Geneva Convention, the North Vietnamese did not release the names of their prisoners.

Then on April 15, 1966, she walked back to her home at 547 A Avenue, sifting through the day's mail as she went. Toward the bottom of the stack, she found two thin envelopes with Hanoi postmarks. One was addressed in Jim's handwriting. She froze. She could scarcely believe what she held in her trembling hands. Then she began to wonder about the second letter, addressed by a different hand. What if it contained bad news? She didn't want to open it by herself and she raced to a neighbor's house. Both letters were from her husband. He was alive.

In his letters, he had included heartfelt messages to his wife and boys and let them know he was okay, relatively speaking. He also included several hidden messages he thought the prison's censors wouldn't notice. First, he included the phrase "there was cold and darkness, even at noon," a reference to the 1940 novel *Darkness at Noon* by Arthur Koestler, which tells of state-sanctioned torture and horrifying gulags in Joseph Stalin's Russia. He also urged Sybil to say hello to his "old football mates," Baldy and Red Dawg. Aviator call signs have another function—Jim was letting Sybil know his fellow aviators Harley "Baldy" Chapman and Ed "Red Dawg" Davis were alive. Stockdale's letter gave Naval Intelligence an idea. They devised a plan to send Sybil's letters on carbon paper that Jim could use to encode messages in his replies. Then the team devised a way to write a message "inside" a photograph. Jim could access the message by soaking the photo in water. They cleverly gave Jim clues in Sybil's next letter. Sure enough, he understood.

The message inside the photo instructed Jim to write a normal letter, then place the letter from Sybil (written on carbon paper) on top of his letter, along with a cover sheet. Anything he wrote on the cover sheet would be "encoded" in invisible carbon on his letter to Sybil. Participating would put him at great risk, but Jim didn't hesitate, as Sybil knew he wouldn't.

When Naval Intelligence reviewed Jim's next letter from Hanoi, they discovered he'd used the carbon paper to write, "Experts in Torture. Hand and Leg Irons . . . 16 hours a day."[3] He also included a list of fellow prisoners' names, perhaps the most valuable information he could provide since many were listed as Missing in Action—their fates had been unknown to the government or their families. After Jim received Sybil's next message, his response mentioned the regular torture, then listed the names of more than forty additional U.S. POWs that he'd memorized. He had just swallowed the telltale cover sheet when the guard walked in to take the letter. The date was January 17, 1967. Sybil would not receive another letter until March of 1968.

During those trying months, Sybil Stockdale became the POWs' greatest advocate. After she first learned Jim had survived—in April of 1966—she began working to ensure the Departments of Defense and State were doing all they could to bring the prisoners home and, until that happened, ensure their well-being. She abided by the Pentagon's "keep quiet" policy and didn't make public statements about her husband or his fellow captives, but she pushed Ambassador Averell Harriman on the issue. She received the first of many noncommittal responses from Washington, and she pressed the issue with the Chief of Naval Operations. By 1968, however, she began to sense that nobody in the government cared enough about the prisoners to push the North Vietnamese and make their inhumane and illegal practices public knowledge. She smartly realized that only world opinion would force them to release the names of their prisoners and end the torture.

She stepped into the role of a commanding officer's wife and became a true force for her husband and his fellow captives. She organized the League of Wives of American Prisoners in Vietnam and fired her opening salvo on October 27, 1968, in the *San Diego Union Tribune*. She flagrantly broke the military's "keep quiet" policy and shed light on the Democratic Republic of Vietnam's refusal to abide by the Geneva Convention.

"The North Vietnamese," she told the reporter, "have shown me the only thing they respond to is world opinion. The world does not know of their negligences and they should know!"[4]

She finally got the attention of the nation's leaders and California governor Ronald Reagan personally assured her that he would carry the League's message to President-elect Richard Nixon in Washington. But in the early days of the Nixon administration, she still saw little progress. The League began to grow as more families became disillusioned with the Pentagon's inaction and "keep quiet" policy. Sybil became the organization's leader and mobilized members across the country to bring their stories to the editorial writers of influential local newspapers; she wanted everyone in America to hear their story. On March 26, 1969, the League blasted a delegation of State and Defense Department representatives sent to San Diego to appease them.

"There was no question about our feelings by the end of the meeting," Sybil recalled. "The three men from Washington were somewhat wide-eyed. I couldn't help but feel a little sorry for them; they had walked right into a hornets' nest."[5]

Those men apparently carried Sybil's sentiments back to the Nixon administration. Less than two months later, Secretary of Defense Melvin Laird leveled America's first public criticism at North Vietnam over their violation of the Geneva Convention. He had requested that Hanoi soften its stance on the POW situation, and he reacted to their negative response at a May 19, 1969 press conference.

"I am deeply shocked and disappointed by this cruel response of Hanoi's representative to such a basic request for humanitarian action," he said. "Hundreds of American wives, children, and parents continue to live in a tragic state of uncertainty caused by the lack of information concerning the fate of their loved ones. This needless anxiety is caused by the persistent refusal by North Vietnam to release the names of U.S. prisoners of war."[6]

As the government firmed its stance, Sybil Stockdale saw support increasing both at home and abroad, even as her husband and his comrades continued to suffer. Her small group of wives had grown to several hundred and renamed itself the National League of Families of American Prisoners in Southeast Asia. That September, Sybil led a high-profile National League delegation to Paris, France. The group of young wives and one father aimed to meet with North Vietnam's delegation to the Paris peace talks. They held a press conference before their flight departed New York's John F. Kennedy airport, then flew across the Atlantic, hoping the Vietnamese might see them.

Once in Paris, Sybil persistently reminded the North Vietnamese embassy that their delegation was waiting. She called every other day, but received no assurances, just a regular clipped response. She spent many hours in her hotel room, waiting for the call. It finally came on Saturday morning, October 4, 1969.

That same afternoon, her delegation walked into the North Vietnamese embassy. They each read letters—their own and those of other League members—detailing plights of loved ones being held or listed as MIA. The hosts listened stone-faced and gave no assurances or answers. Sybil recalled their only concrete response came when she suggested more POW/MIA wives might visit their embassy. They answered with an emphatic "not necessary." The North Vietnamese didn't want any more publicity. The League members left the room disappointed but satisfied that they'd had their meeting.

As Sybil spoke with the reporters who had gathered outside the North Vietnamese embassy, she realized that while their visit may not have pried any information or immediate concessions from her husband's captors, she had brought international attention to the POW/MIA situation that existed in Southeast Asia—and both she and the North Vietnamese knew it.

After she returned from Paris, Sybil Stockdale became the epicenter of the POW issue, receiving mail and invitations to share her message on air and with groups throughout the country. She began traveling to Washington more frequently and met with President Richard Nixon, Senator William

Fulbright, General Alexander Haig, and Secretary of State Henry Kissinger—each time pressing them to make North Vietnam abide by the Geneva Convention and help end the suffering of so many families and prisoners.

In 1970, her television and speaking engagements continued and Senator Bob Dole organized a POW tribute in Constitution Hall on International Justice Day, May 1. That night, an overflowing Constitution Hall audience gave Sybil Stockdale a standing ovation for her devotion to America's imprisoned warriors.

By the time of the Constitution Hall tribute, the ripples of Sybil's activism had reached Hoa Lo Prison in Hanoi. The days of torture ended as the North Vietnamese government bowed under the spotlight of international opinion, which the League's advocacy had focused upon them. In late 1969, the Alcatraz Gang returned to Hoa Lo prison from their isolation. Jim Stockdale had his first roommate since his captivity began, and solitary confinement ended for other prisoners as well. By the end of 1971, the prisoners visited with one another often and they spent their last two years as standard detainees, treated appropriately under the rules of the Geneva Convention.

In the winter of 1973, the United States, North Vietnam, and South Vietnam signed the Paris Peace Accords, ending U.S. involvement in the conflict and securing the release of all prisoners of war. Five hundred ninety-one men were released during Operation Homecoming in 1973. On February 12 of that year, Jim Stockdale and 115 fellow POWs from the Hoa Lo prison boarded U.S. Air Force C-141 Starlifter cargo planes in Hanoi. Cheers erupted as each plane lifted off the ground and started the long journey back to America. The twin ordeals faced by the individuals in Hanoi and their families at home finally came to a close.

What makes an individual extraordinary? Sometimes, pure circumstance. No American POW arrived in Hoa Lo prison by choice. Nobody wished for that loneliest of assignments, but Fate or Fortune dealt it to a small group of aviators. More than 2.5 million Americans served in Vietnam. Of those, 58,156 never returned. Seven hundred sixty-six were held as prisoners throughout North and South Vietnam. In that sense, the POWs under Jim

Stockdale's command were statistically extraordinary. But their conduct behind the prison walls made them truly elite. They were strong as individuals. They were nigh unbreakable as a unit. Their mutual suffering, their common hopes, and their pledged unity inspired them to persevere under circumstances that would have surely defeated lone men. They resolved to return home with honor and they did.

In February of 1971, Jim Stockdale and his fellow POWs in Building Seven of the Hoa Lo prison staged the "Church Riot of 1971." They assembled for a Sunday church service—a gathering that was quite explicitly forbidden—and when their captors arrived to break up the meeting and haul away the instigators, the entire prisoner population began belting out "The Star-Spangled Banner" in open defiance of their captors. Surely then, if not before, the North Vietnamese realized they weren't holding men who were merely good. They were dealing with men who were truly great.

PART FIVE

THE PACIFIC

15

SURVIVORS

C HIEF PETTY OFFICER HAROLD DIXON scarfed down a hasty 11 A.M. lunch in the chiefs' mess aboard the USS *Enterprise* on January 16, 1942. He ate most of his food, then wiped his mouth, stood up, and began to leave. He hesitated at the doorway and went back for two more bites of celery. He later came to wish he'd also had another drink of water.

After lunch, Dixon went to his squadron ready room and began preparing for an antisubmarine mission over the South Pacific, large swaths of which the Japanese navy still patrolled. Dixon had joined the navy twenty years earlier and entered the Naval Aviation Pilot program, which trained enlisted sailors to fly. He held the designation of chief aviation pilot and belonged to the esteemed group of enlisted men who served as pilots during naval aviation's earlier years; the navy ended the program after World War II. At two o'clock, the enlisted aviator heard the call over the loudspeaker: "Pilots, man your planes," and he hustled to the flight deck to join his crew—Petty Officers Gene Aldrich and Tony Pastula. He knew both by sight, but had never been formally introduced to either; he often had a different crew for each flight. Twenty-two-year-old Aldrich, the radioman and gunner, had already taken his place at the rear of the 1937 Douglas Devastator torpedo bomber they would fly that day. Pastula, the twenty-four-year-old bombardier, greeted Chief Dixon at the plane's side. Soon, all three men were strapped into the Devastator's long cockpit, and with its nine-hundred-horsepower engine humming loudly, the torpedo bomber unfolded its wings and taxied into position for takeoff. The launch officer signaled Chief Dixon to rev his engine. Then with a wave of a flag, the officer signaled him to release the brakes. The plane gathered speed, floated off the bow, and carried the three men into the sky.

The patrol proceeded as usual, with plane and carrier observing strict radio rules to reduce the chance of Japanese forces intercepting messages and learning the location of the *Enterprise*. The unintended consequence of this procedure was that the Devastator had little communication with its home base and drifted off course. When Chief Dixon ended the patrol, he began searching for the carrier and soon realized that they had become hopelessly lost over the expansive Pacific Ocean, somewhere 1,900 miles south of Hawaii. The *Enterprise* simply wasn't anywhere near where he thought it would be waiting. He couldn't raise anyone over his short-range VHF radio, nor could he locate the carrier's homing beacon. The sun was quickly dropping toward the horizon—about as rapidly as his fuel gauge was dropping toward empty. With no carrier or land in sight, he had one remaining option.

The plane's crew received Dixon's instructions over their headsets at 6:30 P.M. He calmly instructed Pastula to secure the emergency rations, water, and the life raft. Aldrich readied the first-aid kit, signaling mirrors, and anything else useful that he could find.

With the fuel tanks almost dry, Dixon told his crew, "I'm going to make a landing in the water, and wait for them to come back and find us. Ready, Aldrich? Pastula?"[1]

The two crewmen, both in their early twenties, were as calm as circumstances could allow. Dixon turned the plane into the wind and settled the propeller-driven torpedo bomber toward the sea. The seasoned, forty-one-year-old aviator made a perfect water landing just as the sun ducked below the western horizon.

The Pacific Ocean covers more square miles than all the Earth's landmass combined, and the vast sea south of Hawaii ranks among its emptiest. I remember flying southwest from Honolulu toward the Marshall Islands—not far from the ditching site of Dixon's plane—and gazing across this expanse of water, a dazzling and infinite blue sheet, entirely undisturbed by land. Even moving at hundreds of miles per hour at thirty-five thousand feet, hours could pass with no land appearing on the boundless horizon. The azure sea struck me as beautiful but terribly lonely.

For Harold Dixon, the sea that had appeared peaceful and alluring from five thousand feet now seemed dark and greedy. Bobbing on the black swells, he and his crew were completely alone. Night climbed across the sky from east to west, and the last remnants of daylight soon disappeared.

Dixon stood up on his seat and checked his crew: no injuries. The pilot stepped onto the left wing and Tony Pastula passed him the inflatable life raft. Dixon began to inflate the raft, but the CO_2 canister failed.

Then suddenly, the wing began sinking rapidly and within seconds, he was immersed in the ocean, hanging by his life jacket with salt water assaulting his mouth and nostrils. He gasped at the chill of the ocean and desperately held on to the raft. The plane had sunk with astounding speed, dragging all the crew's carefully assembled survival gear toward the deep ocean floor, more than three miles below the waves.

"The sinking of the plane was like a magician's trick," Dixon later recalled. "It was there, and then it was gone, and there was nothing left in our big, wet, darkening world but the three of us and a piece of rubber that was not yet a raft."

Finally, Dixon triggered the stubborn CO_2 canister and the rubber quickly became a raft, although it floated upside down. Twenty minutes of trying to right the cumbersome raft while being dashed about by the sea found the three airmen still in the water and now in the pitch dark. Neither Gene Aldrich nor Tony Pastula could swim, adding to their frenzy. Finally, Tony calmed down and thoughtfully suggested they make a rope from their shirts and tie one end to the thin cord that ran along the gunwales of the raft. Once they had assembled and anchored their improvised rope, they threw it across the raft's beam. Struggling against the sea, they groped their way to the other side of the raft, found their rope of shirts, and pulled. By bracing the near side of the raft, they created enough leverage to flip up the far side. With a loud slap, the rubber raft landed on the water, ready for its crew. The three men struggled over the sides and flopped onto the floor, exhausted. They were safe for the moment, ready to sleep and worry about their predicament when the sun rose the next day.

Their first harsh lesson came quickly: the raft and sea would offer them little rest. "We soon learned that we could not sleep," explained Dixon. "The raft was only four feet long by eight feet wide . . . The dimensions inside were eighty inches by forty inches. We discovered almost at once that it was impossible for three men to dispose this space so that any one of us would be comfortable.

"Imagine doubling up on a tiny mattress," he expounded, "with the strongest man you know striking the underside as hard as he could with a baseball bat, twice every three seconds, while someone else hurls buckets of cold salt water in your face. That's what it was like."[2]

No one slept that night, or on many nights to follow.

On January 17, 1942, the sun rose quickly, as it does in the tropics, lighting the sky and surrounding sea. From their vantage point low in the waves, however, the castaways could spy no ships or planes on the horizon. Their spirits lifted around 8:30 A.M. when they saw a plane, so distant they first mistook it for a bird. The plane came toward the raft and the men began frantically waving their arms and shirts; their other signaling devices were beneath 16,500 feet of ocean. The plane closed to within half a mile, but its pilots never saw the three castaways. Either the yellow raft was hidden in the dazzling, golden path of the rising sun or, more likely, was just too small to attract any notice in the immensity of the Pacific. As the plane disappeared from sight, the castaways sat in silence, painfully alone once again. Dixon broke the quiet, saying, "Boys, there goes our one and only chance."[3]

Their thoughts turned to their options and tools. Upon inventorying the boat and their pockets, they found they had no flashlight, pump, oars, food, or water. They *did* have a strong raft, a police whistle, pliers, a pocketknife, a can of rubber cement, patching material, a pistol and three clips of ammunition, two life jackets, the damp clothes that presently clung to their bodies, their training, their wits, and their will.

Their story, then, becomes one of three men pitting their will to live against the unforgiving Pacific Ocean, for the airmen had virtually no other resources. They would ultimately endure thirty-four days afloat, and each day brought more disappointment, misery, and loneliness than most souls could bear. Yet their spirits persevered. Dixon assumed the role of captain and ran his vessel as best he could. A disciplined crew did as he asked, never losing hope entirely.

Harold Dixon, Tony Pastula, and Gene Aldrich were men who believed they controlled their destiny. Born to Polish immigrant parents, Tony enlisted in 1939, shortly after giving up on formal education; he thought he'd earned high marks in an early college class, but instead received an F. Furious, the headstrong young man walked out of the classroom and never returned. He lived and worked with his parents for a time then began seeking independence and a chance to prove himself; the navy offered both. Gene Aldrich hailed from a strong but poor family in Missouri; he and his father sometimes rose at 4 A.M. to hunt squirrels for breakfast. He put himself through a year of school then decided to find a better, more exciting type of education in the navy. Dixon was an avocado farmer with a ranch near La Mesa, California; his thoughts aboard the raft would often turn to his family's land. But in choosing naval aviation, he set out on a path different from that of his parents and friends. He wanted adventure and he certainly found it. All three men had come to the navy with a purpose. Now another purpose united them: survival.

The sun bore down with brutal rays that first day afloat and the crew cut up a jacket to protect their heads. They wet these rags often and eventually wet all their clothes to fend off the heat; sharks made swimming too dangerous. They repeated the ritual every fifteen minutes as the sun would dry the fabric in about that time. With each cycle of wetting and drying, however, the salt stiffened and coarsened their shirts and pants, adding immeasurably to their discomfort. The raft, their most precious asset, became nearly too hot to touch under the blazing sun.

Sunset on their first full day afloat left the crew grateful for the cool and dark of night. Their relief quickly dissipated as a maddening new set of problems replaced the old ones: their wet garments now became sticky and clammy; they huddled together for warmth; incessant pounding still deprived them of sleep; and they'd had neither food nor water since lunch aboard the *Enterprise* the previous day. The raft's size of course crowned this set of difficulties. It would have proved tight for just a single person, let alone three. These conditions would never improve during the coming days. Each day brought its own particular struggles, but their root tormentors—the blazing sun, salt water, the pitching sea, hunger, and thirst—never granted them quarter.

By the third day, the crew realized the fleet had surely moved on, having neither the time nor resources to search any further for the three missing aviators. The men never spoke of that reality, but it became silently understood. They were entirely on their own. Once they accepted their situation and mourned their circumstance, the threesome resolved to remain positive and control their fate as best they could.

Chief Dixon explained, "Controlling our craft's progress was my first concern because, while we were entirely without food or water, there was nothing any of us could do about this but wait for the Lord to send us a shower and bring some food where we could catch it. I figured the Lord would help those who helped themselves, so I set out immediately to take every bit of advantage that I could of the few materials available to me.

"I had studied the charts," Dixon continued, referring to countless hours of flight briefings aboard the *Enterprise*, "and had a mental picture of where every island was. So I knew from the beginning just where I wanted to go.

"To the west and north of our position were Japanese islands," he explained. "I wanted to avoid them at all costs because the Japs, I knew, were in no mood to take prisoners. To the east were uninhabited islands which would not do us much good to reach. Our only hope seemed to be in maneuvering our boat some five hundred miles to the south and west where there were inhabited friendly islands. Also along such a route I thought we might be able to pick up an American convoy or perhaps even a naval task force.

"I had no intention of letting that raft drift aimlessly, guided only by the shifting winds. We were without rudder, oars, or canvas, but still I was determined to sail that raft if I could. And I maintain that I did sail it. I worked like the devil to sail it, and I resent anyone's saying we 'drifted.' "[4]

With no real means of steering, the craft would sail in the direction of the wind, its eighteen-inch sides acting as satisfactory sails. Two decades in the navy had taught Dixon about navigation and he divined a method for tracking their speed and position. He used bits of floating cloth to gauge the raft's relative speed and how the wind affected it. Then he used a small pencil and a small aerial navigator's scale to sketch a rough map on the back of a life jacket. Each evening, the crew dutifully and ceremoniously updated the map and charted their progress.

For the first days, the wind cooperated with their plan, blowing them south and somewhat west toward the Phoenix Islands, the Samoa Islands, and Fiji. When winds shifted and blew them northward, the crew improvised a sea anchor out of a life jacket and the cord strung around the raft. When they deployed it, the life jacket sank several feet below the surface and its drag reduced their rate of drift to almost zero. Dixon also took great care to keep the raft's bow, not its beam, pointed toward the unfriendly wind. In truth, their makeshift navigation likely had a larger effect on their psyche than their raft, but that may have been more important.

As days wore on, food and water began to outrank navigation in their immediate concerns. Their mouths were cotton dry by the fifth day; it hurt to swallow. They each knew their systems would soon stop working without fresh water. Gene, the most religious of the three, suggested that they pray. The men bowed their heads and prayed reverently and earnestly. Then, with slightly less reverence, they began to sing hymns. They knew few hymns well, so—with no reverence whatsoever—this choir of castaways began singing into the heavens the tune "Ain't Gonna Rain No More." For the first time in many days, they laughed. And that night, for the first time since they ditched, it rained.

They used their life jackets to collect the water, and Dixon drank greedily. He immediately spat it out; the fresh rain would first have to rinse the accumulated salt out of the fabric. The tropical deluge provided enough force for the task and soon they were drinking and collecting every drop they could, until the shower ceased a short time later. They felt renewed with their mouths wet and the salty grime washed from their clothes and bodies. Another prayer session occurred the following night, but providence was not as kind. No rain fell for the next several days. In the interim, their hunger became almost unbearable. They were slowly starving.

They noticed a gathering crowd of fish around the boat and Gene spent much of the seventh day trying to snare one. Finally, with a quick stab of the pocketknife, he speared a fish and flipped it onto a sleeping Tony, who quickly woke and held down the catch. The men scaled their victim and divided every ounce of edible flesh among them. They put as much of the raw fish into their shrunken stomachs as they could and saved the rest for later. Soon thereafter, it rained.

By the second rainstorm, the three had devised a better method for snaring the precious water. They had cut their cotton underwear into strips, which proved very absorbent. They would wring out the strips in a lifejacket, which would funnel the water into a zippered bag that became their water bottle. They used this method for the remainder of the trip until all their rags—and clothes—were gradually lost to the sea as treacherous waves capsized the raft several times.

Before that memorable seventh day ended, Gene used the .45 to shoot an albatross that alighted on the raft's bow. Thankfully, the bullet found its mark and missed the raft—had it punctured the raft, their voyage and lives would have ended quickly and tragically. Dixon dove into the sea without hesitating and retrieved the bird, which the men divided and devoured like the fish. The small morsels aroused their hunger in full, however, and hunger pangs gripped them with sharper claws than ever.

On the morning of their eighth day afloat, a school of sharks gathered around them. Gene went to work with the pocketknife. A shark closed toward the raft's side. Gene struck swiftly, the crew heard a sound like a punch or puncture, and Gene turned pale. The men looked at each other, fearing the blade struck the boat, not the shark. Then Gene's arm thrashed along with the speared shark and he hauled the big creature in, the knife blade still in its gills. The four-foot shark struggled for some time, but eventually succumbed. They ate the liver first, then several sardines from the shark's stomach before attacking the rest of the creature. Soon, for the first time in eight long, hot, thirsty, hungry days, their stomachs were full. They wouldn't be full again for two weeks.

The sharks had their revenge the next night, as one bit Gene's fingers as he trailed them in the water. He yanked his hand out of the sea with the shark still attached and flung it across the raft before it let go. Thankfully the wound wasn't severe. Soon, Gene was back to fishing—granted, there was little else to do. But he didn't spear another fish until the fourteenth day. On the fifteenth night, the chief came through. A slight noise attracted his attention and he discovered a tern had alighted on the raft, just above his resting head. Quietly, he slipped his arm toward the bird then grabbed for it. He snared the small bird's leg and his crew sprang to his aid, wrestling the tern into submission and dispatching it with the knife. Raw food no longer fazed them and the tern became breakfast the next morning. Five days later, they devoured a waterlogged coconut and snared another on day twenty-eight as it floated by. They would have no other food. Rain proved rare, although they often spied tantalizing squalls passing by them in the distance.

Not long after they caught the tern, Dixon had grown displeased with their ability to control the raft's course. They needed propulsion—and distraction—but their hands and feet were insufficient. A long, flared coconut stem floated by in a clump of flotsam, and the men surmised it had been used as a paddle by an islander. The sea had long since sapped its resiliency, however, and it broke quickly when put to use. But it did give Dixon an idea. He began cutting the leather uppers off his useless shoes. Soon, he had two soles, with just enough leather to reinforce them and make a cup. He bored a hole in each heel, through which he ran a shoelace that would tether his improvised paddle if a rower should drop it.

Fifteen minutes after the men began digging the soles into the water, a wake stretched out behind the boat and the spirits of the three oarsmen lifted immeasurably. Two would row while one would rest. "Sometimes the man resting in the stern acted as coxswain," Dixon recalled, "counting the stroke and calling hilariously for 'ten big ones for deah old Hahvahd!' "[5]

They rowed throughout the night with the wind at their backs. The morning found them fatigued from exertion and lack of sustenance, but they were sharper, more optimistic, and immeasurably proud. Dixon gauged their mileage by stars and his drift calculations; he found it quite satisfactory. The next day, unfavorable winds erased all of their progress.

Their thirty-third and thirty-fourth days at sea brought the high winds that run before a hurricane, and the gusts roiled the seas around them. Gallons and gallons of water poured into the raft yet somehow the men found the will to bail. After such a long ordeal and with a storm gathering, however, they realized their end was near, one way or another. They were dehydrated, starving, weak, cramped, and sunburned, with little energy or hope of salvation remaining. Waves had flipped their raft three times, gradually ridding them of most of their tools, resources, and clothes. They were naked and badly burnt, almost helpless beneath the unrelenting tropical sun, which shone down from the sky and glared up from the water. Conversation had mostly ceased. Even Gene, who had so often entertained the others by fictiously cooking elaborate meals, was mostly silent. They closed their eyes as much as possible during the days; opening them to the ubiquitous brightness became increasingly unbearable. Gene had been enduring the sunlight for about an hour on his watch—the trio still dutifully stood watch for land, coconuts, or rescue—when the raft crested a wave and momentarily expanded their typically sea-bound horizon.

"Chief," Gene said calmly in his Missouri accent, "I see a beautiful field of corn." Nobody reacted; their minds seemed as adrift as they themselves. The raft slid down into a trough and nobody said anything more. Several minutes later, the raft crested another wave and Gene exclaimed, "Sure enough, Chief—I see something green in the distance!"[6] That roused the others from their daze. The rows of corn were in fact rows of palm trees lining a distant beach.

The trio couldn't know if the island was friendly or occupied by the Japanese, but they immediately realized it offered their only chance for survival. They couldn't last much longer, mentally or physically. Dixon gauged the wind, took a bearing on the island, and estimated they would pass ten degrees to the island's right. He issued orders to correct their course.

Dixon manned the port side with their one remaining shoe paddle; the others paddled on starboard with their hands. They rowed fiercely all day to correct for this dangerous drift, their hunger and cramps forgotten. If they floated past the island, they were doomed and they well knew it. One mile from the island, they finally rested; the wind and waves were now carrying them straight toward the gleaming white beach and the green trees beyond.

The crew was completely exhausted; they had rowed for the island on willpower alone. They rose above their physical weakness long enough to reach safety. Fortune at last smiled upon the trio and they passed over the jagged barrier reef during a lull in the menacing thirty-foot waves that routinely broke there; they might not have survived the heavy rollers. Just past the reef, a smaller wave caught the raft from behind and spilled the men into the shallows. Their legs were too atrophied and cramped to stand, but they floated along for several hundred yards with the inbound current. Once the water became too shallow to float, they pushed through the gentle surf and across sand and sharp coral until, cut, exhausted, and immeasurably grateful, they lay on solid land at last.

"We still didn't know, of course, whether the island was friendly or Japanese," Dixon recalled. "So, although we could barely stagger and none of us could stand up straight, we marched in military fashion, stark naked. If there were Japs there, we did not want to be crawling. We wanted them to have to shoot us, like men-o'warsmen."[7]

Fortunately, the threesome had washed up on the Puka Puka atoll, the only inhabited island for many miles. The natives were American allies. When the locals first discovered the castaways, who resembled skeletons more than men, they couldn't determine their ethnicity; their skin, which clung to their famished bones, had been too badly burnt by the sun. Eventually, the locals identified them as Americans and brought them to the local commissioner. The commissioner and his wife alerted the allies and began the slow, kind process of resuscitating the three emaciated men that fate had battered so fiercely before bringing them to their island's shore. That evening, the natives had to turn their attention to other matters as a full hurricane slammed into the island. The storm ravaged Puka Puka and the surrounding seas. Dixon, Pastula, and Aldrich realized that had they not made landfall when they did, the angry sea would have certainly taken their lives, if hunger, sun, and thirst hadn't already claimed them. Seven days after they arrived on the island, the seaplane tender USS *Swan*, a veteran of the Pearl Harbor attack, appeared offshore to carry the three sailors back to the fleet. Their ordeal had ended after thirty-four days—more than eight hundred hours—and nearly one thousand miles. Their story would become one of the twentieth century's greatest accounts of survival at sea.

Today, the navy trains its aviators for long-term survival in environments made hostile by Nature or by enemy presence. Before they deploy, aviation personnel must endure the navy's Survival, Evasion, Resistance, and Escape (SERE) program. Its motto: "We train the best for the worst."

In the wooded hills of Maine and in the remote mountains near Warner Springs, California, the navy prepares its aviators and crew to survive behind enemy lines. The programs teach individuals how to carry the navy's code of conduct into the worst of circumstances, and not just survive any ordeal they might face, but to endure it and return home with their code upheld.

Students enter the SERE program before their first deployment, so most students range from twenty to twenty-five. They initially undergo classroom training that teaches them how to survive, improvise, and evade capture in the wilderness. They also learn how to persevere under the duress of captivity and interrogation, in theory. The next phase of training takes place in the field and builds on classroom work. Anything a sailor or officer didn't learn in Scouts, they learn here. Teams of students receive objectives just before instructors strip them of anything that would make survival too easy; they're simulating the conditions aviators could face after being shot down. The students have to trek through the woods and hills, undetected, to reach their objectives. If roving instructors discover them, everyone receives an entirely different set of lessons, none too pleasant.

Next comes more wilderness survival—and more evasion, this time on an even less-full stomach. Eventually, everyone is caught and students become POWs; the tricks of Jim Stockdale's tormentors in Hanoi serve as the instructors' models. They endure interrogations and considerable duress in a prison compound—every action mimics something they might experience if ever captured on the battlefield or behind enemy lines.

As they survive in the wilderness, figure out how to endure life in a prison camp, and in some cases escape, they learn to improvise and endure the most trying conditions. By the end of the ten-day SERE program, everyone has lost a noticeable amount of weight and collected more than a few cuts and bruises. But when they leave, they're at their best, ready to deploy and face the worst.

The castaways aboard the raft had no such training, but they had the same sense of inventiveness that the SERE program aims to instill in modern aviators. Their ability to make do and maintain focus led to their survival on the hostile swells of the South Pacific.

The most well-known improviser in naval aviation history took a very different view of those swells. Jim Lovell, commander of Apollo 13, could not have been happier to find himself floating on the warm blue seas of the Tropic of Capricorn. For three days in 1971, the world had held its collective breath, afraid that Lovell and his crew would become the first American astronauts lost in space.

When Oxygen Tank Two exploded aboard Apollo 13 on April 14, 1970, vibrations pulsed through the spacecraft, knocking Lovell and his two fellow astronauts into the walls and instrument panels. Lovell looked wildly to his crew, command module pilot Jack Swigert and fellow naval aviator Fred Haise. When their eyes met, they all reflected bewilderment. Klaxons began to sound. Warning lights illuminated, one after another until a veritable Christmas tree of red, orange, and white lights lit the interior of Apollo 13's command module.

Jack Swigert called NASA Mission Control in Houston, some 178,643 nautical miles and fifty-six hours of flight time below them.

"Okay, Houston," he radioed. "We've got a problem here."

"This is Houston, say again please."

"Houston, we've had a problem," Lovell confirmed.

Indeed they had. Instruments showed one oxygen tank had disappeared, taking with it half of the ship's life-sustaining supply. Pressure in the second oxygen tank nosedived. Two fuel cells returned readings of zero. Electrical systems crashed; communication systems failed; the computer restarted. Technical malfunctions caused erratic bursts from the hydrogen peroxide maneuvering jets, which jolted the spacecraft from side to side, pitching it up and down.

Then Lovell looked outside and discovered the full scope of their problem.

"It looks to me that we are venting something," he told Houston. "We are venting something into space."

The three astronauts looked through the porthole and helplessly watched their life-sustaining oxygen leak steadily from the ship's ruptured side. For a moment, the crew in space and the team in Houston fell silent. Everyone realized the severity of the spacecraft's problem.

Apollo 13, which was composed of the Command/Service Module *Odyssey* and the spidery Lunar Module *Aquarius*, confronted a situation so dire that NASA had never developed procedures to address it. The spacecraft had suffered simultaneous electrical, fuel, and oxygen system crashes, which engineers assumed would doom any spacecraft. Survival then, depended on the ability of Lovell, his crew, and Mission Control to remain calm, improvise, and work together.

"We could have panicked and bounced off the walls for ten minutes," Lovell said later, "but then we'd be right back where we started. As long as it wasn't a catastrophic situation like *Columbia* or *Challenger*, but one where we were still breathing and the spacecraft was not violated by a meteor, we just had to think. You had to be objective and positive in your thinking, not looking at your hands wishing for some miracle to happen. If we'd all gotten in a fetal position to wait for a miracle, we'd still be up there."

Despite his outward calm, Lovell quietly assessed their odds; they weren't good. The fuel and oxygen situation was as bad as the instruments indicated. They had lost their chance for a lunar landing and were now just hoping to survive. The command module *Odyssey* was dying and the crew had to shut it down quickly and retreat to the lunar module. If they couldn't restore *Odyssey*'s power before reentry, they could never get home. Further, if the explosion had damaged the protective heat shield, they would disintegrate upon crossing from space back into Earth's atmosphere. But those problems would have to wait.

"As long as we were still breathing," Lovell said, "we were going to go as long as possible. If you want to put it in percentages, there was a ten percent chance we'd make it home again when the tank exploded. As we solved one problem after another, the percentages went up until at splashdown it became a hundred percent again."

For the three days after the explosion, Mission Control in Houston and the astronauts aboard Apollo 13 would work together, meeting and overcoming challenge after challenge. But despite the considerable assistance rendered by Houston, the mission's fate and the astronaut's lives ultimately lay with three men who were in two tiny conjoined spacecraft more than 200,000 miles away from Earth. Their actions onboard *Aquarius* and *Odyssey*—and their ability to improvise—would lead the mission to end with a successful splashdown or with terrible tragedy.

"People always think that the navy follows manuals or orders," Captain Lovell said. "They think there's no initiative. That's absolutely incorrect.

Naval aviation offers more opportunity to be creative and exercise initiative at a young age than anywhere else. From the very beginning, you're given a job to do and left alone to do it. It takes creativity and initiative to succeed in the military, and that's of course what it took to bring Apollo 13 home."

Jim Lovell had a wife and four children to see again; failure was not an option for him, just as Flight Director Gene Kranz famously stated it wasn't for Mission Control. Lovell rose to the challenge of manually flying the lunar module *Aquarius*, which was exceptionally unwieldy with *Odyssey*'s sixty thousand pounds of deadweight attached to it.

Trying to fly the unwieldy ship in a way it was never meant to be flown, Lovell harkened back to his first weekend at the navy's Pax River test facility, where he had walked down to the flight line for some extra practice. The only plane on the ramp was an antiquated propeller-driven AD Skyraider used to spray for mosquitoes. Pilots had nicknamed the big single-engine plane "the flying dump truck." Lovell hadn't flown prop planes since he was a student pilot, but the plane captain helped him inside and gave him a quick overview. As Lovell taxied out to the runway, he heard the plane captain shout, "Use right rudder." Unlike jet engines, the Skyraider's big 2,700 horsepower engine created heavy torque that pilots needed to use their right rudder to correct.

"Sure enough," Captain Lovell said, "When I poured the gas on, I had to jam the right rudder just to keep it straight on the runway!"

Years later, Lovell found himself having to wing it yet again. Three separate times, the veteran navy test pilot positioned the conglomeration of *Odyssey* and *Aquarius* precisely for engine burns that set their course and critical reentry angle. With so many miles to cover, the tiniest deviation at the outset would send the ship thousands of miles astray.

As they sped through space, the crew conserved every amp of power they could. Their cabin stayed cold and dark and the ship used as much electricity as a coffeemaker. Even so, Mission Control was unsure if enough power would remain to restore life to *Odyssey*, which served as the reentry vehicle—their only way home. En route to Earth, another complication arose when the lithium hydroxide devices that removed toxic carbon dioxide gas from the air in *Aquarius* became saturated. The similarly capable devices in *Odyssey* would not fit into the environmental systems of the lunar module *Aquarius*. The team faced a challenge of literally fitting a square block in a round hole. But together, the crews in Houston and space collaborated to construct the very picture of improvisation: a contraption of paper, plastic, tape, and cardboard that scrubbed the air. They dubbed it the "the mailbox." The team had solved another problem with a feat of improvisation that has few equals in aviation history.

They continued overcoming challenges one by one, until at 11:53 A.M. on Friday, April 17, 1970, Apollo 13 crossed into Earth's atmosphere. For the fourth and final time in his storied career, Jim Lovell felt the heavy Gs, heat, and vibration of a reentering spacecraft. The world waited breathlessly to see if the heat shield held and the three astronauts would survive the six-day ordeal. Then over the South Pacific appeared the tiny silver command module, swinging gently beneath a canopy of striped parachutes. Cheers went up in Times Square and around the world as millions of people heard the news.

From Mission Control: "*Odyssey*, Houston. Welcome home. We're glad to see you."

The amphibious assault ship USS *Iwo Jima* was waiting to recover the Apollo 13 astronauts, just four miles distant from their splashdown point. Three Sikorsky Sea King helicopters were airborne as the capsule floated down and they were overhead seconds after *Odyssey* settled onto the waves. A team of rescue swimmers in full dive gear was in the water moments later. Soon they were helping three tired but happy astronauts into an orange raft that was not too much larger than the one Dixon, Pastula, and Aldrich had sailed on those same waters twenty-eight years earlier. Flying its fifth and final spacecraft recovery mission, Aircraft Sixty-six of Helicopter Squadron Four (HS-4) hoisted the astronauts aboard and brought Lovell, Haise, and Swigert to the waiting *Iwo Jima*.

During World War II, hundreds of aviators and aircrew went down over those deep blue waters, but very few found ships or helicopters awaiting them. They had to survive until they floated ashore like Dixon, Aldrich, and Pastula, or until they were rescued. Long-distance PBY Catalina flying boats and U.S. submarines did most of the rescuing.

Twenty-year-old Lieutenant George H. W. Bush, still one of the youngest aviators in the fleet, had sustained severe damage to his TBM Avenger during a raid over the notorious island of Chi-Chi Jima on September 2,

1944. Despite the crippling damage to his plane, he completed his attack and laid 4 five-hundred-pound bombs into his target; he later received the Distinguished Flying Cross for his actions. But he wasn't thinking about medals. He was thinking about getting his wounded Avenger away from Chi-Chi Jima. He raced for the sea, but he didn't make it far. Flames and smoke were engulfing the plane by the time he hit the coastline.

"When I saw the flame along the wing, I said, 'I'd better get out,'" America's forty-first president recalled decades later. "I told my crewmen to get out. I dove out onto the wing. I hit my head on the tail—a glancing blow—and was bleeding like a stuck pig. I dropped into the ocean and I swam over and got into this life raft. I was sick to my stomach, I was scared. If someone didn't pick me up, I'd be captured and killed. They were very brutal on Chi-Chi Jima."

Unfortunately other planes saw only one of Bush's two crew members bail out and his chute never deployed. The loss of those two men still haunts President Bush to this day. His first thoughts after splashing into the water were of his crew. Then he realized a Japanese patrol boat was closing on him. He began to paddle his raft fervently, hoping against hope to outrun his pursuers. As it turned out, he outran them long enough for his fellow aviator Charlie Bynum to arrive in another Avenger and strafe the approaching boat. Shortly after the seas were cleared, Bush saw a periscope slicing through the water. A submarine began to surface and Bush just hoped it was American. It was the USS *Finback,* and soon Bush was on board, cruising away from the island beneath the sea. When the *Finback* returned to Pearl Harbor thirty days later, she deposited five grateful aviators her crew had rescued.

"People say you're a hero," the former president reflected with noticeable sadness. "Well, there's nothing heroic about getting shot down.[8]

"I wonder if I could have done something different. I wonder who got out of the plane. I wonder—wonder why the chute didn't open for the other guy. Why me? Why am I blessed? Why am I still alive? That has plagued me.

"Now, getting older and much, much, much, much older, and I'm at this stage; I look at all of this as a blessing. I look at all of this as having made me a better man. Little kid made into a man, by a series of circumstances over which he had no control."[9]

———

Of the hundreds of aviators who were rescued from the Pacific, most found salvation in the navy's graceful PBY Catalina flying boats, which patrolled vast distances throughout World War II, ever vigilant for airmen or sailors lost at sea. They rescued countless men. In one action, a PBY piloted by Lt. Adrian Marks rescued fifty-six survivors of the USS *Indianapolis* from their terrible three-day plight through shark-infested seas; it was July of 1945, just weeks before the war's end. But perhaps no single rescue mission was more daring than that flown by Lt. Nathan Gordon in his PBY, the *Arkansas Traveler*, on February 15, 1944.

Throughout that day, American B-25 Mitchell bombers had been raiding the Japanese stronghold of Kavieng on New Ireland, an island off the eastern coast of Papua New Guinea. The defenders took their toll and several of the big four-engine bombers ditched in the sea, some not far from the heavily fortified coastline. A circling B-25 sentry directed Gordon's PBY to one of them.

The young lieutenant settled his plane into heavy seas and had to cut off one propeller so the high seas wouldn't damage it. The twin propellers sat atop the PBY's wings, so the swells were exceptionally high, which ironically may have saved the plane.

"Gunfire from shore was hitting around us," Gordon remembered decades later. "Luckily, none hit us, and I think the swells helped us here, as the plane would have disappeared behind a swell to anyone trying to shoot at us from the shore. We pulled right up to [the six survivors], and Kelly at waist position threw out a rope and Joe Germean pulled them inside. Joe was the strongest guy in our crew, and pulled in all of the B-25 crew."

Gordon guided the flying boat through the wave troughs and got his precious cargo airborne. They had flown twenty miles when they received another radio transmission from the same B-25 sentry. Another crew needed rescuing. Gordon turned around.

He found the surviving crew just one mile from shore and already taking fire from Japanese batteries. He settled the PBY down carefully then watched his P-51 Mustang fighter escorts leave the scene as their gas tanks ran low. He became a sitting duck for vicious waves and deadly shells while Kelly and Germean pulled in three more survivors. Once they were aboard, he got his increasingly battered plane airborne. Again, twenty miles from the scene, the sentry called. The *Arkansas Traveler* and its cargo of nine wet and wounded airmen turned around another time.

"We would have to land closer to shore this time," Gordon said. "I did not consult with the crew; there was no time for making decisions. I just did it, and nobody complained. That is what had to be done; there was no time to discuss things.

"We made our final landing, only six hundred yards from shore. We had to make our approach over the town, where later I was told some of the heaviest AA fire was coming from. There was a lot of fire coming at us from the shore: small arms and machine guns as well as larger stuff. Again, none hit us. The swells helped us here, as the plane would disappear to anyone trying to shoot at us from the shore when we were behind a crest. We did the same thing and took the [six survivors] in through the waist hatch."[10]

Still under heavy fire, he plowed through the rolling swells and willed his leaking, battered, and overloaded Catalina into the air. He rose slowly and winged toward the allied base at Finschhafen, New Guinea, where he deposited fifteen B-25 survivors. By the time Nathan Gordon and his crew returned to their home base at Samarai, they had been flying and rescuing aircrews for ten hours. Five months later, the crew all received the Silver Star. As mission commander, Gordon received the Medal of Honor. After receiving the medal, he left directly for another mission.

Time and again, I saw adversity calling forth the very best in the men and women of naval aviation. They'd trained and prepared, then endured and triumphed—although not necessarily in a glamorous fashion as the three castaways showed. Regardless, they survived because of their own mettle and the character of those who brought them home. And once rescuers and rescued alike had reached safety, they reported straight back to work. Fellow servicemen still faced danger and new missions; their place was alongside them.

16

CHIEFS

A FRAMED PRINT OF THE USS *Abraham Lincoln* rocked back and forth on its hanger, in rhythm with the rocking of the ship herself as she rode the Pacific swells that had seen so many dramatic rescues and ordeals. Typically, ninety-seven-thousand tons of displacement kept the big *Nimitz*-class aircraft carriers steady, but the seas had kicked up that evening as storms raced across the ocean, stirring the waters beneath them. Below the swaying print, on a simple but comfortable couch, sat Rear Admiral Mark Guadagnini, the former Chief of Naval Air Training. Just three months earlier, Mark had left his training command in Corpus Christi, Texas, and returned to sea as Commander, Carrier Strike Group Nine.

"We're certainly feeling it tonight," said the admiral in his ever calm voice, "but for the Pacific, these swells aren't too bad. I've seen it much worse." He sipped from a glass of water and replaced it carefully on the end table.

He was glad to be at sea again—it was where he belonged. In the thirty-four years since he received his first military haircut, he had become quite accustomed to rolling seas, such as the ones presently heaving beneath the *Lincoln*'s keel. He'd flown missions from twelve different aircraft carriers on deployments around the world, and unlike many high-ranking officers, he hasn't stopped flying. He was scheduled to fly the very next day.

"You're a lucky man," I said, knowing how senior officers dread finding themselves in cockpits less and less frequently.

"I am," he said and let out a gentle laugh. "Now, my flying is largely leadership by example, but I don't go out and joyride; it's too expensive. When I fly now, I give back to the strike group. I fly the Super Hornet tanker. I'll be giving gas to someone else, so my missions provide value. But it's not the flying that keeps me in.

"Our purpose here is truly grand," he explained. "It's the United States of America. After I graduated from the Naval Academy, which I'd attended for the selfish reasons of getting an education and a job afterwards, I found myself in this organization that's filled with wonderful people and has a grand purpose. That grand purpose is the defense of our nation and the freedoms enshrined in the Constitution of the United States."

He reached across the end table and from his desk, retrieved a small blue book, a copy of the Constitution.

"This little book has guided the course of our history," he said, flipping through the pages. "That is the purpose to me. Since I've been in the navy, I've been to forty-nine different countries and there is no other country I'd rather live in than this country right now, and it's worth defending.

"Now, there's an adventure as well," he confessed. "You can go all over the world and you do. Anytime you go to sea, there's adventure—wind, waves, new ports. Then you add to that flying an airplane, which I think is the grandest of adventures, particularly off a ship at sea."

He laughed again. "There's no ride at Disneyland that compares to what we do on a regular basis!"

While Mark still flies occasionally, he more often hears the roar of jets on a catapult from his oh-three-level office, one level below the flight deck, where he spends much of his time commanding the eight aircraft squadrons, four destroyers, three frigates, cruiser, submarine, and carrier that comprise Carrier Strike Group Nine. He endeavored to lead the strike group like a conductor leads a symphony, making many talented individuals perform together as one.

To do that, he has to convey important high-level strategies and messages to all those teams and individuals under his command, from squadron skippers to department heads to the newest recruits on the lowest decks of his escorts and carrier. And those he commands must convert his tactics into action. To make that happen, he relies on chief petty officers.

"Nothing gets done until sailors take specific action, either in an aviation squadron or on a ship," Mark explained. "It takes a third-class petty officer, or airman, or seaman *doing* something to make that end goal happen. The chiefs take this highfalutin language and they turn it into something understandable so a sailor knows what he or she needs to do in terms of a specific task so we can accomplish our mission. Without that translator role played by the chiefs, nothing ever gets done and we never succeed."

The navy considers chief petty officers its senior noncommissioned officers—that is, "chiefs" serve as top leaders in any ship or squadron, but they do not hold an officer's commission. Instead, they rose through the enlisted ranks. They typically have more than ten years of experience and have earned the respect of their superiors as well as the younger sailors they lead. They know their job inside and out, having learned by doing the tough, dirty work themselves as they progressed from walking out of boot camp to earning the anchors that mark the collars of a chief's khaki uniform.

The title of "chief" has existed in the navy since 1776, but its meaning varied until 1893 when the navy officially established the rank of chief petty officer, giving it status above all other enlisted ranks. A board of senior chief petty officers and master chief petty officers selects new chiefs, who must also pass an exam and show proficiency in their rate, or job. Their subordinates generally cease calling them by their first names or rates; they're simply called "chief." And officers and sailors alike realize the chiefs make everything happen aboard ship.

Admiral Mike Mullen, Chairman of the Joint Chiefs of Staff, observed, "I believe that the chiefs run the navy . . . It is the formation of that whole command around the chiefs' mess that really makes it all come together—CPOs form the nucleus."[1]

Former Master Chief Petty Officer of the Navy Joe Campa echoed those sentiments when he addressed a class of new chiefs, saying, "Never again will individual accomplishment define your effectiveness. From this day forward, the number one indicator of your success will be the success of the sailors who look to you for leadership."[2]

Chiefs are trainers as well as leaders. By definition, chiefs are experienced sailors and skilled professionals. They know the basics of keeping their shoes polished and getting to work on time. But admirals don't want simple sailors in their command.

"Being a maritime warrior, which is what we are, takes a lot more than keeping your boots polished," Rear Admiral Guadagnini said. "Our chiefs train people to be maritime warriors. They also train them in the technical aspects of their rate, which is their specific job. The chiefs are technical masters of their given trade. No one individual person will see everything that might go wrong with a piece of equipment until they've been in for a while. The chiefs are the ones who have that experience and they're trying to impart that to the junior sailors. Chiefs are there to teach and oversee because they've done it."

The next day, the admiral was scheduled to talk with the Chiefs' Mess, a term I'd heard several times. The name stems from the separate mess hall for chiefs that each ship maintains. Since the early days of the navy, chief petty officers have always slept and dined in separate quarters from the rest of the crew, owing to their experience, age, and skill. The dining arrangement conveniently lends itself to group problem-solving and better coordination among departments, as chiefs share challenges, advice, and information.

"There are myriad problems I never see or hear about," Mark said, "because the chiefs solve them. They get together and figure them out because they want to get the job done."

The next morning, I was standing by the maintenance office of Strike Fighter Squadron Two (VFA-2)—the Bounty Hunters. Petty Officers Elizabeth "Kruzer" Kruzan and Sammy "Homer" Holmes were talking with me quietly when a stocky chief petty officer approached Sammy from behind and grabbed him in a bear hug. Sammy blinked with surprise as Chief David Price released his grip, laughed, and asked, "How ya feelin', Homer?"

"That's his way of saying good morning," Sammy told me as Price walked away. "But you noticed the first thing he asked was, 'How you feelin'?' He knows I've been a little sick and he'll always ask how I'm doing. And usually if he calls you a nickname, it's going to be a good day."

"He's always been a positive role model," Elizabeth Kruzan said as the three of us began walking to the Parachute Rigging shop, where she oversaw the maintenance of all the aircrew survival gear. Her station was the last stop pilots made before climbing up one floor to the flight deck.

"But you know when you tick him off! He's very vocal about it. Generally you know when he's angry because you have no idea what he's saying! He'll be so angry, his Arkansas background comes out and he just uses random words and collections of weird phrases. It's outlandish!"

"Like 'buttermilk pancakes,'" Sammy interjected. "It's a very good term."

"Like he's having 'a buttermilk pancakes kind of day.'"

They both laughed, then Sammy continued, "Or if people don't know what he's saying, they'll just respond, 'Roger that, buttermilk pancakes.' They don't understand anything else he said!"

"He's also the creator of nicknames. He dubs you one thing and you stay that forever. He's Homer. I'm Kruzer. Martinez Hayes was Marty. He calls the chiefs names too—there were three Johns and he named two MJ and LJ—Middle John and Little John. It went by height."

"But really, he's been a very positive role model and a very strong leader," said Sammy. "He's very up front and straightforward. He'll never lie to you—and definitely never lie to him! That's probably the worst thing you could do. He wants to know what's going on so he can know the best way to help you. If you ever lie to him and he finds out, he'll never be your friend ever again. Tell it like it is the first time and he'll fix it."

Each squadron has several divisions and each division has a lead petty officer. The Maintenance department houses the plane captains and other young deckhands (collectively called the line shack), as well as the power plant, aviation electronics, and other maintenance-related divisions. All the people who fix the planes and prepare them for flight fall under this group. The Operations department houses several divisions including safety, administration, and the officers in charge. They make sure the squadron runs smoothly. Everyone rolls up under the skipper and XO. In single-seat fighter attack squadrons, sometimes just fourteen officers will have responsibility for two hundred people, which presents quite a managerial challenge. Helicopter, two-seat fighters, and other aircraft with two or more flying officers can spread out the work among more managers. Regardless of their numbers, the officers rely on their chiefs to bring two hundred squadron personnel into line.

Chief Price owned responsibility for the entire Maintenance department of the squadron, and when he first became department chief, he admittedly knew little about the small Parachute Rigger shop where Kruzer worked; he had been an airframer, working on the nuts and bolts of fighters. But Kruzer reported that Chief Price visited the PR shop regularly to see if everyone was doing okay and if he could help them in any way.

"When I took over the PR shop," she said, "I had absolutely no idea what I was doing! He wasn't my division chief at the time, but he pulled me aside and said, 'Hey, it's not about knowing everything. It's about knowing where to go when you have problems, and knowing that you can always go find a khaki—me in particular—and we'll lead you through it.'" Sailors often call chiefs "khakis," since they're the only enlisted personnel authorized to wear khaki-colored pants.

"He's setting an example for [the younger maintainers]," Sammy added. "[He says] this is what you want to do: take care of your people, make sure they have what they need, and it's amazing what they'll do for you. They'll work the extra hours. If you need them to come in and work a weekend, they'll do it because their chief goes to bat for them. You need time off? You got it. You have problems at home, go take care of them and we'll get somebody to cover your shift. You take care of your people this way and it's amazing what it'll do for you later on. When you need to count on them, they'll be there. That's something that you wouldn't really expect from an eighteen-year-old airman out of boot camp, but Chief Price can count on these younger guys to do it just because of the way he's been bringing them up. He sets the example as a leader."

Kruzer noted that Chief Price dutifully defends his people from chiefs in other departments as well. If another chief tries to commandeer a junior airman without Chief Price's approval, he steps in. He also takes a sincere interest in helping his airmen improve themselves. Since the navy helps its enlisted personnel pay for college, each airman has a special opportunity to pursue an advanced education. And Chief Price has helped many of his subordinates see the wisdom and value of furthering their learning.

Kruzer laughed and said, "That chief from rural Arkansas who never went to college himself has gotten so many people in our squadron to go to college!"

Sammy contributed another observation about the chief's leadership.

The previous day, Chief Price had been at Catapult One near the bow. The squadron was short several people on the flight deck during a launch and the chief heard a jet near the island needed a part from a jet on the fantail.

"Chief Price did a Herschel Walker sprint from the bow of the ship to the fantail, got this fifty-pound piece of equipment, and ran with it up to the island to get it changed into another aircraft," Sammy said. "In my eyes, that's leadership. He was listening in on the radio, knew we were short-handed, ran back there and grabbed that part, and took it to the other jet so we could make our launch.

"He's supposed to be leading the whole launch and he's in the middle of it grabbing parts, taking them to other jets. He made it happen and that jet launched on time. That's how he leads."

That's not out of the ordinary for Chief Price, who Homer and Kruzer reported often walks the flight deck carrying chains—a tough job typically reserved for the newest members of the squadron.

"He's up there carrying nine chains like everybody else," Homer said with no small trace of admiration.

"He's not afraid to just do it if it needs to be done," Kruzer said. "And his uniform is never clean!"

"He's just a great leader based on his enthusiasm, emotion, and his passion for the job," Homer said. "He loves what he does. He lets everybody know it. He's rubbed off on me in very positive ways. I was one of the first people to shake his hand when he made chief. I whispered in his ear, 'There was not a better mech that could've been picked to make chief.' Chief Price is by far one of the best chiefs I've ever seen in the navy." Clearly, Chief Price knew how to motivate his sailors.

I met the man himself in the *Lincoln*'s hangar deck late one evening. It was nearing taps and he'd been up since 4:00 A.M., which I learned was fairly typical. Chief Machinist Mate Price—his formal title—had short brown hair matched with a neat moustache. He wore heavy-duty khaki pants and a brown long-sleeve T-shirt stenciled with CPO (for Chief Petty Officer) and VFA-2 (for his squadron). Like Rear Admiral Guadagnini, he'd long ago become accustomed to the swaying of a carrier on the high seas.

"I went through a hurricane on *Kennedy* back in ninety-six," the sixteen-year veteran said. "That was a lot; that was bad. This? Naaah."

Dave Price was born and raised in a small town in Arkansas, nowhere near the ocean. "We didn't even have our own zip code," the chief told me. "We had to use the one for the next town over. I had thirty-seven people in my graduating class and I joined the navy to get the hell out of there."

Like most every fresh enlistee, Dave found the work hard and low-level. He figured he'd suffer through his commitment then get out. But during his first enlistment he got married, and the stability of the navy suddenly became more appealing. Then he began advancing, his assignments improved, and he promised himself that if he made the rank of petty officer first class in ten years, he'd stay for good. He made it in seven and a half. He told his wife they were in it for the long run. She had laughed and told him, "I knew that when I met you."

"And to me," he said, "this is the best job I could ever have . . . There's always something that changes. There's always something going on—a jet turns the wrong way and you gotta grab a guy, or a jet turns the wrong way and somebody has to grab you!"

When Chief Price enlisted in 1994, he went to Fighter Squadron 101 (VF-101)—the Grim Reapers—an F-14 Tomcat squadron based at NAS Oceana in Virginia Beach. I remembered Sammy Holmes telling me about the love affair between Chief Price and the F-14 Tomcat—a sentiment shared by many of the men and women who flew and maintained the big fighters during their thirty-six years of service before their sunset in 2006. The Tomcat developed a cult following that didn't disappear when the planes retired, and the film *Top Gun* has forever enshrined their legend. Since Chief Price had spent his first years maintaining the twin engines of the sixty-thousand-pound fighters, he had developed quite an attachment. The first time he saw a maintenance crew testing the engine with a full power turn, Dave Price found his calling. The scream and thunder of the engine and the rumbling vibrations it sent coursing through the maintainers standing nearby captivated him.

"The feeling that I had sitting next to the airplane while it was doing that full power turn was unbelievable," he remembered, "I was like, 'Oh yeah, I want to do *that*. How do I get my high-power qual?' Being a mech was the easiest way to do it, so I did it. Next thing you know here I was and the first qualification I got was my turn qual so I could sit up there and turn jets, start 'em up. I could do everything but fly the damn thing. That's a hellluva feeling, helluva feeling."

I don't think Dave Price ever set out to become a chief petty officer, but it happened while on deployment aboard the *Lincoln*, three years before we met. Chief Price recounted the story.

"Skipper came down and knocked me off my chair and said, 'Congratulations, Chief.'

"I said, 'You're out of your mind. They don't make guys like me chief anymore.'"

The chief always spoke his mind, didn't watch his language, and generally didn't kowtow to superiors. In his mind, he wasn't the ideal candidate. But the squadron's commanding officer thought just the opposite; Price was exactly the right guy.

"You've got the wrong name," he protested once more. "It can't be me! I've stepped on too many toes and I've told too many people to go screw themselves for them to make me a chief. No way.

"Well, sure enough, the results came out and seven weeks later I'm getting those golden anchors pinned to my collar."

Who knows how his straightforward nature played in the promotion board's discussion, but the number of people who have reenlisted because of Chief Price perhaps speaks to his character more than anything else. At least five airmen have asked Chief Price to stand next to them at the ceremony where they announce their commitment to extend their service. He seems genuinely surprised, or perhaps amused, that he has received so many such requests, each of which he regards as an honor.

"To be able to stand up there and have this guy continue his naval service because he respects me is pretty awesome and pretty interesting," he said. "I never coddled anybody. I was always stern. I'm gonna tell you exactly how I feel when I feel it and if you don't like it, piss off. That's just the way it is.

"But I guess they know what they're gettin' with me. I may chew your ass when you mess up but I'll be the first one to have your back. I've always got their back. If anyone is going to chew their ass, it's going to be me. You don't mess with my people. You've got a problem with my people, you come to me. That's the way I've always been coming up through the ranks. That's why I'm here. That's my only real job right now: I take care of my guys. Ten fingers and ten toes at the end of the day; that's all that matters. They come home at the end of the day and I'm good. Evidently a lot of the junior folks—couple of senior guys as well—have liked that outlook and they'll come to me and ask me to stand beside them when they reenlist."

At the moment, he had lost track of how many times he'd reenlisted—he estimated three or four—and as soon as the *Lincoln* returned to her home port in Everett, Washington, he would sign up for an additional six years.

Many times during my travels, I heard the phrase, "Chiefs are the backbone of the navy." The more enlisted personnel and officers with whom I spoke, the more I understood how true that statement rings. Chiefs turn orders into action and serve as an invaluable and trusted source of knowledge for young sailors and officers alike.

"Every one of these kids you see that's not wearing these peanut-butter-colored pants are taught one thing," Price said. "Ask the chief. You got problems, you got questions? Ask the chief. Period. We gotta know the answers or know where to find the answers. And we don't blow smoke up their butts. No—do not lead these kids the wrong way. Maybe that's why it fits me to a T. I've never been that guy to blow smoke up somebody's butt. I'll tell you exactly what I'm thinking when I'm thinking it. When the kids come up and they've got problems, I'll fix them. One way or another, I'll fix them."

Chief petty officers typically range from their young thirties up well into their forties. In rank, they are below the greenest commissioned officers in the fleet. In experience, they far surpass them. Among chiefs' jobs lies training and mentoring junior officers—those ensigns and lieutenants who are learning how to navigate within their new squadrons on their first tour. It requires a delicate balance since all officers outrank any enlisted sailor, no matter his seniority. Technically, a junior officer could reprimand a chief or assert his or her rank. Practically, however, a more senior officer would most likely redirect the upstart lieutenant and show him the value of the chief's point of view. So the delicate job of training these junior officers (JOs) falls to the chiefs. They must help them appreciate their enlisted counterparts, who are so critical to their unit's success. They teach the young officers the fundamentals of operating a squadron, which is like operating a two-hundred-person business.

"I have a good time with training the JOs," Chief Price explained. "The JOs are nothing more than a bunch of young airmen. The only difference is the enlisted guys are fresh out of A-School and the JOs are fresh out of flight school. There's no real difference; somebody has to teach them the ways of the world. Somebody's gotta teach the JOs how to handle these eighteen- or nineteen-year-old kids. And they're not but twenty-three or twenty-four themselves.

"What's expected of them? How are they supposed to act? I'm training them to be a division officer or a department head one day. Or training them to be an executive officer or a skipper. If a JO has a bad experience with a chief or if a chief has never taught him anything when he's an ensign or JO, when he grows up to be a skipper, he's going to be a raving lunatic and not have any trust in his chiefs. Then his squadron is going downhill. You don't trust your chiefs and don't trust your chiefs' mess, things will go downhill quickly. When you give your chiefs' mess a chance to work and do their job and take care of the squadron the way they're supposed to take care of their squadron, life is pretty good."

Before I left the *Lincoln,* I asked Elizabeth Kruzan—Kruzer—to help me find one of the airmen Chief Price had reenlisted. We wove through the endless corridors of the ship, weaving from the VFA-2 maintenance desk forward and to the port side of the oh-three level. In the Quality Control shop, she introduced me to six-foot-five Nick Davis, who hailed from an even smaller town then Chief Price—Raywick, Kentucky, population 142.

A smile spread across his thin face when I asked him about the chief.

"Chief Price is one of those good leaders who can be hard," Nick said, "but he'll teach you what you need to know. If you're being stupid, he'll let you know. For me, he'd always let me know if I was doing something wrong. He'd also show me the right way to do it. Sometimes he might not be the nicest about it . . . but we're in the navy, it's real life.

"He's always helped me out and he backs you up; he protects you. Even if you've done wrong and you come honest with him, he'll let other people know, 'Yeah, Nick screwed up, but look at all the good stuff he's done.' If they try to screw you over, he'll do his best not to let it happen—and he's done that for me before. So I have no doubt in my mind that if he can help you out, he'll do it.

"I wouldn't be here today if it weren't for him. They keep telling me I'm one of the top people in the command—that's what they tell me anyhow—and if he wouldn't have trained me and helped me out when I first met him, I'd still be struggling. The chiefs sure work us hard sometimes, but they're fair and make sure we do it right. They know we'll take their place one day."

When I awoke to another day, the *Lincoln* rode on much calmer waters, which I watched glide peacefully by the ship's side from the hangar deck where I stood with Command Master Chief Susan Whitman, the highest-ranking noncommissioned officer aboard. The aft port elevator was raised and we looked out through the enormous opening across a sea glowing softly with the sun's first rays. It was time for an early breakfast and we headed below to the fabled chiefs' mess.

By 6:30 A.M. the serving line was already full, as it had been since much earlier. Morning often comes early in the navy; Chief Price usually woke up around 4:30. I stood next to one of his counterparts from VFA-2, Chief Petty Officer Chris Bolin. As we watched food service attendants pile breakfast onto our plates, the tall Tennessean explained that the mess—and ship—hummed around the clock.

"You can't let this ship run itself," he said. "For us aviation guys, we only man-up for flight operations, but the ship's producing power twenty-four hours a day. It never sleeps and someone is always on duty.

"In the chiefs' berthing, we pretty much never turn the lights on. You don't walk into a chiefs' berth and turn the lights on unless you want your tail kicked. You don't know who's on what shift, who's asleep, and who's had a hard day."

Since sailors' shifts run around the clock, chiefs' schedules vary; someone is always in their rack, as bunks are called aboard ship. They shut dark curtains and rig improvised shields to keep light out of their narrow bunks so they can sleep regardless of others' schedules. The system holds true in the chief petty officer berthing, which sleeps up to 100 men, and in the enlisted berthing, which sleeps up to 225. The two-, four-, and eight-man officers' quarters often have similar setups.

"But *here* is where we solve problems," Chief Bolin explained as we sat down with our trays at a table with several other chiefs. "It's not about how smart how *I* am; it's how smart we are together—those of us sitting at the table. Now, we may argue about the best solutions to a problem, but when we leave the chiefs' mess here, we're on the same page."

Many of the challenges that get a hearing over breakfast or dinner in the mess have little to do with specific skills or functions. Each chief has unquestionably amassed the knowledge and experience to become a subject matter expert in a particular area. But so often, their general leadership skills matter most.

"When we put our khakis on," Chief Bolin said, "it's less about the skills and more about the people. As chiefs, our job is about managing, leading, motivating, and helping our sailors."

And the navy's chiefs do that like few other groups of leaders. A carrier's 200 chiefs keep more than 4,000 enlisted personnel focused and motivated, contributing to a ship that remains at the ready day and night until the mission ends.

After breakfast with *Lincoln*'s CPOs, I climbed a series of ladders to the Air Transfer Office where I put on the now-familiar cranial and olive horse-collar life preserver. A sailor escorted me outside the island into the din of flight operations, which easily seeped through my headphones and foamies, as earplugs are called aboard ship. We walked through the heat and fumes of jet exhaust to the waiting COD. Its crew, who were members of the West Coast's fleet logistics support squadron—the VRC-30 Providers—directed me to a seat by the porthole and the gate began to close. Again, I felt the aircraft roll toward the catapult, maneuver into position, and gun its turbo-prop engines. Seconds later, the catapult engaged and through the porthole I glimpsed a rainbow of colored shirts rushing by. The cat stroke sent us hurtling off the carrier's bow and our twin propellers strained to pull us away from the waves. We rose into an impossibly clear sky and banked away from the ship.

I watched the magnificent Pacific spread out below me and remembered taking in the vastness of those same waters from a catwalk near the stern of the USS *Nimitz*. Chief Rob Palmer of VFA-14 had been with me.

The day's flight operations had ended and a relative quiet had fallen over the deck. All I could hear was the ever-present hum of the ship and the hissing of the parted waves against our hull, sixty feet below. The ocean view was supremely peaceful; for a minute, I forgot I was aboard a warship. When Rob joined me on the catwalk, he had just insured that the last of his squadron's jets had been properly spotted on the deck and tightly secured. He had removed the white cranial that identified him as the chief in charge of everything and everyone on deck that belonged to the Tophatters. If something went wrong with any of the squadron's aircraft or if someone made a mistake, Chief Palmer would receive the first call from the Air Boss and would bear responsibility. Throughout his career, his superiors had groomed him for this very position. He was ready for it.

He had been working flight decks since he joined the navy after a short stint as a carpenter and cabinetmaker in New Jersey. He spent his twentieth birthday in boot camp. He entered the fleet as an aviation machinist mate and had worked his way up for seventeen years, doing what he loved—fixing jets.

"I've always loved working with my hands," he said. "I've worked on cars ever since I was old enough to work on them. I used to hang out at the local gas station and do oil changes and things like that. It was basically free labor—the owner might give me five bucks after I'd put a few hours of work in. I always liked tinkering with things. I always had a screwdriver and wrench in my hand as a kid. It was just fitting to become a mechanic.

"But now I have to drop the wrench and let the other guys do it. That's been the hardest thing. Now I'm in a managerial position, where I'm not the first one to grab the toolbox. I have to make sure the second-, third-, and first-classes are out doing it."

His role had changed as he progressed in rank. New and greater responsibilities were placed on his shoulders. He wasn't just responsible for himself or one particular jet. He had to oversee more and more aircraft and personnel.

"With rank comes responsibility," he said. "There's a lot of responsibility to make sure the younger guys are led properly, especially as a chief. If I want to *stay* the senior leader, I'll make everyone else fail, then I'll have no replacement. But I want to train each guy to do the next guy's job. I should be looking to do a senior chief's job where my first-classes should be looking to do my job; a second-class should be looking to do a first class's job. Essentially, someone should put me out of a job.

"And the higher you get in rank, the more of an example you are. If they see that the chief did it, they think, 'Why can't I?' We have to reflect what we say. The flight deck isn't a 'Do as I say, not as I do' place. You've got to instill the proper attitudes and proper ethics if you want to help the person better themselves."

The chiefs I encountered on the Pacific evidenced the characteristics that seemed to mark the people of naval aviation—they were doing their job to make the next guy better. They came to work, honed their skills, and passed them on for the sake of their unit. Like Chief Palmer, they all were preparing to hand over their tools, but not before showing that aspiring first- or second-class petty officer how to use them. And like Chief Price, their motivation and example could make a real difference in the lives of others.

Once, I had understood almost nothing about the men in the grease-stained multicolored shirts marked with CPO. They seemed to be ever-present on carrier flight decks, mess decks, hangar decks, and corridors. And everywhere they walked, sailors would address them with one name only: "Chief." But I didn't recognize the hard work that earned that title; I didn't understand their role in this great shipboard play. Then I discovered how they prepare aircraft and crew, lead by example, and make launches happen on time, again and again, sometimes by dragging the chains themselves. I learned that crucial skills don't necessarily come from a college degree; dedication doesn't require an officer's commission; and leaders don't always receive a salute, the gesture of respect rendered only to officers. Chief petty officers run a proven personnel management system that has kept the U.S. Navy strong for more than a century. By serving as mentors, coaches, experts, disciplinarians, hard workers, father figures, and examples, chiefs motivate and train the youngest and newest members of the navy. They take raw but willing recruits and make them into capable individuals, dedicated team members, and true maritime warriors.

17

SACRIFICE

Dawn was breaking over the long-silent Diamond Head volcano that watches over Honolulu, Hawaii, when the final liberty of the USS *Nimitz*'s Western Pacific deployment ended. All hands reassembled on Hotel Pier at Pearl Harbor and began filing back onto the ship that had been their floating home for the past six months. Some were sunburned from the warm but unrelenting sunshine that falls on the beach at Waikiki. Others were groggy from celebrations at Duke's and other traditional establishments of call in Honolulu. But the entire crew gathered with an air of anticipation—they were finally heading home.

A small flotilla of tugboats was soon pulling *Nimitz* away from her moorings and carefully turning the great ship around in the tight confines of the harbor. Her stern swung past the modern pier and her bow pivoted toward memorials to sailors of another war and another generation.

I stood on the large number "68" that marked the foremost section of *Nimitz*'s 364-yard-long flight deck. The number signified her place as the sixty-eighth fleet carrier built by the United States. She entered service in 1975, fifty-three years after the first aircraft carrier, the USS *Langley* (CV-1). Standing on the deck's forward edge, I watched the mystic green mountains and hillsides of Hawaii pass before our turning bow. They now stood sun-washed, warm, and quiet, but on December 7, 1941, waves of Japanese aircraft had swarmed down their very flanks toward this unsuspecting blue harbor at their base. Those planes and their successful mission redefined the entire discipline of naval warfare.

On that Sunday morning in 1941, Japanese aviators flew over waters just as quiet and clear as those that bore the *Nimitz* on this particular spring day. Then their guns, torpedoes, and bombs roiled the harbor and blackened the sky as they brutally and methodically destroyed U.S. bases on Oahu and the battleships that formed the backbone of the American Pacific Fleet. That day, America entered World War II—and our navy entered a new era, one defined by carrier aviation.

In the early battles of the Coral Sea and Midway, opposing ships never sighted one another; carrier aircraft pressed the attacks and won the day. The USS *Hornet* sailed its mobile airfield toward the coast of Japan and from several hundred miles beyond the horizon launched sixteen Army Air Corps B-25 bombers under the command of Lt. Col. Jimmy Doolittle on a surprise raid over Japan that stunned the Japanese public. As the Americans pressed westward, hopping from island outpost to island outpost, fast carriers and their planes cleared the skies and seas, and readied the beaches for the marines. Carriers became the deciding factor in the Pacific campaign and so they have remained. Today, whenever an international crisis erupts, America's leaders immediately ask, "Where are our carriers?"

I watched *Nimitz*'s long shadow pass by the USS *Arizona* Memorial, a gleaming white monument that gracefully spans the sunken hull of the once proud battleship. Tears of oil still rose to the surface from the ship's tanks, a poignant tribute to those 1,117 men who died on board that morning in 1941. Rusted gun placements broke the surface of the crystalline water. An American flag flapped softly from a shiny pole bolted to the *Arizona*'s weathered masthead, which still stood above her sunken bridge.

The tugs continued turning our massive ship around in the harbor and her bow swung toward the decommissioned battleship USS *Missouri*, where on September 2, 1945, the Japanese surrendered to Fleet Admiral Chester Nimitz and General Douglas MacArthur. From the bow of the admiral's namesake ship, I looked over the war's beginning and its end.

We soon left these monuments in our faint wake as the tugboats ushered us down the narrow channel, toward the open sea, and toward home.

As Oahu's last mountaintop sank into the ethereally blue Pacific and the carrier began plowing the ocean's long swells, I thought about how much had transpired on those waters in such short order. In December of 1941, Pearl Harbor lay in ruins along with America's pride and hopes for victory in the Pacific. Just six months later, all that changed on a swath of ocean not far to our northwest.

In May of 1942, the U.S. military cracked Japanese codes and learned that a significant force was converging on Midway Atoll, a small American base thirteen hundred miles northwest of Pearl Harbor. If Japan could gain a foothold at Midway, it could stage strikes against Hawaii and eventually, the West Coast of the United States. With this serious threat in mind, Admiral Nimitz dispatched naval aviator Vice Admiral William "Bull" Halsey's Task Force Sixteen. The task force sailed under command of Rear Admiral Raymond Spruance, filling in for an ill Halsey, to confront a force of more than two hundred Japanese ships divided into several task forces, which included eight carriers, eleven battleships, twenty-two cruisers, sixty-five destroyers, twenty-one submarines, and roughly seven hundred aircraft. Japan's First Air Fleet, the component that would soon engage the Americans, sailed with four carriers and 261 aircraft. Just two U.S. carriers—*Enterprise* and *Hornet*—fifteen escorts, and 158 aircraft formed the initial American opposition. Repair crews in Hawaii had worked for three straight days and nights to repair a third carrier, the USS *Yorktown*, which had suffered severe damage in the Battle of the Coral Sea. She set out for Midway two days later with Task Force Seventeen, which had eight escorts and seventy-five aircraft; crews were still making repairs as *Yorktown* steamed northwest. Rear Admiral Frank Jack Fletcher took command of the combined American force and hoped that with his ships, submarines, three carrier air groups, and the garrison at Midway itself, he stood a fighting chance against the Imperial Japanese Navy.

Fletcher's hopes and fortunes would turn almost entirely on one hour of battle during the morning of June 4, when tremendous sacrifice made way for ultimate victory. It was that sacrifice, more than the victory it enabled, that preoccupied me as I looked out over the Pacific from the deck of the *Nimitz*. It was a perfect morning at the beginning of June, just before the battle's anniversary. I imagined the aviators aboard *Yorktown, Enterprise*, and *Hornet* walking onto their wooden flight decks under these same skies nearly seventy years ago. Many would never see another sunrise.

At dawn on that morning, several waves of aircraft left Midway to attack the four carriers of the recently located Japanese fleet. Six new TBF Avenger torpedo bombers and four B-26 Marauder bombers outfitted with torpedoes were among them. Foreshadowing a day of terrible losses for American torpedo bombers, only one Avenger and two Marauders would survive the early morning attack; twenty-nine men were lost. Just as the Midway-based strike was being savaged by the Japanese fleet's defenders, the American carriers began launching their first strikes, using the navy's antiquated Devastator torpedo bombers. Torpedo Squadron Eight from *Hornet*, Torpedo Squadron Six from *Enterprise,* and Torpedo Squadron Three from *Yorktown* were soon airborne. By the time they approached the Japanese fleet, none of these forty-one torpedo bombers had fighter escorts. Poor decision making, aircraft limitations, and confusion en route conspired to put the fighters nowhere near where they were needed.[1]

Between 9:30 and 9:40 A.M., two hours after they launched, the twenty-nine TBD Devastators of Torpedo Eight and Six sighted the Japanese fleet, dove toward the sea, and began their torpedo runs. They flew low, slow, and straight toward the carriers. The pilots focused on completing their methodical runs, just as they'd trained. But in real combat, they were effectively sitting ducks. Rear gunners in the Devastators had little chance of defending their obsolete aircraft against the agile Zeros that pounced upon them from every quarter. Pilots saw friends shot down in flames, yet onward they flew, through the flack and smoke until they too burst into flames or crashed into the sea. The Japanese Zeros flying combat air patrol downed every plane from Torpedo Eight.

Of the thirty pilots and airmen in Torpedo Eight's fifteen planes, only Ensign George Gay, who was rescued by a PBY Catalina patrol plane after thirty hours afloat, survived. Next, Zeros sent ten of fourteen Devastators from Torpedo Six into the sea. At 10:00 A.M., the planes of Torpedo Three from *Yorktown* began their runs; only two planes out of twelve escaped. Even had American fighters escorted the Devastators that morning, they would have suffered heavy losses too; Japanese Zeros far outmatched the obsolescent F4F Wildcats used in early 1942.

In all, fifty-one planes tried to torpedo bomb the Japanese fleet that morning. Only seven returned to their bases. Of 128 pilots and crew involved, 29 survived. Not one torpedo exploded against a Japanese ship.

Regardless of the wisdom behind the torpedo attacks, which has been debated, the aviators and crew did their best to complete their missions, even as they knew odds leaned against them. They didn't flinch. They took their slow, outmatched bombers into the enemy's teeth without fighter cover. They stayed on course through a hail of flack until they were shot into the sea, one by one.

The minutes following their attacks would make their sacrifice one of the most important of World War II. One of American naval aviation's darkest hours became one of its finest.

The torpedo bombers had pulled the Japanese fighters down low to near sea level. Likewise, Japanese lookouts trained their eyes low on the horizon, scanning for more torpedo planes. They failed to notice the approach of another group of aircraft high overhead.

Dive-bomber squadrons from *Yorktown* and *Enterprise* arrived above the Japanese force just as the torpedo attacks ended. Wade McCluskey, who commanded the SBD Dauntless dive-bombers from *Enterprise*, had miraculously found the Japanese fleet by following a trailing destroyer, the *Arashi*. He led his planes in the direction indicated by the destroyer, even though they'd neared bingo state—the point at which their planes would not have enough fuel to return to their carriers. They were risking their lives, knowing someone had to eliminate the Japanese carriers. If they didn't do it, who would?

High over the melee, McCluskey's dive-bombers from *Enterprise* met those from *Yorktown*, commanded by Max Leslie. Finding the skies above Japan's carriers undefended, the leaders divided the targets and began their attacks, screaming down upon *Akagi (Red Castle)*, *Soryu (Green Dragon)*, and *Kaga (Increased Joy)* from on high and planting bombs squarely into their flight decks, which were packed with fueled planes and munitions. Within minutes, the Japanese carriers were hopelessly ablaze. These three veterans of the Pearl Harbor attacks—along with a fourth Pearl Harbor veteran, the nearby *Hiryu (Flying Dragon)*—would soon sink, joining the planes of America's valiant torpedo squadrons. As the Japanese carriers sank into the depths, they dragged with them any realistic hope of victory for the Japanese Empire in the Pacific.

Before and since those days in 1942, sacrifice and tragedy have punctuated naval aviation's story. Some sacrifices have come in combat, like the destruction of Torpedo Three, Six, and Eight; the death of Jesse Brown in Korea; the shoot-down of famed Hellcat ace and Medal of Honor recipient Butch O'Hare; and the loss of the USS *Yorktown*'s charismatic E. T. "Smokey" Stover over Truk in the South Pacific.

Other deaths have occurred in peacetime. Hoser Satrapa's best friend Jim Cannon crashed when a sudden downdraft sent his F-8 Crusader into a mountainside. Pete Booth's best friend Bob Gale was lost at sea shortly after his jet's engines malfunctioned on takeoff. Barbara Ann Allen Rainey, the first female naval aviator, died in a training accident as she taught a new student how to fly. Sixty-six people lost their lives in 1955 when a Douglas C-118 Liftmaster transport crashed in Hawaii, the worst disaster in naval aviation history. Mission pilot Captain Michael J. Smith died in the 1986 *Challenger* disaster. Commander Willie McCool perished as the space shuttle *Columbia* disintegrated upon reentry in 2003. The pursuit of naval aviation has always come at a price.

None of these tragic deaths had touched me personally, however. When I sailed from Pearl Harbor aboard the *Nimitz*, I had not yet known the pain of loss or had to ask the question "Why?"

Five days and two thousand nautical miles after watching the Hawaiian Islands disappear into the foaming wake of the *Nimitz,* the great ship at last came to rest off the coast of California. A six-month deployment had almost ended. The air wing would depart the ship the next day and the carrier would sail proudly into San Diego Bay soon thereafter, her sailors manning the rails in their white summer uniforms. On their final night aboard, several aviators and I had gathered in a dimly lit passageway near the forward wardroom. Taps had already been announced. A hush had fallen over the ship and most crewmen and pilots were sleeping; no late-night landings or echoing catapult shots would disturb their rest on this most quiet of nights. Soft red lamps glowed in the long port corridor where we stood talking, our voices hushed. For most, it was their last night aboard after six months at sea. Each was overtly anxious to return home, but at this late moment, I sensed a reluctance to leave the constant camaraderie of friends—almost like that mix of emotions students experience on the last day of school. When these aviators flew their aircraft off the deck the next day, another chapter would come to an end. They would soon forget the hardships of deployment and remember the friendships instead.

Among the group was a dark-haired helicopter pilot named Allison Oubre—call sign "Cholula," or "Lula" for short. The young Louisianan had reminded the skipper of her squadron, Helicopter Antisubmarine Squadron Six (HS-6)—the Screamin' Indians—of the woman adorning bottles of Cholula hot sauce; the nickname stuck.

Allison had grown up with the navy. Her father served as an officer aboard an amphibious assault ship and like many children of military families, she attended more schools than she could count on one hand—in her case, seven different schools before ninth grade. She had never set out to become a naval aviator but she joined the NROTC program at Vanderbilt University, where she was a member of the Class of 2003.

When she began considering aviation as a career, her parents subtly tried to steer her toward safer endeavors. Her father had seen two helicopters lost on one of his Western Pacific deployments and never forgot those tragedies. Like most parents, Don and Judy Oubre encouraged their daughter to excel in the path she ultimately chose, but held some worry, much like parents of firefighters or police officers.

After she graduated from Vanderbilt, Allison entered the navy's flight training program with her best friend from NROTC, Andrea Alvord. When she and Andrea arrived at Pensacola, they began hearing the term "Type A personality" used to describe pilots. Well, the twosome never felt they belonged in that category.

"We had none of that Type A organization," Andrea said with a laugh as she recalled her friendship with Allison from her home in Norfolk. "We did everything at the last minute—and we always had fun. We said we were B-plus personalities."

But they certainly had the spirit that marks so many aviators and their exploits together included sailing, backpacking in Europe, and witnessing the running of the bulls in Pamplona, Spain.

"I've never met anybody more similar to me than Allison," Andrea said.

"We always joked about what a terrible decision it would be on the part of the navy to let us fly together. For Allison and me, there'd be no checks and balances! If one of us thought something was a good idea, so would the other. That's not what you need in a cockpit!"

During flight training, Allison met fellow helicopter pilot Colter Menke and on October 23, 2004, Colter took Allison on the first of many dates. The pair complemented each other and their relationship deepened, enduring training and deployment schedules that would have submarined many budding romances.

After my cruise on the *Nimitz*, I met Colter, who described the beginnings of his relationship with Allison. "Our underway periods didn't align since we were assigned to different battle groups," he said. "She was assigned to the *Nimitz* and I was on the *Abraham Lincoln*. One time, I watched her pull into port from the pier and talked to her on the phone and then had to rush to another pier to get on my ship, where she came over and watched me leave while we talked on the phone. I have never counted the days we were apart for the two or three years that we dated and were engaged but I'm sure it was well over half."

Colter proposed in October of 2007. They were married a year later in a San Diego courthouse so they could receive collocation orders for future assignments. They planned the big wedding for summer 2009 in St. Louis Cathedral, which famously anchors Jackson Square in New Orleans.

Sometime after midnight on that last night aboard *Nimitz*, the small group finally disbanded and we retreated to our respective racks. The next morning, pilots and NFOs assembled in the wardroom for an early breakfast, then prepared to return to their home bases on land. Up on the flight deck, yellow-shirted shooters kept four catapults busy all morning, firing off more than fifty aircraft—F/A-18s, E-2C Hawkeyes, and EA-6B Prowlers. The constant din of jets roaring at full power assaulted the crew on deck and everyone watching the activity from Vulture's Row and the superstructure's decking. The bow withstood the unrelenting assault of the catapult shuttle, which sent a dull thud resounding through the ship every time it slammed into the hydraulic pressure brakes. By early afternoon, the noise and vibration had subsided; the jets had flown home. The shooters ending their tour ceremoniously launched their brown boots over the bow with the catapult. Then they disappeared from the deck arm in arm; a full celebration would no doubt soon take place at an appropriate establishment on North Island or across the harbor in San Diego. Only six Seahawk helicopters remained on deck, and they too soon left one by one.

I watched Allison and her crew emerge from below deck in their green flight suits, dark visors, and shining helmets. They walked to their waiting bird, performed a final preflight check, and climbed inside. Exhaust puffed from the engines and the blades began to spin until they created a dark halo above the gray SH-60F Seahawk. Soon thereafter, Allison powered up and lifted the last of Carrier Air Wing Eleven's aircraft off *Nimitz*. She pitched her nose toward San Diego and disappeared from sight.

Just before going to bed on May 19, 2009—a year after Allison had flown that last helicopter off the deck—Lt. Carl Ellsworth of Electronic Attack Squadron 135 (VAQ-135)—the Black Ravens—aboard *Nimitz* got word that a helicopter from the ship's air wing had gone down off San Diego. As Coast Guard cutters, an E-2C Hawkeye, and another *Nimitz* helo reported details, the ship began understanding the scope of the tragedy. The crew wasn't bobbing in a life raft waiting for rescue. All five crew members had perished.

Twenty-five-year-old rescue swimmer Naval Air Crewman 2nd Class Aaron Clingman of Bend, Oregon, left behind his wife Ashley and ten-month-old daughter Aiden. Naval Air Crewman 1st Class Grant Kerslake from Hot Springs, Arkansas, had two boys, Justin and Samuel Ryan. Lt. Commander Eric Purvis also had two sons. The small community of Lovelock, Nevada, lost Naval Air Crewman 3rd Class Sean Ward, who had graduated high school just two years before the accident.

Then there was young Lt. Allison M. Oubre of Slidell, Louisiana. That night, Allison—Cholula, Lula, Don and Judy's daughter, Colter's wife, Andrea's best friend—had been killed.

She would never return to her squadron ready room, the *Nimitz*, or her home. Her fellow Air Wing Eleven pilot Lt. Ellsworth remembered, "Throughout the day following the accident, we kept wondering, 'Where is Allison?'" They did not immediately release the names of those involved in the incident, but everyone soon feared the worst.

Allison's best friend Andrea was in Peru, taking two days of liberty from the frigate USS *Carr*, when she heard about a crash. She thought little of it until two days later when she saw that a friend had posted a note on Allison's Facebook page, saying he knew Allison was in Heaven. Suddenly, Andrea understood. She realized why her parents had unexpectedly sent a message to call them the previous day. When she reached her father, she learned the few available details and immediately returned to the *Carr*.

Almost a year to the day later, Andrea battled soft tears as she shared her memories of that tragic event. She recalled, "During the hour-long bus ride back to the ship, I was thinking, 'She has to be okay, she has to be okay.' But the worst part was being a helo pilot and knowing that it wasn't good that they hadn't found the survivors yet. Then I thought about how it was only a month before her wedding, and I'd been thinking about what to say at the reception. I was suddenly hoping that I wouldn't have to say it at her funeral."

Within an hour of reaching the *Carr*, Andrea learned that Allison's body had been recovered. "I fell to the floor in the O-Country hallway [the officers-only passageway]," she remembered. "Literally, my knees buckled. I really had been holding out such strong hope until that moment."

When Andrea reached Miami, she heard from the military liaison assigned to help Allison's family; she wondered how the liaison had known her number. She learned Allison had listed her on her emergency form. Then Andrea reread an old text message from her best friend. The two always called each other whenever they heard Lee Greenwood's song "Proud to Be an American," and months earlier Allison had sent Andrea a text at 3 A.M. Eastern: "It's too late to call, but 'Proud to Be an American' is on and it's tradition :)." The full reality finally struck her; Allison was gone.

"When Allison died we had been legally married for seven months," reflected Colter, "but we still referred to each other as fiancés. So on May 19 of 2009, just a month before her 'real wedding,' I lost my fiancée and my wife.

"I think we were still operating under the assumption that *it* couldn't happen to either one of us. In 2007 we both attended the memorial service for a fellow female helicopter pilot and friend who was killed along with her crew when their aircraft lost control off the coast of San Diego. The young woman's husband gave a speech at the service and could barely get a word out without breaking into sobs. Allison, Andrea, and I walked away from that service deeply affected and I remember thinking to myself that I was glad that wasn't me on that podium asking what I was supposed to do next."

Andrea's department head had encouraged her to go to that particular memorial service, saying, "This is your first one, so it's really important to go."

His words struck Andrea: "First one? There are going to be more than this?"

Later, an admiral had told her, "When I was your age, I would go to about six of these a year. People older than me will say they'd go to nine or ten a year."

Thousands have lost—or given—their lives while flying for their country, and many of those deaths have occurred in training, not in combat. Thankfully safety practices and better equipment make crashes less common today. Despite the risks that do remain, young men and women continue to volunteer and continue to sacrifice.

"There are a lot of sacrifices that go with the military," Colter said. "In our jobs we don't necessarily sacrifice our lives any more or less than anyone in any other branch of the military and it's probably safer to be in naval aviation than in the forces that are literally fighting on the front lines. That doesn't mean that sacrificing time, youth, and love for the military is any easier but it's a part of what we want to do to ensure we've done our part for our country. I think it's interesting to talk to friends of mine that have given almost a decade of their lives serving in the military and yet want to sign on for more time because they feel they haven't given enough.

"Allison used to always say, 'There's always someone who has it worse,' which is really true and helps to put things in perspective when you think that you just can't help out anymore."

Allison couldn't have given more, nor could Colter in a sense. The entire military community recognizes that type of sacrifice and support for the family poured from all quarters.

"Regardless of the tragedy that occurs or the branch of the military that experiences it, we are all on the same team," Colter said. "I received heartfelt condolences from someone in every branch of the military and was told by numerous stalwart men that they broke down in tears when they heard of Allison's accident . . . The military family is very tight."

"Both our families were—and are—supportive of what we do and are so proud of us," explained Andrea, whose sister Nicky flies with the VAW-115 Liberty Bells—the E-2C Hawkeye squadron aboard the USS *George Washington*. "My mom finally made herself stop worrying about the risks, but she thought of Allison as a third daughter. She was devastated, just like me. I thought, 'How could I continue flying and take that risk, knowing that my parents could have to go through what they did for Allison all over again?' Then I thought, 'I could die in a car accident tomorrow.' You accept risks in life and do your best to manage them and trust your crew does the same. But I do think about it when I fly, although I shouldn't. When something goes wrong, the community comes together like no other."

Allison's father Don explained, "There is a saying that 'the navy takes care of its own,' and it is definitely a truism. Not only in times of crisis such as Allison's death, but in everyday navy life. Having spent twenty years in the navy and now fifteen years in civilian jobs, it is a different culture in the private sector, and that positive aspect of military life is often taken for granted or not understood."

Her mother Judy added that most people have difficulty comprehending the everyday risks and sacrifices—great and small—that accompany shipboard flight operations, which are more dangerous and demanding than most every other occupation. As a result, she thinks that military families and members tend to avoid discussing those risks. Instead they just accept them once the decision has been made to pursue the naval aviation path.

"I think Allison was extremely proud of what she was doing in serving her country," her mother reflected, "and she fully realized and accepted the unique sacrifices a career in the navy—and flying in particular—presented."

Presiding at Allison's funeral, Father Mark Lomax said, "I don't think most people understand the sacrifices that Allison made—and so many people of our armed services make every day—the peril of their own lives, to protect, to serve, to take care of us all."[2]

Until 2009, I had to count myself among those ranks—I had never known anyone who had died in the line of duty, nor had I spent enough time with active duty men and women to see the sacrifices they make on a daily basis.

I had been among those millions of Americans who never fully understand or realize what the individuals in our armed forces sacrifice for us, for our freedom, and for our country. In fact, I thought about it rarely. That has all changed.

Sacrifice made for country and duty doesn't remove the pain of loss, and those close to Allison are still enduring a pain shared by too many other military families. And while I didn't know Allison like her family, lifelong friends, and squadron mates did, I'm still haunted by the infinite sadness of the memorial service, where Allison's fiancé and mother sat side by side, faces streaked with salty tears, each receiving a folded American flag that represented Allison's service. Uniformed sailors fired a salute, H-60 helicopters flew overhead in the missing man formation, and the lonely notes of "taps" carried over the stillness of a warm afternoon.

Too often I forget how many people share the burden that comes with military service. During the short time I spent in the naval aviation community, I saw the effects of three tragedies, including the loss of Allison Oubre's Seahawk.

I had arrived aboard the USS *Dwight D. Eisenhower* on a particularly somber Easter Sunday. Whether in religious services held between the anchor chains of the forecastle or in private moments throughout the ship, members of the crew and air wing were remembering Lieutenant Miroslav "Steve" Zilberman. Steve's family had emigrated from the Ukraine to the United States and he'd enlisted in the navy after graduating high school. After two years, he entered the "seaman to admiral" program, graduated college, received an officer's commission, and earned his wings. Four days before I landed on *Eisenhower*, Carrier Air Wing Seven had lost the bright thirty-one-year-old aviator over the Arabian Sea, only five miles from the ship.

One of his E-2C Hawkeye's two engines failed and the prop wouldn't feather properly. So instead of being able to fly on one engine with the dead prop spinning harmlessly, the pilots had to contend with a dead prop that acted like a barn door, creating drag that made flight impossible. Steve ordered the three members of his crew to bail out as he fought the locked propeller and held the plane steady while they escaped. The plane crashed into the sea before he could follow. He left behind a young wife, a four-year-old son, and a two-year-old daughter.

While I was at NAS Pensacola with the Blue Angels and the SAR rescue swimmers, two instructors and two students took off in a T-39 training jet from Forest Sherman field. Two hours later they crashed in the mountains of North Georgia. None survived. These two crashes—a world apart—happened within a month of each other.

Tragedy will strike the navy family again, but the men and women who fly the aircraft understand the risks. They also understand their duty and again and again, they step into the cockpit to complete their missions.

The families and friends of these and too many other young men and women have endured the same hurt and asked the same questions: why their son, why their sister, why their friend? Those questions may have many answers; I believe some of those lost servicemen and women would answer that they died in the line of duty because they volunteered to serve something greater than themselves. They wanted to protect a set of cherished ideals, people they loved, and people they might never even know.

Allison's sacrifice, and the sacrifices made by others past and present, helped me understand the emotion behind the immortal question with which James Michener concluded his novel about Korea, *The Bridges at Toko-Ri*. Upon losing a promising young aviator under his command, Rear Admiral George Tarrant turns away from the flight deck of his carrier as more planes prepare to launch into battle to face the same dangers. The veteran admiral looks to the heavens and asks, "Where do we get such men?"

Today, both men and women fly into harm's way, and upon losing lives in the line of duty, friends and families still raise Rear Admiral Tarrant's same plaintive yet grateful question, "Where do we get such heroes?"

18

GENERATIONS

Denver Amerine and I walked up to the USS *Carl Vinson*, which was moored at her new home port on the Pacific Coast, just across the bay from downtown San Diego. The radars atop her island rotated smoothly and the ship hummed with activity as crew members prepared to take her to sea the next day. Denver wore his olive flight suit, khaki garrison hat, and dark sunglasses. The biggest of the three Amerine aviators, Denver stood a solid six-foot-two and had the bright optimism so typical of youngest siblings. A red patch with a yellow lightning bolt was on his right chest—the emblem of Electronic Attack Squadron 129 (VAQ-129), the Fleet Replacement Squadron for the new EA-18G Growler, an F/A-18 Super Hornet modified for electronic attack missions. Over his left chest, a blue patch bore his name and naval aviator's wings of gold. He'd earned the wings when he graduated flight training at Pensacola the year before, and he'd spent the past twelve months learning to fly the $65 million Growler, which was loaded with gadgets for jamming radar, missiles, and anything electrical an enemy might possess. But Denver had never landed the EA-18G jet on a boat, and in naval aviation, nothing else really matters if you can't accomplish that final part of the mission. He'd been preparing to land a fleet aircraft on a carrier his entire career. The *Vinson*'s flight deck would soon be his proving ground.

I first met Denver during his second year at the Naval Academy. He already had expectations to meet since his older brothers, Lee and Travis, had made their marks at Annapolis. When Lee and Travis received plum assignments as Super Hornet pilots, the bar rose ever higher for young Denver. With Lee instructing at the Naval Strike and Air Warfare Center and Travis having earned a graduate degree at Stanford and flying with Strike Fighter Squadron Twenty-Seven (VFA-27)—the Royal Maces—aboard the USS *George Washington*, Denver hadn't escaped the high expectations he'd known his entire life. But he didn't dwell on it. His tour at the Academy was marked with slightly less academic accomplishment than his predecessors, but he enjoyed more lighthearted exploits. Denver had a talent for having a good time while still making the grades he needed, and during his years in Annapolis and after, he never lost sight of Travis and Lee. He earned a spot in flight school at Pensacola then graduated from the prestigious jet training program in Meridian, Mississippi, where he streaked over forests and farmlands piloting white and orange T-45 Goshawk training jets, just like his brothers—now ages thirty and twenty-eight—had several years before. To complete his training, he landed the Goshawk on the USS *George H. W. Bush*. He never missed the wires. Then he received orders to fly the Growler—cousin to the Super Hornets flown by his brothers. Now he was about to join them as an equal—as long as he could land the jet on the boat . . . at night.

He had reached the last week of his training and all that remained was his carrier qualification, considered among the most difficult tests a student aviator faces. By week's end, he aimed to become the third Amerine brother to join the ranks of the navy's fleet aviators—the only pilots in the world qualified to perform that demanding feat of landing aboard ships, at any hour, in any weather.

Denver and I walked up the steep stairs leading to the *Vinson*'s quarterdeck, where we passed a stone-faced sailor carrying an M-16; he could not have been older than nineteen. Denver paused at the last step of the gangplank and asked a white-uniformed petty officer for permission to come aboard. The formality granted with a salute, Denver and I walked inside CVN-70, the third of the *Nimitz*-class carriers. The *Vinson* was christened in March of 1980, in the presence of her ninety-six-year-old namesake, Georgia Congressman Carl Vinson; he would not live to see her commissioning two years later. A fifty-year congressional veteran, Vinson chaired the House Armed Services Committee for twenty-nine years. When approached about becoming President Dwight D. Eisenhower's Secretary of Defense, Representative Vinson had once replied, "No, I'd rather run the Pentagon from here."

We walked through the now-familiar corridor along the oh-three level of the ship—the layouts for all *Nimitz*-class carriers are largely identical. Just before we reached the forward wardroom, we turned into a ready room where Lieutenant Ian "Huff" Hudson stood before a whiteboard, leading a briefing for the squadron's newest aviators and Electronic Warfare Officers (EWOs), as backseat naval flight officers in the two-seat Growler community are known. The students, clad in their flight suits as usual—aviators seem to wear little else—sat in classroom-style rows of steel chairs with folding desktops. Dark brown leather cushions like those that have been used in ready rooms for decades padded the chairs and added a slightly clubby atmosphere to the room. For most of the pilots—all lieutenants junior grade and around twenty-five years of age—it was their first time aboard a carrier since being a student. For many EWOs, this was their first visit to a fleet carrier.

Huff made sure the students understood the rules of the boat since they were *Vinson*'s guests on this detachment, and that they had a fighting chance at navigating the impossible maze of corridors that interlaced the ship. Many sailors are still discovering new compartments at the end of a six-month deployment; others simply stick to those routes they know. To save sailors and officers alike from becoming hopelessly lost, every corridor or room inside a carrier has a bull's-eye stamped on its wall that identifies a precise location. For example, a lost airman viewing the numbers 03-88-4-L would be on the oh-three level of the ship, three decks above the hangar, one deck below the flight deck. He would be standing eighty-eight compartment frames from the bow, roughly underneath the forward catapults. The even number four indicates he would be four frames to the left (port) of centerline (the acronym PESO—port even, starboard odd—helps experienced sailors and first-cruise nuggets alike). The letter L indicates he'd be standing in a living space.

Before leading the group to the flight deck for an orientation walkaround, Huff reminded them not to let the carrier's deck intimidate them.

The squadron had spent the past two days performing touch-and-go landings at Naval Air Facility (NAF) El Centro in the California desert, some eighty miles east of San Diego. While El Centro's 9,500-foot runway was significantly longer than *Vinson*'s 700-foot strip, the pilots would be flying the same ball—that is, they'd still be following the signals of the standard Fresnel lens, which had been guiding them on their practice approaches. Huff reminded them to simply fly the ball as they'd been doing all along.

When Huff dismissed the group, Denver and I followed the line of students toward the flight deck. He seemed more relaxed than I would have imagined, but then again, Denver would exude confidence in almost any situation. In this instance, several months of training at Whidbey Island, Washington, had considerably helped prepare him for the first test of landing at NAF El Centro in the California desert. From all reports, he had performed well and he was bucking for the chance to prove himself at sea.

"That first look at the boat will be a different picture than we're used to," he said, "but really, you're just looking at the ball. You just block out the idea that you're landing on a 135-foot section of a 700-foot strip versus having an entire 9,500-foot runway. It's pretty simple: two touch-and-gos, then it's time to put the hook down and make things happen."

Denver and I emerged onto the flight deck, which stood empty except for our group of aviators. We walked toward the stern, over the landing area that would determine the future of each olive-clad individual among us. A white, downward-sloping section of deck perhaps ten feet long marked the very end of the landing strip. At its end was a drop to the water below. If a pilot puts his hook—or plane—into this space, he could lose his active flight status or worse, his life. Many aviators have died behind the boat, bringing their aircraft in too low and striking the ship at the deck's end. Not all were rookies. I remember Andy "Huck" Hoekstra, Carrier Air Wing Two's Landing Signal Officer—"CAG Paddles"—aboard the *Abraham Lincoln*, showing me two hook gouges, one on the white ramp, the other just five feet forward. Neither was made by a first-timer. Both pilots found themselves in serious trouble for landing so short and almost crashing into the carrier's stern. Regardless of their experience, naval aviators must remain ever alert when they're on final approach.

The danger wasn't lost on Denver and he knew that during the coming days, that deck would test his skill and put his family reputation on the line. If he botched his CQ, he could lose his wings. Worse, he'd face his brothers. While they'd of course love him regardless of anything he did in an airplane, they'd certainly remind him of his shortcomings for the next several decades. Thanksgiving and Christmas with his chiding brothers would be hard to stomach.

"With Lee and Trav in the fleet, I have some big shoes to fill," Denver said. "Naval aviation is a small world. It's very seldom that I walk down a squadron space or have a drink in an O-Club that people won't come up to me and say, 'You're IPOD or Sweet-T's little brother.'

"Both my brothers are exceptional aviators, and everyone expects me to be as good or better than they are just because I carry that name. Hopefully I'll live up to it this week."

Halfway around the world, off the coast of Japan aboard the USS *George Washington*, Travis Amerine was thinking about his little brother and how far all the Amerine brothers had come from their Arkansas boyhood. Regardless of what would happen on the *Carl Vinson*'s flight deck, Travis knew that Denver had beaten all the Amerine brothers in realizing their boyhood dream of flying. During Travis's freshman, or plebe, year at the Naval Academy, his parents told him that Denver had begun taking civilian flying lessons back in Arkansas.

"I was amazed at the idea," Travis said. "And the first thought in my mind was 'Why didn't I think of that?' The kid was doing everything he possibly could to scrounge up enough money to pay for one tank of gas and one instructor fee after another. Knowing that he didn't have the time, or most importantly the money to mess around, he not only soloed in record time, but he also got his private license in the Federal Aviation Administration's minimum amount of time required. I think it was a Thanksgiving break when I first saw my little brother fly. I'll never forget sitting on a piece of asphalt watching Denver roll down the runway and pull his Cessna into the air. I don't think one brother could have ever been so proud of another. So, most people like to think that Denver, being the youngest of us all, followed in our footsteps. Not true. He was the first one out of all of us to reach out there and grab his dream. Regardless of whether Lee and I followed through on *our* dream of flying jets off an aircraft carrier, Denver was going to. And he did."

Of all the brothers, Denver seemed like the most natural pilot. His experience might be less, but he was busting to prove himself. He already knew the details of his aircraft cold, just like he did the mechanics of flight. Same for the patterns and nuances of a carrier's air space, even though he'd yet to fly the Growler behind the boat himself. He could instantly call distances, altitudes, and patterns for a host of scenarios. But as his instructor reminded me, he hadn't proven himself just yet. VAQ-129 instructor Kelsey "K-Mart" Martin was still nervous.

Kelsey had completed several tours in the EA-6B Prowler, the antiquated jet that has been the navy's primary electronic attack aircraft for decades. Deadly effective on the battlefield, it earned the nickname the "flying drumstick" for its looks. The Prowler began taking over the navy's electronic attack duties in 1971. Since then it has taken part in most major navy actions, often going into combat first to neutralize enemy ground radar, knock out surface-to-air missiles, and gather electronic intelligence before the main strike arrives. In Iraq and Afghanistan, the planes have helped identify and jam improvised explosive devices and roadside bombs. And even though they have no afterburners, Prowlers are the loudest aircraft on the deck. By 2013, they'll all be gone, replaced by the EA-18G Growler.

Kelsey Martin had transitioned into the Growler a year before, training with the F/A-18 Super Hornet Fleet Replacement Squadron to learn the new jet and its tactics. On this carrier qualification detachment aboard the *Carl Vinson*, he was serving as both instructor and evaluator. He took Denver's success as his responsibility and hoped the rookie could back up his confidence.

"Denver is a great pilot," Kelsey said, "but he's young and aggressive. He wants to be as good as his brothers right now but he just doesn't have as much time in the aircraft. He'll get there, but he'll need to focus hard on that flight."

Despite his relaxed facade, the youngest Amerine took the upcoming challenge seriously. Like most aviators, he might be joking and all smiles the night before, but he'd arrive on the flight line early, supremely prepared, and focused. On the night of July 11, he blew off steam and relaxed with his friends. The next morning, he made it happen.

On July 12, Denver and his EWO, six-foot-five Ian "Wilt" Chamberlin, took off from the airfield at NAS North Island and roared out over the Pacific, full of optimism. Then they hit weather as they neared the *Carl Vinson*. "Mom"—as they termed the carrier—called for a Case Two recovery, which meant that planes would fly the established landing pattern for scenarios where clouds were above one thousand feet but below five thousand feet. The carrier reported the cloud ceiling at twelve hundred feet. Visibility was five miles—not exactly the clear weather for which Denver had hoped.

"We had to shoot an instrument approach to below the clouds," he said. "Then we started a break pattern. We were flying our instruments and we were still in the clouds at twelve hundred feet, a thousand feet. At eight hundred feet we were barely able to see the water and we were seven miles behind the boat.

"We dropped on through to seven hundred feet. Sure enough, at five miles, we see the boat through the haze. It was crazy. We came in and the weather dictated flying the break pattern at six hundred feet, so we put it down for two touch-and-gos and then trapped."

Once safely aboard, the students had dinner in the officers' wardroom. Then Denver briefed for his first nighttime carrier flight in the Growler. He reviewed the pattern and plans: two touch-and-gos, one trap. He'd fly straight in on a long approach that would lead him to the ship—no breaking turns around the ship after sunset. When the brief concluded, Denver picked up his flight bag and walked out the door and across the hall to the PR shop where his helmet, g-suit, and survival equipment hung, maintained by the parachute riggers. He pulled on his g-suit and life vest, and cradled his helmet under his arm. He took a deep breath and walked toward the starboard side of the ship. He emerged into the inky darkness that blanketed the Pacific Ocean and walked up a short ladder to the flight deck, near the Number One catapult. Then he walked aft toward the spot where his Growler stood ready, waiting to see how this student would handle it.

When he'd taxied the jet across the deck, Denver found the catapults surrounded by personnel wearing cranials and reflective float coats, safety vests that would also serve as life jackets should the wearer fall overboard. The plane directors used glowing wands to direct Denver toward the catapult shuttle, which he could barely see. To his left and right, he could make out the faint deck and twenty-five men and women with glowing cranials and coats.

"Now, I gotta tell you about cat shots at night," he said later. "Everyone talks about night landings, but I thought the cat stroke was more exhilarating than trapping at night. I was much more nervous for the bow cat shot.

"You're sitting in your jet and see the deck hands with their wands and reflective coats floating all around you. Beyond them? Nothing. You're waiting to get shot off and you see absolutely nothing beyond the boat. When you're flying a Super Hornet or Growler, the cat is loaded for fifty-five thousand pounds—four times the force they launched our T-45 trainers with. The force of a cat stroke in a Super Hornet is so tremendous, and at night in particular, it can really disorient you because you have no reference. You go from zero to 170 miles per hour in three seconds and you're in total blackness. You might as well be in space."

That night, Denver was the only student pilot flying, and he faced the blackest night he'd ever seen. "It was dark and then some," he said. "There was no moon, just starlight. And you only saw that above the clouds which were between five hundred and a thousand feet. We navigated our approach on top of the clouds, went into them at a thousand feet and broke out at five hundred, a mile and a half behind the boat. There was absolutely no light below the clouds, so it was a pretty sporty first night.

"I called the ball at three-quarter miles and four hundred feet. At that distance, the boat is a little group of lights in a black abyss and you'll be over the deck in about twenty seconds."

He executed two touch-and-go landings then trapped. The plane directors taxied him to his appropriate spot and he climbed down. He'd seen flight deck crews organize chaos during the day. Seeing them do it at night impressed him even more.

The next day brought a second round of daytime landings, then one more series of night exercises. Flying Aircraft 565, he took off for his final CQ mission. He flew the now-familiar nighttime approach pattern and nailed two touch-and-go landings. Then he circled around for his last approach. He guided the Growler along the glide slope, putting his head in that imaginary one-foot square box that would mean he was in position to catch the number three wire. Seconds later, his hook grabbed the cable and his jet came to a halt. While he was taxiing out of the landing area, Paddles called over the radio.

"565? Paddles."

"Go for 565," Denver responded.

"Welcome to the fleet."

The next month, Denver would join his brothers as a fleet aviator. He would pilot the navy's newest airplane for the VAQ-141 Shadowhawks aboard the fleet's newest supercarrier, the USS *George H. W. Bush*. New aviators, new aircraft, and new carriers; the navy always makes way for the next generation.

Travis was immeasurably proud of his brother Denver, who had become part of a family much larger than just the one in the Amerine household.

"Without question," Travis said, "the three of us followed the same career path because of family. Our bond as siblings established the constant desire to belong to something that represented what we were able to share together—brotherhood. Anyone who has ever spent one minute in a squadron ready room knows exactly what I'm talking about. The guys you serve with become your family and that same banter, backslapping, and good times that I shared with my brothers growing up—and still today—I'm able to share in a larger context with my fellow squadron mates. Family, the guy flying off your wing—that is what naval aviation is all about. Anyone who has ever worn a set of golden wings can run into a fellow naval aviator and I guarantee you that the atmosphere surrounding the two will be akin to a family reunion. It is for this reason that naval aviation becomes a family affair. It is just an added bonus that I get to be part of such an amazing extended family with two brothers that share my same DNA."

Few families have naval aviation ingrained in their genetic fiber like the Kilclines. And four generations of tradition now rested on the shoulders of twenty-four-year-old Tom Kilcline III, who seemed supremely at ease with any expectations others might have for him. His flip-flops, shorts, and red T-shirt, which bore the faded phrase ENJOY LIFE, were quite befitting his relaxed demeanor. He wore an easy smile on his face as he gazed up at four Blue Angel jets gracefully looping over the runway at NAS Oceana in their Diamond formation, their wingtips just eighteen inches apart. Saturday afternoon spectators shielded their eyes from the sun and devoted their full attention to following the Diamond as it exited stage right. That gave

Lt. Commander Frank Weisser an opportunity to sneak his Number Five jet around the rear of the flight line unnoticed. Then just as the Diamond was disappearing, Blue Angel Number Five burst over the crowd from behind, flying low and fast. The engines issued a deafening boom that shook the ground. Everyone in the crowd jumped. Seconds later Frank was soaring into the sky and was gone. The Blue Angels were proving yet again that they were the navy's consummate showmen.

"So, do you ever want to fly with the Blues?" I asked Tom, who had only recently arrived at the East Coast Super Hornet Fleet Replacement Squadron. It was one of those obviously premature questions that get asked anyway.

"I haven't thought about it too much yet," he answered, still looking into the clear sky, "but can tell you that I love ACM [Air Combat Maneuvering]. It's so exhilarating. It's the ultimate sport. ACM is like a game of chess combined with a boxing match: you have to outthink the other guy and use strategy, but you also have to fight against gravity. Every time you pull Gs, you're flexing your muscles in order to keep the blood in your head and stay conscious—especially a taller guy like me."

Tom stood six foot five, just short enough to fit into a navy cockpit.

"I used to come out of an ACM flight and it would look like I'd jumped in a pool! But I've gotten used to it and gotten in better shape. It's the best sport there is. It's awesome to watch air shows, but imagine being up in the air five hundred feet away from a guy doing that and trying to fight him. It's amazing."

We craned our necks again and continued watching the Blue Angels perform. They flew their maneuvers even more precisely than those I'd witnessed months earlier in Pensacola. A season of practice and performance had honed their skills to a point I didn't think possible. In Blue Angels Five and Six, Frank Weisser and Ben Walborn streaked across the sky for their final act, pulling their jets into high-G turns before joining up with their squadron mates for a final six-plane fly-by. Then the Blues peeled into their landing sequence. It was Frank's third and last season on the team; the next season, Ben—whose brothers Jason and Steve also flew F/A-18s—would take Frank's place as lead solo pilot in the century-old pattern of young aviators replacing their mentors.

Likewise, Tom had replaced his father in the air, just as his father had replaced his grandfather, and Tom's grandfather had taken the place of his great-grandfather. As the Blues' demonstration ended, Tom and I turned away from the field and walked among the aircraft on display at the air show, which included World War II–era planes like those flown by his great-grandfather Tommy Thompson, who started the family business. I watched Tom contemplate his ancestors as he ran his hands along the aircraft that were so familiar to them.

"Early on in Primary, I felt a lot of pressure," Tom said, helping me understand what it was like to be part of such a lineage. "But it wasn't from my dad at all. It was all internal. I realized I was the fourth one. I worried, 'What if I go in and I'm the worst in my class?' That'd be extremely embarrassing. Plus, everyone knows who my dad is. I worked as hard as I could those first weeks of flight school. Then as I got into it and started learning how to fly, I finally relaxed and began enjoying it. And people never treated me any differently than anyone else."

He laughed when I asked him about his first thoughts of going navy. He had followed the family path from as far back as he could remember. Even before then, his baby clothes had navy logos and airplanes hung over his crib. Around age three, he began launching toy planes from coffee table aircraft carriers while watching videos his father sent home from cruise. As he got older, he and his father played flight simulator games on their home computer. At age sixteen, Tom flew the real thing, soloing in a Cessna and earning his pilot's license. From then until flight school, he regularly scrounged money to pay for lessons and gas. His father complemented his prop training with jet simulator time whenever he could sneak Tom in.

Tom's father never pressured him to pursue aviation, but he came to it naturally. Tom would see his dad always return home from a day—or six months—at work, radiating energy and a love for flying. He wanted the same passion in his own life.

On the flight line, we came across a dark blue F8F Bearcat, the first plane used by the Blue Angels. It had entered service just as World War II was ending. As we listened to the "Bear" rev its big 2,250-horsepower engine, Tom began talking about his great-grandfather and the tradition he started.

The long association between the navy and the Kilclines began in rural

North Carolina during the early twentieth century when Tommy Thompson ran away from his family's small Appalachian farm. It was 1919 and he was seventeen. He set out to find adventure and opportunity in the broader world. He lied about his birthday and joined the navy. By the time his superiors discovered his real age he was almost eighteen, so they let him remain as a machinist.

In 1922, the navy expanded its aviation program to include enlisted personnel. They needed pilots and Tommy jumped at the chance. He traveled to Pensacola, earned his wings in 1926, and became a Naval Aviation Pilot. In 1929, he became a chief petty officer—and thus a Chief Aviation Pilot— better known as a member of the Silver Eagles. He was soon flying torpedo bombers from three of America's first aircraft carriers, the *Langley*, *Lexington*, and *Saratoga*. He piloted an assortment of planes and miraculously survived seven Class A crashes—meaning his planes were totaled and by all rights he shouldn't have lived. A lingering injury from one of his brushes with mortality caused a fatal blood clot in 1945, and Tommy passed away suddenly in Key West, Florida. His wife and three children, including daughter Dornell, moved from the Keys to Pensacola where, eventually, a young naval aviation student named Tom Kilcline would bring a new last name to this family story.

Chief Thompson's daughter Dornell grew up happily along Florida's Gulf Coast, winning the crown of Miss Pensacola along the way. At age eighteen, she began working as a petty officer at the naval air station and soon became the executive assistant to Rear Admiral Jimmy Thach, Chief of Naval Air Training and tactician of World War II fame. In a rare midcentury feat, she learned to fly and taught students the fine points of aviation in Link trainers. Her adventurous spirit caught the attention of flight student Tom Kilcline from Kokomo, Indiana.

Tom had arrived in Pensacola for flight training after graduating from the U.S. Naval Academy in 1949. Not long after he met the lovely and accomplished Dornell, the two married and started a family. They would have two sons and two daughters. After flight school, Tom began a legendary career that took him into the skies over Korea as a new pilot and over Vietnam as a squadron commander. As a test pilot, he also managed the Strike flight test programs at NAS Patuxent River. As an admiral, he commanded U.S. forces in the Philippines and served as the navy's Chief of Legislative

Affairs. He ended his career as a three-star vice admiral, in charge of all naval air forces in the Atlantic.

His sons Tom Jr. and Patrick followed his path and flew navy fighters. Of his two daughters, Kathy became a navy doctor and Mary married a navy pilot, Bob Novak, who had a distinguished career flying the P-3 Orion maritime patrol aircraft, working as the chief engineer on the Joint Strike fighter, and commanding the navy's Tomahawk missile program. Tragically, the first documented F-14 Tomcat flat spin took Patrick's life in 1978. An automobile accident claimed Kathy's two years later.

Growing up in a navy family, Tom "Killer" Kilcline Jr. always felt the influence of his father's profession and remembers deciding on his life's course at six years of age—in 1957. Upon greeting his father after a long deployment, he asked him what he did for months at sea. His father replied, "I eat ice cream during the day and fly at night." Young Killer was sold. He graduated from the U.S. Naval Academy in 1973 and flew F-4 Phantoms, F-14 Tomcats, and F/A-18 Hornets at sea; he piloted A-4 Skyhawks and F-5 Tigers as an adversary pilot. Like his father, he earned three admiral's stars and served as Commander, Naval Air Forces from 2007 until 2010. He oversaw all of naval aviation—a job that earned him the title of "Air Boss."

Killer met me in the hangar bay of the USS *Midway*, just two months after he'd passed on the mantle to a new Air Boss. Trim and six foot three, he looked every bit the avid basketball player he was, and with the weight of the fleet's air force off his shoulders, he seemed supremely relaxed.

As a young aviator, he had flown hundreds of missions from *Midway*'s sister ship, the USS *Franklin D. Roosevelt*, and happily recalled his first deployments as we walked through familiar junior officer staterooms and ready rooms; the *Midway* now serves as a public museum and San Diego landmark. He remembered cruises where bands of new junior officers learned how to fly, tried to buck the establishment, entertained one another with antics and devilish pranks, slept up to eight in the JO bunk room, and developed friendships that never faded. Killer was back in his element.

Memories of a different sort emerged when we walked past *Midway*'s restored aircraft, which included an SNJ Texan trainer, sleek North American A-5 Vigilante, and the ungainly A-3 "Whale," all flown by his father, Tom Sr.

"I have memories of Dad flying all the way up until his retirement, just as my son Tommy has of me," Killer said. "My dad was very intelligent, top of his class at the Academy. Then he earned a masters degree from the Massachusetts Institute of Technology, so there were some technical interests we didn't share! But there were two places where we matched up, where we were on the same level. One was basketball. We both loved basketball and played all the time. Considering our ages, it was unusual that we played together, but we loved to do it—not that we were good!"

Joking and modesty aside, they were good. Tom Sr. played on the Senior Olympic team and was still playing just months before he passed away in 2002 at age seventy-seven.

"The other thing we shared was naval aviation," Killer continued. "The passion we shared—the same passion my son Tom and I share—allowed me an entry point where we could talk with each other and support each other."

But early on, Tom Sr. harbored concerns about Killer becoming a naval aviator. During his deployments in Korea and Vietnam, he'd learned how demanding that career path becomes. It inevitably siphons time away from family and puts constant pressure and serious responsibility on aviators themselves at such a young age. Would he wish naval aviation on his son, and would his son be ready?

"I remember getting a letter from Dad while he was in Vietnam," Killer said. "He wrote that he wasn't sure if naval aviation was the right thing for me to do. He was worried I wasn't ready. It's funny; I remember thinking the same thing about my son Tom when he was a youngster! But he was more than ready when he started to fly. He worked hard and saved his money to take flying lessons while he was a teenager. It seemed that he was in a holding pattern in high school, just waiting for his chance. When he was accepted to the Naval Academy, he matured unbelievably fast and then kept clearing all the hurdles on his way to earning his wings.

"I understood how hard it was for him to get to each point on that journey. I knew he wanted to fly jet fighters like his grandfather and me, and I had confidence in him, but I was constantly wondering if he'd be able to get there. Could he make it through all the academic and physical cuts? Can he get into Annapolis where there are around twelve thousand applications for just over one thousand spots? Can he be ranked high enough in his class to get selected as a pilot? Can he get the grades for jets? His mother Deb and I always wanted the best for him, but we realized what's best might not necessarily be what he wanted. But each milestone became a celebration and another point along that good-to-great journey that is naval aviation."

Killer's pride in his son was evident, but carefully measured. Tom was becoming a fine pilot, but academics and flying were only one part of a naval aviator's job. Tom also had to become a naval officer.

"If you look at your fitness report you're graded on seven different things," said Killer. By this time we were sitting at a table on *Midway*'s port elevator looking over the sunny harbor. "Only one of them is how well you fly an airplane. The other six are about being an officer: how well do you speak, write, lead a team, what's your military bearing. Tom hasn't really had to do that yet. You can be the world's best pilot but you'll never move up the rank structure unless you're a good officer also. That's his next step. Once he learns how to fly this airplane, and gets good at flying around the boat, the squadron will start giving him new challenges—leading other officers or leading divisions of enlisted folks who are working on the airplanes. That'll be his job—and he'll be flying airplanes. To me, that's what makes a naval officer and a naval aviator. You gotta do both."

As a father and an aviator, Killer had enjoyed watching Tom pass the milestones of naval aviation, meeting challenges and rising above them, on his way to becoming a pilot and officer. Then in June 2010, father and son reached important milestones together. The day before Tom received his aviator's wings, he and his father climbed into a fighter cockpit together, repeating a scene that had happened a generation before with Killer and his father, Tom Sr. Although Tom would not undergo the formal winging ceremony until the next day, this flight would be his first as a winged aviator. It was also his father's last.

For Killer's final flight and Tom's first winged flight, they flew a two-seat Northrop F-5 Tiger II fighter, an adversary jet from Composite Fighter Squadron 111—the Sundowners. When father and son walked onto the tarmac at NAS Meridian they both stopped at the first sight of their jet's new paint job. Under the rear canopy in red letters was: LTJG THOMAS J. KILCLINE. Under the forward canopy, also in red: VADM THOMAS J. KILCLINE/KILLER/AIR BOSS. Neither had expected that personal gesture.

Killer strapped into the familiar F-5 and the plane captain briefed his son on the unfamiliar controls. Once the canopies closed and engines started, Killer guided the jet to the runway where the two Kilclines watched their opponent take off in a T-45 Goshawk. They followed in the Tiger, ready for a day of combat.

"The first fight my dad took," said Tom. "Then he let me try the second one from the backseat. I was getting killed until Dad started helping. The T-45 was rolling in getting ready to shoot and Dad starts yelling, 'Rudder right! Roll right!' I wasn't entirely sure what we were doing but I did what he told me and it worked out perfectly. He's been flying for thirty-seven years. I guess you learn some things in that time."

When they'd returned to base and the engines had powered down, Killer climbed out of an F-5 cockpit for the last time. His son followed and soon joined him planeside. They shared the exhilaration of the flight and embraced each other in the good-natured way of old friends. Killer knew this was all part of life's great cycle. Now it was Tom's turn.

As the newest naval aviator in the Kilcline family walked to the showers after the flight, sweaty from the intense workout, he thought about what he'd just experienced. He had never expected to fly with his father, although he always hoped he might. His father had flown with Tom Kilcline Sr., and Tom III wanted the same chance, the same opportunity to share something so unique and special. That day's flight also showed Tom something new about his father, who spent so much time on deployments as his family was growing up.

"Dad didn't get the chance to come home that much," Tom said. "I knew him, but not that well. I played different sports growing up, so we never connected there, like he did with my grandpa. Going up and flying with him, I finally understood a very large part of his life. It was a very different dimension to my father that I hadn't seen before.

"Before flight school, I didn't understand how much effort Dad had put into flying," Tom continued. "I only thought of it as a fun job that required long hours. Between our flight together and my time going through the training command, I'm realizing he knows more than I can imagine right now. I only hope that with enough work I'll be able to follow in his footsteps. Flying with him that day and doing aerial combat maneuvers, I realized he was an artist. Dad was amazing."

The very next day, Tom's parents and three sisters joined him for his winging ceremony in Meridian. His father brought a special pair of gold wings along with him—the set worn by Tommy Thompson, Tom Kilcline

Sr., and Tom Kilcline Jr. During Tom Kilcline III's 2010 ceremony, his mother Deb pinned the family wings above the left pocket of her son's uniform while her husband stood by in his summer whites, remembering the moment in 1975 when his mother and father had done the same.

Yet another generation had come to naval aviation.

EPILOGUE: GREATER EACH DAY

A CROWD HAD GATHERED ON the sunny tarmac at NAS Oceana in Virginia Beach, just outside the expansive hangars that house most of the navy's East Coast fighter attack squadrons. Women wore sundresses; children wore the nicest clothes their mothers could convince them to wear. Parents shared stories with each other while media milled about carrying cameras and microphones. Inside the hangar on a long table sat buckets of iced beer, each with a colorful name tag for an aviator. Everyone engaged in that preoccupied style of chatting that arises before a highly anticipated event. It was July 27, seven months after Carrier Air Wing Seven left this same airfield, bound for the skies of Afghanistan aboard the USS *Dwight D. Eisenhower*. Soon, the air wing would once again be overhead.

Around 2:00 P.M., cheers began coming from the crowd on the tarmac as they watched twelve small specks in the southern sky become twelve distinct F/A-18F Super Hornets. The chorus grew as more family members and friends rushed out of the shaded hangar and looked up. American flags waved, cameras snapped, happy tears ran from many eyes. Arranged in three Diamonds, the VFA-103 Jolly Rogers roared overhead, announcing their long-awaited return from the Arabian Sea.

One by one, the four planes from the first Diamond peeled from the formation, banked hard to the east, circled behind the hangar, and entered the landing pattern. The crowd watched them on final approach, which they made with landing lights shining brightly through the summer heat. They each touched down to more cheering and taxied toward the flight line in front of the hangar. There, twelve air crewmen waited, marking the twelve spots where the nose of each jet should stop. Soon, eleven Super Hornets idled in two rows. When the twelfth and last plane joined its row, the squadron's twenty-four turbofan engines whined to a stop and fell silent.

On the skipper's command, twelve canopies opened simultaneously to great cheers from the crowd. Wives and girlfriends gathered near the flight line, straining to identify the olive-clad figures who were removing their white helmets and stepping from the cockpits. Two by two, pilots and WSOs from the far jets began walking toward the hangar, with another pair joining them at each successive jet. High fives and handshakes were exchanged after this first landing on solid ground in seven months. When the aviators from each row had met at the jet closest to the hangar, the two groups converged in the middle of the flight line. More gestures were exchanged. They were home—almost.

They turned in unison and began walking toward the hangar and gathered crowd. The line of wives and children burst forward, sprinting to meet them. The women jumped into the outstretched arms of their loved ones and spun in an embrace both had dreamed of for seven long months. From one side of the flight line to the other, jubilant couples hugged and kissed, fathers held children, proud mothers and fathers stood by and smiled. Now, at last, the long deployment was over.

Among the reunited couples were Ed and Brie Hine. It was Brie who'd first accompanied me aboard the *Eisenhower*, just before her husband deployed. And it was Ed who'd welcomed me aboard the same ship after it had taken up its post in the Arabian Sea. Brie and Ed had imagined this reunion for months, wishing for it daily. They were indescribably glad that it had finally arrived. They both glowed with happiness.

After thirty minutes of conversation with friends, family, and squadron mates, Ed left the hangar with Brie on his arm. They would return to their Norfolk home, where Brie had lived alone for more than half a year. She hadn't been able to sleep the night before and had been clearing and straightening since 3:30 A.M. Ed would walk across a freshly mowed lawn—courtesy of Brie's brother Tim—and under a colorful welcome home banner that bore an enormous picture of a Super Hornet. Ed would open the door to their spotless house and see their dog, relax on their couch, and fall asleep in their bed for the first time since January 1. For Ed, Brie, and the rest of the VFA-103 Jolly Rogers, all was once again right with the world. They were finally home.

While the Jolly Rogers traded their aircraft for their family cars, most of the *Eisenhower*'s five thousand men and women had one more night at sea. Now it was their spouses' turn to battle the butterflies of anticipation and struggle to sleep during this last night in an empty bed, knowing their loved one was just over the horizon. With her parents and grandmother asleep nearby, twenty-one-year-old Casey Patterson wondered what the next day would bring. Four weeks earlier, she had given birth to her first child, a son. Casey had been just three months pregnant when Austin's father Rob sailed east with the *Eisenhower* strike group. Austin was born six months later on July 3. Now, Rob was sleeping just hours offshore and would meet his son before noon the next day. With so many thoughts running through her head, Casey couldn't sleep. Like Brie Hine, she spent the early morning hours cleaning and organizing the house so everything would be perfect when her sailor returned.

The next morning, Casey waited with her family under a white tent on the *Eisenhower*'s pier. With her and Austin were other babies who were about to meet their fathers for the first time. For all the new mothers, this deployment had been particularly long and taxing.

"The first two weeks he was gone, I couldn't stop crying," Casey said, then laughed at the memory. "We e-mailed almost every day and it got easier day by day. Before I knew it he was almost home. Those first days were really hard, though! Him not being there for birth of our firstborn? That was difficult. But the ship definitely made provisions for new dads to talk to their wives. And when Austin was born, Rob's grandmother and mom, my mom, and a whole bunch of my best friends were there to support me.

"But you know, what I've missed most—and this will sound crazy—is his snoring! As I fall asleep at night, I'm just waiting to punch him and I miss that! Now I'm excited for him to be back—and experience being up at 2 A.M. with the baby!" She laughed again.

"The new dads are the first ones off the ship so I'm really excited and nervous. But mainly, I just can't wait for him to be here."

Looking at baby Austin, whom she cradled in her arms, she added, "And this little guy can't wait to meet his dad."

By 10 A.M. on July 28, the hot summer sun was baking the three thousand people gathered dockside at Naval Station Norfolk. The head of the *Eisenhower*'s pier was a veritable carnival. Military uniforms mixed with every other sort of attire—pressed pants and golf shirts, colorful sundresses, T-shirts and flip-flops. Friends and relatives gathered in groups, on grandstands, and under enormous tents that offered food, drinks, souvenirs, and shade. The squadrons that had flown in the previous day hosted tailgates like those at a college football game and waited for their remaining squadron mates to join them on land. Many families had made signs and banners to welcome home their sailor. The anticipation and emotion of homecoming gave the crowd a special energy easy to sense.

Shortly after 11 A.M. cheers began erupting from the crowd as people noticed the gray bow of the USS *Dwight D. Eisenhower* slowly emerging from behind the quietly moored USS *George H. W. Bush,* whose mass had been blocking the view of the harbor channel. Since the returning carrier had entered the Chesapeake Bay an hour before, the crew had been manning the rails in the classic and dramatic fashion that has marked homecomings and port visits for decades. The sight of several thousand sailors dressed in white, standing shoulder to shoulder at parade rest along the high deck of a carrier never fails to draw chills and tears. Adding to the sight were the flags of each U.S. state and territory, which were carried by the men and women standing across the bow and along the forward sides of the flight deck. The mosaic of flags blew gently in the wind and brought another lump to many throats. The supercarrier began turning slowly toward her pier. Her foghorn bellowed across the warm water, announcing her return.

Two tugboats began nudging the ship toward her berth and soon, *Ike* loomed over the pier. From the towering black mast flew brightly colored flags, telling all of a mission well done. A great wreath hung from one side of the bow to the other. The crew continued to man the rails as mooring lines were dropped to small craft that ferried them to the dock. Teams of five sailors wearing bright orange life vests and navy camouflage fatigues began tying the lines to black cleats along the pier. They wrapped the lines and, in unison, pulled mightily to secure them.

From behind the dark windows of the bridge, a proud captain and staff surveyed the scene below. With his ship finally moored to her pier, the captain's voice came over the loudspeaker: "*Eisenhower*, salute!"

The lines of white uniforms instantly straightened and snapped their right hands to the corner of their right eyebrows. They held the rigid salute until the next command: "To!" Their arms fell to their sides. They stood at attention ready for the next order.

"Secure from man the rails," came the final command of the cruise. "Well done. Well done."

The crew unleashed a cheer that cascaded from the high deck down over the pier and across the throngs gathered on the dock. The crowds responded with a roar of their own.

The sailors retreated from the rails and headed belowdecks, more than ready to leave the ship. Soon, the starboard elevators were lowered and two mobile cranes maneuvered four gangplanks into position. Then the exodus began. Following navy tradition, men whose wives gave birth while they were on deployment led the way. A wave of white-clad fathers rushed toward the special pier-side tent where they knew their wives and babies waited. They anxiously searched the crowd of families until they spotted their loved ones—or their loved ones spotted them. Cries of joy erupted. Couples embraced one another; children leapt into their mother's or father's waiting arms; tears flowed freely. New fathers kissed and held their wives. They hugged their young children, who had changed so much since they were last together. Then they scooped their newborns into their arms for the first time. In the crowd, Rob found Casey and met his son, Austin. Together as a family for the first time, they left the dock to begin a new life.

As the remainder of the ship's company followed the new fathers, the pier became a endless river of sailors and officers—all dressed in their white summer uniforms—surging toward the cheering crowd waiting at the dock's end. There, the river of white collided with family and friends who rushed forward to greet loved ones they had not seen in seven months. Tears were soon replaced by laughter and families left the dock behind to resume the life that had paused on the cold January morning that seemed so long ago.

Presiding over the scene was the great warship that had carried these men and women across thousands of miles, into combat, and safely home again. She had stood her guard, completed her mission, and served her country. Her hard-earned battle flags snapped in the breeze coming off the Chesapeake. At last, her engines rested quiet and still. From the clear sky above, the noontime sun washed over the joyful scene.

Ike was home.

When I last saw Captain Dee Mewbourne, he had stood on *Eisenhower*'s bridge, looking over the Arabian Sea, dressed in his blue-gray camouflage fatigues, captain's eagles modestly sewn into his collar. But when he strode down the gangplank from the lowered aft elevator, he was blinding in his summer whites: white shoes, white pants, white shirt decorated with ribbons, and black shoulder boards bearing the four golden stripes of a captain.

I met him just after he stepped onto the pier, returning to American ground after seven months abroad. Above us towered his carrier and its island. Toward the rear of the island sat the ship's giant crane. I noticed the words painted along its arching white boom: IKE: GREATER EACH DAY.

We looked up at the words together and I thought about the cycle I'd watched his ship undergo. I'd stood on this same pier just before she deployed in the dead of winter. I'd stood with him on the bridge as she'd launched sorties over the Arabian Sea and into Afghanistan. And now we had returned to this pier under a cloudless summer sky, the journey over.

Every day of their deployment, the crew aboard the *Eisenhower* had become a little more proficient, a little faster, and a little more seasoned. Under the pressure of war, plane captains endured the impossibly thick air of the sunbaked, exhaust-washed flight deck to keep jets ready to support American troops, day after day. Aviators launched off the bow, flew long missions, returned under moonless night skies, and landed on a rolling deck, time and again. Helicopter pilots and rescue swimmers laid everything on the line to save the lives of others. And five thousand men and women gave their best on every level of the ship while five thousand families back home did their best to support them from afar.

"Excellence is a journey," Captain Mewbourne said as we looked at the crane's words. "It's not a destination or port of call. We commit ourselves to becoming better each day."

Suddenly, I saw that common thread that tied together everything I'd witnessed. When new navy recruits or officers pledge to bear true faith and allegiance to the Constitution, they embark on a long voyage. In the years to come, some will find themselves on the drill field at the rescue swimmer schoolhouse. Others will line up behind a carrier, making their first night-time approach. Some will work freezing flight decks; others will work steamy galleys. A select group will earn a chief's anchors or an admiral's stars, then help others along their same path. The courses these individuals pursue will always vary, but every step along that course makes them a better person, a better shipmate, a better leader, and a better citizen.

I'd experienced the drama of *Top Gun*; I had stood transfixed as the Blue Angels spiraled overhead with impossible grace; and I had witnessed the mesmerizing pageant of flight operations. In those moments, I sometimes forgot that the business of naval aviation is ultimately war, which is unequivocally brutal and harsh; it necessarily brings times of great distress. But the very worst of circumstances have always summoned the navy's best, and through stories born in times of peace and war alike, I'd learned how great challenges have inspired individuals to accomplish the extraordinary. I'd seen great leaders encourage sailors, squadrons, and ships to complete missions large and small. I'd observed how naval aviation itself has protected our freedom in every trial. And it all happened day by day, across eras and oceans, on a journey of one hundred years.

I realized naval aviation now faced a second century; another hundred years with challenges unknown. I felt confident that new generations would overcome them. As Tom "Killer" Kilcline and I had walked slowly down the brow linking the USS *Midway* to its San Diego pier, we had talked about his son, Tom, and about the future of the discipline they both loved so deeply. The pier was nearly deserted; the museum had closed and the sun was beginning to set. I asked the just-retired Air Boss, the leader of all U.S. naval aviation, about the emerging enemies, types of warfare, and new technologies already changing his world. Computers, satellites, and joysticks were guiding unmanned drones from land and ships alike. America was fighting primitive insurgents armed with rifles and shoulder-launched missiles, not Russian MiGs with complex weapon systems. Budgets were tightening, new powers were emerging.

"The guy who rules the air will always be in control," Killer responded. "And there will always be ships at sea, and even small ships will have aviation. There will always be a naval air presence." But who—or what—would provide that presence? And how?

A debate has emerged about the merits of remote-piloted aircraft, like the Predator drones used over the Middle East, and whether the navy should adopt them. Should they replace the spirited individuals who have, for so long, stepped into aircraft and piloted them off carriers? Tom pointed out that because the technology exists already, the questions become: Is that something we want, tactically and morally? Are mechanical systems or individuals better suited to execute missions efficiently, assess situations, and make decisions? Beyond that, how can the navy do it more cost-effectively, while also addressing new threats.

With those questions in mind, we stood on the pier, looking across San Diego Bay. The sun settled toward the western horizon, sinking behind the tower that marked the North Island office Killer had occupied for the past three years. The carriers *Nimitz*, *Carl Vinson*, and *Ronald Reagan* were moored quietly across the harbor, subtle in their majesty. We looked into the sunset and the admiral gave me the bottom line on naval aviation's future.

"This culture of caring, courage, and commitment will always endure," the veteran aviator said. "We'll always look after our wingmen. Those are the culture and values. They've been there the whole time. They're the most important facet of this great enterprise, this great journey, and they're not going away."

My own journey into naval aviation began with *Top Gun*, and after the *Eisenhower*'s homecoming and my visit with Vice Admiral Kilcline, I watched the classic film one more time. But on this occasion, I watched it with the new perspective that came from immersing myself in that special culture born on mighty aircraft carriers during long deployments made in times of peace and war alike. I had been honored to meet figures from the past and also walk modern flight decks with a supremely devoted team as they sailed the world's oceans. They had taught me about their calling, their values, and their mission. They had revealed the essence of naval aviation and I would never again watch *Top Gun* with the same eyes.

In the film's climatic scene, Maverick and Iceman land on the *Enterprise* after fending off a section of hostile Soviet MiGs. When their F-14 Tomcats taxi to a stop and their canopies open, the pilots and RIOs look out over a cheering crowd of crewmen. Men wearing green, brown, white, blue, purple, yellow, and red shirts throng around the jets, cheering, clapping, and pumping their fists into the air. Behind their goggles, their eyes crinkle as proud smiles spread across their faces.

The camera follows Maverick as he descends the ladder and steps onto the deck in the midst of the surging crowd. Just like I'd seen Lee Amerine do those many months ago aboard *Nimitz*, Maverick begins shaking the hands of these hardworking young people.

Once, I thought they were shaking his hand. Now, I realize he was shaking theirs. Once, I thought this hardworking supporting cast was just celebrating the pilots, those heroes who had slain dragons and returned home triumphant. I now realized that they were also cheering for each other. Together, they had readied the deck, loaded the weapons, and launched the jets. Together, they all shared the victory. It was *they*—a spirited team of all ranks, roles, and shirt colors—who had vanquished the dragons and who shared pride in a mission well done.

Together, they were—and will always remain—naval aviation.

SELECTED BIBLIOGRAPHY

AcePilots.com. "Lt. Guy Bordelon." www.acepilots.com (accessed September 8, 2010).

Atta, Dale Van. *With Honor: Melvin Laird in War, Peace, and Politics.* Madison, WI: University of Wisconsin, 2008.

Booth, Peter B. *True Faith and Alliegance: Journals of a Naval Officer—Three Decades of the Cold War.* Milton, FL: Trent's Prints, 2004.

Bush, George H. W., interview by Paula Zahn. *CNN Presents: A Flyboy's Story: George Bush in World War II* (December 19, 2003).

Bush, George H. W., interview by U.S. Naval Institute. *Americans at War* (2007).

Cardinale, Krista. *Overview of Project Mercury.* 2007. http://www.encyclomedia .com/mercury_project.html (accessed June 12, 2010).

Christmann, Timothy J. "Vice President Bush Calls World War II Experience 'Sobering.'" *Naval Aviation News*, March–April 1985: 12–15.

Christopher, Ralph and Chief Jim Davy. *Iron Butterfly: The True Story of an Elite Group of Men Who Wrote a Page in Naval History.* Bloomington, IN: AuthorHouse, 2010.

Clements, Dennis, interview by Petty Officer Second Class Andrew Kendrick. *Coast Guard, Navy Rescue Man from Sunken Sailboat off East Coast* (January 3, 2010).

Collins, Jim. *Good to Great: Why Some Companies Make the Leap . . . and Others Don't.* New York: HarperBusiness, 2001.

Danger Zone: The Making of Top Gun. Directed by Charles de Lauzirika.

Denger, CW2 Mark J. *Eugene Burton Ely: The California National Guard's First (Naval) Aviator.* http://www.militarymuseum.org/Ely1.html (accessed September 14, 2010).

Dixon, Chief Machinist's Mate Harold F. "American aviators, forced down in mid-Pacific, survive 34 days of thirst, starvation, sun, wind, and sharks . . ." *Life*, April 6, 1942: 70–75.

Elder, Adam. "Top Gun: Forty Years of Higher Learning." *San Diego Magazine*, October 2009: http://www.sandiegomagazine.com/media/San-Diego-Magazine/October-2009/Top-Gun-40-Years-of-Higher-Learning/.

F-16.net. *The Web's Largest Collection of Call Signs stories.* http://www.f-16.net/call-signs.html (accessed July 14, 2010).

Files, Paul. "Chosin Reservoir: Epic of Endurance." http://www.koreanwar-educator.org/topics/chosin/index.htm (accessed March 19, 2010).

Finback vet talks about rescuing George H. W. Bush: Interview with Cavin McPhie. http://www.youtube.com/watch?v=cU5v6vbhDrs (accessed August 25, 2010).

Fuchida, Mitsuo and Masatake Okumiya. *Midway: The Battle that Doomed Japan.* Annapolis, MD: Naval Institute Press, 1955.

Goat Locker. "Chiefs Should be Leaders." September 2005. www.goatlocker.org (accessed September 15, 2010).

Goodspeed, Hill, and Rick Burgess. *U.S. Naval Aviation.* Pensacola: Hugh Lauter Levin Associates, 2001.

Gordon, Nathan G., interview by Justin Taylan for PacificWrecks.org. "Nathan G. Gordon—PBY Pilot & Medal of Honor" (2003). http://www.pacificwrecks.com/people/veterans/gordon.html (accessed September 19, 2010).

Hill, Melvin B. *Carl Vinson: A Legend in His Own Time.* http://georgiainfo.galileo.usg.edu/c-vinson.htm (accessed July 24, 2010).

Hiller Aviation Museum. *The Curtiss Pusher.* http://www.hiller.org/curtiss-pusher-story.shtml (accessed August 15, 2010).

Holloway, James L. III. *Aircraft Carriers at War: A Personal Retrospective of Korea, Vietnam, and the Soviet Confrontation.* Annapolis, MD: Naval Institute Press, 2007.

Houlihan, Senior Chief Mass Communication Specialist (SW/AW) William. "Sailors of the Year Advanced to Chief." July 17, 2008. www.navy.mil (accessed October 15, 2010).

Hoyt, Edwin P. *McCampbell's Heroes: The Story of the U.S. Navy's Most Celebrated Carrier Fighters of the Pacific War.* New York: Van Nostrand Reinhold Company, 1983.

Kernan, Alvin. *Unknown Battle of Midway: The Destruction of the American Torpedo Squadrons.* New Haven, CT: Yale University Press.

Liewer, Steve. "Crew faulted in blaze on carrier." *The San Diego Union-Tribune,* October 2, 2008.

Lovell, James A. and Jeffrey Kluger. *Apollo 13.* New York: Houghton Mifflin, 2000.

Mahan, Lewis F., "Eugene B. Ely—His Racing Days." *Naval Aviation News,* February 1981.

McCampbell, David, interview by Paul Stillwell. U.S. Naval Institute Oral History Program (July 16, 1987).

Moore, John Hammond. "The Short, Eventful Life of Eugene B. Ely." *Proceedings,* January 1981: 74.

NASA. "Apollo 13 original flight communication transcript." www.insideksc.com, 1971.

———. "MR-3 original flight communication transcript." www.insideksc.com, 1961.

———. *U.S. Navy E-2C Hawkeye.* http://www.nasa.gov/centers/dryden/news/X-Press/E-2C_Hawkeye.html (accessed August 24, 2010).

Naval Historical Center. *Desert Storm: The War with Iraq.* September 17, 1997. http://www.history.navy.mil/wars/dstorm/ds5.htm (accessed September 8, 2010).

Navy IT. *Navy Advancement Study Aid.* 2007. www.navyit.com (accessed May 5, 2010).

New Orleans *Times-Picayune.* "Navy pilot laid to rest in Slidell." Slidell, LA, June 9, 2009.

Nick Del Calzo, Peter Collier. *Medal of Honor: Portraits of Valor Beyond the Call of Duty.* New York: Artisan, 2003.

Reagan, Ronald W. "Remarks at the Tuskegee University Commencement Ceremony in Alabama." Tuskegee, AL, May 10, 1987.

Reich, Robert, interview by WHYY, National Public Radio. *Fresh Air* (September 11, 2007).

Reynolds, Clark G. *Admiral John H. Towers: The Struggle for Naval Air Supremacy.* Annapolis, MD: Naval Institute Press, 1991.

Shepard, Alan, interview by Academy of Achievement. Houston, Texas, (February 1, 1991).

Shepard, Alan and Deke Slayton. *Moon Shot: The Inside Story of America's Race to the Moon.* Atlanta: Turner, 1994.

Shepard, Alan, interview by Charlie Rose. *Charlie Rose* (July 20, 1994).

Shepard, Alan, interview by Roy Neil. *NASA Interview with Alan Shepard* (February 20, 1998).

Speed and Angels. Directed by Peyton Wilson. 2008.

Stockdale, James B. *A Vietnam Experience: Ten Years of Reflection.* Palo Alto: Stanford University Press, 1984.

Stockdale, Jim and Sybil. *In Love and War.* New York: Bantam Books, 1984.

Taylor, Theodore. *The Flight of Jesse Leroy Brown.* New York: Avon Books, 1998.

Thomas J. Hudner Jr., interview by Ed Tracy. *Pritzker Military Library Medal of Honor Series* (February 22, 2007).

Thomas J. Hudner Jr., interview by Gene Pell. *Veterans Chronicles* (February 10, 2008).

Thompson, Neal. *Light This Candle: The Life and Times of Alan Shepard.* New York: Three Rivers Press, 2005.

Tillman, Barrett. *Clash of the Carriers: The True Story of the Marianas Turkey Shoot of World War II.* New York: NAL Caliber, 2005.

———. *Hellcat: The F6F in World War II.* Annapolis, MD: Naval Institute Press, 1979.

Top Gun. Directed by Tony Scott. 1986.

Trumbull, Robert. *The Raft: The Courageous Struggle of Three Naval Airmen Against the Sea.* New York and Annapolis: Henry Holt and Naval Institute Press, 1942.

Wilcox, Robert K. *First Blue: The Story of World War II Ace Butch Voris and the Creation of the Blue Angels.* New York: Thomas Dunne Books, 2004.

Wolfe, Tom. *The Right Stuff.* New York: Farrar, Straus and Giroux, 1979.

NOTES

1. A Journey Begins

1. "Ely got . . . fired him": Moore, John Hammond. "The Short, Eventful Life of Eugene B. Ely." *Proceedings,* January 1981: 74.
2. "The battles of . . . in case of war": Denger, CW2 Mark J. *Eugene Burton Ely: The California National Guard's First (Naval) Aviator.* http://www.militarymuseum.org/Ely1.html (accessed September 14, 2010).
3. "The most important landing . . . Ark": Hiller Aviation Museum. *The Curtiss Pusher.* http://www.hiller.org/curtiss-pusher-story.shtml (accessed October 15, 2010).
4. "I am sure many . . . commit suicide": Reynolds, Clark G. *Admiral John H. Towers: The Struggle for Naval Air Supremacy.* Annapolis, MD: Naval Institute Press, 1991, 32–33.
5. "The effect on all . . . great big H": Ibid., 154.

3. High Trust

1. "I don't think . . . teamwork": Wilcox, Robert K. *First Blue: The Story of World War II Ace Butch Voris and the Creation of the Blue Angels.* New York: Thomas Dunne Books, 2004, 182.

4. Sharpening the Sword

1. "The rest of the navy . . . come out there": Elder, Adam. "Top Gun: Forty Years of Higher Learning." *San Diego Magazine*, October 2009: http://www.sandiego-magazine.com/media/San-Diego-Magazine/October-2009/Top-Gun-40-Years-of-Higher-Learning.
2. "This is *Star Wars* . . . make it": *Danger Zone: The Making of Top Gun*. Produced by Charles de Lauzirika.
3. "This was not just flying . . . in any situation": Ibid.

5. Esprit de l'aviateur

1. "The fleet's other carrier . . . eight other aircraft": Tillman, Barrett. *Clash of the Carriers: The True Story of the Marianas Turkey Shoot of World War II*. New York: NAL Caliber, 2005.
2. "When I tried . . . all right": McCampbell, David, interview by Paul Stillwell. U.S. Naval Institute Oral History Program (July 16, 1987).

7. Rescuers

1. "There was nothing . . . another day": Clements, Dennis, interview by Petty Officer Second Class Andrew Kendrick. Coast Guard, *Navy Rescues Man from Sunken Sailboat off East Coast* (January 3, 2010).

8. Freedom Seven

1. "Even at that age . . . pause for reflection": Shepard, Alan, interview by Academy of Achievement. *Academy of Achievement Interview*. Houston, Texas, (February 1, 1991).
2. "I think the one thing . . . in myself": Cardinale, Krista. *Overview of Project Mercury*. 2007. http://www.encyclomedia.com/mercury_project.html (accessed June 12, 2010).

3. "Well, there I am . . . hard as I had": Shepard, Alan, interview by Roy Neil. *NASA Interview with Alan Shepard* (February 20, 1998).
4. "All he'll say . . . right guy": Shepard, Alan, interview by Charlie Rose. *Charlie Rose* (July 20, 1994).
5. "I think all of us . . . things to go right": Shepard, Alan, interview by Academy of Achievement. *Academy of Achievement Interview* Houston, Texas, (February 1, 1991).
6. "Believe me it's a lot . . . piece of cake": Shepard, Alan, interview by Roy Neil. *NASA Interview with Alan Shepard* (February 20, 1998).

12. Orders to Execution

1. "Dude we gotta make . . . still firing": *Speed and Angels.* Directed by Peyton Wilson. 2008.
2. "I pulled the stick . . . would have hit us": Ibid.
3. "We don't really . . . completely gone": Reich, Robert, interview by WHYY, National Public Radio. *Fresh Air* (September 11, 2007).

13. Brothers in Arms

1. "Brown, I want to tell . . . you to the limit": Taylor, Theodore. *The Flight of Jesse Leroy Brown.* New York: Avon Books, 1998, 79–80.
2. "Does not use enough . . . altitude emergencies": Ibid., 122–44.
3. "I realize I was more . . . treatment or training": Ibid., 123–49.
4. "Good hop . . . fine pilot": Ibid., 159.
5. "Over so fast": AcePilots.com. "Lt. Guy Bordelon." www.acepilots.com (accessed September 8, 2010).
6. "By the campaign's end . . . 65,000": Files, Paul. "Chosin Reservoir: Epic of Endurance." http://www.koreanwar-educator.org/topics/chosin/index.htm (accessed March 19, 2010).
7. "So he could concentrate . . . catching fire": Thomas J. Hudner Jr., interview by Ed Tracy. *Pritzker Military Library Medal of Honor Series* (February 22, 2007).

8. "When [Jesse] hit . . . in the airplane": Thomas J. Hudner Jr., interview by Gene Pell. *Veterans Chronicles* (February 10, 2008).
9. "I could see that . . . just frozen stiff": Ibid.
10. "Ah don't know . . . big words": Taylor, Theodore. *The Flight of Jesse Leroy Brown.* New York: Avon Books, 1998, 237.
11. "We finally had . . . to do it": Thomas J. Hudner Jr., interview by Ed Tracy. *Pritzker Military Library Medal of Honor Series* (February 22, 2007).
12. "Knowing that he's . . . in his tracks": Taylor, Theodore. *The Flight of Jesse Leroy Brown.* New York: Avon Books, 1998, 269.
13. "I look back . . . to be Americans": Thomas J. Hudner Jr., interview by Gene Pell. *Veterans Chronicles* (February 10, 2008).
14. "Now I would like . . . were in trouble": Reagan, President Ronald W. "Remarks at the Tuskegee University Commencement Ceremony in Alabama," May 10, 1987.
15. "My biggest fear . . . going to survive": Christopher, Ralph and Chief Jim Davy. *Iron Butterfly: The True Story of an Elite Group of Men Who Wrote a Page in Naval History.* Bloomington, IN: AuthorHouse, 2010, 94–95.

14. Returning with Honor

1. "the brutal facts . . . current reality": Collins, Jim. *Good to Great: Why Some Companies Make the Leap . . . and Others Don't.* New York: HarperBusiness, 2001, 85.
2. "[The men] demanded . . . conscience at night": Stockdale, Jim and Sybil. *In Love and War.* New York: Bantam Books, 1984, 247.
3. "Experts in torture . . . hours a day": Ibid., 206.
4. "The North Vietnamese . . . they should know": Ibid., 300.
5. "There was no question . . . hornets' nest": Ibid., 306.
6. "I am deeply shocked . . . prisoners of war": Atta, Dale Van. *With Honor: Melvin Laird in War, Peace, and Politics.* Madison, WI: University of Wisconsin, 2008.

15. Survivors

1. "I'm going to make . . . Pastula": Trumbull, Robert. *The Raft: The Courageous Struggle of Three Naval Airmen Against the Sea.* New York and Annapolis: Henry Holt and Naval Institute Press, 1942, 17.
2. "Imagine doubling . . . it was like": Ibid., 5, 27.
3. "Boys, there goes . . . chance": Ibid., 8.
4. "I had studied the charts . . . we drifted": Ibid., 31.
5. "Sometimes the man . . . old Hahvahd": Ibid., 119.
6. "Chief I see . . . in the distance": Ibid., 176.
7. "We still didn't know . . . men-o'warsmen": Dixon, Chief Machinist's Mate Harold F. "American aviators, forced down in mid-Pacific, survive 34 days of thirst, starvation, sun, wind, and sharks . . ." *Life*, April 6, 1942: 70–75.
8. "People say you're . . . shot down": Bush, George H. W., interview by U.S. Naval Institute. *Americans at War* (2007).
9. "I wonder if . . . no control": Bush, George H. W., interview by Paula Zahn. *CNN Presents: A Flyboy's Story: George Bush in World War II* (December 19, 2003).
10. "We would have . . . waist hatch": Gordon, Nathan G., interview by Justin Taylan for PacificWrecks.org. "Nathan G. Gordon—PBY Pilot & Medal of Honor" (2003).

16. Chiefs

1. "I believe that chiefs . . . the nucleus": "Chiefs Should be Leaders." September 2005. www.goatlocker.org (accessed September 15, 2010).
2. "Never again . . . for leadership": Houlihan, Senior Chief Mass Communication Specialist Bill. "Sailors of the Year Advanced to Chief." July 17, 2008. www.navy .mil (accessed October 15, 2010).

17. Sacrifice

1. "At dawn on . . . they were needed": Kernan, Alvin. *Unknown Battle of Midway: The Destruction of the American Torpedo Squadrons.* New Haven, CT: Yale University Press. 2005.
2. "I don't think . . . care of us all": New Orleans *Times-Picayune*. "Navy Pilot Laid to Rest in Slidell," June 9, 2009.

ACKNOWLEDGMENTS

As I TRAVELED ACROSS OCEANS and through generations, the men and women of naval aviation shared their stories and opened their lives to this uninitiated author. As they did so, I began uncovering a legacy richer than I'd ever imagined. I only wish I could have heard every story that sprang from daring missions and busy flight decks throughout the past century. *Fly Navy* truly belongs to the men and women whose stories are within its pages—and beyond that, it belongs to all the individuals who have proudly worn the uniform of the U.S. Navy and put their life on the line. I just hope I've done them justice.

What started as a simple journey became quite the odyssey, and I appreciate the many individuals and groups who made it possible—and, honestly, so much fun. Above all, I'm grateful to the men and women who graciously shared their time and story for the book. Thank you.

Specifically, members of the Blue Angels, HS-5 Nightdippers, HS-11 Dragonslayers, VFA-2 Bounty Hunters, VFA-14 Tophatters, VFA-103 Jolly Rogers, and VAQ-129 Vikings opened up their hangars, homes, and ready rooms and taught me something about spirit, camaraderie, and how to stay entertained on a boat. Officers and crew aboard the *Nimitz, Dwight D. Eisenhower, Abraham Lincoln,* and *Harry S. Truman* were gracious hosts. The Rawhides and Providers always got me there and back.

The U.S. Navy and its public affairs teams ashore and afloat helped at every turn and I'd particularly like to thank Mike Maus, Jason Pollock, Aaron Kakiel, John Supple, the talented Katie Cerezo who went above and beyond, and Matt Allen who introduced me to Shawarma Alley.

Special appreciation goes to Walleye, Missile, Elwood, Killer, Mongo, Sleepy, FUNGUS, IPOD, Sweet-T, BASS, Cricket, Cheech, Oggie, Huck, LUDA, K-Mart, Huff, Balls, Hot Carl, Smash, Spooky, Robert Gates, Pete and Carolyn Booth, the Oubre family, Barrett Tillman, and Richard Latture. Hill Goodspeed and Rich Dann always pointed me in the right direction, and friends in the Scouting and W&L communities helped at every turn. Mary Ellen Wiggins and Andrea Alvord had insights beyond compare, and I will always owe Stacey Horton McElrath for the ideas and encouragement she gave at the very outset.

More friends than I can mention helped me along the way. I'm particularly grateful to John, Mimi, and Ellen Rogers who loaned me their porch and a sea breeze; Matt, Mary, and Caroline Sawhill provided friendship and a Blue Ridge retreat; Donnie and Susan Boyd always had a bed ready. Kathleen Stark and the ever-gracious Stark family took special care of me on the West Coast, and many other friends across the country supported me in countless ways.

In New York, my editor Peter Joseph at Thomas Dunne Books along with Tom Dunne, Pete Wolverton, and Margaret Smith, helped me venture into new territory. My agent Jack Scovil always gave the right counsel.

When I began writing, I think my family and close friends saw it as a passing phase, but I'm glad they've stuck with me as it has become something more. They have truly made this journey possible and gave me something to look forward to at the end of each cat shot and every flight home. I'm supremely fortunate to have them in my life.

Finally, I wish that those who read this book will find the same inspiration as I did in these accounts and in the great enterprise of naval aviation. And I hope that they will turn this last page with a greater appreciation for those men and women who have always given so much to serve and protect us all.

INDEX